Journey of a Thousand Steps

Book Three
A Whisper of a Mystery
Trilogy

M.A. APPLEBY

Copyright©2017 ~ M.A. Appleby

Journey of a Thousand Steps
By M.A. Appleby
Printed in U.S.A.

ISBN: 978-0692921340

2nd Edition 2017

All rights reserved solely by the author. The author guarantees all contents are original and do not infringe upon the legal rights of any other person or work. No part of this book may be reproduced in any form without the permission of the author. The views expressed in this book are not necessarily those of the publisher.

Information regarding permission, contact: info@maappleby.com
Visit Author website: www.maappleby.com

Cover, graphics, layout design, and all inserts by M.A. Appleby
Photo by V. M. Little

Fictional Novels by Author: *A Whisper of a Mystery Trilogy*:
The Ancient Whisper, Book One ~ ISBN: 978-0-6929-2129-6
Whispered Dreams, Book Two ~ ISBN: 978-0-6929-2133-3
Journey of a Thousand Steps, Book Three ~ ISBN: 978-0-6929-2134-0
Award Winning Non-Fiction: ~ ISBN: 978-1-4984-9873-9
    RAISING DAVID AGAIN
    A Guide To Understanding The Uniqueness of Brain Injury
    And How Our Faith Sustains Us

Dedication and Acknowledgement

I dedicate this final book in the trilogy to two strong women. One was my biological Mother named Evelyn (not her real name) Davis) and Sylvia I. Richter (my adopted Mother) who were close family friends.

They were so influential that these two fascinating individuals imparted little idioms, which I sporadically incorporated throughout all three books. My mother's wisdom and 'lectures' pop into my mind on occasion or I find myself saying something as she would say it when situations arise, and it gives me pause.

My Mother always said, 'to follow your dreams' and Sylvia said on more than one occasion that, 'you should do everything in moderation.'

Madam Sylvia, as we called her, told me to take notes after reading the first book; it must have a sequel, because the story was not over, which added to the mystery and adventure. We will forever miss these vibrant, humorous, and occasionally snarky Ladies!

Table of Contents

Chapter One	We Shall Carry On	1
Chapter Two	New Standardbred Horses	23
Chapter Three	A Real Murder Mystery Party	45
Chapter Four	Disturbing Dreams	71
Chapter Five	News – Some Good, Some Bad	84
Chapter Six	The Sky is Falling	101
Chapter Seven	Never Give Up Becomes a Slogan	129
Chapter Eight	The Will to Win	155
Chapter Nine	Life Plans	174
Chapter Ten	The Courage to Change the Things We Can	199
Chapter Eleven	Challenges and Fierce Competition	220
Chapter Twelve	The Road to the Championship	244
Chapter Thirteen	Journey of a Thousand Steps	266
Chapter Fourteen	Determination, Fortitude, & Resilience	289
Chapter Fifteen	Final Absolution	317
Epilogue		350
Postscript		353
Books and Resources		357

Foreword

A skillful storyteller captures the reader in the first paragraph and keeps him entranced until the very end. Keeping a reader engaged throughout a trilogy compounds aptness needed to transition one book to the next while, at the same time, delivering sufficient backstory for the reader who has not read a previous volume by employing narrative not appearing repetitive for those who have.

With this final book of her trilogy, *Journey of a Thousand Steps*, M.A. Appleby succeeds on both accounts and provides an enjoyable reading experience filled with intrigue and characters the reader will find empathy with (and villains to detest).

This mystery, filled with sub-plots, red herrings, twists and turns, portrays a mother and her family overcoming a life turned upside-down by world politics, organized crime, bureaucracy and fate. It deals with efforts of a lady who aims to bring normalcy to everyday family life, but normalcy is often disrupted by unexpected events and crisis. Her psychic is constantly bombarded by concern for her son who turned up missing in Saudi Arabia.

Is he dead? She doesn't know, but her intuition says he's alive. Over objections from her family and the CIA, she has to find out.

As an author, I found myself amazed by Ms. Appleby's ability to constantly surprise this reader with unexpected, yet logical, twists in an amazing story. It is well worth the read.

Terry L. Wilson

Introduction

My story revealed itself when my family experienced a real life-altering event. Finding peace and closure has not been easy. In the last chapter of book three, I share our caregiver tips in the form of *10 Keys to Recovery* that help us get through our day. No one can predict with any certainty what life will bring, but when one door closes, another opens, as God does not abandon you; he gives you only what he knows you can handle.

The Ancient Whisper, Book One of the trilogy is fast-paced, laced with mystery and suspense, with a splash of international intrigue. As the main character, Ellen narrowly escapes a plane explosion, she is kidnapped during a botched murder attempt and goes into the Federal Witness Protection Program with her family. With no income and a new identity, she needs to generate money quickly. Thus she enters the perilous world of horseracing, wagering, and high-stakes betting!

Whispered Dreams, Book Two, segues to another part of the world, where the story shifts to Ellen's son, Jason. It takes the reader on a journey of discovery as the plot thickens. As the family continues to meet challenges head-on, it stretches their patience to their limits, yet shows how close family ties bind them together. Complacency becomes the 'norm' around Ashwood, but they pick up for Jason, who is now living with his uncle. When opposing factions within the Monarchy of Obagur threaten, he is compelled to become involved. Ellen starts to worry when Jason misses their usual time to connect each week. Days pass without a word, and then the unthinkable happens.

The ***Journey of a Thousand Steps*** concludes the trilogy. As life continues, Ellen flips a coin; stay on the path to the Championship, or go to find her son. After the coin toss puts her on the racing circuit, Ellen vows that after it's over, she will seek closure and adopts the motto that she will never give up without a good fight. Book three takes the reader on a roller-coaster ride of emotions, as Ellen embarks on the journey to find her son, but does this without her husband's knowledge.

"Man will occasionally stumble over the truth, but most times he will pick himself up and carry on."
~ Winston Churchill

Chapter One

We Shall Carry On

The day starts as usual, but the dread of what's to come is what honestly terrifies me. Dr. Laurel has chosen today to begin my journey toward confronting my deepest fears. She hopes that the realization that specific events were not preventable will start the healing process. My family has voiced their opinion that I must move beyond this to fully embrace life without my son. It's time to let him go and move on with my life.

Perhaps they're right.

For as long as I can remember, my mother and sister have accused me of being a cockeyed optimist who not only lives in an ivory tower but continuously looks through rose-colored glasses.

Perhaps they are correct in this view.

Have I closed my eyes to pretend that things don't exist to cope with reality? When something unexpected happens to alter the course of your life, how you handle it is what truly matters. Haven't I been treating it okay?

Dr. Laurel insisted that I submit a questionnaire before beginning our new sessions. She mentioned it would help her understand my present anxiety; however, I have anxiety walking into her office because I want to turn around and run the other way.

While filling out the questionnaire, it reminded me about the glass half full/half empty thing. Am I a pessimist with a tendency toward a myopic view of the world? One that my nearsighted views lack tolerance and understanding? Or, am I an optimist, who believes that only good will ultimately prevail over evil?

"Hello Ellen, how are you today? Have a seat in the chair or recline on the sofa, kick your shoes off and make yourself comfortable."

"I'm fine, Dr. Laurel, just looking through my rose-colored glasses today, hoping things will look better. I'll sit over here, thanks. The sofa makes me think you might hook me up to some elaborate mechanism and suck my thoughts out through my ear."

Laurel opens the door and sticks her head around the corner to signal to her assistant. Closing it quietly, she sits down at her desk to press the buttons on her tape recorder. "I haven't heard that expression about glasses for a long while, Ellen. You have a vivid imagination. And the sofa thing only happens in hospitals. Have you been getting enough rest? Any problems there?" she asks, smiling.

"Mother always said I had a wild imagination. I think I'm getting enough rest and dreaming a little too loud for Adrian. Do they hook people up to machines and shock them? Mother keeps reminding me about the rose-colored glasses thing. Does it mean delusional?"

Laurel is a striking woman who wears a blue on blue sweater-set and a black pencil skirt. As usual, her short brown hair frames her oval face, and her makeup is impeccable. "Let's explore that a minute, Ellen. Occasionally the subconscious mind plays out in dreams. Perhaps it helps you to cope with what is stressful to you."

"My dreams are certainly in technicolor, very vivid, along with a lot of action. Now and then, I have the sensation that I'm flying in my dreams. Adrian has to push me over to my side of the bed several times a night. I practically smother him and hit him with my fists. When I wake up, he's sleeping on the sofa pit."

"Dreaming in color is perfectly okay, Ellen," she says, reaching for a pen. "Many people experience their dreams that way. It's the roughness that is worrisome. Are you sure you're getting enough rest? Are you taking that sleeping aid I suggested?"

"I'm getting as much sleep as possible. I do wake up several times a night. Maybe it's all that wrestling in my sleep. Do I look tired to you? And no, I don't need that stuff you prescribed."

Dr. Laurel stops writing to look directly at me. "Let's go back to when you first came to Virginia. We may not have done a thorough job when we talked about it before."

"Are we starting at the beginning? What part did I leave out? If you listened to the CD Adrian gave you, you already know how much I detested those two idiots that passed themselves off as FBI agents. They dumped us at Ashwood and took all our possessions. I still don't understand how they were able to do that."

"Yes, I know all that, nevertheless, when you repeat things, it sometimes helps to resolve issues. It might trigger something that wasn't said before. It's apparent to me that you still harbor resentment toward the FBI agents."

"Wouldn't you if your whole life turned upside down and everything you knew to be right and wonderful in your world suddenly evaporated?"

"Yes, Ellen. I probably would feel as you do. Would you like to talk about that?"

"No. Talking about those idiots only makes me crazy."

"Let's explore something else, then. Any pleasant memories you want to discuss?" Laurel asks gently.

"I told you about the antiques we found in the house, and then Jason found that old car in the barn that was worth a small fortune. I was thinking of that as I was driving here."

"That sounds like a good memory, Ellen. Please expound on that."

"Jason was so pathetic when he found out that we were going to sell it. Then he hounded and pestered me for months until I gave in and bought him a used car. We still have that car. My youngest daughter drives it now. Then we paid off the debts we inherited with the money I made at the racetrack, and we renovated practically every room in our house. What more do we need to talk about?"

Laurel stops to stare at me, then leans forward, saying, "You seem more stressed than usual, Ellen. How can I help you today?"

"Stupid things keep popping into my head and I can't get them to stop! Can you suggest a pill for that?"

Dr. Laurel sighs. "You know it doesn't work like that. Let's talk about how Jason might have felt when he first came to Virginia. Do you think he adjusted to the upheaval that came with moving and leaving all his friends?"

"I think he had an okay time with that. His big shock was finding out that the mother he thought was dead, wasn't. Of all of my children, he was, what I mean to say is that he is the most stable."

Dr. Laurel is thoughtful for a moment. "When a child goes missing, Ellen, the parents might think they're responsible. They typically question why such a thing could happen to their family. They wonder what prompted someone to act maliciously toward them. Do you feel as if you did something to warrant such behavior against Jason?"

Trying to control my sudden anger, I start to laugh instead. "In the case of the missing Jason L. Thompson, age twenty-three, I do not think I'm responsible. I do, however, blame his incredibly insensitive Uncle Dimmy who lives far, far away, in a land I don't ever wish to mention! I would like to point out that it was Jason's father who involved us in that whole mess in the first place. You read the file. Was that part in there?"

"We can't talk about certain things, Ellen, due to the National Security protocols your husband, Adrian, and I discussed. I believe you mentioned in a previous session that you wished you had done more to talk him out of going to that faraway place." Dr. Laurel tilts her head and raises her eyebrows slightly.

If this is my cue to spill my guts, she's in for a surprise. "No. I wish you knew the entire story. I don't blame myself. I'm convinced that Jason would have gone with or without my consent."

Dr. Laurel presses the stop button on her recorder, standing to open the door for her assistant, who is holding a clinking tray. It instantly reminds me of a distant memory. Taking the serving tray, she silently closes the door with her hip. "Would you like a cup of tea, Ellen?"

"Sure."

Is drinking tea supposed to make one feel better? Is it a prerequisite for shrinks to offer this beverage instead of coffee? How about a sugar-high brought about by drinking a soda? On the other hand, why can't she offer me a bottle of water, maybe a scotch and soda?

"Ellen, you look a million miles away," Dr. Laurel says starting the recorder again.

"My mind goes off in different directions, and I can't get it to stop."

Dr. Laurel jots something down on her steno pad, glances up at me, and says, "Shall we get back to why you think Jason's Uncle is responsible for his disappearance?"

"Wow, where do I begin this ridiculous tale of woe? It's so bizarre that I couldn't have made it up."

"Ellen, why don't we let that go for now, and we'll move on to something else? Can you tell me what you've been doing to keep yourself busy?"

"You still think I'm delusional, don't you?"

"I do not believe that was ever my assessment, Ellen. I would never have said that to you. Is that how you feel right now?"

"I wanted you to help me get out of my funk, but all you've done is say I can have some drugs that allow me to have a restful sleep and we keep going back to useless stuff. I don't want to sleep through my dreams, because they're the only connection I have to Jason. Am I the only one who thinks my son is still alive?"

Dr. Laurel tries to steer away from that line of thinking. "Do you have a hobby that would take your mind off everyday things?"

"Do you want me to take up knitting? You think I have a gambling problem, and you're trying to get me to admit it, right?"

"Did I say that I thought you have a gambling problem, Ellen?" she says bluntly. "You seem very jittery today."

"Sorry. I lost my interior design business some years ago, as you know, and it did keep me busy to renovate every room in our house. What I want to do is race again."

"Do you think if you raced again, that you would be happier?" she asks.

"So now you think I'm not happy! You think that's the root of my problem?"

"No, Ellen. All I'm saying is that everyone needs to vent, for many, hobbies help to do that. Some find that punching a bag or taking an exercise class does the trick."

"I don't *need* to race to keep me happy!" Looking directly at her in her perfectly coiffed hair, manicured fingernails, and expertly applied makeup, a snide remark erupts from my lips. "Underneath that persona of professionalism, I'll bet you play competitive bridge."

Dr. Laurel's face slowly transforms into a soft smile. "That is an astute observation, Ellen. Is that how you win so successfully at the racetrack?"

"First, tell me if I'm right! Then maybe I'll share my deepest, darkest secrets with you."

"I'm an avid bridge player with aspirations of gaining enough points to become a Life Master."

"How close are you to that?" I ask, watching her face.

"I'd like to go further, perhaps to either achieve an Emerald or Platinum level," she says.

"How many points do you need to get to that level?"

Dr. Laurel hesitates, leaning forward in her chair, saying, "Are you equating my bridge playing to your horse betting?"

Leaning toward her, I say, "Are you answering my question with a question?"

"Alright Ellen," she says, folding her arms around her notepad. "If it will help to talk about myself, then my goal is to be a Grand Life Master."

"How close are you to reaching your first goal of Life Master? Will it take years, months, or will you get them in your lifetime?"

Dr. Laurel contemplates this for a few seconds. "There are several levels to gain masterpoints. I'm currently at the NABC Master level. Without going into the entire procedure, one must attend sanctioned events to win points. It's rather complicated, so I'll try to keep it brief. I need to accumulate a certain number of black, silver, red, gold, and platinum points to move forward in these events."

"I can tell you're driven to win. How long will it take you to get to the Grand Master stage?"

Dr. Laurel seems pensive, then says, "That would be my ultimate achievement."

"How many points do you need to get to that level?"

"That would most likely take the rest of my life, Ellen. That requires 10,000 points of various events or tournaments. I would have to retire and do that full-time."

"But, you have a goal. I'll bet you won't stop until you reach that goal, am I right? How many points away are you from your first big goal?"

Dr. Laurel picks up her teacup, taking a sip, she looks me straight in the eye. "Alright Ellen, I only need four gold and three platinum points to reach Life Master, but then again it would spur me on for the rest of my life to get to the Grand Life Master status. What I believe you're saying is that everyone should have something to look forward to and you think that bridge is my addiction."

"Bingo! Give the lady a prize! Everyone needs an out, even you. If you think gambling is my addiction, then you don't know me. I only bet on a sure thing and not without doing a lot of serious studying. I do not smoke or drink to excess, and I don't shop until I drop. It's not as if I have to go to the racetrack every day. I only did that when we needed cash, which we don't do anymore. We make money the old-fashioned way. We earn it."

"Let's get back to you, Ellen. You mentioned racing. Didn't you tell me that you gave that up some time ago due to an injury?"

"Yes. I wanted to take Ashwood Stables up in prestige, up in levels as you do for your points, yet, my goal seems almost as elusive as finding my son."

"I don't understand. I thought you had two racers that compete for Ashwood. It sounds to me that they might help you reach that goal even if you aren't doing the actual racing." Dr. Laurel starts thumbing through her notes. "Here it is. Was it winning the Triple Crown of Harness Racing?"

"Yes, I want to win the Triple Crown of Harness Racing. Would you pay someone else to play bridge for you and they earned your masterpoints?"

Her face suddenly registers comprehension. "Ellen, of course, you're right," she sighs. "It takes all the fun out of it if you don't win it yourself."

"You think I need a hobby; something to take my mind off my troubles? Adrian keeps after me to go away on trips. I don't feel like celebrating anything when my heart feels like it's about to explode!"

"Ellen, your heart is heavy with sadness. It's a natural feeling when you lose someone close to you. In your case, you've had more than your share. In time, this feeling will dissipate as we work it out. In the meantime, allow yourself to grieve and carry on as best you can."

"As *we* work it out? Do you have a mouse in your pocket, Doctor? How do you figure this is *we*? How long will this take if *we* are going to do this? Are you going to help me before I grow old, or do I have to figure it out myself?"

Dr. Laurel laughs, "How did you come up with that saying about a mouse?"

"Daddy always said things like that. I had almost forgotten it."

"You are using humor to mask how you feel. It's okay, Ellen. No one knows how long it will take to work things out; each person is different. Perhaps a year from now you'll look back and say it didn't take as long as you once thought."

"A year is a long time. A lot can go on in a year."

Another year could go by without one word about Jason, and this abruptly annoys me. I don't want to think that Jason is gone forever. In my heart and gut, I know he's out there.

"You don't think Jason is alive and I can't talk about certain things, so what's left to talk about?"

Dr. Laurel glances at her wristwatch, declaring that our time is up for today. When she does this, Jason's unique wristwatch pops into my mind, the one I gave him before he left to study martial arts the first time.

"We can pick this up next week, okay Ellen?" The click of the recorder triggers a sensation, and I turn toward her, and for a split-second, it reminds me of another distant memory.

"Ellen? See you next week?"

"Yes, Dr. Laurel, I'll see you next week."

Are my rose-colored glasses obscuring my vision? Although Mother didn't say it, she probably thinks it's time to throw the glasses away.

In the weeks that follow, I struggle with simple decisions, and can't seem to focus. During the next few visits with Dr. Laurel, she tries to extrapolate my darkest secrets, then finally concludes that I'm not willing to accept simple facts. The more accurate description is that everyone runs the other way when I mention my ideas about looking for Jason.

After this information comes tumbling out of my mouth, Dr. Laurel ponders this revelation for a few minutes, glances down at her notepad, and then lets out a heavy sigh. "You seem more stressed than last week, Ellen. I can only help you learn how to cope with what has happened to you. It's quite amazing how you've managed to get through the traumas in your life thus far. You must know that there is no magic formula. It takes time, and your ability to talk things through that will help you over the hurdles."

"You mean it's a wonder I didn't go nuts before now, with the stress, you mean?"

"Interesting how your mind works, Ellen. That's not exactly what I meant."

"Then what did you mean?"

Dr. Laurel sighs again. "I can only lead you to discover how you can help yourself through the steps of therapy. There is no magic pill for grief. Although you may not think so, you are making progress; however, there is irrefutable evidence to suggest that Jason is gone. And there is no way to change this. I can only help you cope with your loss. I'm sorry, Ellen, that's the best I can offer you."

"Do you mind if we end our session now? I don't want to think about this."

"I understand Ellen, will you come back next week?" Dr. Laurel pleads with her eyes. "I think we're making progress."

"Of course, Dr. Laurel, I'll see you next week."

As I drive home, I try to look on the bright side of things; however, there isn't any. Could my optimistic self be changing into a pessimistic one? For the first time in over a year, doubt surfaces.

Could I be wrong in thinking that Jason is alive? Why is there an overwhelming feeling that he's out there waiting for us to find him? And why can't I home in on where he might be? Why didn't we put a chip in his head? But then, Jason vehemently refused to allow Jewel's to put it into his wrist. It could have led us straight to him.

Why, why, oh why didn't we insist upon this?

The words scream silently in my head. No parent intends to have a child abducted. As a precaution, we put a DNA kit together along with fingerprints when Jason, Melanie, and Curlie first enrolled in their new schools here. It's little comfort when these can't help us find him.

Automatically looking into the pasture next to the barn, I maneuver my car past our entrance gate and pull into my spot in the garage under the Carriage House. It seems so long ago. So much has happened since we first came to Virginia. Aside from our missing Jason, we've settled into the house built by Sara Ashwood, and grown comfortable with the new life we have established here.

We have everything we need: family, friends, a steady income, and a gentle whisper from time to time, from one of the resident ghosts that have cohabited peacefully with us. Because of this, we no longer need to go to Billingsworth Racetrack to wager for large sums of money, even though Adrian tries to coerce me into doing so since he doesn't bet effectively.

This undesirable doomsday feeling must go away before it consumes me. Everyone around here, including Dr. Laurel, thinks Jason is dead. I know in the recesses of my mind and heart that he's out there; we merely haven't found him yet!

During our usual nightly banter and commentary around our dinner table, I bring up the possibility that Ashwood Stables might benefit from acquiring a new Standardbred horse. It might be time to explore this idea, but no one offers to help, they simply let me talk about it.

Did Dr. Laurel speak with Adrian? Did she mention that my family needs to appease and agree with me so I won't go off the deep end?

Mother thinks that we should adopt a new motto: we shall carry on, which sounds like a good plan, and in spite of all that we have endured, *we shall carry on.*

"Ellie, are you telling Dr. Laurel what's troubling you?"

Adrian fumbles to turn the pages of his newspaper, dropping it slightly to stare at me. We are lingering in the Morning Room since we have no immediate plans for today.

"She thinks I'm delusional even though she doesn't use that exact word. I do feel a little better when I talk, and she is a good listener. She asks leading questions, and I mostly answer them. She probably thinks that I've made it all up."

"She doesn't judge you, Ellie. She's a professional. She knows how to help people go through emotional things like this. It's what she does, my darling."

"You had a few sessions with her. Did you talk about us?"

"I had one session with her a long time ago and, of course, we talked about us. We also talked about the rules she needs to follow during your sessions with her. She thinks you're sad, maybe a little depressed, because of what happened."

"Sometimes I get sad. With all the things that go on in our lives Adrian, now and then I am sad and depressed all at the same time."

He drops the paper to look directly at me. "You never said how Dr. Laurel reacted after she listened to the CD we gave her."

"Didn't I? I thought I did."

Adrian frowns. "I remember my reaction the first time I listened to it, and I'll bet she thinks the story is beyond strange. I listened to it again before I gave it to her and it made me cringe when I heard your voice describing what happened to you."

"We all know how you bet, Adrian, but you might be right this time. She was quite surprised and only referenced it a few times. Oh, Lord, there was all that stuff that happened right after I made the CD. Should I tell her what else happened, Adrian?"

He folds up the newspaper. "Clear it with me first, would you? That's not the reason you're going to see her, so why would you have to talk about that stuff?"

"I'm guessing that background is something that triggers depression. The crux of the matter is that you all think Jason is dead and I don't. She keeps steering me back to what she calls my 'reality.' You wouldn't have anything to do with that part, would you, darling Adrian?"

"Ellie, I'm not part of your therapy sessions, if that's what you're suggesting."

Suddenly remembering a poem, I start to say it out loud, "Somewhere out there, a Mother mourns…"

"What is that, Ellie, a poem you remember?"

"Yes, high school English Literature, if memory serves. It's about a mother who wrote about her son, her husband, and fellow soldiers when they went off to war and never came back."

Adrian gives me his full attention. "I'd like to hear it. What else do you remember about it?"

"Let me think." Allowing my mind to go blank, somehow the poem finds its way to the surface. "*'somewhere out there a Mother mourns, 'tis impossible to explain, somewhere out there his soul is calling me, let go and banish pain. For love is rare and can't be lost, God gave that gift to us. And know for all eternity, we'll never lose that trust'.*"

"That was beautiful. You're right, it's sad."

"I know there are more lines to it, but I can't remember them."

"My father enlisted at the end of the Korean War, and then went to Viet Nam in fifty-six. It was during the early days of the uprising. Did you know that it lasted from 1955 to 1975? None of the soldiers who came home got a warm welcome when they returned. They didn't get ticker-tape parades, marching bands, or ceremonies as there was after World War Two ended. He didn't like to talk about it. That's for sure."

"Both Daddy and Mother kept their childhoods secret, until Terre and I begged them to at least tell us about possible relatives we could look up if we ever went to Europe. They weren't forthcoming with the information. It was a bad time for them, so we eventually stopped asking."

"Let's not be sad anymore; we have so much to be thankful for, my darling Clementine. There's always a silver lining!"

"Isn't that a song?"

We often go in search of things we are discussing if they elude us. It could be anything from the weather to when hot air balloons race in the area. Adrian has his cellphone handy.

"*'There's always a silver lining somewhere in the sky, to bring your troubled soul new hope and lift your spirits high. When disappointments come your way, accept them with a smile, for deep down in your heart you know they only last awhile. Do not believe you walk alone because you never do. Hold out your hand, and you will find that God is there with you,'* by Harold F. Mohn."

"Isn't that beautiful. I'm going to try very hard to get past this depression, okay? It's time to let it go for now."

"That's my gal!" Adrian pulls me into a hug. "You'll feel better if you do. I'll help you."

Saying you'll overcome something doesn't automatically make it go away. Some mornings, it's a challenge to get out of bed. Dr. Laurel says to concentrate on something productive, as she thinks it will take my mind off the things that make me sad. Then gradually, the realization sets in that most of us are powerless to change the things that we have no control over.

At every opportunity, my family tells me to let go and live. I will never give up hope of finding Jason and wonder if his guardian angel is watching over him. A guardian angel prayer pops into my mind, but it's not specific enough, and instead, I modify it to:

"*Angel of God, My Guardian Dear, find Jason and keep him near. Help him to find the light, guard him from harm, and guide him tonight!*"

From time to time, small pieces of paper make their way to my nightstand; my bible might be open to a passage on the dresser, or an inspirational bookmark suddenly appears on my desk. Near my reading glasses is one called, *Footprints in the Sand*.

Reflecting on the sad events that took place over the last year or so, I've decided that Jason's memory will live on in my heart. It's also my opinion that the X-Andress slash Thompson dash Sellers family has had enough pessimism and certainly more than our fair share of imprudent occurrences, and it's time to turn it around.

It is now time to move on with the business of living.

My next visit to Dr. Laurel's office brings me face-to-face with my grief. I'm not as overwhelmed with Jason's disappearance and apparent death as I once was, but it's still difficult to let it go.

We have tried hypnosis, and it merely did not gain the results she hoped for, so we are seeking a new technique. She will take me into a meditative state, with the intention that I can speak transcendentally to Jason. Before the session, Dr. Laurel asked me what I might say to Jason if he were here. She will use this information as a prompt should I run into trouble.

Soft, relaxing ocean sounds are playing in the background as Dr. Laurel murmurs, "Listen as the music takes you on a journey. You feel your body relax. You are standing in your bare feet and can feel the warm sand between your toes. It is a calm place; a place where the ocean is peaceful. It is serene; it is tranquil. You are very relaxed now, as the ocean beckons to you. You hear my voice fade as you listen to the music and then all you hear is the ocean. The music and the ocean merge as they create a safe and calm place for you. Take in a breath and let it out slowly."

Dr. Laurel stops talking as the sound of the water laps lazily on an imagined shore, then continues, saying, "Listen to the ocean, feel the water soothe you; feel the calmness of the ocean as you hear a voice. It's Jason's voice. He is calling to you, and you walk toward him very slowly, as he walks toward you. He is now standing in front of you, and you put your arms around him and hug him."

Trying to imagine Jason standing in front of me, music merges with the swish of the ocean, as his image (or what my mind formulates) suddenly appears as he does in my disturbing dreams. I also imagine myself moving forward to embrace him, while the ocean and the music play in the background.

Dr. Laurel's soft voice interrupts, saying, "You are calm. Jason is calm. Jason says something funny and you both laugh. You feel good, and you feel happy. You are relaxed. He is relaxed. He is here with you." She stops talking as the music continues to play softly in the background.

In my mind the words formulate as, "Where are you Jason? We have all been looking for you for a very long time. What happened to you? Why haven't you called? **Jason, what happened to you that you went**

away?" When my voice startles me, Jason's image fades. I open my eyes to Dr. Laurel's exasperated expression.

At this point, she sighs as she presses the button on the tape recorder. "Ellen, this will not work if you do not remain calm and in a happy place. You need to meditate properly."

"Can't we try this again? I saw Jason. What did I do wrong?"

"When you encounter the person you wish to communicate with, you are supposed to ask your questions quietly. Didn't we go over that part? If we didn't, I apologize. Most of my patients don't say anything at all, and keep it in their minds only."

"I don't understand. Why would you record this if no one says anything?"

"It's a matter of procedure, Ellen. I believe what I said was that most people keep it to themselves. On occasion, others may utter something quite significant."

"Do you always have to be right? You know I'm a betting woman, and I'll bet you were first in your class."

Dr. Laurel smiles, "I think what you mean to ask is, am I competitive? No more than you are, Ellen."

"Can I try this on my own? I have some CDs with music like this. I felt a little odd doing this in front of you."

"Yes, you might try this yourself. I suggest you go into your office, turn off your cellphone, put some soothing music on, and relax. It might work if I'm not around to distract you. Then again, we might try an alternative therapy."

"Okay, what else do you have in mind?"

Dr. Laurel turns to consult her appointment book, glancing up at me, saying, "It wouldn't be effective if I told you. See you next week."

After posting a DO NOT DISTURB sign on the door, I shut myself in my office; however, Adrian ignored the warning and popped his head in out of curiosity. I had to tell him that under no circumstances should anyone interrupt me for at least two hours.

Putting the CD into my computer, there are ocean sounds with seagulls squawking in the background, and all that happens is, I fall asleep.

Two hours later, Adrian is gently shaking my arm. "Ellie, time to wake up, sweetie."

"I must have fallen asleep."

"Isn't that why you posted a sign on the door?" Adrian snickers. "Maybe you won't beat me up tonight."

"Oh yes, I do feel better. And I haven't stopped doing that?"

"No, I know better than to snuggle with you, because you start flailing and kicking me!"

"I'm sorry Adrian; I don't know how to control that, especially in my sleep."

Adrian grins. "Isn't that one of the reasons you're going to therapy? Are you feeling better?" He pulls me close and starts to stroke my hair.

As is our custom at dinnertime, the adults get into ridiculous conversations over the most mundane subjects. It is where my youngest daughter and her two cousins can't wait to leave. They either prefer kitchen duty, or they merely don't want to partake of our silliness.

My Mother starts right in with her opinion about wearing rose-colored glasses, and we all have a field day with that one! Then she segues into something she found in the newspaper yesterday. An outbreak of a new strain of bacteria has stricken a country on the other side of the planet. "It's unfortunate more isn't done for that country."

"What do you expect us to do?" Terre asks.

"Now is your opportunity to expound on your thesis, Ellen. Tell your sister how you really feel about that," she says, looking directly at me.

"You mean about my dichotomous' slant of the world? The one that says we should never go to war? And the other one that should protect and feed hungry children?"

"Yes, that one," Mother says.

"My thinking also leans toward world powers; they should band together to cure cancer, the Ebola virus, and other life-threatening diseases. And, why don't we concentrate our efforts to wipe out AIDS instead of each other? Is this asking too much? Is world peace that unattainable?"

Dennis chimes in with, "There will always be some type of war in certain parts of the world, that's a given."

"You see, that's what it's like to look through those glasses," Mother quips, looking straight at me. "Right, Ellen?"

"Mack and I aren't exactly following this tonight. Mind if we go back to the barn?" Danny suggests as he and Mack stand to leave.

"No, go on. We'll take it from here," Adrian says waving them off.

"Since it is inherently within human nature to control itself, there will be disruption to the order of things," Mother adds. "That's not a new concept, Ellie, it's how God intended and how the world works, Darling. When they cure one disease, another will appear."

"Talk about disruption, look what you all went through the last several years," Terre says, looking around the table.

Terre is right, over the last several years, my family faced insurmountable odds, and we could have easily gone down with the ship, but instead, we chose to rise to the occasion, because that is who we are. Thinking back, the story of how we all came to live in Virginia is more unfathomable than anything. Even after we discovered some terrifying information about some of our family members, and when we thought things worked out, we were still caught off guard several times.

The intensity seeps back when it's least welcome. Is it some forewarning of something else to come? Could it be more than eight years since a massive curve ball hit my family and our lives turned upside down?

Little did we know that our lives were about to change that fateful day my husband, Ravi, boarded the plane for home, as I languished in the restroom. Waking briefly to witness an explosion, I believe it was what began our twisted and challenging journey. That memory haunts me to this day, which can be triggered by a familiar scent of lemon, a particular taste or sound, or word that instantly reminds me of the vile drug they gave me.

Ravi and I had achieved a monetary level of accomplishment and comfort; he came up through the ranks of his company, and I had a successful interior design business. We had a spacious house in suburbia, three healthy children, a dog, and we were content.

After our funerals, my Mother went into emergency mode and moved in to care for our children. That's when an Executor of the Andress Estate came to settle and get our affairs in order. This executor fabricated a story that my children were moving to Montana to live with their father's relatives. Their Grandmother Francesca was moving into an assisted living complex in Florida, and no one questioned this.

It could not have been farther from the truth.

None of what they said was true. My husband boarded that fateful plane with a woman who impersonated me. Since my laptop and cellphone went missing, there was no way to contact my family, and they went on to believe I died with Ravi. It occasionally comes back in the form of horrifying nightmares. These dreams are vivid reminders of how our lives changed in the blink of an eye.

Several months after our funerals, Special Agents of the FBI, named Lenard and Gene, visited Mother while the children were at school. They told her that I was alive and relocated to an old dairy and horse farm in Virginia. We learned later that the person who passed himself off as our executor was Lenard in disguise.

Lenard gave Mother a choice: she could either stay in Chicago or move to Virginia to live with us, and be included in the Federal Witness Protection Program. She didn't hesitate, telling my children that because they had been through so much trauma, it was time to have some fun before school started in the fall and they were going to a dude ranch.

A day after they left on their trip, Jason, Melanie, and Curlie's bedroom furniture (along with their possessions) went into a moving van which included select pieces of Mother's furniture.

Everything Ravi and I owned went to buy half of the property called Ashwood Farms. We learned that private investors purchased the other half, which, we also discovered, were partly behind some of the shenanigans that went on here in Virginia.

The next session with Dr. Laurel finds me as anxious as the previous one, but with one exception. I am angry about something trivial.

"Please have a seat, Ellen. I'll have some tea brought in, and we can get started. How was your week?"

"I had a little meltdown."

"Can you describe what led up to it?" she asks gently.

"I wasted two hours looking for something I was sure came with our stuff from Illinois."

"And you are angry for wasting two hours, or angry with not finding the object?"

"Everything is gone from the time before we came here. It's as if we never existed. Now and then anger gets the better of me, and then I chastise myself for thinking that way. I don't need material things. I know what's important. We don't need them to make us happy. However, it's maddening to look for something, only to recall it's not here!"

"Would you like to talk about that time, Ellen? It sounds as if you have unresolved issues."

"Maybe you're right. Where do I start?"

"How about when your Mother and children first arrived at Ashwood. How did they find out you were alive?"

"It was Curlie, my youngest child, who saw her grandmother's white baby grand piano in the living room. But, it was Jason who noticed the chip near the pedal that made him realize something was off."

"How did you explain being put into the program?"

"They took this mostly in stride, except the part about never having contact with anyone from their old life, which included their friends and relatives. All traces of our former life would merely vanish. It was more as a way to ensure our safety than keeping them in the dark about what happened to us. They changed our identities and gave us new I.D. cards, birth certificates, social security cards, including medical and dental records, and our surname changed to Thompson."

"So, you told them about what precipitated this move to Virginia?" Dr. Laurel asks.

"Most of it. Over time, we realized Lenard and Gene were phony FBI men, and the real CIA came to our rescue. That's when I met Adrian. The volatile information on the CD I gave you explained most of it. The consensus was that there was an obvious threat to our lives, especially when ties to the Middle East surfaced."

"You've grown fond of Mr. Levi and his group, haven't you?" Dr. Laurel says, smiling.

"Yes, Levi has become a trusted friend. He gave us declassified information. Specifically, a letter that was found sealed in their vaults at CIA Headquarters. It explained in detail that both my Daddy and Ravi were CIA Agents, and this single piece of paper shed light on our situation. Once Levi and his teams dissected and put it back together, they found damning evidence to suggest my family was part of an elaborate plot that had been in motion for many years. It was not a simple scheme, and it involved both International and U.S. Foreign Policies."

"What do you think is the worst part of all this, Ellen?"

"I think it was finding out that my dead husband and my captor were brothers. This revelation was extremely hard for me to grasp, and as the teams followed the trail of crumbs, they were able to link the ancient documents (that belonged to my husband Ravi's family), old currency (that once belonged to my father's adoptive uncle), right to my son Jason. Things spiraled out of control from there. As one event ended, another would appear. Mr. Levi described it as the most peculiar and intriguing adventure in CIA history, but I wouldn't call it that!"

"You've made remarkable strides, Ellen. Let's talk about positive aspects. You started a new business and moved on with your life."

"I suppose you're right, Dr. Laurel, but sometimes, this all comes back to me in nightmares. Some unseen hand is always chasing me, and I wake up in damp pajamas."

"It's quite remarkable how you got through it, Ellen. You and Adrian fell in love and married in Saudi, correct?"

"Yes, in a lovely ceremony in the one place I vowed never to set foot in again--the Royal Palace of my brother-in-law, one King Ak-dim-er Abdul Major Pain-in-the-Ass. Wouldn't you agree that the last event is so unbelievable and so wretched that it saps my strength thinking about it? It twists me up, and comes out as depression; my son Jason is missing and it's a wonder that I'm able to function at all!"

Dr. Laurel stares at me. "Yes, I do agree with your assessment."

"Will I ever be able to let this go?"

"In time, I hope to help you work it out," she says quietly.

"It has subsided over the years. It's the random flashes of anxiety and sadness that permeates my thoughts during the day. There are other times, where it sucks me into extreme mood changes where I laugh aloud when things are not especially funny, or cry when things are. It's as if my brain does a flip-flop and two people inhabit my mind, the old Ellen Andress, and the new Ellen Thompson-Sellers."

"That's a normal response from someone who has gone through trauma such as yours. You did a marvelous job of keeping yourself busy."

"Renovating every room in the Manor House was a welcome challenge. It gave me back a sense of pride and accomplishment. After that, I immersed myself in harness racing, until an old tailbone injury made it so painful, that it was impossible to go even a mile on the race bike seat."

"Do you think things would have turned out differently if you had insisted Jason *not* go to Saudi?"

"Jason would have gone, with or without my consent. We did try to warn him, but he wouldn't listen."

"How is the rest of the family coping with their issues?"

"The rest of the family seems to be coping better than me. I know they miss Jason, but they've been able to go on with their lives with little trouble. The past events don't seem to bother them as they do me. Every so often little things creep into my mind, and I get annoyed with myself for letting them invade my thoughts. Trying to concentrate on the future, and dwelling negatively on what happened is what disturbs me the most because I'm not a true pessimist!"

"You mentioned that your nephew and Jason's best friend are your harness drivers. How is that working out?"

"It's been good. When my nephew, Danny, was inadvertently brought into our drama, it heightened our awareness of potential danger. The CIA made the unprecedented decision to bring my sister and her family to Virginia and include them into the program. When Jason left for college, his best friend, Mack, came to train with us. Then Danny surprised us by wanting to join the racing team."

"It sounds as if they are an integral part of Ashwood Stables."

"They and their trainers all make it work. You know, Adrian pushed me to come here. He said it's why God made psychiatrists. That sleeping aid dulled the sensation, it didn't resolve it, but reliving our incredible story does help to recall things that have remained unresolved. The problem doesn't stem from my childhood, does it?"

"No, I'm convinced it's the extenuating circumstances that brought you to Virginia in the first place," she says pensively.

"How many years will it take to wash away the dreams that haunt me?"

"There is no timetable for grief, Ellen."

"If only I had trusted my gut about those two idiots who passed themselves off as Special FBI Agents. They were far from special. I'm so angry with myself. I should have known better."

"That's what we need to work on, Ellen. It's called unnecessary baggage. Everyone has some, not all of us know what to do with it. Are you still able to meditate?"

"Yes and no. It's not always easy to shut the world out and keep a business running at the same time."

"I understand. Our time is up for today, Ellen, but see you next week?"

"Sure."

Getting through the rest of the afternoon is difficult. I try to suppress my negative thoughts, but somehow, our after-dinner subject tonight is meditation.

"How's that comin along for ya Missy?" asks Glen, as he shovels food into his mouth. "I hear that stuff makes ya sleepy."

We can always count on Glen to chime in with something whether it's pertinent to the subject, or otherwise. He and his wife, Mona, came with the property, stayed on when the estate dried up and never thought the place would prosper again until we showed up. He's been our trainer, barn manager, and paternal father figure for some time now.

Our cook Nancy shares kitchen duties with Mona. Mona continues to supply the bakery in town with her amazing pastries, pies, and bread. Mother is her sidekick, helps with the menus, baking, and shopping, along with supervising the children, and delegating the household chores as she sees fit.

"It's not a medication, Glen; it's called meditation. Anyway, that's what it does to me."

"I think Dr. Laurel wants you to meditate," Mother volunteers, "so you can get more rest. Maybe you won't be so crabby then."

"I'm not crabby!" Everyone starts to grumble with this assessment. "Am I that crabby? Oh boy, I am so sorry for doing that everyone!"

"Meditation," Terre muses. "Isn't it supposed to relax you and take you on a journey? Wasn't that called transcendental meditation?"

"Does meditation transport you somewhere? Can it take us to Paris?" Adrian suddenly realizes that he has said the P word. "Sorry sweetheart, I meant the Mexican Riviera, anywhere but there, honestly."

"It doesn't work that way. The meditation we're doing now is different from the transcendental version. You put yourself where you've seen your loved one. You imagine hugging and talking to them. Anyway, if this doesn't work, she said we could try something else."

Danny starts to laugh. "Did she give you a meditation mannequin to practice with?"

"You should seriously think before you open your mouth, Danny," his sister Ginny says, shaking her head as she pushes the little tea cart around the room. She stops, then says, "To explore strange new worlds, meditation seeks out new life and new civilizations. It boldly goes where no one has gone before."

"OH!" Lindy exclaims, "that's good. Star Trek, of course."

"Hey, is meditation like a placement something?" Mack mutters.

"You mean placebo," Mother offers. "Do you need a piece of clothing, like a bloodhound would need to sniff to do this meditation thing?"

"Boy, I wish I had Dr. Laurel's tape recorder. She would have a field day with you people."

Adrian waits to vindicate himself, "Hey, is anyone up for a cruise? We could sail around the Caribbean, snorkel, do a little fishing, sightseeing. We could eat, drink, and be merry while we meditate."

"Didn't work, did it?" Dennis mumbles my way, and then he looks at Terre, as she shakes her head.

"Not so far, but the nap part works great! It should only take a few more meditation sessions to get back to normal."

"Yeah, no one can disturb her Royal Highness for at least two hours," Adrian cracks.

"Please do not call me that! I will give you Royal Highness." Throwing a roll at Adrian's head, he mechanically turns toward me, and then reaches up to catch it.

"How did you do that, Uncle Adrian?" Danny asks in amazement.

"Yeah, how did you know she was gonna throw that roll at you?" Mack stammers.

"Have ya practiced that a long time?" Glen chortles. "You two b'long in the circus. One's comin to town in a few weeks. Bet they'd hire ya."

Adrian laughs, as he chews on the roll. "Instinct, fellas, pure and simple instinct."

"Okay, the show's over for tonight. Don't you have somewhere else to go boys?"

Adrian, Terre, Dennis, and I walk toward the library, as Mother goes up the staircase to her room. We've not ventured out of Virginia since Jason disappeared except for an occasional visit to Melanie's college. Was I afraid he would show up and not find us here?

"Adrian, you mentioned a cruise. Are you serious?"

"Would you like to travel, Ellie? I thought you couldn't tear yourself away from here."

"Maybe. I've been working on a little adventure."

As I start to feel better mentally and physically, Adrian and I discuss a little trip that might help us focus on ourselves. So far, I have kept the details a secret. It gives me the right amount to motivate myself out of bed each morning.

The home meditative sessions continue, and when Dr. Laurel hears about the naps, she's not at all surprised about the outcome. In her opinion, any kind of rest that allows me to overcome a sleep-deprived, foggy brain, is beneficial.

"Instead of giving myself reasons why I can't,
I give myself reasons why I can."

~Unknown

Chapter Two

New Standardbred Horses

Although our horses, *Lester's Best* and *Raindrop Dew,* have performed admirably and moved up in class with Danny and Mack to guide them, they are aging nonetheless. And as Jason predicted, before he left for Saudi more than three years ago, they are not what will take us to the championships and beyond.

A few nights after our discussion about travel, most of the adults are lingering at the dinner table enjoying one of Mona's mouth-watering desserts and having one of our more enlightened post-dinner discussions about time travel. After we exhaust this topic, I decide it might be the opportunity to segue into another subject with the family.

"I've located a few horse farms in Kentucky that I want to visit. Adrian, are you up for a trip with the horse trailer?"

"Is that my surprise?" he says, in a disappointed tone. "We're going horse shopping? I was so hoping for something else, you know, like a fancy hotel kind of surprise that's way outlandish. Or maybe a romantic getaway to a warmer climate, like a sandy type beach thing, exotic like Hawaii maybe."

Glen starts to chuckle, "Ya ain't gonna try doin that again are ya, Missy? Ya don't think we have enough stuff 'round here to keep us busy?"

"Are you trying to rain on my parade, old man?"

Reed says, "We could use a few runners, Glen."

Reed and Glen share training duties. He and his wife Dr. Jess, and their two children reside in the Carriage House. He's having dinner with us tonight while they are away visiting her family.

Nathan, Reed's best friend from college, excused himself to go to the barn right after dinner. He isn't keen on our nightly conversations and is uncomfortable when we make him sit through our banter.

Glen mutters, "She don't mean that she means about the horses, don't cha, Missy? Ya don't think we did a good job bringin home *Lester* and *Raindrop*."

Reed starts to laugh. "We don't mean for it to sound like we're complaining, right Glen?"

"No hard feelings, fellas, but I'd like to be involved this time. You did a great job of bringing *Lester* and *Raindrop* back to the stables. I want to do something useful again. We could be training our champion now if we had a couple of new Standardbred horses."

Glen begins to snort, saying, "I'm glad you're feelin better, but ya thought *Lester* or *Raindrop* was gonna be your champions? Now that's darn right funny, Missy. Almost as funny as…"

"Don't go there, Mr. Glen. I know what you're about to say. *Lester* and *Raindrop* are not the horses that will take us to the championship. We need new blood."

Danny chuckles. "Aunt Ellen, are you going to hire new trainers and drivers, too?"

"We're good with the teams we have now, Danny Boy. We're looking into other possibilities, that's all. If Ashwood Stables wins a significant championship, it will gain more prestige. That prestige means higher earning power. You potentially could earn a substantial increase."

Danny glances over at a quiet Mack who stares wide-eyed in my direction. "I didn't know that."

"Ain't ya gonna talk her outta that, Adrian?" Glen says, shaking his head.

"This time she happens to be right fellas, and I am happy to oblige. We need a little time away even if it is to sniff at horses," he says laughing.

"Sniff at horses? Where do you come up with this stuff, Adrian? We do need a change of scenery. We might be gone about a week maybe more. Think you all can handle things while we're away?"

"Maybe Terre and I could join you," Dennis says, looking at his wife.

Terre shakes her head. "We've talked about this, honey. If they wanted us to come along, they would have asked us."

"Sorry for not including you and Dennis this time. We'll plan something else, okay? There are a few stables I'd like to visit, and I do not intend to come home without a prize or two."

Everyone has been anxious, as my temperament has been less than stellar lately. Dr. Laurel suggested a different type of over-the-counter sleep medication; however, it carries over to the next morning and leaves me foggy-brained. I'm also prone to mood swings, but this is more likely due to the lovely change in-life-status, which presents an entirely new set of miseries.

Adrian sees our journey to find new horses a welcome respite to the tragedy that seems to linger around here. Even our resident ghosts have been quiet, an occasional breeze here and there, with a shadow that passes the sizeable upstairs window when I glance at it while getting into, or out of my car.

My research narrowed down to three stables that are all within a hundred miles of each other. With capable hands, it will be business as usual at Ashwood Stables while Adrian and I go off on our little trip. Glen, Reed, and Nathan will keep everything in excellent working order, so Danny and Mack can race while we're gone.

Since we never had our Paris honeymoon, I'm determined that this little excursion will be memorable for Adrian, at least that's the plan. I have booked us into some expensive hotels along the way, adding extra days, which will also give us some quality time alone.

With everything squared away at Ashwood, we embark on the first leg of our journey that takes us to a quaint little town in rural Kentucky called Charmed. We ask the owner how the small town got its name, but Mr. Smith laughs, says it's a funny story, and then changes the subject. He's more anxious to show us his bevy of Standardbred horses than he is to kibitz with us. Less than impressed, I politely tell Mr. Smith we are not interested, thank him, and then retreat to our truck.

"What was wrong with those horses, Ellie? I mean, what are you looking for in a horse?"

"That's a good question, Adrian. I don't know how to explain it to you in terms you'll understand."

"Come on Ellie, try it. The horses looked okay to me. How do you know that the horse will be a winner? We weren't there very long. All you did was watch them run around."

"It has a little to do with instinct and a lot to do with what the horse does when he moves. I'm not sure I can explain it to you. It's almost as complicated as wagering." Laughing to recall the lessons I tried to give him when he wanted to learn how to bet, and how he stubbornly refused to adhere to those instructions, I merely shake my head.

"Never mind, on to our next destination. Are we stopping soon, because I'm getting a little hungry."

"We have to go about forty miles yet. You're always hungry. Hang on; I'll get something out of the cooler to tide you over until dinner."

"I hope Mona packed some of my favorites," he says, rolling his eyes.

"You mean like her famous chicken?"

A memory flashes of Jason. When he and Mack went to New York the winter after they graduated from high school, he started to study martial arts and didn't indulge in a bunch of junk food. He ate whatever Mona and his Grandmother Francesca had on the menu. Dr. Laurel said it's healthy to remember things about Jason, as long as I don't ruminate about them.

Our next stop is a fancy hotel where Adrian raises his eyebrows, "What's going on? Is this where we're staying tonight?"

"It's one of your surprises. I thought since we don't have any horses to worry about yet, we could stay here a few nights."

After we check in, a bellhop takes us to the presidential suite on the third floor. Adrian admits this is a good idea, for the simple reason that we are never alone. We have almost no privacy except our bedroom, which at times feels like it has a revolving door.

During my therapy sessions we discussed how important it is to reconnect with Adrian. He was supportive when we learned about Daddy and Ravi and their secrets, and she helped me realize that Adrian needs to feel special. She has also helped me to understand that my melancholy is typical, and it's a little different when a child goes missing.

Before we left, Mother took me aside to say that it's time to let Jason go. "Hold him in your heart, Ellie, but don't allow his death to take the wind out of your sails. You have survived worse. The rest of the family needs you. And don't let the tragedies of the past haunt you into turning into yourself. I know first-hand what depression can do to a person; it robs one of so much."

We open the door to the suite to find champagne chilling in a silver bucket. The rooms are excellently appointed; a large vase of fresh-cut, fragrant flowers are arranged on the dining room table while soft music plays in the background. As we move through the room and into our bedroom, the bellhop points out the en-suite, excusing himself after Adrian gives him a tip.

"This is a nice surprise, Ellie. Well done my little chick-a-dee."

"That's not all." Extracting a shimmering black nightie, I move it across my arm in a seductive gesture.

"That's a nice surprise, too! You don't go in for stuff like that. Is that for me?" Adrian rolls his eyes, then puts a finger to his cheek in a comical gesture, which makes me laugh.

"I am so sorry for being somewhere else for so long, Adrian. I hope this makes up for all the bad things I did."

"You didn't do anything bad, except ignore me. What counts now, is that we're together. An ordinary person would have gone off the deep end, but you didn't. I love you, my little Ellie May."

"Are you saying I'm not normal?"

"No. I'm saying you are extraordinary." Adrian dances me around the room, saying, "Oh la la. Soup de jour! Come here, my little fem fatal!" We stumble onto the bed. "What's for dinner, my little sherry?"

"That's *femme fatale*, Adrian."

"Um, what else is there to nibble on besides you?"

"The chef is preparing something special and the *pièce de résistance* will be *Vol au vent* and *petit fours* followed by *café au lait*."

Adrian puts both of his hands on his cheeks and declares, "*Sacré blue!*" I laugh at the way he does this. He can't remember the French words we both studied for our nonexistent honeymoon to Paris. "Was that a fax pox?"

"Oh Adrian, you are such a clown. I have missed that about you."

"I was humorous. You were too busy to notice," he says. "As long as you are *all natural* later tonight, I don't care what we eat."

"*Merci.*"

"God bless you," Adrian says with a straight face, nodding his head comically.

"I didn't sneeze, sweetie. I said thank you."

Adrian's eyes twinkle with delight. "Are you thanking me ahead of time, or are you just being polite?"

After dinner arrives, Adrian remarks how incredible it looks spread out on the dining room table. It reminds us both of New Orleans at Mardi Gras, as everything is plentiful and presented on colorful platters. It also reminds me that we don't get out much.

"Do you miss single life, Adrian? I mean, do you miss being with your friends at the CIA and traveling?"

"I see the friends I want to see, Ellie. As for traveling, I've had quite enough of that, thanks very much. If you have another trip in mind, though, let's talk about it."

"You know where I want to go, Adrian. I'm beginning to think that it's a dream, not reality."

Adrian studies me. "I can't help you get past that. Dr. Laurel is the only one who can help you unlock that mystery." He raises his glass and smiles. "You are an amazing person, Ellie. I am so glad that you came into my life, and you want me to share the rest of it with you. I love you more than you will ever know."

"That was beautiful. You came into *my* life just when I needed you. You have always been here for us, and I am grateful for that. You said it would never be dull. We both have to admit it's been a hell of a journey."

"Yes, I believe you're right. Thank you for this, Ellie. Pass that platter, *s'il vous plaît*."

"Thanks are never needed, Adrian. I love you always."

Adrian grins, "I don't know how to say this in French, but when dinner's over, can we test-drive your nightie?"

"Why certainly!"

The next horse farm we visit has miles and miles of white picket fencing, which is along a scenic, tree-lined driveway. As we approach a large covered arena, a ranch hand motions us toward a parking lot. He introduces himself as Harry. He takes us around one side of the barn and says the owner will bring out several horses that he feels might be right for us.

"Take a seat, and Mr. Campbell will be out directly."

Something caught my eye as we drove up the driveway and I turn around to watch a mare with her colt frolic in an adjoining pasture. Adrian taps me on the arm and asks what I'm looking at, as he thinks I'm ignoring the horses we came to see.

The owner introduces himself as Boyd Campbell. He knows right away that I'm not interested in what he has to show us, as I have turned around again to watch the mare and her colt.

"How old is that little fella out there, Mr. Campbell?"

"That there's *Shoo Fly Pie* and that's *Buttercup Delight's* foal. Please call me Boyd, Ma'am."

Mr. Campbell's lazy drawl immediately reminds me of Glen. "I would like to take a closer look at them if I may, Boyd. They might be what we need."

Boyd glances from Adrian to me and back to Adrian again. "He's not what you want Ma'am. He's too young to leave the farm. I'd say, if you want that one, you have to either wait a while or take 'em both."

Without hesitation, I say, "Then, we'll take them both."

"You're gettin a good deal with those two, Ma'am and you won't regret it, I assure you."

"We could use a mare to train with the other horses we have. We lost a good runner a while back and this would be a good addition to our stables. The little one will attract youngsters that come to our property."

"Are you thinking Reed would like to do his therapeutic riding for children again? Didn't he used to do that at a dude ranch out west before he came to Ashwood?"

"That's a great idea, Adrian. I'll bet that he would like this little one, for sure. He did work with children with disabilities. We'll talk to him about that when we get back."

After we negotiate a price, we ask Mr. Campbell to hold the horses a few days, as we have another stable to visit. Competition is keen for racehorses, and he's curious, asking where we are going next. I don't want this to become an incendiary incident, so we don't say anything, as we've had enough of those to last a lifetime.

Adrian is bursting with questions. "Why did you want the mare, Ellie? And why did you pick that little horse? Boyd said he wasn't ready to train yet."

"We were going to use *Truly Yours* as a practice horse so *Buttercup* will do nicely for that. And you know how *Lester* likes to train with other horses. The little one has spunk. We don't have to train him now;

he'll learn as he goes. We'll let him go loose around the track with the other horses. Then Glen and Reed can take over. Besides, *Shoo Fly* is perfect for children."

Adrian knows better than to keep asking questions when it comes to my 'horse sense.' When I don't elaborate further, he goes along with my decision.

At the last horse farm, the owner is known as one of the most reputable breeders of Standardbred horses. Mike personally takes us into his barn and talks on about the care and attention each of his horses receives. My research has turned up some interesting facts that several of his stock has gone on to win some very large purses.

As I glance out one of the open barn windows, something catches my eye, and I move closer to watch a beautiful bay colt that is standing near a fence.

"Is that one out in the pasture for sale, Mike?" I am already walking toward the horse.

"You mean *Peanut Brittle?*" Mike says, a little startled. "I can't sell you that horse, Mrs. Sellers. That one ain't going to be a winner. He's too high-strung, and no one likes to train with him and it ain't for lack of tryin. He's plain mean, and he don't like bein with the others if ya know what I mean."

It reminds me of Glen's exact words of a few years ago, as the memory of *Didgeridoo* surfaces. "I've heard that before, Mike."

Mike persists. "Maybe he's a bit too young yet. He's only a one-year-old. He's not too friendly, either, kinda took a chunk outta the last hand that tried to put a bridle on him."

"Again, Mike, I have also heard that before."

Mike cautions, "Don't say I didn't warn ya, Mrs. Sellers."

"Do you mind if I say hello to him?"

Mike takes off his hat and waves it in a little arch, saying, "No, Ma'am, go on ahead and see for yourself."

Adrian knows from experience that I need to talk and perhaps touch the animal, so he engages Mike in conversation about a subject he knows only slightly, betting on the ponies. Laughing to myself, I stroll toward the horse and stand near the fence, and then pull a carrot out of my bag and hold it out, so he can't nip my fingers.

"Hello, *Peanut Brittle*." The big horse lifts his head, stares straight at me, pricks his ears, and for a split second, a horse named *At Lightening Speed* flashes before my eyes. It was the day I came to live at Ashwood. My eyes fill with tears at the memory of how we discovered that he was named *Didgeridoo*. I remember thinking that he would be a good horse to train. The horrible way he died was as senseless as what happened to *Truly Yours*.

The fact that our local Sheriff never caught who did these deeds still troubles me. Is this one of those unresolved issues that I need to discuss with Dr. Laurel? Will this horse be able to live up to what *Didge's* potential might have been?

Peanut Brittle slowly moves toward me and stops about three feet away. As I whisper to him, I wiggle the carrot, and he moves closer. Lowering his head, he starts to nibble. I stay still so that he won't spook, and when I feel he's ready for me to touch him, I reach up to stroke his nose with my free hand. His big brown eye is level with my face, and he surprises me by nuzzling my head, disengaging when a farm tractor backfires.

Mike mumbles behind me, "I'll be darned. He don't ever do that for nobody – not even if he's offered a sugar cube!"

Adrian proudly states, "She has that effect on them, my little wife, the horse whisperer. She will want to buy the horse now."

We negotiate a suitable deal for *Peanut Brittle* and arrange for his pickup, and then drive to a local hotel that caters to the rich and famous (or as rich and famous as they pass through here, anyway). The lobby has framed photos of movie stars, presidents, and notable dignitaries hanging on the walls.

"I doubt very much if all these people stayed here. What have you planned for us tonight, Ellie? I'm not sure you can top what you did yesterday!"

"It's a surprise. We're not staying here; I'm meeting someone for directions. And I can't tell you, because then I'd have to, you know the rest."

Adrian starts to laugh. "Never mind, I like surprises. I like your surprises, anyway."

"We're going on a little adventure. It's a sunset sailing cruise complete with dinner. I'm sorry it isn't more elaborate."

"I don't see any water!" Adrian declares.

"It's on a private lake, silly. Come on, and I'll show you."

As it turns out, our dinner consists of a picnic basket filled with gourmet food, a bottle of champagne, and a rowboat tied to a walkout pier built near a cozy cabin in the woods. The setting is spectacular and the sunset colorful and quiet.

We've been gone over a week, stopping to explore sites we passed on our way to look at horses, and have stretched it out to relax and enjoy ourselves. We are now ready for our trek home.

After we pick up our new horses and settle them into the trailer, Adrian gives them a mild natural medication Dr. Jessica said would help in their transport. Horses don't like being in the confines of a horse trailer for extended periods, as it rocks, rolls, and is generally uncomfortable for them. So the sooner we can get them home, the better.

Two hours into our trip, Adrian's cellphone chirps and we know by the ringtone that it's Levi. Adrian pulls over at the next rest stop and gets out of the truck.

"Tell Levi I said hello...."

He nods his head and walks toward the sidewalk, jumping up on the fence as he does so often back home. While he chats with Levi, I get out to stretch my legs and check on the horses. *Buttercup's* nose is sticking through the open window of the trailer and I absently pat it.

As I reach for the door handle, Adrian suddenly jumps off the fence and starts to pace back and forth in front of the truck, every so often moving his lips. Mostly, he waves his free arm around, and I get the feeling that something is wrong. When he climbs into the cab of the truck, he squeezes the steering wheel so hard that his knuckles turn white. I know better than to drill him and wait for him to speak.

Adrian lets out a long breath, then says, "Houston, we have a problem."

It is one of our codes that means something is very wrong. These codes came in handy several times, but in the intervening years, have mostly gone unused.

"What did Levi say?"

"I'm not going to beat around the bush, Ellie. He said that the Solana person called Andrea Simmons is still alive."

"What? How could that be, Adrian? I thought she was dead. Levi said she was dead! What does this mean? Will she come after us? Why didn't she stay dead?"

Adrian puts his arm around me. "No one is more shocked than Levi, Ellie. His teams never mess up like this. The person we all thought was Andrea Simmons was a decoy. The woman impersonating her must have had plastic surgery. The real Solana surfaced about three days ago."

"Surfaced? Where is she?"

"I'm not at liberty to say. We thought this part of the case was over."

It is freakishly unbelievable.

"We can't go back to my family and tell them bad news is on the way! We have to do something! It is not what we need now. When you think it's safe to go back into the water, something happens, and you're afraid all over again. Why now, why couldn't she stay dead? Why isn't this over yet, Adrian? After all the crap we've been through, why isn't this over?"

"I don't know, Ellie, somehow we'll get through it, I promise you. Try not to think about it."

"I'll try." But in reality, we don't know what's coming. "A crystal ball would come in handy right about now. Or the ability to accurately predict the future would certainly be helpful. Then of course, if we had those, we could find Jason."

Adrian steers the truck away from the parking space and proceeds toward the freeway slowly, so the horses aren't shaken unnecessarily. I can't squelch the funny feeling that comes over me. It isn't foreboding this time, and it isn't that odd *déjà vu* thing that we've been there and done that, and it's about to happen again. It's more like anticipation.

Most of the unsettled particulars have worked themselves out over the years, while others continue to linger. The inscrutable phony FBI agent named Lenard went deep into the penal system after our government extradited him to Germany. Both Gene (also a phony FBI agent) and their supposed leader named Solana/Andrea perished years ago, each in a strange-type accident.

"Do you suppose that Gene isn't really dead too? If Andrea isn't dead, maybe he's still alive!"

"Levi can only speculate on some of the information. Jewels thinks she might be unhappy that we caught Uncle Ruggeri so quickly and he's behind bars. Maybe she wasn't paid for her part in all this, and she wants revenge."

"Revenge! What a great word. I'll be happy to give her revenge. How about Ellen's Revenge?"

"You mean Montezuma's Revenge?" he adds with a chuckle.

"No, I mean Ellen Thompson dash Sellers' revenge. If anybody deserves retaliation, I certainly do. Maybe she's also furious that Lenard told you everything. Do you think she will stalk us now? She can't think I'll give her money. I will most assuredly not give her money!"

"We can't figure any other angle. Except, now that Fariq is gone," Adrian says pensively, "it could mean that she's after her part of the fortune."

"Why would this Solana person want part of that fortune?"

"I told you, sweetheart, you don't remember. You have been somewhere else for a long time, Ellie. We figured Solana might know Fariq and he must have promised her something. Fariq was the one who was behind the whole thing."

"What whole thing? You mean that he was behind Jason's disappearance?"

"Ellie, where have you been? You were told about all this."

"I certainly would have remembered a little detail like that. How would Solana know Fariq? Wait a minute; I thought she worked for that crazy Uncle Ruggeri!"

"And then bamboozled Uncle Ruggeri into thinking that she worked for him when all the time she was working with Fariq, you mean?" Adrian concludes.

"Where was I when you disclosed this information?"

Adrian looks thoughtful and then bites down on his bottom lip. "You might not have been receptive to our conversations. Without rehashing all the details, Levi suggests we use extreme caution."

"Why would she be mad at us? She should be mad at Fariq. Maybe she's the one behind all the incidents we haven't quite explained away. She might be the one who took Jason. Maybe he was already gone when she got to the palace. When Fariq wouldn't give her any money, she figured she would come here and take Melanie or Curlie to use as bait!"

"No, I don't think she has that in mind. She would be crazy to try that, honey."

"Adrian, you don't think she's crazy enough to do that? I'm scared. All over again. It's happening all over again."

"To be on the safe side, we'll open up the shelter in the basement. You should practice with your little Glock again, too. You know, the CIA is a little like a soap opera when we have to work out plots and subplots when it comes to a case. Levi used to say we have more drama than an action-packed mystery movie. The big difference is that the movie mystery gets solved within two-hours; when we have a big case, it takes years to close one of those."

"May I remind you that it's been years for us, too Adrian. Especially when this ridiculous thing started when Jason was fifteen, and now he's twenty-four. That crazy person could have something to do with his disappearance, you know."

"Yes, it has been years, and there is no way of knowing what this Solana woman is up to, Ellie, we need to keep our eyes open. And I hate to say this, but we may never know what happened to Jason, sweetie. I wish I had the magic words to help you."

"I wish you had a magic wand so that we could wish Jason back home."

"Levi reckons that Jake and Josh should come and stay with us for a while until things blow over and there are no more surprises."

"I think that's a good idea."

The ride home is quiet except for the music playing on the radio. Every once in a while, Adrian and I talk about the events that brought us to today and how those events changed both of our lives. Levi had explained the entire story to us some years ago. He had laid it out in painful detail, once his teams had enough information to share with the family.

Questions start to formulate in my head, so I reach into my bag for a little notebook. It's the one I keep handy to write things down in before they float away. What does Solana have to do with Ravi's past? How did she get involved with the nasty uncle that Daddy tried to avoid for so long?

What does Solana hope to gain by conspiring with the likes of Fariq! It all seems to go back to him and the Royal Palace. Could she be the common denominator that has puzzled us for so long? Could it have anything to do with the ancient documents again? Or why my late husband left the Royal Household in the first place?

"What are you doing, you look so serious," Adrian asks.

"I'm formulating some hypotheses about how this Solana woman fits into our drama."

"What have you got so far? Remember when we used to go back and forth? You always came up with good questions. We haven't done that in a long while. Why don't we try it, it could help?" Adrian reaches to turn off the radio.

"We need a police whiteboard, Adrian. Now there are too many players and timelines to sort through. I know Levi and his teams have gone over everything with a fine-toothed comb, but we're missing something. Somehow this Solana woman is part of this, but I don't know what it is."

"Okay, say you're right, I'm not saying that you are, but if we do this, you have to be upfront with me and not hide things."

"Adrian, I have never lied to you. Besides, I'm only formulating a hypothesis."

Adrian blows out a breath. "I said that wrong. Didn't you keep the ancient documents and the currency a little secret? You didn't put that in your official report when you first came to CIA Headquarters if I recall."

"In my defense, I didn't know you then. So many people lied to us; I didn't know you and Levi could be trusted."

Adrian says with a pout, "You trust me now, don't you?"

"Would I have married you if I didn't trust you? Honestly, we have truly been up a creek without a paddle more times than I care to count, and if you, Larry, Levi, and his teams hadn't come to our rescue, I don't know what we would have done."

"Okay, but if you get the slightest whiff something is either about to happen, or you have that thing you get that tells you stuff in your head, you have to tell me right away, okay?"

"Whiff, Adrian, you think I get whiffs of information?" He still doesn't get the *déjà vu* thing or understand how premonitions work. "Do you think they float out of the sky and I catch them in my brain with a net?"

"Ellie, I didn't mean it like that. Let's try that again. You have a marvelous mind, and you come up with some excellent stuff."

"You mean like the hypothesis?"

"Yeah, that thing. What do you have so far?"

"It's more like a suggestion. What is Solana after, hum? If we can prove what it is, we might be able to figure out how she's involved in all this."

"Hypothetically speaking, it could be one of those things you do when you have those episodes where you go somewhere, and you can't explain it."

"Outstanding, Adrian. Hypothetically speaking, it's an assumption rather than fact, or reality. I'll bet she knows more about this than anyone gives her credit. Maybe she knows more than that goofy Lenard or Gene put together. She could be behind this whole thing, you know. Hey, a good mystery always points to the person that is the least obvious to do the murder."

Adrian shakes his head. "That's not how it works in real life, my little tangerine. It only happens in the movies when the scriptwriters write it that way. And I don't think she knew everything."

"How do you know it doesn't work like that? I met her before Lenard and Gene showed up, remember? Maybe she had all this planned out and didn't include them in her plans when they started to screw things up. Or, maybe she didn't trust them, and it didn't come to me in an episode; it came to me in my brain alone."

"First of all, Lenard is buried so deep inside a mountain in Germany that it would take a crane to lift him out of it, metaphorically speaking, that is. We can rule him out for now. And we're convinced that Gene is dead. They found his body in the Potomac, remember? He's off the grid."

"Adrian, you get a gold star for that one, but you missed the entire point."

He doesn't often miss the point. This banter back and forth usually leads to productive conversation, as he knows it helps to develop questions, which mostly lead to decent conclusions. "What did I miss?"

"You forgot the top player in all this. The king from across the ocean named Ak-dim-er, aka Uncle Dimmy, aka the Most Royal Pain that ever lived. And I would be slapdash if I didn't mention his giant sidekick G-man. I can't connect the dots yet. It's not the fact that Dimmy and Ravi were brothers, either, it's something altogether different."

"What the heck does slapdash mean? Anyway, for once, Ellie I don't agree with you. Akdemir went out of his way to bring us all to the Royal Palace for our wedding. He wanted Jason as his rightful heir. I honestly don't think he would allow harm to come to him!"

"Oh, now you're taking his side, are you?"

"I'm not taking his side, darling, but he paid for Jason's college. I can't see where he has an ulterior motive other than the fact that he was your brother-in-law and uncle to your children, and wants desperately to be your family. Why would he jeopardize that?"

"Something isn't right about all that, and we may never know what it is. Jam-ale is the only connection we have to the Royal Palace now, and I can't bring myself to talk to him. I get so emotional thinking about what happened."

"Hold that thought, we'll have to talk later, Ellie. The traffic's getting worse."

Due to our heightened risk, Levi sent a female CIA Agent to make sure Melanie remains safe while she attends college. Not an hour after the agent arrived, Mel called to rant her displeasure about how unfair life is and can't the agent stay near her, but not in the same apartment? I had the feeling the agent may have cramped Mel's style, and to that, Adrian concluded, "That's too bad the agent stays!"

The rest of the trip was uneventful. As we approached Ashwood, the front gate swung open, and Nathan waved, pointing us toward the barn,

where the family waited to welcome us home. When Reed pulled *Peanut Brittle* out of the trailer, we watched as Glen solemnly removed his hat, where he remarked that for a moment, he thought *Didge* had come back to life!
Bless my soul, perhaps he has!

Dr. Jessica examined the little colt named *Shoo Fly Pie,* whom we coaxed away from his mother with a gentle hand and a treat. She then moved on to *Buttercup,* without saying a word. After she checked all the horses, Danny and Mack stepped in to take the mare and colt to the south pasture.

Rosie waited patiently until the horses moved off, and then put her snout under my hand so that I would pet her head.

"The little medication I gave you worked okay for the trip home?" Dr. Jess asks in her matter-of-fact-way as she snaps her medical bag shut.

Adrian says, "They took that stuff with no problem. What do you think of them, health-wise?"

"They are in excellent health. Their owners did a good job in caring for them. Their teeth and ears are clear, coats are shiny, and there's no evidence of malnutrition. They've been fed well, no fat in the neck or around the tail-head. I'll try to get a stool sample and runs some tests, but in my opinion, they're fine specimens. You did fine in choosing them, Ellen."

"Why thank you, Dr. Jessica."

"You are quite welcome." She then moves away and into the barn in her usual, no-nonsense manner.

Jake and Josh arrive and settle themselves into the extra bedrooms vacated by the ostracized Akdemir and his entourage. Since I forbid Dimmy from ever stepping foot into this house again after he failed to keep Jason safe, it seems fitting that they make themselves comfortable. It's a slight disruption of the order of things, nonetheless, a necessary precaution under the circumstances.

Since no one knows the whereabouts of this Andrea/Solana woman, Levi instructed them to comb the area, check out our equipment, and make sure the shelter in the basement is secure and ready for possible habitation. When the family hears what we're doing, they naturally moan their displeasure but continue going on about their lives as if nothing is amiss.

Danny figured that he might as well take up residence in Jason's old room. I was glad that he felt comfortable enough with the resident ghosts to do that. I have also told him not to get too comfortable, as Jason could pop out of nowhere and demand eminent domain. Danny laughed, as he knew I was trying to lighten a difficult situation.

As we discussed on our trip home from Kentucky, we will come at this latest threat like a police investigation. As Adrian works on his theory, I work on mine. It also gives me something to focus on, other than feeling helpless about Jason. A whiteboard will be hard to hide, so the family tree I drew a while ago will have to do. As information became available, I added it on and when things changed, crossed some off. Then I copied it and gave it to Adrian.

Although the odd occurrences that once plagued us have almost stopped, we have never found out who murdered *Digeridoo* or *Truly Yours*. Will this come back to haunt us? Will something happen when we least expect it? Maybe I'm carrying a slight grudge against some people who rubbed me the wrong way when we started to race.

We have had few altercations with drivers and owners down at the racetrack the last several years, but my gut feeling is that we should stay away from our neighbor Lassiter, as we do with Jenkins and his lot. So far, we have been amicable with the other people we have to deal with, including the racetrack manager, but as we have discovered, anything is possible.

Now that this Solana woman is our current threat, my thoughts keep wandering back to those two despicable FBI men for some reason. How are Miss Shenanigans fitting into things? Adrian and I went through several scenarios where they interconnect. The perplexing thing is that the pieces do not fit, puzzle-wise. The common denominator is still missing, and without new information, it looks as if the mystery will remain a mystery.

Three days after we arrive home, Mr. Lassiter pays us an unexpected visit. I'm trying to hide in Glen's stinky office when the walkie-talkie squawks. When I poke my head out to get Adrian's attention, he's coming out of the tack room.

"Mother says Lassiter's on his way to the barn. He rubs me the wrong way. You talk to him. I'm busy."

"Francesca told you to be more neighborly, Ellie. I heard her say that myself. What could he want, I wonder?"

"I don't know, and I don't care!" As the words leave my mouth, Lassiter practically runs into Adrian. I'm trying to sneak away when Adrian quickly grabs my arm.

"Can I help you?" Adrian chirps, putting his arm around me to keep me next to him.

"Mr. Sellers? I'm Emil Lassiter, from down the road a bit. You might remember me from Billingsworth Racetrack?" Lassiter extends his hand to shake Adrian's outstretched one. "Mrs. Thompson, good to see you." He extends a hand toward me, but my hands stay in my pockets.

"Hello, Mr. Lassiter."

"Please, call me Adrian. What can I do for you, Emil? Let's talk out here, okay?" Adrian steers us out of the barn, and we walk toward the fence, all while he keeps a firm hand on my arm.

"Sure. I was hoping to um, to give you something in person," Lassiter says quietly.

Adrian squeezes my arm as we walk toward the garages. Danny and Mack are standing near the practice track and poke oddly at the wood on the fence. By this time, Glen and Reed are standing inside the barn door.

"I came in person because quite frankly, I didn't think you'd refuse me to my face. I have come to extend an olive branch, so to speak," Lassiter says quickly.

Glen and Reed move toward the boys, presumably, so they can eavesdrop, but not so close they'd get sucked into our conversation. Lassiter seems uncomfortable since there is now an audience.

"Isn't that interesting. I didn't peg you for a Christian man, Lassiter. Do you go to church?"

Lassiter looks confused. "I felt that it was time to be more neighborly is all, Mrs. Thompson. We haven't welcomed you properly to the neighborhood. My wife and I thought you'd like to socialize with some prominent members of our community."

"We know most of the pillars of our community already. They're the ones who turned their noses up at us when we first came here. Most or all of them wanted their money, immediately, as I recall, and they weren't very generous when we needed time to come up with the funds. Sorry, I don't think we're interested."

Adrian stares at me and then releases my arm. "Her last name is no longer Thompson. Her name is Mrs. Ellen Thompson dash Sellers. She does have a point."

Lassiter nods. "Oh, yes, I'd heard that you married a while back. Pardon my mistake. I wanted to set the record straight, so to speak."

"I'm not following you. What record do you want to set straight?" Adrian asks.

My patience wanes with this lengthy conversation. "Cut the crap, Lassiter. Why are you two dancing around the real issue?" Turning toward Adrian before he can say anything, "Say, do you think he knows anything about our dead horses?"

"Ellen, let the man speak," Adrian says, lightly pinching my arm.

Lassiter has an envelope that he transfers from hand to hand. "Thank you, Adrian, Mrs. Sellers, I wanted to congratulate you and Ashwood Stables on a fine showing this season. I'm sorry that you feel that you haven't been treated right, but with your drivers and obvious talented trainers and such, I wanted to tell you that in person."

"It took you all this time to come over here to say that? What do you really want, Lassiter?"

"Emil, please call me Emil, Mrs. Sellers. Might we talk somewhere more private?" he pleads with Adrian. "I don't have enough, um, invitations for everyone."

I've about run out of patience. "Whatever you have to say, you can say it right here."

Adrian grabs my arm again, as he's probably afraid of what else might come out of my mouth. "Sure, Emil," Adrian says, "Why don't we take a little walk? Come on, honey, walk with us."

Lassiter looks embarrassed, as he thrusts the envelope into Adrian's hand. "Yes, that would be fine. I came to give you this invitation. I do hope you'll come. Much planning has already gone into it. It should be great fun."

"You could have put it into the mail," I say.

Adrian lets my arm go to peer into the envelope, and stares up in surprise. "What kind of invitation is this?"

Lassiter laughs. "It's not a regular Halloween party, mind you. It's a murder mystery, a who-done-it-party. For the whole thing to work, we can only have so many people, so I brought this invitation in person. I need to know if you intend to come."

By now, Danny, Mack, Nathan, Glen, and Reed are all standing next to the fence. It's like watching the *Three Stooges* as they poke and vie for a good view.

"Murder mystery who done it." I roll this around a minute. "Nope, that's not something I want to attend. Thanks for coming all this way, Lassiter, looks like you came for nothing."

As I try to walk away, Adrian says, "Wait a minute, Ellie, I've heard of these parties. They're supposed to be fun, right Emil?"

"You mean like we'll find out who killed our horses, Adrian? That would be wonderful! That mystery who done it can finally be solved." Adrian stares at me, giving me his best-irritated face.

Lassiter looks a bit muddled. "I don't know what you're talking about here. Let me explain. We have to limit the number of people so we can do the mystery part of the game. We have to have so many main players to do it right. Am I making myself clear? It's not about horses at all, Mrs. Sellers. You thought this was about horses?"

"Emil, what my lovely wife is trying to say, is that we would love to come, right Ellen?" I imagine that Adrian is mentally trying to convince me that we should go to the party. "Consider this our RSVP."

"Speak for yourself, Adrian. Thanks, Emul, but no thanks, I don't wish to attend your party. Regardless of why you came, you'll have to find other people to play your little game because I'm not interested."

"Don't mind her, we'd love to come," Adrian says, laughing. "I'll convince her she'll have a good time. You can count us in."

"How do you intend to convince me, Adrian? There, that leaves room for you to invite more people. Now, if you'll excuse me, I have important work to do in my office."

About an hour later, Adrian sneaks in and sets the invitation on the desk. "Come on, Ellie, this is a fun way to take your mind off things. Lassiter said the party isn't for a while yet, and he would appreciate it if we didn't say anything to anyone. We're supposed to get our instructions in the mail to keep up the mystery."

"Who else did he invite to this not Halloween party?"

"He didn't say."

"If we don't know who's invited to this shindig, how will we know who *not* to discuss it with?"

"Ellie, he said he knew nothing about how or why our horses died. And he also doesn't understand why you're so mad at him. I don't remember if Lassiter's name came up during our investigation."

"I think he's somehow connected to at least one of our dead horses. I don't like him, Adrian. I think he's evil and I think he's in deep with the boys down at the racetrack. Isn't that a good enough reason?"

"Haven't we got past that yet? He turned white when I told him about some of the stuff that went on here and at the racetrack. Then, he kept saying how sorry he was about Jason and that he had no idea who might be responsible for the awful things that happened to this family. Before he left, he said to tell you that if you ever need anything, don't hesitate to call on him or his wife. He seemed sincere."

"Why did you tell him about Jason? You want me to forget about what he might be involved with, go over to his house, and pretend that it never happened? I'm not sure I can pull that off!"

Adrian comes around the desk and pulls me into a hug. "Yes, sweetheart, that's what I'm asking you to do, exactly. I have a plan."

"I do not intend to let that man into my head. He is malicious, and so is that blow-hard friend of his, Jenkins. I do not trust either of them—and for a good reason. What sort of plan are you concocting, Mr. CIA man?"

"Ellie, you are so bitter. It isn't like you," Adrian says, stroking my hair. "Plan A is that we could do a little snooping to find out what happened to *Didge* if we go. Maybe we might find out about *Yours Truly*, too."

"You have a point there, Adrian. Do you remember when I was researching horse farms? Lassiter's name came up, and it wasn't good news. But then, you probably uncovered that during the investigation you and Sheriff Rocky did when our horses were murdered. I get bad vibes from him, okay? I'll think about going to the party. The horse's name was *Truly Yours*."

"Ellie, we could make it a real CIA caper. We could call it, *'murder at the Lassiter Estate caper.'* Or, we could call it the, *'whatever happened to Didgeridoo caper.'* Or, it could be the, *'let's go have some fun for a change caper.'* Whattayasay?" Adrian grins, raising his eyebrows. "Wasn't the horse named *Yours Truly?*"

"What are we snooping for, Adrian, a drug with no name? Do you think he keeps that kind of thing around his house? Or, maybe it's in the barn."

"You won't know until we go," Adrian pleads. "It's the perfect opportunity to get into his house without calling undue attention to what we're trying to do."

"I'll think about it. But you're wrong, darling; the horse was named *Truly Yours*. Yours Truly is the name of a restaurant."

"Sheriff Rocky stopped his investigation when there was no evidence that pointed to him. It would give us the perfect opportunity to poke around his house, now wouldn't it?" Adrian smiles and I throw a pad of paper at him.

"I'm not promising to go; I'll think about it okay? And the horse was named *Truly Yours*."

"Good. I have time to work on you. Evidently, we're a big part of it."

"What are you talking about, Adrian?"

"The only hint Lassiter would give is that he needs exactly thirty people for his party to work, and we are some of the key, or main, players."

"I do not give a rat's behind what he needs, Adrian."

"He wants us all to swear to keep our mouths shut, until it's time to reveal the 'who done it' part."

"Did he invite Terre and Dennis? How about Dr. Jess and Reed? Hey, you can sneak Josh and Jake into the party. They're really good at uncovering stuff."

"He did not mention who he invited. It's supposed to be a mystery, Ellie. And it should be a surprise."

I hate surprises.

"Not every puzzle is intended to be solved.

Some are in place to test your limits.

Others are, in fact, not puzzles at all."

*~ Vera Nazarian,
the Perpetual Calendar of Inspiration*

Chapter Three

A Real Murder Mystery

Adrian shoves the invitation in my hand, waiting as I open the envelope. "Lassiter did say that you and I are some of the main characters. And if you consent to go, we'll come up with a plan that includes Josh and Jake, okay?"

"It's ridiculous. The lunatic wants us to dress in roaring twenties costumes. Oh, hell no, Adrian, there's no way I'm doing this!"

"Come on Ellie, it could be a lot of fun," Adrian grins.

"Or it could be a terrible idea. I don't see how Lassiter's party could in any way, shape, or form be construed as fun. I don't like him, and the prim and proper Mrs. Lassiter snubbed me at a function last year. She doesn't strike me as the friendly, what can I do for you kinda gal. How do you expect us to move around his house, without anyone knowing what we're doing? How can you possibly come up with a plan for that? You'll need more than one."

> # WELCOME TO THE MURDER MYSTERY WHO DONE IT!
> (Please arrive between 7:00 to 7:30 p.m./Dinner @ 9:00 p.m.)
> Your host and hostess for this evening is:
>
> ## *Mr. & Mrs. Emil Lassiter*
>
> Key (or main) characters are linked to the murder, along with secondary characters. Each play roles that intertwine into the 'who done it part'.
>
> During the get together portion of the party, you might want to:
> 1) Try to identify all of the characters
> 2) Choose the murderer from amongst the guests
> 3) Guess who the Victim might be
>
> All guests, whether Main or Secondary Characters, are welcome to participate. A prize of $1,000 goes to the person who names the murderer first.
>
> **Dress: Roaring Twenties Costumes.**
> More information will arrive via email or snail mail.
>
> Thank you for your participation. Keep the mystery going by not taking about this party to members of your family, neighbors, etc.

Crumpling the invitation, Adrian grabs it. "Don't destroy it, give it to me. When was the last time you went to a Halloween party?"

"I thought Mr. Evil said it wasn't a Halloween party?"

"Why are you so ornery, Ellie?"

"It's a costume party on October 31st, that's All Hallows Eve, so it makes it a Halloween party. I hate dressing up."

"You need to get out and mingle with our neighbors."

"Hey, why don't you take Jake, or Josh, or Mother. How about Terre, anyone but me, Adrian. I honestly don't want to go."

"It's a way off yet. I bet I can convince you to come. I have whiles you can't avoid."

"You can try all you want, Mr. CIA man. And I'll bet you can't talk me into going to this ***not*** Halloween party. Do you honestly want to bet against me, Adrian?"

"I win sometimes. What do I win, if you lose the bet?"

"We are not having this conversation, Adrian, we all know how you bet."

Glen and I are standing along the fence watching the horses run around the practice track. "You did a fine job of pickin 'em out, Missy. I never would've thought of takin that little one and the mare. *Buttercup*

loves bein out there with *Lester* and *Raindrop*. *Peanut* even looks like he's enjoyin himself. I thought ya said he was shy and unmanageable?"

"That's what the owner tried to tell us. Hey, was that a compliment, old man? You know how some horses like to train alongside each other. And *Shoo Fly* is a natural. He's going to be a winner someday."

"*Peanut's* the one for ya right now, Missy. I hope ya won't argue with me about usin them hopples for trainin this time."

"No argument from me about using them, Glen. Did you see his legs move when he went out with *Buttercup* yesterday?"

Glen lets out a laugh. "That was pretty excitin ta watch, Missy. They was tryin ta keep up with *Lester* and *Peanut* if ya can believe that. Didn't ya say the owner didn't train *Peanut* yet? He sure don't have much trouble fittin in with this bunch."

"That's what they told me, but they might not have known what he was capable of so he's going to give us a run for our money, Glen, I'm sure of that."

"I'm proud to be a part of Ashwood Stables, Missy," Glen says softly, touching my head in an endearing gesture. "Me and Mona, we might not have said enough thanks, for all ya do for us."

"Are you getting misty on me, Dad?" I poke him in the arm; often refer to him in that way, because he does remind me of Daddy at times.

"Just sayin b'fore I forget ta tell ya."

Mona told me not twenty minutes ago that Glen's eldest son, Alec, called to ask them if they wanted to move to Arizona when they retire. They're building an addition on their house for them. They got a little older when no one was watching. So did Rosie, as she seldom ventures up the stairs now, preferring to spend her time near the fireplace in the library, whether there's a fire blazing in it or not.

After much discussion, Josh, Jake, and Adrian convinced me to go to Evil Lassiter's murder mystery party. They said it was for 'the greater good.' In one plan, Jake and Josh will nestle themselves into the tree opposite Lassiter's first-floor office, should Adrian not be successful with his first plan to gain entry to Lassiter's computer.

We all feel there will be ample opportunity to do our information gathering before or after the party starts, and then we can finally put our suspicions about Evil's participation in our horse's deaths to rest. What they have not considered is the barn. Since none of them have brought it up, it falls to me to do the snooping in that area while they are otherwise concentrating on the inside of the house.

Adrian figures that we have nothing to lose and everything to gain. I'm already regretting my decision as my costume is very unflattering. The band is too tight on the synthetic blonde wig, and I don't dare cut it or my dark hair will start to fall out from the bottom. My thumb got stuck in the left stocking as I tried to line up the seam and the small hole is getting larger. Luckily, it's not noticeable when I'm standing; however, I'll have to keep my knees together.

"Ellie, are you ready, OVER?" Adrian set the walkie-talkie on the dresser before he went downstairs to keep us from bumping into each other while we dress. "Ellie, come on down, OVER? We're going to be late, OVER." Adrian stomps up the staircase and pops his head into our closet. "You look great, my little Annie, The Flapper! How do I look?"

He grins, and it makes me laugh. The striped red and black suit has a long jacket with bulky exaggerated pads at the shoulders. The high-waist trouser pants, held up with wide suspenders, are so baggy that he appears short in stature, even though he isn't. A black shirt and matching striped tie completes his costume. He has placed a hat on top of a salt-and-pepper wig, which reminds me of a funny Bugs Bunny movie.

"Are you sure that's part of the roaring twenties? The wig is so you, Adrian." I'm laughing so hard I practically fall over trying to fasten my shoes.

"What! Don't you like it? It was a steal doll; I got it online from the same website you found your dress and stuff. If it's not, who's gonna argue with a gangsta? The suits all looked the same except the one that was all black. It looked like an undertaker's suit. The only other suit looked like a bumblebee, so I chose this one because it goes better with my shoes. Whaada ya think, sweetheart? Don't I look like a gangsta?"

"Yes, you do, Adrian. Did men wear pointy shoes like that back then? By the way, someone will have to feed me, if I can't hold my fork. These stupid glue-on fingernails are ridiculous. I can't pick anything up with them! They keep falling off."

"They're wingtips. And don't worry, little Annie Flapper, I will feed you with my own two hands if need be."

"Adrian, we look ridiculous. Can't Terre and Dennis go to this party in our place? Oh, my God, you look so funny! Do you have to wear that hat all night?"

"No, my little buttercup, *we* are going. Come on, Ellie, we need to go to this party, if we ever want to get into Lassiter's house. Think Plan A, besides, I've been practicing all day walking in these shoes. The hat keeps the wig on, without the hat, the wig looks bad, so the hat stays on." He looks down at the pointed shoes and laughs at himself.

"We don't have to stay for the whole thing, right?"

"We stay for as long as we need to. Now stop complaining, okay? It's the perfect opportunity to gather information and get into Lassiter's house without Sheriff Rocky breathing down our necks."

"What if he's there too? Can't you invent a reason to snoop without us doing this? I have a better idea, why don't you dress Josh up in this getup, and you can take him."

"But darling, he would never fit into those stockings, let alone the dress you're wearing. Come on, Ellie, it'll be fun. You need fun. You haven't had any lately. Besides, the boys already left, and our *caper* has begun."

"Okay, Adrian, you win this time, but I will not promise to have fun. Would you help me with this necklace? My instructions said to wear diamonds. Someone is supposed to steal them. I wonder what else Lassiter has planned for us."

Adrian looks concerned. "These aren't real diamonds, are they? These are fake, right? Tell me these are not real. Trust me, okay, it's gonna be great, you'll see."

"No, they aren't real, they're Austrian crystals. They look pretty real though, don't they? Why would Evil make us his main characters? Do you think he has an ulterior motive, Adrian?"

"That's funny, Ellie! Ulterior motive for a murder mystery party. Is that the best you can do? And please don't call him Evil to his face. It makes me uncomfortable when you do that."

The instructions for Lassiter's party came in the mail. I checked out the company he found online that put his mystery party together. It described our characters and gave helpful hints; how to dress and how we should 'act' during the party. When Adrian found out about the sumptuous dinner, he wouldn't stop his relentless pursuit, so I caved.

I don't get why we're integral to the party scheme, but Adrian is okay with it. His plan to slip in and out of the party without too much notice will be easy, as part of his instructions has him as a secret FBI agent. Josh and Jake are on the property already, in the event one of us gets into trouble. They have worked out several scenarios and several plans.

It will either be a very short or long night depending on whether one of us gets caught.

My fake eyelashes keep peeling off, and the bright red fingernails seem to jump off my fingers at the slightest touch. I have pocketed three of them, and we haven't left the house yet. The instructions go into my purse, along with some extra fingernails, glue for when they fall off, and adhesive for the eyelashes.

INSTRUCTIONS for Main Character: Annie, The Flapper:

You see a man coming out of the library. When he moves out of site, you go in to view the body.

- All you want to do is dance the Charleston with your boyfriend, Al Apone when you hear it. He knows something, but keeps it to himself.
- Al Apone mysteriously disappears for about thirty minutes, and when he returns, there is lipstick on his cheek.
- You mingle with the other guests and act as if nothing is wrong.

Dress in roaring twenties flapper attire, diamond necklace, earrings, red lipstick, rouge, long red fingernails, short bob-style hair, and long gloves.

NOTE: Someone will steal your necklace when the lights go out. Allow them to take the necklace. You are to say nothing about the murder, but faint when the lights come back on.

"Suck it up, Ellie, we're going to have fun."

"I wish I could be the murder victim, Adrian."

"No, you don't, the victim has to stay dead until the mystery is solved. Honestly, I don't think you could stay still for that long. And besides, you might miss the dinner Lassiter has planned for us."

"That's the real reason we're going, isn't it? You want a free meal. Hey, we can both sneak out when the lights go out, and someone supposedly steals the necklace."

"I don't think the lights stay off long enough, Ellie. We have to go with plan A."

"And what if Plan A fails, Adrian?"

"Then we move on to Plan B."

Journey of a Thousand Steps

"And if Plan B doesn't work?"

"We're trained to deal with extreme duress, my little pumpkin. Josh and Jake know their stuff and I'm supposed to be with the FBI. They always have a plan."

"Yeah, I know about FBI plans, and I don't trust them."

"Then pretend I'm with the CIA. You do trust them, don't you? Come on, plaster a smile on your face and get in the car. We're going to have a good time if it kills us."

"Are you trying to be funny, Adrian?"

"Yes, is it working?"

"I'll let you know in about an hour."

"Let me see your instructions," Adrian says with his hand out.

"No way, mister. If I have to go to this thing, I want to win."

"Are you taking this as a challenge, Mrs. Thompson dash Sellers?"

"Maybe..."

INSTRUCTIONS for Main Character: Gangster Al Apone:

You are actually with the FBI and the HOST is under suspicion of money laundering and have uncovered a plot against the government during your clandestine search of the premises
- You suspect your girlfriend knows something about the murder, because you were standing in the hallway.
- You are fooling around with the banker's wife.
- You disappear for about thirty minutes to search for evidence.
- You gave Annie diamond jewelry (the necklace is stolen when the lights go out).
- When the lights come back on, Annie has fainted.

Dress in dark suit, dark shirt, tie, and hat (mustache is optional).

GATE CODE:1234

Mr. and Mrs. Emil Lassiter's sprawling estate sits on a lovely parcel mere minutes from Ashwood Stables. A tall fence majestically surrounds it, and a fancy grill-work gate grants us access once Adrian puts in the code.

"Look at his lawn, Adrian. It's so perfect that it looks like AstroTurf. Can you buy it in large quantities to do that?"

Adrian laughs. "It's real grass, it's probably that stuff they use on golf courses. We're going to have fun. You wait and see. It'll be a night to remember."

As we approach the house, two young men dressed as valets in black pants, vests, and white shirts (rolled up to the elbows) step forward to open our doors. One young man takes my hand to escort me to the front door, then he turns, smiling sheepishly. I get an uneasy feeling about him trying *not* to stare at my necklace. The other valet gets into Adrian's side of the car to drive it off.

"Stay focused and alert, sweetie. We're supposed to receive more information about our characters once we enter the party," Adrian advises. "Remember, we have to stay in character the entire time."

"I'll try."

As Adrian is about to say something, the front door opens. A woman dressed in a black and white server's uniform greets us. She then motions us into the vestibule and asks Adrian for his hat, but he politely refuses, because he knows what his wig looks like without it. We chuckle at each other, and wonder if she's one of the guests, or hired for the night; it's difficult to judge.

The woman points solemnly toward a door on the left marked OFFICE. I almost expect Lurch (from the *Addams Family*) to open the door. Neat rows of packets are lined up on a table with our character's names. Adrian finds his right away, yet I don't see one for Annie, The Flapper.

A man with a black-streaked wig and fake-looking mustache walks around a shoji screen. He's dressed in an old dark blue smoking jacket. His ghoulish grin is alarming enough, but he is also making clicking sounds with an unlit pipe. At first, I don't recognize Lassiter, then realize that he would be the first to greet his guests. He hands me a packet and a sharp pencil.

"Greetings, Annie, The Flapper, and Mr. Apone. So glad you could join us this evening," the man says in an odd accent.

Adrian takes Lassiter's outstretched hand, saying, "Hello Emil, Ellen and I have been looking forward to this. Haven't we, my dearest?"

"I don't want to be here, but my husband made me come."

"Please join the others in the parlor. We'll get underway shortly when everyone has arrived. Put your ballot into the box before eight thirty." He points to the box marked 'WHO DONE IT?' and then motions toward the door on the opposite wall.

"Thanks, Emil," Adrian says.

"I think you'll be pleasantly surprised at what we have in store for your entertainment this evening."

We find the room marked PARLOR, and make our way to chairs along the window where we open our packets to find a welcome card, a small pad of paper, another set of instructions, and a ballot for voting.

"Who's he dressed as, himself? I want to go home Al, this is ridiculous."

INSTRUCTIONS: Annie, The Flapper

1. You witness the murder in the library. You get close to investigate and leave one or two red fingernails near the body.
2. Go to the ladies' room and act nonchalant.
3. Gangster Al Apone is getting too friendly with the Banker's Wife, so you haul him onto the dance floor to do the Charleston whenever you hear it.
4. You will hear a loud scream and the lights will go out
5. Stay in character no matter what happens next

(Fill in the names of the other characters when you ascertain who they are.)

"Quit griping, Ellie. Hum," he says, looking at his information.

"We're supposed to dance the Charleston every time we hear it. And I don't know any of these people."

"You'll have to teach me, and you *do* know some of these people. That has to be Gladys over there. I would know her by her hair alone. She looks like the Real Estate Broker. Let's jot that down."

Poking at my wig with the sharp end of my pencil, I say, "Hey, you're right Al."

"Look, Annie, just observe. Our Host did this for a reason. Look at your list again and then look closely at the people in this room. There are people here we both know."

Gazing around the very huge room, I am slightly impressed with the size of it, not so with the décor. The Charleston begins to play, and Adrian grabs my arm. As we jump around the dance floor, a server passes him, and he snitches a canapé from the tray.

"Hey, Al, isn't that Mr. Allen?"

"Who's Mr. Allen?"

GUEST CARD: MATCH NAMES WITH OTHER GUESTS IN THE ROOM	
Annie, The Flapper:	Antique Dealer:
Baker:	Baker's Wife:
Banker:	Banker's Wife:
Bar Tender:	Diamond Expert:
Doctor:	Gardner:
Gangster Al Apone:	Host:
Librarian:	Lawyer:
Maid:	Pharmacist:
Society Male:	Society Socialite:
Real Estate Broker:	Valet # 1:
Valet # 2:	Victim:

Welcome To The Murder Mystery
Who Done It! Party

Your Host and Hostess for this evening wishes that you enjoy the hospitality! There are many players, main along with secondary, who have been assigned 'character' roles. Your acceptance to join us this evening means that you have studied your instructions and will stay in character until the reveal once dinner has commenced.

Each of the main and secondary characters have been given 'special clues'. Take the opportunity to mingle with the other partygoers to ask them questions. Then, when you think you have solved the mystery and you know, Who Done it! – Put your selection into the WHO DONE IT BOX no later than 8:30 p.m.

Dinner will be served promptly at 9:00 p.m.

Followed by homemade desserts and coffee.

Tear here ⇧

BALLOT: fill in the MURDERER'S NAME HERE:

_____

Guest Name:

"He's the crooked executor and *last will* lawyer for Old Miss Abigail's estate. What's he doing here?"

Adrian stops to stare at me. "Really? I thought he and Mr. Yancy were both in jail."

"That's him in the Banker's suit, and that must be his lovely wife sitting next to him, so she must be the Banker's Wife. He keeps looking at me, and it gives me the creeps. Do you think Fancy Yancy is out of jail too? Ooooh, the plot thickens. I told you Lassiter was in thick with these people."

The music stops, and we leave the dance floor to flop down on the nearest sofa. "Let me see your card, Al."

"No peeking, you're not supposed to know what I know. I'm, with the BFI, you know."

"What exactly does BFI mean? Best Friends to Infinity?"

"That's code for something."

"Code for what, Adrian?"

The music starts to play the Charleston again. "Come on, Annie**,** we need to dance. I've almost got the hang of it." Adrian pockets his card and grabs my arm to swing me on to the dance floor.

"If I'd have known we were going to do this much dancing, I would have worn different shoes. Why is Allen staring at us?"

"Don't look at him. I don't remember being notified that he was out of prison. And you already know too much, sweetheart. I ain't tellin ya nothin more." Adrian is definitely in the swing of his character. "I'm supposed to be involved with the Banker's Wife. Who would know if we're not sticking to the script? I wonder if she's supposed to go missing, too."

"I thought Allen wouldn't show his face in this town again, after what he did! I know you want to win this thing. It would be pretty bad if you, the trained CIA man that you are, isn't the one who solves this thing."

"Shush, keep your voice down, if it's a competition you want Annie, don't get distracted. You need to concentrate. Who else do you see?" Adrian whispers as he pulls out his card to scribble on it.

"Are you gonna let me see your card?"

Adrian pulls his card toward his chest to hide it from me. "Heck no. You're right, my little loquat, I do want to win this thing." His cellphone vibrates, and he pulls it out of his pocket. He then whispers in my ear, "The boys are near. Stay alert."

"That's Dr. Hamilton. How did he swing an invite to this sorry soirée? He's dressed as a doctor. That was hard. No imagination there whatsoever." As I say this, the Charleston starts to play again, and Al grabs my hand to pull me back on to the dance floor.

"We should go dancing more often, Ellie. This is great exercise."

"If we have to dance every five minutes, this is going to get pretty wearisome. I think the hole in my stocking is getting bigger, and I have to use the restroom."

"Is that the truth or are you trying to follow your plan? Wait." Adrian glances at his cellphone. "Don't go yet. Josh is trying to open the window in Lassiter's office." As Adrian bounces us around the room, his eyes are darting from person to person. "Let's keep track of everyone, okay?"

"Sure. That has to be Gerald Tillman as the Antique Dealer, no mistaking that bald head."

"And the woman with him must be the Librarian, his assistant Jenny," Adrian adds.

"Nicely done, Al, that is Jenny alright, I would recognize that red lipstick anywhere. It doesn't look like anyone went in for deep disguises as we did."

The music stops, and we make our way to empty chairs. "You're doing great, Annie. I recognize the Lawyer as, no that's not who it is. The Bar Tender looks strangely like the racetrack manager. Whadda ya think, Annie, doesn't he look like the racetrack manager to you?" Adrian says softly. "Hey, we're doing great; one of us might even win that prize. What I mean is, I want to win that prize."

The Charleston music starts again. "Are you serious? I am not doing that again unless I hit the restroom, Al. I really have to go." Everyone slowly turns in my direction. "Did I say that out loud? Carry on...."

Adrian smiles at the people who have turned around and follows me to the doorway saying, "She's having a good time, honest."

"Why would the racetrack manager be here? I knew he was in deep with that man. It's so lame Al; I don't know who the other people are. Wait a minute; the Maid looks a little familiar. Of course, she's the baker's wife. Honestly, she's the real baker's wife, Charlotte. Now I'm all goofed up. Lassiter mixed people up, and I won't be able to keep them straight now."

"See, you know more than you think you do. Quit pissing and moaning, Annie, did you bring your gun?"

"Why Al, that's so romantic. Sure did, how about you?"

Adrian starts to laugh, as I hit him on the arm. "Want a drink, gangsta's Moll?"

"Sure, but I need to use the restroom first. I'm supposed to witness the murder, and I'll have to leave the room to do that. It must happen soon, so I'll be back in a few minutes."

As Adrian saunters over to the bar to get us a drink, he trips over his shoes making a loud sound to get everyone's attention as a distraction. He looks down and starts to laugh at himself. He touches the brim of his hat, and talks with a funny accent to anyone who will listen. That bulge under his jacket means he brought his revolver.

"So, you must be Annie, The Flapper," a voice behind me says. "I would like to ask you some questions. Got a minute, Toots?" I turn around to see a robust man wearing a Keystone Cop uniform that looks familiar, though I can't quite place him, nor his voice.

"Oh, sorry, I'm going to find the ladies' room. I'll be back in a jiffy. We can chat then."

He looks a little miffed, says okay and then ambles off toward the bar. Several people are in the hallway now, and Lassiter is talking with guests near the front door. I'm about to turn right when a male server says that the restroom is down the opposite hallway. He looks familiar; could he be one of the valets?

A sign taped to the wall indicates that the library is behind a pair of french doors; however, the filmy curtains are too cloudy to see into the room. I'm about to put my hand on the knob to let myself inside when a voice behind me says the lavatory is the next door on the left. Another server motions for me to move along.

How am I supposed to witness the murder, if I can't witness the murder?

When I find the lavatory door, a woman pushes the door open with such force, that one of my red fingernails flies off. The woman rushes past me into the hallway, muttering something to herself. At this point, I only want to relieve myself, glue on another fingernail, and try to take a peek into the library again before the anticipated scream takes place. When I exit the lavatory, there is a different server guarding the library doors.

"This way back to the party, Ma'am," he says, taking my arm gently, almost pushing me toward the large room marked PARLOR.

"I think I'm supposed to go in the library, so if you don't mind stepping aside, please?"

"Not gonna happen, Ma'am. Instructions are that no one goes into the library. Please go back to the living room and have yourself a wonderful evening."

I'm silently fuming. How am I supposed to witness the murder if I'm not allowed into the library? Are these people following a different script? Back in the large room with the other guests, I spot Adrian at the bar as a dazzlingly dressed woman, dripping in what looks like real jewels, is sauntering around the room. She bends to speak quietly with one man, who looks strangely like my brother-in-law Dennis and then moves on to someone else. I'm trying to glue another fingernail back on when she stops in front of me. Who might I be, she rudely inquires.

"Are you blind Lady? I'm Annie, The Flapper, can't you tell?"

"You must be *the* Ellen Sellers I've heard so much about. So glad you could join us this evening," she says nattily.

"Not right now Lady. I'm in character, shouldn't you be too?"

The woman sniffs so loudly that Adrian turns around to stare at us. He's probably correct in thinking that I've been rude, however, her attitude is somewhat offensive. She must be Mrs. Lassiter, Society Socialite, as there is no one on the list named Hostass!

Antique Dealer waves at me as the Librarian reaches for a canapé that the Maid is serving on a large silver tray. None of us has figured out who we all are, but several have taken to writing down names on their cards as I have, while some have wandered around the room to ask questions.

Glancing out the window, I observe a gardener lightly raking at the AstroTurf. It's rather odd that someone would be working around the yard on a Saturday night while a party is in full swing. Then it dawns on me that the Gardener is our local car dealer. As I chuckle to myself, I look around the room again, when it suddenly fills with more people. Out of curiosity, I move to the open doorway to see two guest packets that remain on the table.

"I take it you met Mrs. Lassiter." Al's back with our drinks and whispers near my ear, "Any luck seeing the Victim?"

"No. No one's going anywhere except the restroom. I couldn't get near the library; there was someone standing guard."

"That's unfortunate. So you didn't see a body in the library, hum?"

"Who said the murder happens in the library, Al?"

"Isn't that where you were going? They always happen in the library, my dear. Either with a candlestick or a knife, or some other sharp, but suitable weapon. Maybe there's been a change in the program."

"I'll show you my card if you show me yours. See, I know how to share. Why can't you show me yours, Al? Are you afraid I'll win?"

My sister's unmistakable laugh echoes from across the room, and her hand shoots high in the air to wave in my direction. How she didn't let it slip that she would be here tonight, is quite remarkable. That is unquestionably Dennis sitting next to her. I have concluded that my sister is the Lawyer and Dennis is the Pharmacist. Then I spot Reed and figure that he's the Baker and that Dr. Jess must be the Baker's Wife, judging from their white starched aprons and unflattering hair nets.

Adrian snatches my card and gives me a wink. "Hey, that's pretty good. Want to know what I found out?" He tries to kiss my cheek but his hat gets in the way.

GUEST CARD: MATCH NAMES WITH OTHER GUESTS IN THE ROOM	
Annie Flapper: me	Antique Dealer: Gerald Tillman
Baker: Reed	Baker's Wife: Dr. Jessica
Banker: Mr. Allen	Banker's Wife: Mrs. Allen
Bar Tender: race track manager	Diamond Expert: local jeweler
Doctor: Dr. Hamilton	Gardner:
Gangster Al Apone: Adrian	Host: Mr. Evil Lassiter
Librarian: Jenny	Lawyer: Terre
Maid: real baker's wife	Pharmacist: Dennis
Society Male: ?	Society Socialite: Mrs. Lassiter
Real Estate Broker: Gladys	Valet # 1: kid from feed store
Valet # 2: can't place him	Victim: unknown

"Sure, does it have anything to do with dinner, because I'm starving."

"No," Adrian says, looking around the room. "Annie, why don't you have another horse's do overs?"

"I already had six of them. I had to stab them with my pencil since I couldn't pick them up with these ridiculous fingernails. And besides, you made such a fuss over our supposedly scrumptious dinner. I didn't want to spoil my appetite."

"Okay, I'm not gonna tell you then! Come here, sweetheart." Al's hat pokes me in the face in another attempt to kiss me, so I bat it, as he straightens up and starts to laugh.

"Al, weren't you supposed to disappear for a while? Did the boys have a successful adventure? Aren't you supposed to have lipstick on your face? You should have come with me to the lavatory. While I distracted that server, you could have gone to the library."

"I'm trying to figure out when to make my exit. You could kiss me with your ruby red lips. Who would know? And I haven't heard from the boys for a while."

The Charleston plays again, but neither one of us move toward the dance floor. Who, besides us, would know about that?

"What did you find out, Al?"

"Why don't you admit that you're having fun, Annie?"

At that precise moment, the lights go out, the music stops, and we hear a blood-curdling scream that sounds very real. A beat later, there is another scream that doesn't. Seconds after that, the music begins again, and the lights come back on.

As if on cue, our creepy Host, Mr. Evil himself, barges into the room clutching a bloody knife. He plops down on the nearest chair, and the guests stop all conversation to stare at him. Smudges of red streak his left cheek that look suspiciously like ketchup. His face, distorted into a horrific glower, seems somewhat comical. He has misplaced his fake mustache.

"Lassiter must have practiced that a long time in front of a mirror. He genuinely looks as if he's seen a real murder. I don't think they're following the script. There was only supposed to be one scream."

"It looks kinda real to me, Annie. You still have your necklace. They aren't following the program, that's for sure."

A large man in a black tuxedo steps into the room. He puts a hand on Lassiter's shoulder and then bends to speak quietly with him. He straightens to remove his jacket, carefully placing it around the back of a nearby chair. We watch in silence as he pulls off his black wig, lifts his glasses, and peels off his fake sideburns and beard. By the looks of him, Sheriff Rocky is Society Male. He reaches for a handkerchief from an inside jacket pocket from the coat on the chair, and gingerly pulls the knife out of Lassiter's trembling hands.

Surprise! There has been a murder!

The guests begin to chatter and turn away from Lassiter to consult their Guest Cards when Sheriff Rocky asks for everyone to be quiet. "No one is to leave this room or the house for that matter. There has been a real murder."

The Sheriff seems to be playing his character rather well, Evil Lassiter, not so well. With this, the guests start to laugh and break into applause. Several guests begin to comment that they weren't ready to guess the 'who done it' part yet, when will dinner be served, and what was the purpose of two screams?

"I'll have your attention!" Sheriff Rocky booms. "There has been a real murder here tonight. The party is over!"

At this point, Society Socialite, aka Mrs. Evil Lassiter, falls to the floor in a dead swoon. Both Dr. Jess and Dr. Hamilton stand up to see what they can do for our ill-fated Host and his charming, but snooty wife. Glancing at Al, and then at my sister, we both shake our heads at the same time. Dr. Hamilton opens his medical bag to extract something. What he has in there is anyone's guess. Was he supposed to come as a real doctor? Then it occurs to me that this could still be part of the party, or it's a diversion.

"Did I miss something here, Al? Aren't we supposed to guess who the murderer is? Why would our Host be the murderer?"

Adrian takes off his hat and wig and runs his hand through his hair. "I honestly don't know, Ellie."

Grabbing Adrian's arm, saying, "That's it? If the party's over, can we eat now?"

"Ellie, I think it's a real murder." He nudges me into a corner so we can talk. "Something is very wrong here. Observe, okay, and keep quiet."

Some of the guests start to grumble, as the faint sound of a siren grows in volume, the closer it gets to Lassiter's house.

"Are you serious? And I suppose that's a real siren, too?"

"Be quiet, will you?" Adrian's face means that the siren is real.

The voices in the room grow in proportionate volume the closer the siren gets to Lassiter's house. Sheriff Rocky has to shout above the din to ask that we all pipe down. He's so livid that his face turns beet-red, and I wonder if he's on medication for high blood pressure. Moments later, someone pounds on the front door.

"It must be Deputy Slim. He wasn't at the party when it started."

"How do you know, Mr. Know-It-All? Maybe he was supposed to show up with the ambulance. I know, maybe he's the Victim."

"It's not him. Josh or Jake would have told me. Even they don't know who the Victim is yet, Ellie."

Sheriff Rocky pulls Lassiter up by the arm, and then turns toward the group, saying, "Stay here and try to remain calm until I get back. You may have to stay a while, so ya might want to make the necessary arrangements."

As he closes the door, cellphones magically appear in over 80% of the guest's hands, and the chatter begins again, asking questions, and speculating on whom the Victim could be. Society Socialite is now sitting in a chair sipping what appears as a shot glass full of whiskey. Moments later, Sheriff Rocky returns to escort the very pale, obviously shaken Mrs. Lassiter out of the room.

Adrian suddenly starts to pace back and forth while he punches numbers on his cellphone. The parlor door opens, and the Gardener and one of the Valets walk into the room and head straight to the bar. Luckily, it has remained open for business.

By now, Dr. Jess, Reed, Terre, and Dennis have joined us on the other side of the room. Terre says near my ear, "Dennis talked with Mother. She'll take care of the girls while we endure the inevitable inquisition. It can't be part of the party. I checked with most of the other guests. No one had instructions that correlate to what's happening now."

"Maybe it is, maybe it isn't. Sheriff Rocky and Deputy Slim could be in on it, and they could still be acting."

"I don't think it's how the party was supposed to go, Ellie," Adrian whispers back. "It looks real to me."

Terre sputters, "Now that you mention it, it could be fake blood. It looks like Mr. Lassiter smeared ketchup on his face and hands. Or its red food coloring, Adrian."

"I don't think so," he retorts. "I would know."

Looking around the room, people have gathered in small groups as we have. "I've only seen horse killings before, never a human, so I can't tell the difference," I say, fingering my necklace.

Adrian adds, "Quite honestly, I don't know if there is a difference in human and animal blood when oxygen hits it. Why don't we ask Dr. Jess to get her take on this?"

"That's a good idea. Can't you do something, Adrian? Can't you show Sheriff Rocky your real badge, so we don't have to stay here all night?"

"I didn't bring it, sweetie. All I have is the fake one."

"I thought you guys were always prepared."

The siren stops, and most of the guests run to the front windows to get a view of what's happening near the front door. Moments later, Deputy Slim throws the doors open and announces that the victim is quite dead. We are all to stay in this room, until further notice. Then he plants himself near the doors to make sure we adhere to his words.

Immediately bombarded with questions, Deputy Slim puts his hands up in the air. When he does this, Barney Fife's face pops into my mind, and I start to laugh. Adrian becomes annoyed and says, "Stop that, Ellen, this is serious."

"As soon as the Medical Examiner releases the body, the Sheriff will start his investigation. You'll all have to be patient until this thing blows over. I suggest you take it easy until then," Slim says.

We still have no idea who the Victim is, or who committed the murder. By Sheriff Rocky's intermittent information, Mr. Lassiter could *not* have done it; he was inconveniently in the library to check on his pretend victim when he pulled the real knife out of the victim's chest.

Glancing at my watch to note the time, I'm surprised that it's nearly nine thirty. Terre mouths the words 'I'm hungry.'

"What the heck, Adrian? I'm not having any fun, my darling."

"It was fun up to a little while ago," he says.

"When you said we would remember this party for many years to come, I didn't think you meant that we would remember it like this! I was looking forward to dinner. And you guys, you never said you got invitations from Lassiter."

"We swore we wouldn't tell each other," Terre says. "It was all part of Lassiter's master party plan."

"And that was hard, let me tell you," Dennis moans, rolling his eyes upward. "You know how your sister has trouble keeping a secret. It nearly unhinged her when she couldn't talk about your wedding dress; imagine what it was like these last few weeks, with this party thing!"

Terre frowns at her husband. "He makes it sound as if I can't keep a secret at all. Only Dennis and I knew about our characters. We didn't know Reed and Dr. Jess were here until we saw their truck. Then we spotted them right away."

"You did not," Dr. Jess says indignantly.

"Honestly Ellie, we didn't think you would show up," Terre says, ignoring Dr. Jess's snarky response.

"You do look great, by the way," Dennis says. "We were taking bets that you would find a way to get out of it."

"Bets? You took bets I wouldn't show up?"

"You don't think this is real, do you?" Terre asks, changing the subject quickly. "The blood could be ketchup. I've seen that on TV before. It could be part of the murder mystery party thing."

"Except that it's real blood," Dr. Jess says nonchalantly. "I should know."

"See, I told you," Adrian adds.

"The stuff on his face did look like ketchup," Reed agrees. "But the blood on Lassiter's hands? I know what real blood looks like too, and he wasn't faking that."

Dr. Jess replies, "I agree; he was horrified. Venous blood remains oxygenated, thus increasing the redness, so it was authentic all right, especially the blood on his hands. If it were not, it would indeed look like ketchup, like the smear that was on his face. What do you think Adrian?"

"I tend to agree with Dr. Jess," Adrian says.

"It all looks fake to me," Dennis mumbles. "It can't be real. Why would Lassiter have a real murder party?"

Dr. Jess purses her lips, shaking her head in his direction. "It's fresh blood, Dennis. I can assure you, it's not even dry, and it takes on a reddish-brown color when it does. I'm telling you it's fresh blood. Now, whether or not it comes from a real murder, we will have to leave it up to Sheriff Rocky and his gang to discover."

"I thought all of us mystery party-goers were supposed to discover the murderer by asking a bunch of questions. Maybe one of us can still win the prize." My stomach growls loudly. "And I'm hungry!"

"Look, the ambulance is leaving," someone remarks as Sheriff Rocky steps back into the room.

He talks with Deputy Slim for a moment and then turns to us. "I know that some of you think that this was all staged as part of the murder mystery party, and it was at first, but there has been a real murder here tonight."

I can't help myself. "Sure there was. I propose that it's the Banker in the library with the knife."

Adrian stares at me. "Ellen, will you be serious? We're not playing the board game CLUE."

"Mr. Jenkins is dead," the Sheriff announces soberly. Mr. Allen's mouth drops open as his wife cries out, then she tries to comfort him.

"I didn't even know Jenkins was here, did you, Adrian? He and his wife must have been guests and didn't pick up their packets. Wait a minute, that rude woman who ran out of the lavatory could have been Mrs. Jenkins."

Adrian chews on his bottom lip. "Allen does look guilty. I wonder why Lassiter invited them, given what they did to this community."

"Yeah, I wouldn't call them prominent pillars. You're mixing Yancy up with Jenkins, Adrian. Now that you mention him, Jenkins hasn't been around the racetrack for a while. Wonder where he's been hiding all this time? He hasn't bothered us lately."

Terre raises her eyebrows. "My, you must have left out some details about how you all came to be in Virginia along with that little program thing you're in, Ellen. Perhaps you can enlighten us?"

Adrian glances at me, and I'm guessing that now is not the time to delve into our past. "You're in that little program thing too, Sis, but I'd be glad to discuss it with you another time."

It's so quiet that all we can hear is a muffled wail coming from somewhere overhead. Murder is not a usual thing that happens in Sheriff Rocky's neighborhood, and it looks as if he's struggling with what he has to say next.

"You will all be questioned individually as soon as the room across the hall is ready. I know that you were hand selected to be here tonight, and I ask that you think about your motive, b'cause according to Mr. Lassiter, most of you had one."

"Can we please have our dinner while we wait?" one guest asks.

Another joins in, "They can't keep that food warm indefinitely. Why can't you let us eat it?"

My stomach growls again, and Adrian adds to the ensuing mayhem. "Maybe you should let the ones you don't need right away eat their dinner."

That's all the people in this room needed to get riled up. I must have chimed in too. Why can't we eat while the Sheriff conducts his investigation? The show, as they say, must go on.

"People, PEOPLE," the Sheriff shouts. "There has been a real murder here tonight. Let's give the grieving woman a chance to recover. The Lassiter's are very distraught over the unfortunate incident that happened in their home. I can assure you that this is *not* what they had in mind for your entertainment."

Deputy Slim consults with the Sheriff. He nods his head, says something back, and then turns toward us again. "Okay. Here's what we're gonna do. As soon as we're ready, Deputy Slim will call your name. And you will come to the room across the hall. The rest of you can go and eat your dinner. No one is to leave this house. Do I make myself clear? Not until I say you can go."

Deputy Slim adds, "Oh, and one more thing. We will be doin a little search of your items, so don't go tryin to get rid of anything?"

Should I worry about the little pistol in my purse? Or the bulge under Adrian's jacket? Do they know about the CIA agents lurking in the shadows?

Adrian stays behind to make a call, as the rest of us move toward the dining room. A female server tells us to please find our character's name and sit down. They will serve the soup once everyone is seated. Since I'm first in the room, I find the cards for Gangster Al Apone and Annie, The Flapper, switching them with other name tags so I can have the best view of the hallway. Terre and Dr. Jess grab their cards to rearrange them so we can all sit close to each other. I note there are five empty seats at the large table set for thirty.

Adrian strolls in and sits down. "I spoke with Jake and Levi. We'll talk later," he whispers.

"Wait a minute, what were you going to tell me about the murder, Adrian?"

"That can wait, Ellie," he says under his breath.

Most of the guests understood that the point of the mystery party was to keep us all in suspense from the front door, through the discovery of clues some of us had, on throughout dinner, until the big reveal at dessert. The facts are just not adding up. And what was Adrian trying *not* to tell me?

"Maybe we shouldn't eat anything, given the circumstances, it could be poisoned, and we could be about to witness another murder!"

Adrian sees my hesitation, snatches a roll, and starts to nibble on it. "If you think the soup is poisoned, Ellie, then don't eat it."

Dennis chimes in with a straight face. "Yeah, wait until everyone else has eaten theirs. If their heads drop into their bowl, you'll have your answer."

Adrian leans forward to stick his knife into the butter. "Or you can eat a roll because those don't usually have arsenic in them."

Deputy Slim waltzes in, and everyone stops to look his way. "We'll have Mr. Tillman in the other room. Mr. Tillman, if you would please oblige us."

Gerald Tillman stands up, wipes his mouth with his napkin, takes a long drink from his glass of wine, and looks up and down the table. "I don't have a motive to kill Jenkins," he says somberly. "Sure, we had words a long time ago over an antique he thought should bring in more money, but it wasn't enough for me to murder him!"

"Come along now. We're gonna question everyone, sir. That's how we do it here. You people go right on eatin,'" Slim says.

One by one, people leave the dining room to go to the inquiry room. By the time we finish eating, there are only a few guests left. Reed looks up to wave as a server presents him with a choice of desserts. The rest of us are now chowing down on either a butterscotch trifle, cherry, or pumpkin pie, and it was definitely worth the wait.

It's nearly eleven when Deputy Slim saunters back into the dining room. He pulls out a chair, sits down, and politely asks for a piece of pumpkin pie. When the server sets it down in front of him, he reaches for a bowl of whipped cream and proceeds to plop several dollops on top of it.

"So, Deputy Slim, have you narrowed down your suspects yet?" Reed asks.

Slim puts a forkful of pie into his mouth, chews it a few times, and says, "We think we have a strong one."

Adrian shakes his head at me. He wants to play detective. "Care to elaborate for us Slim?"

"It could be someone in this very room, Mr. Adrian." Slim puts another piece of pie into his mouth and chews absently. "We *know* it's someone in this room. That's a for sure thing."

"And do you have a name for your suspect?" I ask.

Adrian turns in my direction. "Don't say anything more, Ellie."

Deputy Slim looks straight at me and doesn't blink. "Ma'am, you have the strongest motive. You did have an incident a while back that involved the deceased. Did you not?"

"Are you serious? Did anyone really like that man?"

"It don't matter who did, or did not like him, Ma'am, he's dead, and Ms. Sellers, a crime has been committed here tonight; a crime that don't often happen in this here part of the county. And of everyone who came here tonight, you had the strongest motive, Ma'am."

Adrian shakes his head. "No, that's not right Slim, why would you think my wife had anything to do with it?"

"What did you do on your way to the powder room, Ms. Sellers, if it were not to stop in the library to do the deed?"

"Lots of people went down that same hallway to use the restrooms, Deputy Slim. How could I have done it? There was no way into the library. A man was outside the door, and he wouldn't let me in. Did you find a red fingernail near the body? Do you see any blood on my hands or on my clothes?"

Deputy Slim stops to consider this with his fork in mid-air, then dives into his pie again. "What was your role in these doins tonight, Ms. Sellers? Have a grudge against anyone, maybe?"

"You're focusing on the wrong person, Slim. I was supposed to go into the library and a server would not let me in. Have you questioned all the kitchen staff and servers yet? What happened to the other valet?"

Adrian instantly knows where I'm going with this as Slim suddenly slams his fork down on his plate. "Perhaps my wife has something there. What are you thinking, Deputy?" he asks.

"Stay here, all of ya. I got me an idea." Slim runs into the kitchen so fast he doesn't bother to put his fork down.

Adrian pulls out his cellphone, and says, "I'm calling Josh; I have an idea too."

Since the dining room is near the kitchen, we've heard the usual sounds coming from there throughout dinner, but when it sounds as if someone is beating utensils against heavy pans, we speculate that it might be something odd.

Sheriff Rocky was standing just outside the dining room and heard the commotion. As he runs in, he asks about Slim, and we collectively point toward the kitchen door. Rocky moves at surprising speed for a big man. He has one hand on his holster, which is around his midsection and looks strangely out-of-place on his formal shirt. He motions with his free hand for us to remain in the dining room.

Adrian stands to look out the large window that faces the backyard as lights flicker on and off. Then he moves quickly to the kitchen following Rocky. I'm facing the window when the outside lawn area suddenly lights up like a nighttime football field where it illuminates an amusing scene, as running figures dance in the yard.

Everyone moves toward the window to take a closer look. Jake is on top of someone, pulling at his arm as Adrian points his gun at the person's head. Several people are now milling about talking to one another. People in the kitchen must have fled when the noise started. They are now standing outside with Adrian, Jake, and Sheriff Rocky, but there is no sign of Slim or Josh.

Moving toward the kitchen, Terre is right behind me as Dr. Hamilton and Reed run ahead, with Dr. Jess close behind. When Reed opens the door, the kitchen is in chaos. They call Slim's name, but there is no answer. As we come around a long counter, there is a boot sticking out of a pile of pots and pans. Dr. Hamilton bends to uncover Slim. Dr. Jess feels for his pulse and barks orders to call 911, as a fork is deeply embedded and sticking out of his arm.

It might be the diversion needed that Adrian and I had planned for us. Since he and the guys are busy, and the library is off-limits, and we've been forbidden to go upstairs, there is no way to snoop without being noticed. Or, is there?

Pulling out my cellphone to make the emergency call, I nonchalantly tell my sister that I will direct the medics to the kitchen; however, she astutely narrows her eyes and asks, "Where are you really going, Ellen?"

"I think I dropped my lipstick."

Now is my chance to peek into Lassiter's hidey-holes, while Adrian is busy. Maybe Josh had already thought of this and is already heading toward the barn. It's the perfect opportunity to see if my hunch is correct while everyone else is otherwise distracted.

It takes a few minutes for my eyes to adjust to the darkness. Heading toward Lassiter's barn, it's a little odd when no lights come on, given what security he has around his house. Even though the barn door appears closed, it's not in total darkness, as light is coming in from the side windows. Soft country music is playing from somewhere within, so there might be someone inside tending to the horses.

My shoes have a wide heel so they won't sink into the soil, but sliding through the paddock rails could be a bit tricky in this outfit. Luckily, there's an open door in the middle of the barn, so I slip through it and come face to face with a beautiful chestnut Thoroughbred. Grabbing a handful of oats, he shakes his big head, snorting when I offer him the treat. I'm guessing that he must be Mrs. Lassiter's horse because he's as snooty as she is.

Voices are coming from the front of the barn, but it's too dim to see who is talking from this distance. Poking my head around the stall, an unfamiliar deputy suddenly opens the barn door. He asks the men (who most likely were the ones talking) to go to the main house for questioning, and the door closes.

Moving forward toward the front of the barn, it's dumb luck that they left the door of the office open. On the desk is a set of about twenty keys. Once I find the tack room and fumble with at least six of them, the next one turns easily in the lock. I feel the wall for a light switch to illuminate the room. It looks like a typical tack room, with one exception. There's a picture of Ashwood Stables tacked up on the bulletin board with a large black X and a dart through the middle of it. Usually, this wouldn't offend me, but why it's here is a little disturbing.

What would Adrian do if he were here? What would he look for, or what is out of the ordinary here besides the damning photo? There is a locked cabinet in the corner, so I try the keys again. I'm almost through the keys when one turns in the lock. Opening the doors reveals another surprise – one that Sheriff Rocky will want to see.

My cellphone vibrates. As I reach into my purse, something covers my mouth, and I am instantly incapacitated.

An unpleasant (yet familiar) smell and lingers near my nose and mouth and is the last thing I remember, as I feel myself fall to the floor.

*"Where there is great love,
there are always miracles."*

~ Willa Cather

Chapter Four

Disturbing Dreams

Dr. Jess hovers above me as I slowly open my eyes. A towel and a bag of ice are on my left arm, and it throbs painfully. The memory of how it broke comes back in vivid detail. It is the arm I fell on several years ago when Jason threw a bale of hay over my head, and the rungs on the ladder gave way.

"Ellie?" Adrian's voice calls. "Ellen!"

"Glad you're awake," Jessica says, dryly. "I'm going to step out of the room so you can explain things to her, Adrian. Let me know if you need anything."

The awful taste in my mouth means that someone gave me that vile tasting drug again! "Adrian, I was so close I could have grabbed it. I went to take a picture and the next thing I know, I'm here. What happened?" Feeling for the necklace that isn't there, Adrian hands me a glass of water. "Where's my expensive fake necklace?"

"It's safe," Jake says, behind Adrian. "You gave us a real scare there, Miss Ellen."

"Really, Ellie, while we were out rounding up the bad guys, you must have gotten it into your thick skull to do some detective work on your own."

"I caught the guy near the fence, Miss Ellen. He had your necklace," Josh adds. "And I punched him for you. You're welcome."

Adrian shakes his head. "Why didn't you follow our plan? You could have gone into Lassiter's office, and instead, you went to the barn and put yourself in danger. What were you going to take a photo of in the cabinet beside liniment?"

"I found a cluster of tiny silver bells, right next to a bottle of clear liquid that didn't have a label on it."

Adrian looks irritated, "And that proves what, Ellie?"

"It proves that there's a connection to the long arm of whoever is behind our ridiculous events, which leads straight to Mr. Evil. He has to have some knowledge of what happened to us before Dimmy showed up at the Labor Day fiasco. Don't you remember? Why else would he have those bells locked up in a cabinet in his barn?"

"I hate to break it to you, my little turtle-dove, it proves nothing. Here's a better explanation. Anyone, including Lassiter, could have come across those bells. They could have easily come loose, and anyone could have picked them up. Anyone could have absently thrown them into anyone's cabinet and forgotten about them. Anyone."

"Or, he knows what they mean, and he was going to drive me nuts with them."

Josh's cellphone rings and he steps out of the room to answer it.

"Ellie, he had ample opportunity to do that, and he didn't. Besides, your fake, expensive, fabulous necklace was part of the mystery. That's what I was going to tell you before the lights went out."

Jake says, "I overheard one of the guests, who so happens was one of the main players too. He knew someone was supposed to steal your necklace. You see, he paid one of the valets to steal it when the lights went out."

"Why do things have to be so complicated? That might explain why one of the valets was looking at me so strangely. Was this part of the program?" I question.

"Yes and no," Adrian says. "We went over all of the instructions that listed each guest, their role in the murder mystery and how it was supposed to take place. Valet number one had his own agenda."

Jake concurs. "Valet number one talked valet number two into sticking to you like glue so that he could steal your necklace. He's the one that wouldn't let you into the library. Then, there was another man who attended the party who also paid valet number two to steal your necklace."

"Why would he do that? Oh, they thought they were real diamonds, didn't they? That little twerp drugged me to steal the necklace!"

"When they questioned the second valet, he spilled his guts and even produced the necklace. When things didn't go as planned inside, he followed you outside," Adrian adds.

"Yup," Jake says, "Valet number two said he found the necklace near the paddock fence. He saw you slip through it and figured you were going into the barn. He had what he wanted, so he didn't follow you inside. He said he didn't drug you."

"Are you sure? I'm positive I had my necklace when I went *into* the barn, I remember reaching up to touch it. Where's my purse?"

"It's right here. Can you prove that you had it in the barn, Ellie? Did you see anything that might help us identify the person who did this?"

"No. Can you explain why my cellphone is missing? I said I was reaching for it. I never pulled it out. Adrian, that foul taste reminds me of that awful drug!"

"There was nothing out of the ordinary in the cabinet you broke into if that's what you're trying to say. It contained the usual stuff one finds in a tack room. You know, Lassiter could press charges against you."

"Let him. Something isn't right, Adrian, my cellphone is missing. What do you have to say about that, Jake?"

"While Adrian and I were talking to the police, I told Josh to go and see what you were up to, Miss Ellen. When you weren't with the rest of the guests, he figured you went to the barn. He's the one who found you. There was no cellphone on the floor in the barn," Jake says. "The cabinet door was wide open. There was no one else around, I checked."

"Why don't you call my cellphone and see who answers, Mr. CIA man? Better yet, why don't you track it to see where it is right now?"

"Let's keep this to ourselves, for now, Ellie. We don't want to get everyone riled up over maybe nothing. We'll talk to Levi and get him involved, okay?"

"Sure Adrian. Aren't you at all alarmed that someone drugged me again?"

"Of course I am. But you should not have been where you were, Ellie. We don't have any proof. Until some magically appear, please keep this to yourself."

"Mums the word, Adrian. But I want my cellphone traced."

"Come on Jake, let's see what Josh has."

The next day, Levi called Jake back to Langley to fill out paperwork and to take my fake, yet coveted necklace to their lab for testing. If there is anything to find, their resident genius, Jewels, will discover it. Josh remains with us, due to the unresolved Solana threat.

On their way back from the arraignment that will start the process to put the murderer of Mr. Jenkins away, Sheriff Rocky and a bruised and bandaged Deputy Slim came by to say thanks for helping them solve the murder. They also want us to know how deeply sorry the Lassiter's are at involving us in this heinous crime. We asked them to stay for dinner, but they politely declined.

Our dinner subject tonight is, of course, the Murder Mystery Party, complete with all the juicy details.

"We knew something was going on when no one told us anything," Curlie announces, as she starts to clear away the dinner dishes. "I thought you looked great, Mom, even if you didn't wanna go. How did you keep those fingernails on?"

"I didn't. The darn things kept popping off. Maybe you ate some, Adrian, somehow three of them are missing."

"Is that what that crunch was? I thought it was a cranberry in the salad."

"Mom said not to say anything to any of you, Aunt Ellen," Ginny says laughing. "And you know how she can't keep a secret."

Terre starts to protest, "I'll have you know that I resent that accusation. I can keep a secret. I kept this one!"

"Dad said the same thing," Lindy adds. "It's okay, Mom, we love you anyway."

"You all looked pretty funny, you especially, Mr. Adrian. That suit you wore looked awful. Did men wear stuff like that?" Mack asks.

"I only know what the internet told me, son. Do you know anything about that Glen? Care to elaborate for us?"

Glen chuckles. "Nope, afraid it was b'fore my time. How old do ya think I am?"

Something occurs to me. "Were you all lurking in the bushes when we left?"

"No Mom," Curlie adds, "Grandma said it was okay to peek a little."

"That's right, Ellie," Mother laughs. "It must have been some party."

Danny seems curious. "How did you keep this a secret from each other? I mean, how is that even possible given that we get in each other's business so much?"

"How did Josh and Jake get over there? I didn't even see them leave?" Mack wants to know.

Josh wrinkles his forehead and says with a straight face, "We're just really good at what we do, son. If you must know, we went stealth."

"What does that mean?" Danny asks.

Adrian shakes his head. "Never mind, Danny, don't ask, okay?"

"We're going to remember this party for a long time, right Reed?" Dr. Jess says as Reed nods in agreement.

"It was a mystery for sure!" Dennis declares. "I'm glad the bad guys are locked up, and we can all go back to our boring old life."

"Come on now, our life is anything but boring, and that was a stroke of genius on your part, Ellie. Sheriff Rocky is grateful you gave that tidbit to Deputy Slim, even though his pie fork became a weapon." Adrian raises his glass in salute.

Dennis raises his glass too, and adds, "He's going to get a commendation for it, but honestly, Ellie, that was well played!"

"How did you know it was one of the servers, Ellie?" Terre asks.

"I didn't, not at first. I didn't believe there was a real murder either. Sheriff Rocky belongs to the community theater group, and so does Lassiter and his wife. I thought they were acting."

"I thought we were all acting," Terre says laughing.

"You know, I was the one who was supposed to faint, not Lassiter's wife. It was supposed to happen right after the screaming part, and the lights came back on. Someone was going to steal my necklace."

"Something didn't add up," Dennis says. "For one thing, the blood on Lassiter's face and hands didn't look real."

Adrian sips at his wine. "Not this again. It might not have been real blood on his face, but that was real blood on Lassiter's hands, and he looked terrified. No actor can act that good."

"It's well, dear," I gently tell him. "No actor can act that well."

"Are you picking on my diction Lady? How did you figure out who the murderer was?"

"The moment we got to the party, I had a funny feeling about one of the valets. Then I'm sure he changed his clothes and became a server. He kept jerking his head when he looked around the room like he was nervous about something. It looked odd to me."

"Servers are polite," Mother adds. "They typically move about quietly, and discretely."

"I agree, Mother. He didn't seem to fit in with the rest of them. The ones who served us food wore white gloves. He wore white plastic ones."

"I didn't catch that detail," Dr. Jess says, looking a little surprised. "And I'm usually so good at catching clues and solving mysteries. I should have guessed it. What else did you see that I didn't?"

"It occurred to me that he also looked familiar. For about an hour, I couldn't place his face, then figured out that he was the driver of that race that got him into trouble. Glen, do you remember that driver that nearly put me out of commission a few years ago when we first raced at Billingsworth?"

"I seem ta recall that. Yeah, Missy, I don't remember what his name was," Glen frowns. "Isn't that what ya complained ta the Racin Commission about?"

"That's the one. When this guy caught me looking at him, he practically ran out of the room. It was seconds before the lights went out and we heard that God-awful first scream. Josh, where were you and Jake when that happened? Adrian said you looked in the window of the library about that time. Was there a body then?"

Josh looks thoughtful. "I can't tell you. Then I'd have to, you know."

"Okay, let's move along," Adrian says, trying to change the subject. "You have to admit that the dinner was outstanding."

"You know," Dr. Jess says, "What threw me was the second scream. I reasoned that the screams were part of the murder mystery party and they got their timing off. I did see a tape recorder on the table where we picked up our instructions."

"Okay, I don't suppose Sheriff Rocky will mind if I tell you," Adrian begins. "The man's name is Gordon. The Racing Commission was keeping a watch on him for months, and when another complaint came in, they decided to suspend his license."

"Why would that be of interest?" Dennis asks.

"After another incident happened to a friend of his, Gordon was sure that Jenkins blew the whistle on him, and for that, the commission revoked Gordon's license. Jenkins got to the party way ahead of time. He was supposed to stay hidden in the library and wait for the signal to position himself on the floor. It was later when Josh saw Jenkins on the floor when he looked in the window."

"That's an odd way to start a murder party," Dr. Jess suddenly says. "Why didn't they introduce the victim and the other players so that we could get a handle on the entire situation."

"That wouldn't be fair," Dennis says, "then it wouldn't be a mystery, now would it?"

"It's a little ironic, don't you think? That Jenkins and Gordon came together for this party," Dr. Jess says. "It's a twist of fate, as most mysteries are!"

Adrian leans toward me and picks up one of my hands to kiss it. "You mean it's more like the fickle finger of fate!"

Josh rolls his eyes and says, "Here we go."

"Naw, ya all got it wrong. It's plunk your magic twanger, Froggy." Glen says with a straight face, and then he starts to laugh.

Danny snorts, "Plunk your magic what?"

"Now I know why Nathan leaves the table so quick after dinner," Josh sighs.

"What's a twanger?" Mack wants to know.

Dennis isn't quite following, and his annoyance surfaces. "We're getting away from our subject here. How would Lassiter know that anyone would want to kill Jenkins?"

"I don't think he knew that, Dennis. They had the party part all planned out, right down to the fake murder. Sheriff Rocky had the original script and showed it to us," Adrian replies. "Right Josh?"

"Right you are, Adrian," Josh says, swirling his glass between his fingers.

Dr. Jess adds dryly, "Now that you mention it, I recall walking past the library, on the way to the lady's room. The door was open; there was nobody on the floor at that time. When I came out, Lassiter was standing outside the door blocking it. I could see into the room a little, and a rather robust man was on the floor, but there was nothing on his shirt."

Adrian shrugs, saying, "You must have been there minutes before Lassiter was supposed to spread the ketchup and put the fake knife into his chest. Then someone else was supposed to turn the circuit breakers on and off in the parlor, and another person was supposed to turn the tape recorder on outside the door."

"One of the two screams we heard was a real scream, Adrian," Terre says. "I know a real scream when I hear it. Where was this woman during the party? I don't remember her being in the room with us. Did you see her Josh?"

"No, Ma'am," Josh answers politely.

"That had to be Mrs. Jenkins that nearly ran me over coming out of the lavatory. I lost a fingernail when she slammed the door into my hand. My instructions were to plant one or two fingernails near the body, but no one would let me into the library."

"Ellie, how many boxes of fingernails did you buy? You seemed to produce them every five minutes."

Dr. Jess calmly adds, "Maybe we weren't supposed to know that Jenkins and his wife were there. She could have been in the library all along, so she could tend to her pretend-dead husband. They probably pre-recorded the second scream."

"You're right about that part, Jess. Mrs. Jenkins went to find Lassiter to give him a washcloth to wipe his hands, as she was in on the mystery. She discovered the body before the tape recorder went off. It was going according to the script until Jenkins was really murdered. The real murderer must have panicked when the scream happened."

I'm now having trouble following this conversation. "Wait a minute, was I correct in thinking that the pretend murderer was Lassiter, Adrian?"

"Lassiter **was** the pretend murderer," he begins. "According to the script, his instruction was to smear the fake knife with ketchup, run into the parlor, sit down on the chair, and look mortified. He couldn't tell the difference between the fake knife that came with the party supplies with the real one, so he yanked it out and played his part."

"I'll bet Gordon ingratiated himself into the acting staff, and it was he who pressed the button on the recorder." Dr. Jess says, looking smug.

"Right again," Adrian states. "Mrs. Jenkins startled him, and he moved away as quickly as he could back into the parlor, and then into the kitchen to make it look like he was innocent."

"It was all so real; I kept thinking that everyone was playing their roles so well, we could do this on stage," Dr. Jess says with a laugh.

"Some of it was bad acting. Wouldn't you agree?" Terre volunteers.

Adrian smiles sheepishly. "Say, I have an idea. Why don't we do this as an Ashwood tradition?"

Dennis tilts his head. "You mean we should have our own murder mystery party every year around Halloween?"

"What are you talking about, Adrian? I refuse to do that again. You know I didn't want to go to that thing in the first place, why would you want to do that again?"

Terre laughs, "Oh come on Ellen; it could be fun."

"I'll consent to it if Adrian can be the one I murder because it will be…" As I say this, everyone at the table chimes in with "*over your dead body.*" "Am I that predictable?" Again, everyone says "*yes,*" including Josh.

Adrian grabs my hand and brings it to his lips. "So that you know, Lassiter is devastated over this. He blames himself, as he picked Jenkins to be the victim. Ellie, you don't know how much we love you and have waited for you to play with us again. It's been way too long, sweetheart."

Mother says thoughtfully, "Honey, you and Adrian should have won a prize for the best costume. You two went to a lot of trouble."

"Speaking of prizes, who won the bet?" Everyone suddenly stands up to leave the table. "Wait a minute. I know about the bet you all made about me not going to the party. I demand to know who won."

"Francesca," Adrian says, hanging his head. "Your Mother won the bet. She said you would go to the party."

"I hope you won a good prize, Mother. You all bet that I wouldn't show up. Thanks, Mother dear, for your vote of confidence at least. It certainly wasn't what I expected, but it was entertaining."

"Yes, it was, and it was wonderful watching you having fun for a change. By the way, did you ever find your cellphone?" Terre asks.

"No, I can't find it anywhere."

"I only found you and your purse, Miss Ellen. I didn't look into it." Josh says, shrugging his shoulders.

Adrian combed Lassiter's barn, and my cellphone was not there. Then he had Levi put a trace on it, but it didn't show up, anywhere. And I was so close to getting evidence! When Sheriff Rocky's men went back to Lassiter's barn to check it out, they found none of the items I told Adrian about, nor the photo of Ashwood with the dart through the middle.

The tiny silver bells went poof. The part that is most disturbing; if everyone was inside the house, and everyone accounted for, who was outside in the barn with me? Was valet number two telling the truth? And why would my cellphone be of interest to anyone?

Was my fake, expensive necklace the actual diversion?

Adrian encouraged me to take my little Glock out to the practice range. Most of the time, no one comes with me, however, on occasion,

Josh, or Adrian will meet me there. They usually wager as to which one of us will hit the target the most. Josh knows how awful Adrian is at betting and teases him relentlessly.

During one of these practices, a strange sensation washes over me. There is a distinct impression that someone is trying to connect with me. Could it be the residual from the medication I took earlier to hedge my bet against a migraine headache? Or is it something that's lingering at the back of my mind? Could the sessions of meditation with Dr. Laurel work in reverse?

Is someone from the other side trying to reach me?

Adrian will later tell me that he was out riding one of the boarder's horses when he found me standing perfectly still as one hand held the little pistol, the other hand was on my forehead. When I didn't respond to his questions, he approached quietly, so that he wouldn't scare me. I didn't feel him take the Glock out of my hand.

Adrian's voice brought me back to the present. Standing in front of me with both hands on my wrists, he says, "Ellie? Ellie, can you hear me?"

"Did I have one of my episodes again?"

"Yeah, where did you go this time?" he asks.

"It was an odd sensation, Adrian. I was standing on a big rock or a huge boulder. It was black, like a big hunk of lava."

"Can you tell me where it was, sweetheart?"

"No. There was water all around, and I was sad. I didn't know where I was." Shielding my eyes, I glance up at the sky as Adrian does the same thing.

"What are you looking at, Ellie?"

"When I looked up, the moon was on the right side of the sky. The insane part is that it was not on the left as it is now. How is that possible? I'm sorry, Adrian, my head is pounding, and I'm a little nauseated."

No one can explain why these episodes occur, or what triggers them. Most of the time, I'm not even aware of them and snap out of it. Now and then, there's a flash of something, and at other times, it's tough to relate what I see. Could this be what some have described as an out-of-body experience? Although doctors ruled out epilepsy, it is still worrisome.

Mother told Adrian that as a child, I was a sleepwalker. She, or Daddy, often found the back door of our house wide open. It mostly happened in mid-winter when someone noticed the temperature in the house drop, and naturally assumed that I was responsible.

"Come on, let's get you to the house," Adrian says, steering me to the passenger side of the golf cart. When we get to the house, he gently pushes me onto a sofa. Closing my eyes to tune everything out, when I open them, he's sitting on a chair opposite me.

"Where's my Glock?"

Adrian pats a small bag on the coffee table. "It's right here. You were standing there with it in your hand."

Dr. Stevens brought Adrian up to speed about how we meditate and imagine talking to a departed loved one. Careful not to sound condescending, he gently guides me through the process of discovery as this sometimes helps in the recall of what leads to the episode in the first place. Was this a meditation thing?

"It looked like something distracted you, something about standing on a big rock and looking up to see the moon in the wrong place."

"I don't know how to describe it to you. One minute I was practicing and the next--You know how you see a little puff of smoke when the bullet hits the target? As the little puff of smoke did that, I looked up at the sky and the next thing I knew, I was standing on a big black rock looking at the ocean. I swear to you that I not only felt the sea breeze, but I could also smell the water."

An involuntary shiver runs up my spine.

"Are you cold?" He moves to the sofa and reaches around to pull an afghan down around my shoulders.

"It's an odd thing, Adrian. It wasn't one of my premonitions like I know something is about to happen and it's not a *déjà vu* thing either. It was a little poof, and then I tried to call out, but my mouth wouldn't form the words."

"I'm going to get you a cup of tea. Be right back."

"Adrian? It was like looking at the water through someone else's eyes. How does that even make sense?"

"It doesn't, sweetie. Maybe Dr. Stevens can tell you what it means. Do you want me to call her?"

"No, I'll save it for the next time I see her." What I don't say is that I felt connected to someone. Adrian won't believe me, and I know how that sounds.

Adrian's voice crackles over the walkie-talkie. "The mail came. A registered letter from the Virginia Racing Commission is here, OVER. Never mind, I'll bring it to you. OUT."

Adrian knows that a letter addressed to me from this office never brings good news. He sits on the sofa for the support he feels I might need. As I read the words, my face and neck start to feel hot. It seems that someone filed a formal complaint against Ashwood Stables recently, and I'm to appear in front of the Virginia Racing Commission next week. They suggest that I bring a lawyer for representation. When I glance at Adrian, he merely holds out his hand.

"It's more baloney like before and so bogus, Adrian. We've done nothing wrong. I thought this would stop once Jenkins and Lassiter were out of the picture. Who's after us now?"

"Maybe they didn't get that memo, Ellie," he says, chuckling.

"Everything's a joke to you. I don't blame the commission, because they're only trying to do their job. I do blame the person who filed this complaint, and I honestly don't know who it is this time."

"I'll contact Nicholas Parks. He's the one that Levi put us in touch with the last time the commission tried to do this."

"Would you ask if he can meet with us before next week?"

Could our removal from the racetrack be coming from the banker, Mr. Yancy? He's the only other person who might be causing trouble. Why would his name even pop into my head?

"Don't worry, Ellie, we'll get this straightened out in no time. There's something else. You might want to read this article." Adrian hands me a newspaper clipping and steps out of the room to make a call.

The headline reads: **Banker Yancy Free at Last**. The article suggests that Mr. Fenton C. Yancy feels that he was set-up by someone who knew about insider trading. I was not the one responsible for his demise and sudden departure from the bank. I will not take credit for his stupidity; that was all his doing.

He could blame me for the inquiries that led to the charges of embezzlement that Virginia levied against him when it came to Abigail Ashwood's finances. He and Mr. Allen, the Executor for the Ashwood Estate was responsible for mishandling the funds, as they were trusted friends at the time.

Yancy maintains that he was unaware of the circumstances that led to the dwindled Ashwood Estate Fund. He also feels the punishment he received was unjust, as it was the wrong time to invest, as it was for everyone. They ultimately blamed each other. It was a finger-pointing fiasco, as Yancy said this and Allen said that, in a trial that ended when they both went to prison.

Somehow, Mr. Jenkins was in on their little scheme, as papers surfaced after his death that pertained to stocks and bonds stolen from the Ashwood Estate--that led directly to him. That certainly explains the horrible look on Mr. Allen's face when Sheriff Rocky declared Mr. Jenkins was the murder victim during Lassiter's party.

Perhaps he was relieved the knife didn't make it into *his* chest. The disgrace of the murder of Mr. Jenkins was terrible enough, but Mr. Yancy's reappearance is almost too much for me!

Adrian is back to plop down on the sofa. As he hands back the commission's letter, he says, "Everything's been taken care of, sweetheart. Levi spoke to Nicholas personally. He called the commission for an explanation. They said they're sorry for any inconvenience this has caused you, as it's apparent that they've made a mistake. Please accept their sincerest apology and please come to race at Billingsworth Racetrack, no hard feelings, okay?"

"What? That's it? Everything's fine and dandy?"

"Yup, you can expect a bill for the time Parks spent. He said we should let him know when we're in Washington again, and he'll take us out to dinner."

"We don't have to go to a hearing with the Virginia Commission? You've solved this with one phone call? What magic wand did this Mr. Parks and Levi use? Why didn't we know about him when we went through this stuff before?"

"I don't know. Let's not look this gift horse in the mouth, okay?"

"That's funny, Adrian. I used that expression myself a while back.

"When was that?"

Smiling to myself when the memory surfaces, "It had something to do with Glen and a lot of money."

> *"Today or any day that phone may ring*
> *And bring good news."*
> ~ Ethel Waters

Chapter Five

News, Some Good, Some Bad

Halfway around the world, King Akdemir touched a photo of Prince Jason astride his prized stallion, *Basim's Pride II*. He wondered where he was. Was Jason helped out of the Royal Palace, and he's safe and out of harms' way? Could the news of his death be a fabrication, as Ellen seems to think?

"Your Highness, I must speak to you immediately," Jamaile whispered into the hand-held device he acquired recently. It is a sophisticated apparatus set to a specific frequency only he and his half-brother can use. It is Akdemir's lifeline to Jamaile, as the panic buttons on his desk and wingchair no longer work.

King Akdemir pressed the button and whispered back, "Yes, Jamaile, I am here; come to the library when you are able." He was sitting at his enormous desk in the palace library and glanced around at the rows of books. Then he leaned forward to touch the photograph again, which he slammed down on the desk in frustration. It made a loud crack sound.

"Is something wrong, Highness?" Jamaile asked through the device.

Akdemir brought the device near his mouth and pressed the button, "No, Jamaile, I dropped something on the desk."

"I shall be there shortly," Jamaile replied.

Akdemir turned the frame around, relieved the glass had not broken. Then he positioned it near a shelf so that he could see it from his chair. "Where are you, Jason?" he whispered. "Are you somewhere safe? I hope harm has not come to you."

Akdemir then turned his attention to a mound of papers. When the heavy door at the end of the room opened, it startled him. A person who wore dark clothing came slowly toward him.

"Who allowed you to enter the palace?" Akdemir demanded. His right hand had opened the top drawer of the desk and was already reaching in for his dagger as the dark figure continued to approach. "Stop right there. You do not have permission to be here. What do you want?"

This person looked like any other guard in Jamaile's regimen, and it took Akdemir several seconds to realize that it was a woman dressed as a man. A black scarf covered her face, and she was wielding a menacingly sizeable curved knife.

"I asked you a question. Who let you in here and what do you want?" Akdemir demanded.

"Do not worry. I am not here to harm you. I want to know where you are hiding Jason," the voice spewed in perfect Arabic.

"Who are you to ask about him?" Akdemir glanced at the device and thought that he might have time to touch it to alert Jamaile, then pushed his dagger skillfully out of sight.

The dark figure let out a laugh. "Do not think of throwing that little piece of tin at me," the woman hissed. "It will never make it past your hand. Do go ahead and try. It would give me great pleasure to nail your hand to your desk."

"This intrusion is punishable by law. You speak to me, the King, who has not summoned you here, and you threaten me? We will not honor your demands. Stop where you are."

The dark figure laughed again. "You are not *my* King. I demand only one thing. Tell me where the brat is. If you do that, I will leave and never come back."

"Have you no reverence woman? If you mean Prince Jason, I do not know of his whereabouts. He disappeared many years ago. No one knows where he is, not even his mother." Akdemir shut the desk drawer with a loud bang hoping that Jamaile might be listening. "Who are you? Why would you demand such a thing?"

"I have come to collect a debt," the woman replied, and switched to speak English. "An eye for an eye, so to speak."

"If it is money you want, perhaps we can make a deal." As Akdemir tried to control his temper, he moved around his desk to sit down on the corner to stare at the intruder. He surmised that if he kept the woman talking long enough, Jamaile would have time to alert his guards. He did not understand why the door at the farthest end of the room remained closed.

The woman stopped to remove the scarf that covered her head, which revealed her face. "You think money is the answer to everything. You think it will buy you whatever you want. You and your country's blood oil money. It is not money I want you imbecile! I want revenge."

Akdemir was unsure how to handle this but tried to keep his temper in check. "You do not have the right to talk to me in this fashion. Who are you? We will not tolerate your insolence nor your disrespect in the Royal Palace."

The woman then removed the hat that covered her blond-brown streaked hair which tumbled down her shoulders. She then flung the hat on his wing chair along with the scarf. She stepped closer and Akdemir froze. She did not look familiar to him.

"I have every right to be here," she hissed.

"What kind of revenge do you seek? I have done nothing to you. Explain yourself. Has one of my half-brothers encouraged you to come here? You must go through the proper channels if you want anything from the Royal Palace. The ministers have set the rules. You will need to speak with the Minister of Finance. You can make an appointment with him later this week." To stall her and to defuse the potentially volatile situation, Akdemir calmly said, "Sit down; I will ring for tea and something to eat. Would that suit you, until we have an arranged appointment?"

"NO! It would not suit me. Where is Jason? He is not in Virginia, so he must be here. You are hiding him. Turn him over to me now, and I will leave without incident."

"I cannot do that…" As Akdemir said these words, one of the bookcases along the wall near the end of the room moved outward. Without so much as a breeze, Jamaile came behind the woman to surround her with his big arms. Before she could react, her knife dropped to the stone floor with a clank.

"Now, who are you, and why are you here?" Akdemir demanded again, moving as close as he dared.

"Where did you come from?" the woman stammered. "I know every secret door in this place! You do not have to be so rough! Let me go, and I will tell you why I have come."

Akdemir comprehended the look on Jamaile's face to mean that the woman was not to be trusted.

"It is apparent that you do not know all of them. I will ask you again. Who are you, and who sent you here? He will snap your neck, and thus, you will die needlessly, unless you are forthcoming with your answers."

Jamaile maintained his grip, and when the woman tried to kick him, he pushed her roughly to the floor, tying her hands behind her back so fast she could not comprehend the movements. Standing her upright, he leaned down to whisper something in her ear, which made her flinch and turn away.

"I will not ask again," Akdemir said, slowly running out of patience.

The woman considered this for a moment. "My name is Solana. I was almost Basim's wife. Members of your council will not allow me to claim what is due me."

"That's interesting. A moment ago you were demanding Jason, and now you want money? You said you wanted revenge. My brother has been dead for many years. Why would you come forward now to tell us about this claim?"

Akdemir returned to sit down at his desk, glanced at Jamaile as he picked the woman up with one hand, and slammed her down roughly on one of the chairs to face him.

"You do not have to be so rough!" Solana spit at Jamaile.

"That is not rough…" Jamaile said in his most menacing manner. He is about to slap her across the face, then whispered, "I will show you rough!"

"Jamaile!" Akdemir said to the big man. He backed away from the woman but remained close to her. Akdemir stared at the woman with suspicion. "You had your opportunity to come forward when my father was alive. Why do this now? Do you think I am more lenient than my father? That I will give in to your demands quickly and without much thought? If you think this, you are mistaken!"

"Your father, the great King Basim, promised me that if I left the Royal Palace, I would receive Basim's share of his inheritance along with a small treasure. I've been away from this country for a long time.

I need that inheritance. I am here now to claim it," the woman said as she looked around.

"So your prime motive is money. What do you know of Basim? Were you responsible for his death?" Akdemir watched Solana's face as her expression changed from anger to rage. "Your reaction suggests that you know something about that."

"I do not know anything about his death. It was a long time ago, as you said."

Akdemir calmly said, "I believe you are avoiding the truth. You may claim all you want, however, the time for your request has expired as the Council Ministers will tell you. You will receive nothing of his inheritance, or any treasure, for that matter. When he died, it reverted to the state. I do not have access to it. Only those in authority have that privilege."

"I do not believe you! I lived here in the palace with Basim. He told me that I would inherit many riches. You owe me that for what your kingdom has cost me!" Solana snarled.

"The rules that govern the riches you speak of are not accessible to me," Akdemir said slowly and succinctly. "The Royal Ministers decided that after my father died, that the state treasury needed protection. They put measures in place to keep people like you from profiting without cause."

"You are lying!" Solana screamed as she tried to stand up; however, Jamaile applied pressure to her shoulders, and she sat back down. "You have access to it; you do not want to share it with me!"

"Sadly, that is the truth. The Royal Ministers allot monies for me to live. The Royal Palace and everything you see within it is taken care of by measures they put into place. As for treasure, you would have to be a pirate to claim it."

Solana's face registered outrage. She then started to laugh and talk to herself which made Jamaile and Akdemir uneasy. She moved her body forward in the chair as if she would launch herself off it again, but Jamaile kept his big hands on her shoulders, forcing her to stay seated.

"That is very funny. Perhaps I am a pirate!"

"Take her away, Jamaile," Akdemir said with a flick of his hand. "She does not belong here."

"Yes, Highness, with pleasure."

"Wait! I will tell you. My child died; it was Basim's child. Our child died from the roughness your men made me endure! You and your family have taken everything away from me. It is time to pay up!" Solana said squinting her eyes.

"The men who did this to you were not my men. I would neither have done such a thing nor ordered anyone to do so. That kind of thing is relegated to the Islamic Religious Police, not the guards of the Royal Palace," Akdemir responded.

"They were your father's men! It still falls to you to honor their debt!"

"We owe you nothing. If there was a debt, it was paid many years ago, or should I say a second time, when you set that explosion on the jetliner that killed Basim. It is my opinion that you have had your revenge."

"You cannot prove that I had anything to do with that. I say when the debt has been paid, not you," Solana said resolutely.

"You may not have detonated the trigger; nonetheless, you must have been the one behind it. You are most probably responsible for the strange things that plague Basim's family." Akdemir suddenly realized the implication of Solana's words. "All this time I thought it was Fariq. How long have you two been working and planning these atrocities together?"

Solana started to laugh again. "I do not know what you are talking about, but Basim had a second funeral. My how truly tragic for all of you. Perhaps if you tell me where Jason is, I might feel generous and tell you."

Solana changed thoughts in the hope that Akdemir would relent. She absently glanced around the library waiting for the King to respond. Perhaps she could call his bluff.

"You asked for Jason, and now you say you know where he is? What have you said that is near the truth? You and Fariq. You and he caused much anguish and pain to many people. In your selfishness, you and he have destroyed more than you know. You have had your revenge. I will not be party to more. You have had restitution for whatever happened to you previously. The Royal Ministers and I will give you nothing."

Solana's voice registered her anger. "Your family took everything I valued away from me. I thought it only fair to do the same to yours. I will not stop until I am satisfied!"

"And you have taken enough from mine. I do not care to hear any more. In return for *my* generosity for not having you put to death here on the spot, Jamaile will take you and escort you downstairs, until we can determine our next course of action."

"Yes, Your Highness, the pleasure will be mine." As Jamaile reached for her arm, Solana tried to wiggle away from him, but he was quick to subdue her.

"You cannot treat me like a common person! I know things that are valuable to you!" she insisted.

Akdemir turned his chair to face the wall, and waved his hand in the air. "Take her away, Jamaile. Her face and presence sicken me."

Solana changed her demeanor and asked demurely, "Don't you want to know how poor little Ellen's horse was murdered?" When Akdemir did not turn his chair around, she launched into a litany of profanity. Jamaile hauled Solana out of the chair, making sure she was held away from anything, as she tried to kick him again. "Don't you want to know how I got in here? How about how I get in and out of the country without being seen?"

Akdemir did not respond. Jamaile took Solana through the big library doors where he pushed her roughly into the waiting hands of his most trusted men, and the heavy doors closed with a thud. Then he remembered that there was something important he wanted to discuss with Jamaile. It would now wait for another time.

Did he dare call Mr. Levi or Adrian to inform them that they have the infamous woman in custody? He cannot contact Ellen directly, as she practically threw him out of the Manor House in Virginia, and had refused to take his calls. If Solana did not know where Jason is, perhaps all hope is not lost.

We could all use some good news today. Looking around my office, I reach for our family photo. Then pick up the one next to it. I touch the silver frame where Jason sits astride his mighty Stallion, *Basim's Pride II*, and wonder where he is.

If he made it out of the Royal Palace, how could Dimmy's elaborate security possibly miss Jason's movements? When they held me captive there, I couldn't sneeze, without someone coming out of the woodwork to hand me a tissue.

Questions continue to haunt me. Should we blame Uncle Akdemir for Jason's disappearance? Sources close to him maintain that they don't believe Jason made it out of the Royal Palace alive. Or has the unthinkable happened and he is no longer… I will not allow myself to go in that direction. Where are you, Jason? I know in my heart that you're out there, but where?

It makes me crazy to think that Solana is wandering around out there too. Adrian and his CIA buddies agree that she's probably up to no good. They have no idea where she is at the moment, as all leads have turned up nothing. Should this crazy woman turn her wrath upon us, we have their assurance that we are as safe as possible. They also agree that she is bound to turn up soon.

Josh doesn't always voice his opinion, but just yesterday, he said, "Mark my words, Miss Ellen. Solana will slip up, and when she does, that's when we'll catch her!"

I suppose he's right, but I wish with all my heart that this nightmare ends soon.

"Ellie," the walkie-talkie crackles. "Ellie, are you there? OVER?" Adrian's voice is a welcome interruption, as I haven't accomplished anything of substance today. Bills and stacks of unanswered correspondence sit in several piles across my desk. I'm so frustrated that I start to cry for no reason.

"Ellie, are you there? OVER?"

"Yes, I'm here Adrian, what's so urgent?"

"Are you busy right now? Can you come outside? OVER?"

"Yes, I'm on my way."

"OVER," the walkie-talkie pops, "You're supposed to say OVER when you are giving over to the other person, Ellie, OVER." I'm halfway out of my office when Adrian's voice spits over the walkie-talkie again. "Ellie? Are you coming? OVER!"

"Yes, Adrian. I'm on my way, OVER and OUT."

The walkie-talkie crackles, "Proper radio communication etiquette is either OVER or OUT, Ellie, not both."

Levi's car is near the garages. My crying jag a few moments ago might have been responsible for not hearing him come up the driveway.

"Levi, how are you? You must have something important to tell us, or you wouldn't have come all this way. How long can you stay with us this time?"

Levi bends to kiss me on the cheek and smiles at Adrian. "I had such good news I had to bring it to you myself. Adrian made me promise to deliver it to you in person."

Adrian grins so wildly that it looks as if he's swallowed a frog. "Levi's here to tell you *two* significant things."

"Will you ask Francesca to join us? She needs to hear this, too. It involves both of you. It's all good news, Ellen, trust me. The threat is neutralized now, so Jake and Josh are no longer needed."

Levi reaches into the back seat for his briefcase, which means he has something to show us, then turns to speak to Jake and Josh. "You fellas might want to gather your gear while we talk. I expect you'll be leaving in the morning."

"Does that mean the wicked witch of the east is dead?" I inquire.

"Let's talk in the house, shall we?" Levi replies.

Adrian goes ahead to alert Mother and Mona that Mr. Levi is here for a visit. They are setting up afternoon tea in the Morning Room, and Levi asks if we could postpone that for a few minutes to go to the library for a little chat. Sandwiched between Mother and Adrian on the sofa, they both reach for one of my hands.

"Tell me you found that crazy woman! Did you find Jason? Is that what this is all about?"

"Almost as good," Adrian comments. "Let Levi talk, honey."

Levi sits down on the ottoman opposite us after placing his briefcase on the floor. "I'll get right to the point. Two days ago, we received a call from Jamaile. He was to call us if he had any information to share with us."

"Unless it has to do with Jason, I don't give a rat's patutti what happens over there, Levi. I am no longer concerned with that part of the world."

Adrian looks uncomfortable. "Ellie – let the man talk, please!"

"I know how you feel, Ellen. It's excellent news because I'm here to tell you that Solana, aka Andrea Simmons, is in custody at the Royal Palace in Saudi," Levi says. "As the story goes, Jamaile's men caught her, and there was a scuffle. She gained entrance into Akdemir's library to demand money. The puzzling thing is that no one could figure out how she got in. It is apparent that there are far more passageways and hidden corridors they didn't know existed."

Pulling my hands free, saying, "You came all the way to tell us that? I thought this might be about Jason, or you found my cellphone."

"It doesn't have anything to do with your cellphone. Please hear the rest of it, and after I've told you everything, you can ask as many questions as you like, alright Ellen?"

"Sure Levi, please continue."

"When two of Jamaile's guards were found dead, they went in search of the intruder. It was one of his astute soldiers that had her pegged right from the beginning," Levi smiles. "She was wearing one of their uniforms and filling it out in places only a woman could."

"So you're here to tell us about this Solana person. That's your news? Thanks so much for coming all this way to tell us, Levi, you could have called with that information." I stand as Adrian reaches for my hand.

"Ellie, sit down. Levi didn't come all this way to tell you only that, there's way more," Adrian pleads. "Hear him out, and I promise you will be grateful he came all this way."

"Okay, please continue. I'm sorry for the interruption."

"Solana will stand trial in Saudi if they don't behead her first, and then she'll stand trial here. Her list of infractions is long, starting with international espionage, forgery, impersonating an officer, and murder. She'll undoubtedly be put away for a very long time. The charges against her are longer than Lenard's," Levi chuckles, "and you know how that turned out."

"Now he's getting to the good part, Ellie." Adrian raises his eyebrows and pretends to smoke a cigar.

"Who are you supposed to be, Adrian?"

Mother smiles as she figures it out. "It's Groucho Marx, Ellie."

"Right you are, Francesca, Mom used to sit me in front of the TV when I misbehaved. She thought if I watched Groucho Marx, Laurel and Hardy, and the Three Stooges that I would be a better person," Adrian chuckles. "She thought I'd be a funny person anyway."

"That explains so much, Adrian." Levi shakes his head in understanding. "She was right about one thing; you are a funny person."

"Yes, it does explain so much, Adrian." Mother and I agree.

"Now for the best news. Ellen, Francesca, Jamaile said he tried to call you, Ellen. Jamaile also told us that they know that Jason fathered a child while he was in Saudi. It was evident that the warring factions took the woman out of the Royal Palace soon after Jason went missing. No details as to how they know that. Jamaile's trusted people followed them into the desert, rescued her, and placed her with a family who had recently lost their daughter."

Mother starts to weep as Adrian moves to put an arm around me. "See, I told you it was good news," he mumbles.

"What does this mean, Levi? Who is she? Jason told me about a girl he was fond of and spoke highly of her. Why was she taken out to the desert? What about the baby, is the baby okay?"

Levi laughs, saying, "The young woman's name is Amala. That isn't her real name, but it's the one Jason gave her. Jamaile said she was taken to the desert to die because she shamed her father and their household. That was her punishment. They are both quite fine, however."

"Who did this to her? Can't Dimmy take them to the palace to protect them? What a tangled web they all wove. They didn't harm them, did they? Why are we now just learning of this, Levi? Why didn't we know right away?"

Adrian says, "As far as we know, she's one of Fariq's daughters. Jam-ale wanted to keep this quiet so that no one could trace them back to us. Jam-ale's men rescued her."

"Oh, Lord." All I can do is shake my head as a shiver runs up my spine. "Did Jason know he made this girl pregnant?" When the realization hits me, "I mean--OH MY God!"

"Ellen, listen to me," Levi says softly, taking my hands in his. "We can only surmise that it's unlikely Jason knew about the baby. Amala is shy and quite protective of her son. It was difficult to leave all that she knew to raise this child, in the wake of being left out in the desert. They took her to a village where Akdemir made sure that she would be cared for, but she can never go back to Saudi once she leaves. They informed her real family of her death, and there was evidence left at the scene that leaves little doubt that she died there."

"You're saying she's alive, and so is her baby boy?"

"Yes, Ellen, they are both alive. Amala is having a hard time trying to live a normal life there. She is always looking over her shoulder wondering if her father will come after her. She knows that if her secret is ever known, death would be their punishment. Their future rests on the decision you make, and it affects you all. Jamaile said Amala and her baby are comfortable for now. Akdemir knows of this situation, and he has deferred to you."

"What do you want their future to look like?" Adrian asks. "We can adopt them both, and they can come here to live if you want that. The little boy is already considered a United States citizen, due to Jason being his father."

"Ellen, do you want to leave them there to let Akdemir take responsibility for them?" Levi asks. "Or do you want Amala and her baby to come here to live with all of you? We can make that happen."

My eyes fill with tears. Mother answers for both of us, by saying there is no question that we want them here. I nod my head in agreement, as the lump in my throat will not allow me to speak. Levi squeezes my hands and says he knew what my answer would be; he merely needed a verbal confirmation.

"Did anyone ask her what she wants to do?"

"That's a good question, Ellen. She can't wait to meet all of you and be a part of Jason's family. We have steered clear of talking about what happened to him for now. You can broach the subject once you feel comfortable doing that with her."

"I can't wait to meet her and the baby."

"I spoke directly with Akdemir after Jamaile told us about Amala. When Jamaile brought this to Akdemir's attention, he naturally thought of you. He's willing to send funds to help feed and clothe them. He's remorseful, Ellen. He would do anything to change the past. He mentioned how much he misses all of you."

"I want nothing more from that side of the family, ever! When can they come? How soon can they get here? How old is the boy? What's his name? Will you put them into the program with us?"

Levi laughs at the questions I throw at him. "I told him you want no further contact with him whether or not Amala and the baby come here. Amala has a beautiful baby boy named Basim, who is almost two years old. We still have to work out some of the details. And we will do that as soon as possible."

"You're a grandmother now," Mother says chuckling. "They can stay upstairs with me. We can redo that great big second room for them. I don't need all that space."

"You know, that's a great idea. And you are a great grandma!"

Levi opens his briefcase to extract something. "I thought you might want to see what they look like now. Jamaile had these sent to my office."

My eyes fill with tears when Levi hands me two photos of a woman wrapped in traditional Muslim clothing with a baby sitting on her lap. "He's beautiful. So is she."

Passing one of the photos to Mother, she whispers, "He reminds me of Jason. He looks like…"

"I know, right down to his nose and curly dark hair."

"If it's any consolation, Ellen, when Akdemir saw these photos of Amala and the boy, he had to cancel his meetings for the rest of the day. Jamaile also said that they need to be with you, as the boy reminds Akdemir too much of Jason and he would be a constant reminder of why he isn't there with him," Levi adds.

"Wait a minute, wouldn't this child be considered his heir?"

Levi shrugs his shoulders, saying, "Yes and no. Although he is an heir as Jason was, it would be unfair to subject this child to what may certainly be a tortuous life should Akdemir's other half-brothers discover who he is. Without going into detail, it was an unselfish act for him to allow Amala to leave Saudi."

"Hey, I'm a grandfather! Aren't I too young to be a grandfather?" Adrian sputters.

Adrian and Levi laugh as Mother and I hug each other. How could Levi have known that this would be the ticket to my sanity? Did Dimmy defer to me, because he knew that I would have gone over there to demand my grandchild? Has he really let us go? Good Lord, I hope so. I swear that if we ever do find Jason, we will never tell him he's alive-- EVER!

Of course, it would be over my dead body anyway!

Finally, we will be free of the stigma of the Royal Palace and our desert cousin connection. Will we be able to welcome Amala and her child into our home, without the threat of her family coming after them? Levi assures us that they will be safe. He does say that during all the time Amala has lived with this family, they felt it would be safer to remove her now before the boy finds out about his heritage.

Adrian cautions that it will be tricky to remove them from Saudi, and it may take a few months to work out all the details. Mother and I hope it's soon. We don't want to miss any more milestones in little Basim's life.

"You must stay for dinner, Levi," Mother says, taking his arm to lead him out of the library. We know that he'll take her up on that invitation and possibly stay the night.

"How long have you known about them, Adrian?"

"I honestly only recently found out, Ellie; it was a tightly guarded secret. Don't be mad at Dimmy for not passing this along until now, as he has some other stuff clogging up his brain these days, you know, with him being a king and all.

"I'm not mad at him for this, let's blame Jam-ale this time. I'll bet he's the one that had Amala followed. Do you suppose that he's also the one who caught her in Jason's room? Isn't rebellion like that punishable by death? Do you suppose that Good King Dimmy is guilty of breaking one of his own rules?"

"No, Jam-ale and Akdemir are straight on following their laws. You didn't seem surprised when Levi mentioned Amala. Did you know about her?" Adrian asks.

"Jason told me he was falling in love with a beautiful girl. He didn't know her name, so he called her Amala. It means hope in Arabic. He never said she was pregnant. Maybe he didn't know when we spoke the last time. Maybe that's why Jason went missing. Did that crazy man Fariq find out about Amala and Jason? She is, after all, the opposition's family, if she's Fariq's daughter. I can't wait to ask her about that one!"

"Ellie, I don't think that's a good idea. She's going to have a hard enough time with our language, and coping with the journey here, knowing Jason's gone. Levi mentioned that she has never given up hope he's alive, and she might think he's here with us."

"I've never given up hope either. I know you think he's never coming back. It's incredible. Now we have the chance to bring up his child and welcome his almost wife, don't we? Besides, Curlie and Melanie will be so excited to hear this news. A little piece of Jason is coming home."

Later, a little plaque makes its way to my desk. It has a beach scene with two sets of footprints in the sand. If Amala believes that Jason is still alive, that means I'm not walking this journey alone in my quest to find him.

The real question is, however, why hasn't he been located yet? What happened to his unique (and on the grid) super watch? Did he try to send a signal? I want answers more than anything, and even though the poem brings tears to my eyes, it allows me to forge ahead regardless of the outcome. Come hell or high water; I will never give up!

"Adrian, it's so not fair that you're going without me!" I'm yelling into the walkie-talkie, "OVER! Damn it, Adrian, talk to me! OVER! Please!"

The walkie-talkie remains silent.

Levi and Adrian made it abundantly clear that they would not allow me to go to Saudi with them. They said it was too dangerous. I don't care; I want to go!

Adrian throws a daisy through the open door of my office, and it lands on the sofa. "Don't be mad at me for leaving you here. Come on Ellie, it will be less tedious if I go without you. We can move in and out much quicker if you stay here."

"Less tedious, my eye; I'll stay in the hotel. You won't even know I'm there. Please, you can't leave me here!"

"I didn't mean it that way, sweetie. It won't look as if we're trying to smuggle them out, even though that's what we're going to do. If you come, it'll raise suspicions, and I'll have to worry about you, too. Please don't add to our stress." When I turn away, he comes to place a small box on my desk. "I bought you a peace-offering."

"What could fit in this box to make up for not going with you?" Tearing off the bow and opening the box, there is a bracelet with colorful beads and chunky bits of dangling objects. "What am I supposed to do with this? I like jewelry, but this strikes me as an odd gift, even from you."

Adrian takes the bracelet out of my hands, opening the clasp to place it on my wrist. "Don't you know what it is? Look," he says laughing, "each one of the items signifies something extraordinary in your life, like the births of your children, their birthstones, baby shoes--there's even one for Little Basim."

"I don't know what to say, Adrian. It's beautiful, now that I know what it is."

"I have to go now; I'll call you when we get to the airport. I love you, Ellie May. Please promise me that you'll stay out of trouble while I'm gone."

"I promise."

"I mean it, Ellen! You have to stay out of trouble. I can't worry about you while I'm gone. Jake and Josh are on another case and can't be here. There is no one else available, so you have to promise to stay out of trouble!"

"I promise I'll stay out of trouble, Adrian. What do you think I'll do? I can't fit into your bag, now can I? You better call me a lot."

Touching the pieces on the bracelet, as Adrian hugs and kisses me, there's a horse engraved with the name *Didgeridoo*, a piano with Cuthbertina and her birthstone, a blue and silver riding helmet with Jason's name, his birthstone, and a tiny gun. It is a very thoughtful gift.

By now, Adrian's blue convertible is rolling down the gravel driveway, disappearing in a cloud of dust when it hits the two-lane road. I pick up the bracelet to touch the pieces again; a red convertible with Melanie's name and birthstone, a book that opens to a picture of Adrian, a horse with the name *Truly Yours* along with others Adrian will need to explain. The bracelet jingles slightly, as the pieces hit each other. It sounds like tiny bells. Was this done on purpose?

Mother graciously gave up her sitting room, and the construction workers installed a wall to separate it into two bedrooms. We couldn't move, or add another bathroom, because of the plumbing, and since Mother was not about to move into Akdemir's set of rooms, we all felt this was a better choice.

The window seat remained intact in the balcony play area where I imagine Mrs. Ashwood and Miss Abigail are especially happy a baby will once again live here. When I get to the top of the stairs, Mother is sitting in a chair holding a clipboard waiting for the furniture truck to deliver Amala and Little Basim's new furnishings.

"I'll go down and wait for them, Ellie."

"Okay. I'll stay up here to direct traffic."

Mrs. Sarah Ashwood's rocking chair sits waiting. It makes me smile looking at it. We feel her presence, especially when the chair rocks when no one is near. Sometimes a perfume scent lingers in the hallway, even though none of us wears that brand. Was that a sigh I heard just now?

In two short weeks, Amala and Basim will be here. We hope it won't take any longer than that. Adrian expressed trepidation when he explained how they would be extracted from Saudi. He assured us this type of thing is routinely carried out, and they will make every effort that it all goes as expected with little or no surprises.

The familiar sound of the furniture truck draws my attention to the window. Mother is at the front door to guide the workers upstairs.

"Will Little Basim be happy here, Mrs. Ashwood?" I whisper.

There is no answer. Did I honestly expect one?

After making sure everything's in its place and ready for the newest members of our family, I'm in my office pacing back and forth. Adrian and Levi have been gone for three weeks, and we haven't heard from him in over twenty-four hours. We are all anxious, waiting for word that the extraction went according to plan and they're heading home. The last time we spoke, Adrian said he wouldn't call, until they had Amala and Little Basim safely in custody.

Why hasn't he called by now?

Absently turning on the TV, there is a program on the weather channel that has something to do with oil tankers being moved, due to a rare, yet gargantuan storm brewing in the South Pacific. It wouldn't usually hold my attention; however, it's an uncommon occurrence, as an oil tanker can't rotate that quickly. Add this to the super cyclone named Billy, and you have an exciting story.

Meteorologists around the world began to speculate on the storms' various trajectories. After a lengthy analogy, pictures of the tsunami of the century which was caused by an earthquake in the Indian Ocean in December of 2004 flash across the screen. Then came maps of where ships would generally sail giving examples of shipping lines. Next, they explored what might happen to the shipping companies should their cargo not be off-loaded in time to avoid the storm. The next picture focused on a massive oil tanker, as it maneuvered around Australia trying to avoid the oncoming cyclone.

The sheer size of this 500-foot mega-ship is mind-boggling. Suddenly, my mind flickers back to Adrian and I begin to wonder if this storm will affect their mission. When the phone startles me, I press the STOP button on the remote and glance at the caller ID.

Adrian's tinny voice says in my ear, "The eagle has landed."

"Are they with you? We've all been so worried about you."

"Yes, we're here. I can't talk long. Someone might be listening. I'll call you as soon as we're into a hotel. I don't have my cellphone, so don't try to call me; it's too dangerous right now."

"Is everything okay?"

Suddenly, the phone goes silent. Plopping down on the sofa, I try to pray that all goes well. What is most worrying is Adrian's nondisclosure of what is currently happening. Could that storm have interfered with his cellphone reception and it disconnected? Or did Adrian hang up on me?

Mother beeps the walkie-talkie to let me know that dinner is ready. I'll have to come up with something quick to tell the family tonight. Our topic this evening is what Adrian and Levi are doing now. All we can discuss is that they have connected with Amala and Little Basim. They are in the process of making their way to a hotel, and he'll call when they arrive.

*"Life isn't about waiting for the storm to pass,
it's about learning to dance in the rain."*

~ Vivian Greene

Chapter Six

The Sky Is Falling

Could that cyclone be responsible for Adrian not calling? Thinking that it wouldn't hurt to do a little research into what types of storms affect weather in and around the Pacific Ocean, it lists the hurricane, the cyclone, and the typhoon. From what I can gather, they can all be equally vicious and nasty when they hit a landmass.

News of them often travels faster than the speed of light and slingshots the city it devastates into the limelight, whether it means to or not. They are either a storm chaser's dream or nightmare, depending on how one looks upon it.

Hurricane season is to Florida what typhoons are to Taiwan, according to published information sources. As with most large storms, hurricanes come in several sizes, starting with the mildest Category 1 and ending with the deadliest at Category 5. It's also where they mention the term *millibar* (it measures pressure). It's complicated if you're not a meteorologist.

Running a search on hurricanes, it immediately brings up pictures of Hurricane Katrina. It was initially a tropical depression that formed over the Bahamas, in August 2005. It had a well-defined band of storm clouds that began to wrap around the north side of the storm's circulation center with winds that ran about forty miles per hour. Because of the wind speed, it was only a tropical storm named Katrina, however, by the time it reached the southern tip of Florida, it was a moderate Category 1 hurricane. It weakened as it passed Florida and then downgraded to a tropical storm again as it did so.

When this tropical storm moved over the warm Gulf of Mexico water, it stalled beneath a very large upper-level anticyclone that dominated the entire Gulf, where it rapidly gained in strength. Tropical Storm Katrina was about to become a hurricane again with wind speeds clocking in at 175 mph. It headed straight for the Louisiana coast, and by the time it hit land, it had weakened to a moderate Category 3.

Even with that downgrade, it slammed into Gulfport and Biloxi, Mississippi, devastating both cities and causing catastrophic damage. Further down along the coast, thousands sought refuge in the New Orleans Convention Center and the Superdome, as reporters, meteorologists, and storm chasers braved the incredible elements to capture the footage I was now watching.

This unbelievably on-again, off-again hurricane, was responsible for flooding nearly 80% of New Orleans, along with large portions of nearby parishes. The culprit? The levees collapsed. Why weren't more people evacuated? Who had minded and tended these levees? And why did they fail so miserably?

Some environmentalists predicted that if a strong enough hurricane came in that direction, it would breach the tops of the sea walls, and without question, the age and openness of the area would see massive destruction. The conclusion? No one listened, or no one wanted to.

The filthy water took weeks to recede. The damage to coastal areas and beachfront towns was estimated at a staggering $81 billion dollars! That is nearly three times more than the damage sustained by the famous 1992 hurricane called Andrew.

Additional research about tropical storms, states that they almost never develop within the Mediterranean Sea or the South Atlantic Ocean. It is an even rarer event to have them develop 120 degrees west in the Southern Pacific Ocean. In light of this, there are no official naming lists of storms for that region. By now, I was trying to pinpoint where this was on my atlas. Levi and Adrian were undoubtedly in the vicinity (but not directly in the path) of this impending storm. Am I worrying unnecessarily?

The information takes me to the warning centers for specific areas that are responsible for monitoring tropical lows that *might* intensify into a tropical cyclone. If a tropical depression forms in the Southern Pacific Ocean *and* its intensity reaches 40 mph, *and* it escalates into a tropical cyclone, the Regional Specialized Meteorological Center (RSMC), Nadi, Fiji, will take over the recording of it and put out warnings.

If the tropical depression intensifies in the Pacific Ocean *between* the Equator and 25 degrees south and is *between* 160 degrees east and 120 degrees west, then they will become named storms. The exception to this is if the tropical depression intensifies to the *south* of this 25 degrees. In that case, the Regional Center will confer with the Tropical Cyclone Warning Center in Wellington, New Zealand, and they will name the cyclone and put out warnings.

As I continue to read about cyclones, they are unlike hurricanes in that they are tropical low-pressure systems that develop in the tropics of the southern hemisphere. Australia experiences severe tropical cyclones, due to its proximity to the tropics. This season of storms typically occurs between November and April.

I've spent time on some of these islands toting my umbrella when a surprise downpour happened. The islanders told us that the storms serve a purpose; they drop needed moisture to islands that would otherwise have to rely on shipments of water, which are costly. They are also the reason the islands are so tropical and unique. However, it's frightening to think that tourism solely depends on the beaches being unspoiled and lovely.

The national weather people, storm trackers, storm chasers, and people going on vacation in the areas in question, are the most likely people to check weather reports. Should the threat of a tropical storm prompt one to cancel their vacation plans and vacate the premises? Should one take heed when proprietors pull out plywood to board up their windows? We've been fortunate not to be present during these types of storms, or our travel agent made sure we steered clear of them.

Clicking the TV remote back to the weather again, I decided to record this part of the program. The information could be useful down the road. A few minutes later, a meteorologist begins to talk about a set of islands in the archipelago of a place I've never heard of before. It is west of Fiji, and named storms occasionally affect it. In fact, storms mostly peter themselves out when they blow over the mountainous ranges. Unfortunately, one of the islands happens to lie directly in the path of a named super cyclonic storm, and the news media is playing it up, big time.

The surprising fact is that the information coming out of the weather service still thinks it won't develop into anything except a tropical storm and will dissipate before it reaches known landmass. After all, there have been no such storms, other than the usual heavy downpours, to affect this part of the world. They feel there is nothing immediate to worry about, as its traveling so slowly. However, this depression is picking up speed at an alarming rate.

Hours after the experts wrestle with the suggested direction of this colossal storm, the islands in the cyclone's path are being warned to seek shelter. Again, I wonder if the troubling storm is somehow affecting Adrian and Levi and their mission. Is this the reason we lost communication with them?

Keeping vigil in my office near the TV set to check in on the storm's progress, I wait patiently for the next five days, but there is no word from Adrian or Levi. With no word from either of them, I am between fits of frustration and anticipation. Finally, after leaving six messages on Levi's phone, I contact Jewels at CIA Headquarters as Larry, Josh, or Jake are not available.

"Jewels, I've been going nuts. Have you heard anything from Adrian or Levi?"

"Please wait until Adrian calls you, Mrs. T-Sellers. I'm not at liberty to discuss anything with you. Be patient a little longer."

"I've been patient! What about Adrian's cellphone? Why isn't Levi calling me back? How can I contact them?"

Jewels sighs, then he says in a peculiar voice, "Please, sit tight and try not to worry, Miss Ellen. Mr. Adrian will explain what he can when he sees you." When I ask if he's okay, he says, 'sure.'

I'm sticking close to the phone hoping Adrian will call, but he doesn't. When the phone finally does ring, I practically jump a foot off my chair. "Adrian, why haven't you called before now? We've been so worried about you."

It's difficult to understand him, as there's so much background noise. "My phone was damaged, but I have a new one. We're boarding a plane for D.C. in a few minutes, and we'll be there before you know it." He sounds as peculiar as Jewel's did. What on earth happened over there?

"I'm confused; you were going to call when you got to a hotel. Where have you been all this time? Why do you have to go to D. C. first? Why can't you come straight home, Adrian?"

Several seconds go by before he says, "We have to go there first. I can't talk about that now. He's one of yours, there's no doubt about it, Ellie." Adrian must refer to the DNA sample that was matched to Little Basim's, verifying that he's Jason's son.

"I can't wait to get my hands on him, Adrian. How are they? I mean, is Amala happy to come here?" A child is crying softly in the background.

"You'll get along great together. Jason was teaching her English, and she understands many things already. You're going to love them both. Little Basim took right to me. I have to go. We'll see you soon. Love you." Click. Adrian hangs up before I can say goodbye.

It's as if Jason is coming home, even though it's his son; a piece of him is finally coming back, with the bonus of Amala. Their new papers will show that we've adopted them; her new name is Amala Ceridian Thompson-Sellers.

It reminds me of the time Melanie, Curlie, and Jason jumped on Adrian and me about our hyphenated last names. Little Basim will be Basim Jason Thompson-Sellers. We'll call him BJ from now on because it's difficult for me to keep saying his grandfather's name. How proud they would both be if they knew about BJ.

Maybe they do know.

Two days later, I'm standing on the porch of the Carriage House as it offers the best view of the two-lane road. As soon as I spot Adrian's car, I turn to give Terre a signal. She is standing inside the front doors and has Mother by the hand.

With wobbly legs, I take hold of the railing and descend the stairs. Adrian's car is now at the front gate, and it swings slowly open. *Raindrop* lifts his head at the familiar sound of crunching gravel, as he's near the fence closest to the driveway. As the car comes to a stop, the driver's side window rolls down, and Adrian puts a finger to his lips to signal BJ is asleep.

I sense that something is wrong, but Adrian merely shakes his head. It's his way of saying; we'll talk later. The passenger door opens, and Amala climbs out. She immediately wraps her arms around me, and I hug her back. "Welcome home, Amala," I manage to say.

Amala is about my height, has dark brown hair, and eyes that sparkle. She is beautiful, and it's obvious why Jason fell in love with her. Mother steps forward, then Terre, and then all the rest of the family take turns to hug and welcome her.

Adrian reaches in to gently pull BJ out of his car seat. After he hands him to me, I almost drop him, but he reaches forward to take most of his weight off my arms. As I hug him, my thoughts go to Jason. My son lives in this little boy, and the woman he loved left the country she was born in to bring him here to live with us at great peril to herself. Finally, there is some closure. I'm so grateful that the tears won't stop flowing.

BJ wakes up and lets out a little cry. Adrian must sense how emotional this is for me and reaches to take him. Together we head toward the house, as Amala takes my hand. Once we are inside, she expresses her surprise as our house is neither the opulent version of the Royal Palace nor is it the cramped quarters she's been living in these last few years.

And as Goldilocks once said, "This is just right, Mama T."

Mother takes Amala and BJ up the staircase to rest and settle them in, as their journey was long and tiring. Adrian seems jittery, not his exuberant self. Everyone knows better than to ask about a covert operation, even though they want to.

"Adrian, why don't we go into my office and talk about how things went?"

Adrian's face drains of color as he flops down on the sofa. "There's no need to ever talk about it after today." He is unusually quiet, not full of details he knows I'm eager to hear.

"It's okay if you don't want to talk about it, but I'm dying to know what happened over there."

Adrian's face expresses extreme sadness as if he has to force himself to stay in control of his emotions. It is unusual behavior for the stoic and funny man I know him to be. What occurred to change my mild-mannered CIA man into the despondent person who came back? It's very alarming.

"I honestly don't know if I can talk to you about this," Adrian says quietly, his voice cracking.

"That's not one of your usual responses, Adrian. You know we can talk about whatever you want, or we don't have to talk at all. You look as if you could use a hug. Come here; let me hug you."

Adrian allows me to wrap my arms around him, as I sit next to him on the sofa. He is as stiff as a robot, and neither blinks normally or says anything for so long it starts to scare me.

"Adrian, what's wrong? Can't you tell me what it is? I want to know why you went so long between phone calls."

He inhales and slowly lets his breath out without looking at me. "Ellie, I couldn't call you, because my phone, my phone was damaged during… and I couldn't break down in front of Amala and BJ. It's awful, Ellie."

"You never said anything was wrong. When did this happen? Adrian, this is not like you. What the hell happened over there?"

"Things happened! I had no control over them. You know how in control I am! I was not in control this time." Tears form in his eyes and slowly flow down his cheeks.

In all the years Adrian has been with us, I had never seen him weep except when he laughed at something hilarious, or when he'd try to pull something over on me that he thought was tremendously humorous. Reaching to touch his face, he recoils.

"Are you hurt? Did someone else get hurt?"

"I guess it affected me more than I thought it would," he mumbles.

"Take your time, sweetheart. We have all the time in the world." The red light on the recorder flashes. Thinking that it was already turned off, I reach for the remote on my desk to stop it, then hit PLAY instead.

"Adrian? Where is Van—oo— I can't pronounce where this is."

"Can you turn that off, for now, Ellen?" Adrian almost never calls me Ellen, so I hit the STOP button, turn off the TV, and place the remote control back on the desk. He lets me surround him with my arms and finally starts to relax.

"Everything was going along according to plan…" Adrian says finally.

"What happened?"

Could they have found Jason? Could he no longer be alive and all hope is gone? I stiffen at the possibility while Adrian composes himself.

He starts to talk again, very slowly at first, "Lee… Levi… Levi and I had it all planned, we practiced what we would do; we never slipped up before, never."

My mind is going in all sorts of directions. If he's talking about blunders, what could have gone wrong? "What happened?"

"We contacted Jam-ale. He had one of his men lead us to Amala and Little Basim. We traveled to the city where she lived and stayed to have a meal with her adoptive family." Adrian puts his hands over his eyes.

"It's okay, Adrian, take your time."

"After the meal, we were in our vehicles and close to the hotel. The only explanation for what happened is that we were ambushed. It's the only thing that can explain why this happened. It happened so quickly, Ellie, that we had no time to react!" As Adrian sucks in a breath, a sob leaves his throat as his body starts to shudder.

"Oh my God! That's why Levi never answered my calls. When you didn't pick up, I called him, and I almost panicked. Adrian, tell me he's alright!"

Adrian doesn't say anything and continues to sob. Now I realize that Levi is either wounded or worse, he's dead. How did this happen to one of the best? Nothing like this hit the news. Then, again, it wouldn't be reported, as it was a clandestine affair and its CIA stuff after all.

"I'm still in disbelief. Levi never had a chance, Ellie. It could have been me instead of him. If he hadn't thrown me to the floor and jumped on top of me, or worse, you could have been there, too! It was beyond terrible!"

Adrian had his hands full keeping Little BJ corralled, steering Amala, and juggling luggage. He must have forced himself not to think about what happened until he got home. Perhaps he's in shock much as I was when they first told me about Jason. Maybe now, he'll understand how it feels.

Why do bad things happen to good people?

Levi went out on a limb for so many of us more times than I can count. Was Levi in the right place at the wrong time? Was he in the wrong place at the right time? Maybe it was the right time at the right place. I can never figure that out!

We're staying at a nearby hotel close to CIA Headquarters to attend Levi's funeral. Adrian spent hours agonizing over the words he wanted to say during Levi's eulogy, and I'm wearing the same black sheath dress and pumps Mother purchased for Jason's memorial service.

"It's time to go, Adrian, are you ready?"

"Yes," he says soberly. "I'm glad you're here with me, Ellie. It makes me, Oh God, I can't get choked up like this in front of all those people!"

"Why not, Adrian, you're a human being with feelings. Levi meant a great deal to you. He meant a great deal to all of us, and your acknowledgment will do that."

Shaking his head, he says, "What if I choke and can't talk? What happens then, Ellie?"

"If that happens, then I'll stand up and read it for you. I'll do it if you need me to."

"You'd do that for me?" Adrian frowns. He has prepared a beautiful tribute to Levi. If his courage doesn't fail him today, he will deliver it himself. If he can't, then I'll do it for him.

"Of course; look at all the stuff you did for us? I'm certain you'll be able to do it."

"You're not going to bet on it, are you?" Adrian glances in the mirror to fiddle with his tie and places a handkerchief into the front pocket of his jacket. Then he opens and closes the piece of paper, and then stuffs it inside his jacket. "Okay, Ellie, I'm ready. Please don't feel that you have to say anything."

"You mean please don't say anything. Do you think I'll give away some deep dark secret?"

"No. I know how emotional you get. I thought it would be hard for you because it'll be tough for me."

"I'm your rock today, Adrian. I promise not to get too emotional. I can give Levi's tribute for you."

When we arrive at the church, it's almost to capacity with family, friends, and of course his teams of experts. Some familiar people shake our hands, some hug Adrian, while others hug me. The casket is near the Communion rail, draped with an American flag, a fitting tribute as Levi was a veteran of the Vietnam War.

We take seats near the front, and when the organ starts to play, Adrian grabs my hand and puts his handwritten note in my lap. He will not be able to stand at the podium; his hands are shaking too much.

I decided that Adrian's words are his, not mine. Instead, I pray silently for guidance. *Dear Heavenly Father, let me stand in front of all these people to do this today! It is for Adrian and for what Levi gave up for us.*

Adrian squeezes my hand as the minister walks down the aisle toward the altar. Everyone stands to sing the first Hymn, "Nearer My God to Thee."

As this ends, the Minister asks us to sit down, bow our heads, where he leads us through the 23rd Psalm. When this concludes, the Minister nods to Adrian, but all he can do is stare at his shoes. Standing up to step around him, I walk to the podium, touching the coffin and flag as I pass. The minister wonders what I'm doing, then understands there's been a change in the program. He sits down as do the rest of the mourners in the church. All eyes are on me, so I clear my throat and proceed as if I have rehearsed Adrian's speech for a long time, and then abandon it to speak from my heart.

"Levi was many things to many people. He was a friend, a coworker, a superior boss, a mentor, a brother, an uncle, and a son. However, most of all, Levi was a team player. He made sure his teams knew they were important, and they respected him for the little things he did for them. Many of you know me as Adrian Seller's wife. What you don't know is that Levi was also my friend. He did more for our family than I can tell you. Honestly, I can't tell you."

Laughter erupts, and it startles me, then I glance at Adrian. He's smiling, and then mouths the words 'thank you.'

"Levi had a wicked sense of humor. Many of you were the unsuspecting brunt of some of his pranks. The only ones I can talk about concern my family, and we can't say what they are, except for one. He accompanied Adrian and me on a little trip. All of a sudden, he stood up to tell us that we were going to free fall down to Niagara Falls for our wedding. He instructed us to put on our parachutes, which were located under our seats. Both of our mothers nearly had heart attacks!"

Again, there is laughter.

"All kidding aside, Levi was the Energizer Bunny that kept going and going and going. If his teams were working a particularly difficult case, he would spend endless hours on a solution until the problem was solved as many of you know firsthand. Many of you spent endless sleepless nights under his supervision. I'd like to think he knew how much we all loved him. He knew the risks he took for his job, as do all of you. He went ahead with his capers and never blinked."

"Amen to that," Jake says, as others chime in response.

"We will especially remember him for what he said to us if we went through a tough situation and came out the other side intact. He'd merely say, 'you done good kid.' At one time or another, we all heard those words. It meant that we did a good job and we couldn't do anymore, and to let it go. We felt pride that Levi thought enough of us to notice what we'd done. We will miss him for many reasons, each in our way. He wouldn't want you to mourn his death; he would expect you to celebrate it."

Adrian reaches for my hand, as I sit down next to him. There are tears in his eyes, as he whispers, "You done good kid. Levi would have liked what you said about him."

"He'll always be with us, you know. He's right there in that little secret compartment in our hearts, reserved for those who are special to us. Your dad is there."

"So is yours," Adrian says, "He's right there next to Jason."

After the service, everyone gathered for a solemn, but intimate celebration of Levi's life.

Josh and Jake will stay in Washington until Levi's successor is named. A job that will require some mighty unusual qualifications, because anyone who tries to fill his shoes will have to be superior in every way.

In a remote part of the world in a little-known archipelago in the Pacific Ocean, west of Fiji, and almost due north of Australia, there is little to disturb this set of islands. Except for an occasional tropical storm that dropped needed water for the islander's cisterns. Tourist season would be upon them soon, and many anticipated a reasonable profit for the year.

One inhabitant sat on a stool in the small hut-type office where he glanced out of the window at the heaving sea. At this height, Brian Mansale saw the waves smash the rocks as the water turned a white foam. He followed the frothy spray with his eyes, as it rolled along the beach and noticed that it was higher than usual.

His mother, Kalima, watched him and wondered what he was thinking. Brian hadn't said much since his Uncle Rex brought him home from the hospital almost two years ago. His leg and arm have healed as best they could, but the unfortunate part is that he didn't seem to be any better in the memory department.

Brian did what Kalima asked him to do after she showed him several times, other than that, he took little initiative to do things on his own. It's almost as if he was a stranger.

"What are you staring at Brian? Why do you not remember your mother? Why do you not know your sisters and brothers?" she asked softly, not expecting an answer. "Your friends do not know you anymore. Your best friend, Jamar, says you are different, and he can no longer talk to you, so he does not come around. I do not know the person you are now, but I love you the same."

Brian turned toward Kalima and smiled at her. Did he understand what she said this time? When she asked him questions in the past, he would only lift his right hand to gesture that he did not understand. The odd thing is, she thought Brian was left-handed, then attributed this oddity to his injury.

Kalima sat near him and began to point at objects in the room. She said the word, and then Brian repeated it back to her, although the inflection was strange.

"Good, good! I will teach you the words all over again, as we did when you were a small boy."

When Brian smiled again, Kalima reached to hug him, as she did so often to her children, but this time he hugged her back. He said a string of words which did not make sense to her, although she didn't mind because he was at least finally trying to communicate with her.

Back when her brother-in-law, Rexley, brought Brian home, she had gone through the hospital bag that came home with him. She found several pamphlets that explained Traumatic Brain Injury, and she found it helpful at first, but many of her questions went unanswered; how long would he be like this?

As time passed, Kalima found that she didn't mind so much, because Brian seemed unaffected by his circumstances, almost as if he was happy to wake up each morning. Kalima was also aware of the fact that even if Brian could speak, his words might not come out the way he intended them.

Brian looked out the window and wondered if he should stand on the large rock near the water, or maybe he should sit under the large shade tree in front of the family's resort. He often went to one of those two spots when he completed his work for the day. It's as if he were watching for something, except he didn't know what it was.

Kalima moved to the little shelf behind the reception desk to turn on the radio, then turned it off again when there was only static. "I wonder what is interfering with the radio. Do you think it could be a storm coming?" She talked to Brian often, although she did not expect him to answer.

Brian turned away from the window and smiled at her again. Then he stood up and walked toward her, reaching for her hand, he said, "MUM."

She hugged her son, grateful that he had made such progress. This one word meant so much to her. She knew that it would only be a matter of time before he started to remember other things, but she also knew that he was very different from the Brian he had once been.

The next day, Brian sat in the shade of the giant tree. The wind was rustling the leaves, and he glanced up through the tree branches at the blue sky that was slowly turning a soft grey. People began moving quickly down below boarding up their storefront windows with large pieces of plywood. He did not understand what was going on; could this affect his family somehow?

The White Sands Resort was open for business as usual. It was as modern as Kalima could afford to make it, given the amount of sporadic revenue that came her way. She called her boat-taxi connection (Jonah) on the mainland of Port Vila and assured him that everything would be ready to welcome visitors for the upcoming season. Jonah asked if he could contact her guests to reschedule, as the Office of Tourism received notice that a storm was on its way.

Kalima responded that everything seemed fine here. The storm would blow over; they always did. Everything was perfectly safe on Kakae Luna Island. The Port Vila man asked if she was getting ready for the storm anyway. Why should she? There hadn't been one of those types of storms for many years. Kalima had to think when that was. Of course, it was when Brian was a baby.

Then Kalima decided not to worry about that. She also did not want to send her only guests away, not after having spent the rest of their payment. Steven and Janice Danbury saw the resort website put together by the Vanuatu Tourism and Trade Commission. They fell in love with the idea of a honeymoon in such a remote place where they could fill their days snorkeling, windsurfing, relaxing at the pool, or walking along the beach.

The Danbury's couldn't pass up Mrs. Mansale's deep discounts she had advertised. The complimentary three-course breakfast didn't hurt either. With the bonus of an inactive volcano to explore, the great reviews convinced the couple to come to the resort.

"No need to worry is our motto, be happy," Kalima hummed to herself. As she gazed out the window, she began to worry as her neighbors were scurrying about nailing things over their office hut windows. Then she noticed Brian, who was sitting under the large tree that divided the boundary between her property and the one below it.

Has there been a weather bulletin warning of a severe storm? Has she failed to hear the alarm sound? Slightly worried, she turned the little radio on again, then turned it off, as there was still only static. Because the volcanic ridge of Kakae Luna runs east to west, it had always protected them. How severe could this storm be?

Kalima left her office hut to seek Sammel, the owner of the resort next to hers. He was nailing old shutters over the window on the makeshift hut he used as an office. Glancing sideways at her, he kept working, and said, "You should take this time to get things done; a storm is coming, a bad one."

"When do you think it will get here?" Kalima asked.

"In less than eight hours," he replied. "I only hope and pray that it is speedy, with no loss of life." He turned his head toward Brian and shook his head. "How sad that he has turned out that way," he mumbled.

"We do not have anything to put over our windows, Sammel. Do you have any wood to spare?"

"Close your shutters and secure them. We are using what we have. You will have to take your chances."

The island resorts and hotels have reservations for tourists throughout the season starting in a few weeks. If their guests caught wind there was trouble in paradise; it could affect their revenues. What the resort proprietors fear most is the fact that these tourists could demand the return of their deposits. If there was a lot of damage, how would they get them repaired before their guests arrived? Insurance would only cover so much, and getting supplies to remote islands such as Kakae Luna, was an unbelievable chore.

Kalima returned to her hut to check the guest register. She became anxious as the little cabanas were not ready for tourists. Then her confidence returned at the prospect that the 'no vacancy' status would last for at least six to eight months.

That is if the electricity stayed on and the impending storm didn't damage the cabanas.

Kalima fondly recalled when the White Sands Resort welcomed its first guests. She and her husband had purchased two cabanas when they were first married and added more when funds became available.

Switching her thoughts to concentrate on the list of items to organize the demands of running her resort, while juggling her family, she thought about her husband. He died in a mysterious accident six years ago. Her brother-in-law, Rexley, was the only witness, and he refused to discuss the details with her. With her husband gone, she relied on her children and a woman named Gamete to keep everything in running order. Strange, she had not come to the resort today.

While Brian was missing, she found a local repairman who came to unplug a toilet, fixed leaks in the roofs and did general handy-man tasks. Then when Brian came home, he could no longer help her. Rex used to take Brian on long fishing trips, and when they returned, they brought fresh fish as compensation. During Brian's absence, Rexley took her second eldest son, but when they returned, he said he would never go with his uncle again. When she questioned them, they each walked away without an explanation.

When the shrill alarm sounded, Kalima's eyes widened with fright. Brian had never heard this sound before and didn't know what to do. At the doorway of the hut, Kalima motioned to him. When he got close, she grabbed his hand and called her other children.

"Gather your blankets, pillows, and some clothes…stuff them into a pillowcase. We have to go to the caves."

She loaded Brian's arms with towels, a basket filled with food, and instructed her eldest daughter, Monta, to go back and get rolls of toilet paper, and whatever else she could fit into an extra pillowcase.

Kalima then ran to Cabana No. 3 and banged on the Danbury's door. When it opened, she told them that they needed to gather their things and follow her family to shelter. Their weather-band radio informed them of the storm almost an hour ago, and they immediately began to collect items. When the alarm sounded, they knew something big was about to happen.

At the back of Kalima's mind, she remembered that when she was a small child, a massive tropical storm took the lives of several adults and four small children when a gigantic wave of twenty-five feet swallowed the town built near the water. Because of that disaster, the townspeople decided to corroborate their efforts to keep everyone safe so that it wouldn't happen again. Immediately following the reconstruction of the town, men carved out several caves for emergency shelter.

Through the years, the caves became a refuge for children who went exploring, and tourists who stopped to catch their breath before they headed down the side toward their hotels. It's a fantastic view from any one of them, especially the one that faces the cove, as its framed between the beach and the large black volcanic rocks. From this height, it was a breathtaking sight.

Janice and Steve grabbed their items piled near the door to follow Kalima and her children. They formed a single file behind her, grasped at roots and vines to pull themselves along. Brian brought up the rear, clutched the basket with his left hand, which allowed him to grip the youngest child's hand. His face showed terror, but Brian whispered soothing things, and he smiled up at his big brother, even though he didn't understand his words.

The opening of the cave was narrow. Steve hesitated, looked out at the ocean, and then noticed how it swelled unnaturally and ebbed strangely, as it slammed itself against the rocks near the shore. Instinct kicked in as he reached for his video camera. How could the storm be bearing down on them so quickly?

Once their eyes adjusted to the low light levels in the cave, space seemed more substantial than it looked from the outside. It was fifteen feet deep and twelve feet wide. Soon others joined them, and everyone huddled together to wait out the storm. A makeshift toilet (complete with a curtain) was positioned near a hole. Water trickled in that naturally flushed waste out and down the side of the volcano.

No one knew how long they would stay inside the cave, but most had thought to bring supplies, flashlights, oil lamps, coolers, and a camp stove. As they settled in to wait out the storm, Janice and Steve clung to each other. They hadn't bargained for this to happen while they were on their honeymoon! They were aware of what Hurricane Katrina did; they had seen the aftermath. They didn't talk about that, nor one particular storm, as it was still too painful.

Kalima took charge and instructed all within the cave to make their beds and settle into their space while she gathered what food and supplies each had brought. Assembling a make-shift kitchen, as if she were working at her resort, she propped up crates, turning them to use as shelves. She quickly calculated that their supplies would last three days, but no more.

"How long do you think it will take for the storm to pass?" Janice asked her husband.

Steve drew in a long breath, then let it out slowly. "It could take anywhere from eight to ten hours, maybe more. Did you grab the radio by any chance, honey?"

"Sure did. I got that before I put my clothes on, sweetie. What's your take on this, Steve?"

"You heard the weather-band. Expect it to be wicked. Did you get the extra battery packs? There might not be electricity if this storm does what I think it will do."

"Got them too, and I know we don't talk about this very often, but do you think this will be like that tsunami?" Janice's face goes white at the memory. "It wiped out whole islands. It messed up so many things, took so many lives. I didn't mean to bring it up, Steve, I'm sorry."

"It's okay. Maybe we should talk about it. Jacob knew he was going into the eye of the storm. We can't go back to save him, Janice. We're safe here, sweetheart. We're too high up. I'll bet we can get some great footage for the National Weather Service," he replied.

"You mean we could be on our honeymoon and still earn money? I hadn't thought of that."

Within two hours, the cave grew very dark, and the wind started to generate a screaming banshee-like sound. They hunkered down when Kalima said to hang on. As her youngest child began to whimper, she held him close to her. Brian was near, so she reached for his hand, and then touched each child to assure them, as she started to hum nursery tunes. When Brian joined her, she began to weep.

Steve knew that wind speeds of a cyclone could reach an astounding 186 mph. He also knew that they would be safe if they stayed inside the cave. "Have the camera ready," he whispered. "We might have to move fast once we can get out of here after the storm blows over. We have to capture it right after to make a real impact."

"This could be our big chance. If we can add to the footage we already have, it would make a great documentary. Someone will pay top dollar for this," Janice said quietly.

"We have to wait until the brunt of the storm passes. We can't take the chance our equipment will get ruined. I'm so glad we took all those shots and footage before we went on that volcano trip the other day."

"Me too. This island might never be the same after tonight," Janice mused. "We might not be either. These people may not have a home to go back to."

"Okay, no more talk like that," Steve said, pulling her close to him.

"I'm sorry," Janice whispered.

"We'll be fine. We'll be okay. We have each other, try to sleep." If he could keep his demons at bay, they would be fine, he told himself.

Steve tried to occupy his mind by remembering he was a storm chaser, along with his good friend Jacob. As a rule, if you saw a tornado approach, you would get to underground shelter quickly. On more than one occasion, he and Jacob traveled to experience a tropical storm or hurricane. As a former boy scout, he prided himself on always being ready for most situations. In the likelihood the current storm caused electricity or water to become nonexistent, he wondered about generators. Could water be pumped out of the cisterns without one?

Neither Janice or Steve noticed portable generators anywhere at the White Sands Resort. On the other hand, if there was little chance to use it, why spend precious dollars on so large an item that required upkeep when severe storms are not part of your everyday occurrence? Did anyone take precautions to capture water or lay in a supply of bottled water?

Steve recalled the disagreement he and Jacob had. Jacob had argued that the louder the storm, the more destruction it caused and the quieter it was, the less destruction. However, they both agreed that any heavy rainstorm could cause damage. He recalled the photos of flying debris that stuck in your mind long after the event passed. Someone was bound to have a cellphone or a video camera that captured swaying telephone poles, the bent-over palm trees, and the advertising signs with two by fours stuck through them at odd angles.

Steve will never forget the Indian Ocean tsunami that devastated the tourist-packed Indonesian island of Sumatra and the southern shores of Thailand in December 2004. That devastation took more than one hundred and fifty thousand lives.

He and Jacob were vacationing at a resort near where the killer wave came on shore. When the water began to recede on the beach, Steve yelled for everyone to run to higher ground. His friend Jacob didn't listen and instead grabbed his camera, because after all, he chased storms.

Steve pleaded with him, but to no avail. He then turned to shove his camera into a watertight bag, slung it over his back, and ran for his life. With the loss of such a good friend, Steve swore never to put anyone else in harms' way again. Now, here he is on the cusp of disaster. As he recalled that time, there was no body to put into a casket, and the only recourse was to have a memorial service for Jacob.

A documentary film now exists that covers that event, celebrating Jacob's brief, but award-winning life. The film, plus some photos, are all that remains of Steve's friendship with Jacob. He met Janice the day of the memorial, and she's been by his side ever since. Jacob was Janice's older brother.

When a disaster happened in an obscure part of the world where storms typically do not occur, then it could become big news. The newswires would take this and run with it, which is precisely what Steve and Janice hoped for, not that they wished for damage; they want enough footage to pay for their honeymoon and come out of this terrifying experience intact.

The Island of Kakae Luna, nestled between the Island of Tanna and the tiny Island of Anatom (along the archipelago of Vanuatu), began to quiver as the wind rushed past the opening of the cave.

Steve touched his watch to illuminate the face. The display read nine. Whispering near his wife's ear, he said, "Janice, are you awake?"

"Yes."

"I want to get some video footage."

Janice grabbed his arm to hold him down. "You are not going out now!"

"You're right; the equipment could get wet. It sounds like a freight train whizzing past the opening, doesn't it? Almost like…"

"We're going to be okay. Do you feel water on your feet? Oh my God, Steve, it's coming in the cave."

"Don't wake everyone up. It's a little water. We aren't going to drown or anything. We're too high up. It'll drain out in a little while. I think Mrs. Mansale said someone put drainage in here."

As Cyclone Billy bore down, Steve became skeptical when a large tree branch wedged itself in the opening of the cave. Others reacted to it, but miraculously, it helped keep the rain out as the wind settled down to a dull roar.

"Try to sleep, Janice. Be ready when the storm passes, okay? I want to be the first one out to capture people's reactions," Steve whispered. "When the eye comes over the island, it'll seem like it's over, but it won't because it will get quiet. That's when it'll be directly over us. Then we can expect it to pick up again, as the back wall of the storm hits the island. If I'm right, you count the hours up to that point, and it will be the same number of hours until the storm completely passes. So, we won't know until it gets quiet."

Janice and Steve snuggled together and got as comfortable as they could in the space they shared. Steve was mentally exhausted; mostly due to keeping his mind occupied. The howl of this storm was almost more than he could bear. He hadn't shared his fear of confinement, or that he has *cleithrophobia*. It would make his new bride afraid. He must present a good front, even if panic threatened to overcome him. He tried to tell himself that the cave would not run out of breathable oxygen. The good news is that it was so dark that no one could see his face. The bad news was that light helped to take the fear away.

"Kalima, are you awake?" Sammel called out in the darkness. "Can you hear me?"

"Yes, keep your voice down. My children are finally asleep," she whispered.

"What do you think we will find when the storm passes, Kalima?"

"We will find what we will find," she said to the opposite side of the dark cave.

Sammel sighed heavily. "I hope our Good Lord has mercy upon us because our resorts cannot withstand much more of this wind. What will we do if everything is gone?"

"We will pick up the pieces and do what we can to help each other."

"Will they send help to us?" Sammel asked.

"I hope that we will not need it, but if we do, I hope that someone will help us put our resorts back together." She couldn't see Sammel's tears as they streaked his sad face.

"It may all be gone, Kalima. What will we do then?"

"Sammel, you do not know what we will find. Go to sleep now, and we will all go out when the storm passes," she sighed. "We can do no more until morning."

Kalima cradled her youngest child, pulled up the blanket to keep him warm, as the air had chilled considerably. *Dear God,* she silently prayed, *please keep my family and all those who dwell within this cave safe and protect us, God, from the evil that lurks outside, through Jesus' name, Amen.*

Steve listened in on the conversation between Kalima and Sammel. He wasn't sure what they said, as they spoke too fast for him to understand their dialect. Janice snoozed contentedly beside him, so Steve didn't have her to interpret for him. What a wonder, as she understood their language almost immediately, and every once in a while, he comprehended a word or two.

Steve wondered what they would find once the storm passed and daylight came. He had sheltered during hurricanes and tornados before while chasing many deadly storms but had never been in a cave before. If he could get through this without a full-blown panic attack, he could get through anything. Then he closed his eyes to do the mental exercises his therapist recommended he use when he found himself in tight spaces, repeating his practiced *phrase* over and over.

Once he calmed down and the attack subsided, he wondered what the landscape would look like compared to what it did yesterday. He hoped the other equipment left in the cabana remained untouched. However, it's a good thing Janice insisted they add everything of value to their insurance policy before they left on their trip.

Hour after hour, the wind howled. Most everyone fell back to sleep during the lull as the eye of the storm passed, including Steve. Then it picked up as the backside of the wall of the cyclone moved over the island, smacking into it with a great force.

As the winds abated, the cave began to lighten from the morning sunrise. Steve had been awake for several hours waiting for first light but didn't want to disturb Janice. As Kalima and the others roused themselves, they braced for what they might find outside.

"Janice, are you awake? I'm going out to get a couple of shots from down below looking up toward our cave as people come out of it."

"I'm awake, wait for me."

Steve began to push at the tree branch wedged in the opening. When it popped free, he steadied himself, digging in with the heels of his boots so he could hold the camera without falling down the hillside. Janice was close behind, as he took off the lens cover and did a sweep of the area. The path was muddy and littered with all kinds of debris; things were sticking out of the ground like matchsticks. Upon close examination, the pieces were timber from what was left of the surrounding houses. A haunting wail filtered up from down below.

"Janice, can you see who screamed? What direction did it come from?"

"I think it's a woman and she's too far down. There's too much debris in the way to see clearly."

As the islanders began to survey the sea of carnage, they heard more cries and moans. Janice held Mrs. Mansale's arm to walk down with her. "I cannot believe this," Janice muttered. Kalima said nothing and pulled away to take her small son's hand.

Steve's camera scanned what remained of the White Sands Resort. He asked Janice to describe the scene, but she was so transfixed by what she saw, she was unable to speak.

Janice glanced up to see what she would later describe as an angry looking grey sky. It reminded her of a sky ready to unleash snow, except that the temperature was not cold enough. She made a mental note that there were no other sounds, no wind rustling trees, no birds chirping, no dogs barking, just an eerie silence.

"Janice, can you describe what you're feeling right now?" Steve's hand trembled, as he tried to hold the video camera steady. He was hoping that he could capture what his wife felt as she surveyed the storm damage. "I think it will add to the realism of the situation if you talk about it now."

"No, Steve," she whispered, "maybe later. I need to help Mrs. Mansale and the others."

Janice stepped over debris mindful of where she put her feet, as she made her way toward the last place she saw Kalima. When Janice found her, she felt as if someone punched her in the stomach. The wind picked up random objects as it sucked the water out of the swimming pool. Then it dumped sofas, a TV, small appliances, plywood, shutters, soggy bed linens, and a refrigerator (with no door). It also included several colorful blankets, three cans of paint with their lids still intact and Janice's sun hat, which rested precariously on top of the pile.

Janice looked around for something to retrieve it, as she didn't dare walk on the mess for fear it floated. She decided that the pool pole, still attached by clips to the little shed near it, would do. Then, she wondered how the pool shed survived given what didn't. After she retrieved her hat, she spotted Steve walking toward her. His facial expression said it all, and she reached to hug him.

"Look what I found, sweetheart? Now if I can find some sunscreen, we'll be all set for a day at the beach." Janice tried to lighten the mood, then turned her head so that Steve couldn't see her tears.

"I never imagined this kind of devastation, Janice." Steve's voice faltered, as he choked out a sigh. "I knew there would be some, but not this much!"

"It is unbelievable. I didn't imagine anything like this, either. If we had stayed in the cabana..." Janice didn't finish her sentence.

"We didn't, and we're alive," Steve assured her. "Let's see if there's anything left of our equipment. Maybe it survived somehow. Besides, we have more than these people do; we can go back to our apartment. We can replace our stuff, and we will because it looks like it's all gone."

Janice and Steve are standing in the approximate spot where they last saw an intact Cabana No. 3. All that remained were the poles cemented into the ground to elevate the floor. Oddly wrapped around one of the poles was the netting attached to their bed to keep the bugs off at night. Interwoven were bits of debris, little shells, a bottle of Janice's nail polish, and pieces of broken objects from their bathroom.

Janice started to laugh hysterically. Steve put down the camera and wrapped his arms around her to keep her from touching things. Once she was under control, she sniffed and said, "I don't know why the netting made me laugh like that. It does look rather strange. Look at all the stupid things it did catch. Why didn't it catch our expensive equipment?"

"It looks like the netting trapped light things; our equipment was a lot heavier. I don't know how things are caught or why Janice. I've never seen anything like this. The only things I do know for sure is that the wind speeds must have been more powerful than anyone imagined, and they're random as to what they pick up. We'll replace the stuff, don't worry." He took a lens cap out of his pocket. "I found this sticking out of the sand on the beach. I think it belongs to one of my other cameras. Ah, such memories."

As they surveyed the area, it looked as if someone dismantled the cabanas and stacked the wood against the other side of the pool shed wall that held the pole.

"So that's why the shed wall stayed up." Steve turned his camera on again and made a mental note how odd it looked from this angle.

"I can't find the rest of our equipment, let alone our suitcases. It's all gone, Steve. Oh, wait, is that my shoe?" Janice navigated around debris to a small pile that looked as if they had been placed there for a shoe sale. "It's my shoe, but where's the other one?" She bent to rummage through the pile.

"Gee Janice, do you need a pair of them? How about you start a new trend and wear two different shoes? It could be the next popular craze, honey."

"If I can't find the other one, that's what I'm going to do. Oh my God, Steve, here it is!"

"Let's see if we can find anything else in this mess," Steve said.

Excited voices startled Janice and Steve. When they turned, they watched Kalima and her children comb through the wreckage that was once their home. Kalima systematically moved from one pile to another. She bent to pick something up, examined it, then handed it to one of her children who placed it either on top of a basket or threw it on a pile they had already gone through. They kept going until one of the girls cried out. Kalima hugged her, and the girl shook her head, and they moved on to the next pile.

As Steve and Janice glanced around, other island inhabitants were busy digging through the endless mess. They seemed to be in a trance, as their faces reflected their loss and dismay as they chucked things back and forth. Tourism had been the sustaining revenue for most of them, and it will take millions of dollars to reconstruct what took less than ten hours to destroy. The good news was that it's off-season, so there were few tourists on the island.

If there were no caves to shelter in, and the alarm had not sounded, there would be no one left on the island to witness this ruin. Most everyone fell asleep amidst the crashing and howling because Mrs. Mansale gave them cotton balls to block out the noise. It was little comfort as they waited to know that their world would most likely change when they hiked down the side of the volcano after the storm.

"It's the worst natural disaster I've ever seen, Steve. Look at those twisted signs. Wood is smashed through things, a bicycle embedded in the only tree that still stands on the island. Look what the cyclonic force of a superstorm did to this place."

"That's good, Janice, keep talking." Steve had his camera on trying to capture what he thought would make good footage, knowing that at some point he would edit much of it out.

"Isn't that where that big sailboat was moored yesterday at the marina? There's nothing left of the pier there. All the boats must have blown out to sea. I hope help is on the way. They're gonna need it." Janice slumped against a pile, lost her footing, as Steve grabbed her arm.

"Janice, we have to stay positive. Come on, let's try to help them."

Steve attached the lens cap to his camera, zipped it into its case, and put it into his shoulder bag, then glanced around to see how he could help. He quickly took his camera out again, as something caught his eye. Mrs. Mansale was standing with her mouth agape, as her eldest son tried to comfort her. For a split-second, his face reflected horror, yet when Brian turned his head around again, he smiled at his Mother, touching his forehead to hers.

Steve had his camera fixed on them, and then stopped when the gravity of the situation overcame him, and he started to sob. Memories hidden within the recesses of his mind began to surface. They were of Jacob and how he felt before the water consumed them and he vanished.

"You must have felt this way…" Janice choked on the words. She clung to Steve as tears rolled down her face. "My God, how can they possibly come back from this?"

"I'm not at all sure they can. I know what total annihilation is, and quite honestly, Hurricane Katrina was a kitten compared to this. It's almost as bad as…"

"I wonder if the world is watching. There isn't much clean water, no working toilets. It'll be back to nature, like primitive camping. Luckily, I put two rolls of toilet paper in my backpack."

Steve is in control again. "We'll be okay, Janice, we need to stay positive. We know we'll get out of here, but for these people, they have this to contend with."

The residents banded together, as Kalima took charge by asking them to find dry wood, drinkable water, canned foodstuffs, or anything used for cooking. She and a nurse, from the only clinic on the island, barked orders to find clean linens to dress wounds and asked all non-disabled men to build a makeshift lean-to for shelter. Miraculously, there was only one death; however, there were several injuries, some severe. Others were mostly scratches and bruises from negotiating the mountainside up or down from the caves.

That first unearthly wail came from a woman whose husband refused to leave their home. He told her to go with the others, a stubborn native, who needlessly lost his battle with the cyclone. She found him in the rubble near what was left of their home. Someone gave her a large blanket which the widow washed in the ocean, where it was left to dry on a temporary clothesline. With the help of others, she will wrap her husband within it, and take him to the woods for burial, provided a shovel can be found.

Two days after the storm, Steve was standing on the beach when he noticed a sizable barge-type ship out on the horizon. He wondered if it had come to rescue them. Since the channel was too narrow for the boat to enter the cove, it remained a distance away.

About an hour later, he observed smaller boats being lowered into the water. He started to wave his arms when Janice glanced his way. She nodded in understanding, then touched Kalima's arm, pointed toward Steve where she immediately stopped to pray silently for their impending rescue.

Several flags flew at half-mast from tall poles on the ship; however, from this distance, it was difficult to distinguish the country of origin. As the small boats came ashore at the beach, a dark-haired woman jumped out of the first boat and made her way toward the largest group. She wore green scrubs with a logo with a white circle that contained a red cross. It signaled to Janice that help had finally come.

The woman greeted the crowd and explained that she was from the Red Cross. Others waiting on the oil tanker were from the World Relief Fund. Then she motioned for her crew to distribute water and blankets, asking if they understood her. Janice noticed the struggle and moved closer to the woman's side to offer her assistance.

"I'm Janice. I was staying at one of the resorts before the storm hit. May I help you?"

"My name is Joan. They don't seem to understand me. Are you able to talk to them for me?"

"I can sure try," Janice answered.

"Good, tell that woman in charge that everyone should gather up their things because they can't stay here. We are taking them to the oil tanker. Don't let them protest; they need to move quickly. I've been told there might be another storm headed our way."

Janice did her best to convey to Mrs. Mansale what Joan had told her. Kalima blinked in understanding. Ignoring the pain in her heart, she said that she already had the most important possessions with her, her children. Joan turned her attention to the nurse and what medical needs the wounded might have, then moved into the crowd giving orders like a drill sergeant.

They scrounged until there was nothing left to salvage. One more day—and the food and water would have been exhausted. The villagers had sifted through their debris and would take what was already on the beach. Kalima looked lovingly back toward what used to be the White Sands Resort and imagined a happier time.

Brian had been next to her and took her hand. She clung to him for a moment and allowed herself to weep. When Kalima pulled away, she turned toward the crowd to deliver a little speech. She told everyone to kneel where they were and clasp hands, as she started to pray aloud. Steve got so emotional that he had to put down his camera to join them.

Sammel voiced his opinion, but Kalima shut him down as she calmly told them that they must be grateful for what they have. "You have each other, no loss of life except the stupid man who refused to go to the caves. We are safe, and we will go on with our lives, maybe not here on Kakae Luna, but we will go on."

Janice listened to Kalima's words of encouragement, as the crowd chimed in with gratitude for what they have. As Kalima spoke, Joan surveyed the group, started a count of the survivors, and jotted things down on her clipboard. With Janice's help, she would compile the information for a database to continue the relief effort.

Joan's instructions from her superiors were vague, as they were when unknown variables existed. With some forty-five others on the temporary sanctuary of the oil tanker, the people they picked up today would stay for about two weeks. The tanker would continue its sweep of the other islands, as they made their way north. By then, there might be enough aid and support to put these people on other islands, within the Vanuatu chain.

The hope was that they would carry on their lives with as little disruption as possible. Joan knew that it's something that was said during a disaster. She also knew they would never return; rarely do inhabitants go back to the scene of carnage. She was present for the cleanup after Katrina and remembers it as if it were yesterday. People started to return, although many never did.

Steve continued to capture what was transpiring around him and started to walk to the hill to get a better view when Janice stopped him to ask that he turn off the camera. "What's wrong? It would make great footage."

"Let's be sensitive to what they're going through, okay? Joan said she's taking them to the oil tanker. They don't have much choice and most likely will never come back."

As Janice turned away, Steve picked up his camera again, vacillating between what he should do versus what he wanted to do.

The evacuation would be systematic, as Joan orchestrated who would go first, and so on until everyone was off the island and safely on the oil tanker. As the last to leave, Janice watched Steve as he captured the event. Once everyone was on board the oil tanker, Joan asked Janice to relay the message that, as they passed other islands, everyone should be on the lookout for other survivors.

"Will the world reach out to this remote part of the planet, or will it turn its head to take care of other matters?" Janice said in quiet reflection.

"Bad things happen to good people, every so often," Steve said sadly.

The colossal tanker rumbled somewhere deep within, then started to move forward as the vibrations of the engines mixed with the sweet sound of music. Many stood along the railing to wave goodbye to the only home they had ever known, while others gripped the rails and sobbed.

"Good things happen too, Steve. If it hadn't been for Jacob's funeral, we might never have known each other. They'll bounce back and go on with their lives; you did, we did."

Steve hugged Janice. "I still think of Jacob whenever I look at my camera. It's a constant reminder that things can go wrong when you least expect it."

"I think of Jacob, too; it's always at odd moments. He's with us in our hearts, Steve. Goodbye Kakae Luna, beautiful Island of Vanuatu. May you rest in peace," Janice mumbled.

Steve added quietly, "You will be missed."

"Amen," Janice sniffed.

"Never, Never, Never give Up!"

~ Winston Churchill

Chapter Seven

Never Give Up Becomes A Slogan

"Ellie? Have you heard from Melanie this week? Wasn't she coming home for a break or something?" Adrian asks.

"No, I think she changed her mind. Jered's parents summoned him to their estate somewhere in the Hampton's, and she got her nose out of joint when they didn't invite her. They had one of their arguments, and she threw him out of her apartment. Now she's trying to figure out what to do with all the junk he gave her. It was apparent that she didn't throw everything out with him."

"So she kept the fancy necklace he gave her and threw out all the other stuff?" Adrian puts the paper down to face me. "That's a snooty thing to do. I didn't know Jered was a rich kid?"

"What makes a kid, rich, Adrian? We can afford to send Mel to that private college where other rich kids attend, so I think she could consider herself at least partly affluent."

Adrian ponders this for a minute. "What's the big deal anyway? I thought she was madly in love with this kid. By the way, have you seen the news today?" he asks off-handedly.

"No, I haven't looked at a newspaper for months. It's all bad news anyway, and I don't need anything more to make me depressed; I got enough of that already. Why do you ask?"

Adrian points to something he's reading. "Remember the tsunami that hit Indonesia a few years ago? You must have heard something about that."

"As I recall, it happened the day after Christmas. I don't remember what year, maybe it was 2003, or 2004. What does that have to do with Melanie and her angst with her boyfriend?"

"It doesn't have anything to do with Melanie and her angst. What an odd word to use. I thought you might want to know what's happening out there in the wide, wide world, sweetie. If you don't want to know, don't worry about it."

"Good, that settles that. You can read the article for me, okay?"

Everyone will agree that I've had more than my share of bad news.

Besides, Dr. Laurel says that if normal things freak me out, I should concentrate on things I can manage. The 'tapping technique' she shared with me works when I find myself in bad places. All it takes is a little time to follow the sheet she gave me. She also handed me a copy of the *Serenity Prayer* during one of our sessions. Little does she know that I say this at least once a day!

Amala and BJ have been with us for several months and have adjusted as they can, given the circumstances. Dr. Laurel cautioned me that if we push too hard, resentment could overtake gratitude. It's difficult to look at this sweet little boy and not want to smother him with kisses. Although he's still shy around us, when the girls feed him, he becomes quite animated.

Curlie says that while she and Lindy were dishing out corkscrew noodles to BJ for lunch yesterday, he poured his noodles on the table and put the bowl on his head. When they started to laugh, he wrinkled up his nose and laughed too. Then, he began to throw the noodles at them, and that's when Mother stepped into the kitchen. She calmly put a stop to the monkeyshines, and then quietly, yet firmly, explained there would be no throwing of food, period, end of story. If it happened again, they would all get in trouble, not just BJ.

As the girls relay this story at dinner, a distant memory of a little boy with dark wavy hair comes to my mind. Jason did that very thing when he was that age; only it was applesauce. Terre was visiting that day, and we must have laughed much as the girls did at BJ. I don't remember telling mother about that incident.

Mother, Terre, and I notice that BJ doesn't engage in play by himself. Either he waits for the girls, or he clings to Amala. We think she babies him, often talking for him instead of allowing him to think of the words himself.

Amala is a beautiful young woman who will never see her biological family again, as they were told she died in the desert. We hope that no one will ever suspect that she and BJ are here with us. We realize that coming to live with us in Virginia was difficult for her; it was far easier for us to transition. After all, we didn't have to learn a new language or adjust to another country's customs.

Since I'm Amala's adoptive mother, it falls to me to talk to her about her style of clothes. The possibility exists that she might not want the change. Adrian says to go slow, as her traditions might be hard to break.

Amala and I are in BJ's playroom. It's after his afternoon nap and before Amala needs to help our cook, Nancy, with dinner preparations.

"Amala, are you talking both in Arabic and English to BJ?"

"NO!" she says, her face expressing concern. "Amala never do this thing!"

"Sweetheart, when you came here, we never intended for you to forget where you were born. It's okay for BJ to learn both languages."

"Me do not understand Mama T. Amala not know this. You want Amala teach Arabic and English to BJ?"

"By all means, yes. You can teach him, Amala. That's all I meant. Many people who are in this country now came from somewhere else. Do you understand?"

"Yes, some of what you say. Jason have no time to teach Amala many words. Jason and Amala had no time."

"I think you're doing fine. However, I want to point out that when you refer to yourself, you say me, or I, not your name. Aunt Terre said she would teach you and you can teach BJ. Children learn better when they are younger. If he grows up hearing both English and Arabic, it's likely to come easier for him when he starts school."

BJ is shy at first, standing behind his mother, he clings to her skirt. Every so often, he peeks around, giggles, and then disappears again in the folds.

Sitting on the floor, I've stacked colorful blocks from a plastic tub that Terre found in the attic. Putting them into piles of the same color, I gently knock them over with my hand, repeating this several times. "Hello, BJ. Won't you come and play with me? Come and play with me, BJ. Can you say the word block? You try it, Amala. Say the word block in English and then repeat it in Arabic."

Amala and BJ giggle, and he peeks around her skirt again. When he doesn't come to sit down with me, she grabs one of his arms and forces him to sit down on the floor. Protesting loudly, he runs to wrap himself back in his mother's skirt. She's trying to pry him out when something occurs to me.

"Amala, is this how you were taught to take care of children?"

Her lips start to quiver, as large tears roll down her face. "Amala know only what mother taught I, and what me see other mother do. Is this wrong? Me have angered you. Me am sorry." Then she mutters something in Arabic, and starts to openly weep.

"No, I didn't mean for, hum, maybe if you sit down and play, BJ will get the idea and he'll play as we do. How about if we try that?"

Amala wipes at her face and shakes her head in agreement as she disengages herself from an objecting BJ. Sitting on the floor opposite me, she reaches for a block. BJ then plops himself into her lap.

When she reaches to push him away, I say, "It's okay, we will tackle one battle at a time."

"What is bat tell?" she asks.

"Don't worry, Amala, I will teach you. Wait a minute, I have an idea. Why don't you stack the blocks and say the colors as you stack them? Here, I'll show you. Look BJ, y-e-l-l-o-w," (saying the word slowly), "now you say what it is in Arabic, so he hears both words, that way he will get it little by little."

As I say the word, Amala repeats it in English. She then says the word in Arabic and waits for BJ to say the word. This way, I'm teaching her as she's teaching BJ. So far, she's picked up not only our language but also some of our mannerisms. Our western ways are offensive to some, but our hope is not to offend anyone, we merely want her to fit in more with our lifestyle since she will likely never go back to Saudi.

Adrian and I have discussed this possibility several times. Little BJ could be considered the rightful heir, because of his Obagur origins and we could, in essence, be trading one volatile situation for another. The real question remains: will the stigma of Amala's father's disloyalty toward the crown ever be forgiven? That, in itself, could start the Royal Family on a spiral path toward destruction, if it hasn't already.

Adrian's former partner, Larry, keeps him informed about certain issues. They continue to scrutinize the situation in the Middle East. Most, if not all, of the half-siblings, have voiced their opinions (although they know nothing about BJ). Those who felt left out of the riches and treasures over the years that the oil brought to the nation are especially vocal.

Larry also said that King Dimmy faces some tough decisions in the not-so-distant future. Should he follow tradition, or should he set new precedence? Time will tell whether his plan to rebuild what Fariq tried to manipulate will work. Dimmy knows that something must change. Should everyone share in the country's wealth? That is the real question.

"Amala, I have something for you." Some of Mother's wise words echo in my head. "You know, my Mother used to give me advice once in a while. She said, as soon as you start to sound preachy, your children will start to tune you out. There's a better way, and it's by showing them how to live their lives, by example. I've always tried to follow that. It was helpful to me as my children grew up."

"Amala does not know these words."

"I'll be right back."

Some years ago, Mother came across a beautiful poem, which she shared with Terre and me. It was her way of reinforcing her principles of life lessons. It was so profound that Terre and I purchased small plaques for each of our children.

Standing in Jason's bedroom, I glance at his photos still tacked to the wall and sadness threatens to overwhelm me. Wasn't all this stuff supposed to go to the attic a while ago? One of Danny's socks, thrown carelessly on the floor, makes me chuckle to think that his items mingle so naturally with Jason's. Danny has never asked if he could redo this room for himself. Perhaps it makes him feel closer to his cousin.

BJ is sitting on the floor next to his mother, stacking blocks, knocking them over before they get too high. He attempts a word that sounds like 'do,' looks up at his mother, who is stacking the blocks again. Amala says a word in Arabic and then one in English. BJ says 'boo.' From the side, he looks as Jason did when he was this age.

BJ begins to laugh and throws a block in my direction. Amala immediately launches into Arabic, which I interpret as, "You are a bad boy and don't throw stuff at your grandmother."

Handing the plaque to Amala, I say, "Here, this is for you. It's what helped me teach my children called, *Children Learn What They Live*. We'll add this to our English and Arabic lessons. In time you'll be able to read it to BJ. It's about what happens when we teach our children certain things and what that child will be like when they learn it. It was Jason's. Now it's yours and BJ's."

"Thank you, Mama T," Amala says quietly.

"If you encourage BJ, he will learn confidence. If you praise him, he will learn that he is appreciated."

BJ hands me a block. "Yeddo," he says proudly.

"Yell-ow, *yaSfarru*, Bee Jay," Amala corrects him.

BJ rolls his eyes and mumbles, "Fauu, yeddo, Bee Jay."

Amala and I laugh, and BJ laughs too. "Good job, both of you. I didn't get that snafro word."

So goes our first lesson in English and Arabic. Terre now insists that Amala, BJ, and I become part of the learning process, so that we can understand the basics of each language.

I have trouble with some of the guttural sounds, and when I express my concern that I'll never get it, Terre won't let me quit, reminding me how stubborn us Peters girls are when we're on a mission.

BJ is the only one who gets out of homework.

Since Adrian came back without Levi, he doesn't seem to share my enthusiasm for racing, or my thoughts that Jason might still be alive. He's undoubtedly in a funk, as I was not long ago, yet when any of us suggest he go and talk with Dr. Stevens, he insists that he'll handle things on his own. Why does he have to be so stubborn? Didn't I seek professional help?

As I pass the library table on the way to my office, the word OIL TANKER grabs my attention as it jumps out at me from a folded newspaper. Thinking that Adrian must have left it here, I open the paper out of curiosity. All of a sudden, it occurs to me that I should have pursued this angle more thoroughly, but it was abandoned a while ago when the Adrian/Levi fiasco took place.

I have an overwhelming urge to compose an email and push the stacks of paperwork to the far corner of my desk. This time, I attach a photo at the last second, figuring there's nothing to lose by doing this, sending it on its way via a little prayer.

When there is no quick reply, I figure there must be a difference in time zones, or it needs time to get where it's going. Maybe the Universe will intervene this time, and an answer will come quickly!

The headlines, *"Cyclone Billy leaves twenty-four dead in Vanuatu after the storm!"* was plastered across the front pages of nearly every newspaper across the globe. Several photos accompanied the articles, mostly of people who stood on top of rubble surveying what remained of their homes.

The news out of the Wellington, New Zealand, weather station said the United Nations reported that at least twenty-four people were dead and at least three thousand and thirty people were without their homes as a monster of a storm made its way through the South Pacific archipelago of Vanuatu.

King Akdemir finished reading the news article and wondered if he should join forces with surrounding nations to send relief to this remote area. The Royal Palace typically had not done this in the past, but could this be what the Saudi Government needed to present as change? Would the world even take notice of this gesture?

Jamaile was unaware of what was happening in other parts of the world, as a pressing issue continued to weigh heavily on his mind. He was on his way to inform King Akdemir about how his guards disposed of the despicable woman named Solana. He followed his instructions not to harm her and was to turn her over to the Islamic Religious Police. He had not only struggled with the anguish she caused the Royal Family, but he was also finding it difficult to control his temper. When he reached the library door, he knocked loudly.

"Come, Jamaile."

At the sound of Akdemir's voice, he opened the doors and turned to close them. He walked to within a few feet of the library desk where he performed his usual greeting, bowing slightly, crossing his right arm over his chest.

"Akdemir, you are well?"

The king stood and came around his desk. "It is good to see you, my friend. You have good timing. Lunch was just delivered, and you can join me." The two men moved to the chairs near the desk but did not sit down. "Have you seen the reports of the disaster, Jamaile?"

"No, I have important news, Highness. We have information that Fariq sent the woman named Solana. She did not tell us the entire truth. Fariq did promised her treasure; at least that is what she kept telling us. Basim was never involved, other than she convinced him into thinking he loved her."

"That does not surprise me. What else did you discover?"

"I am certain she knows nothing of Prince Jason's disappearance or who took him. She is a bitter and crazy woman. Akdemir, she is perhaps a little foolish in thinking she could come here and demand things from you. She would not hesitate to harm you; she murdered two of my guards before she slipped in here the other day. You said to let her go. I cannot do that. Her punishment should be severe for what she has done."

Akdemir sat down, and said, "Will you join me, Jamaile? You did not allow her to leave the palace, did you?"

Jamaile nodded his head. "No, Highness. We hold her in one of the cells down in the stable area. We will turn her over to the IRPs, or the Royal Ministers. They can deal with her," Jamaile said. "Should I inform them for you?"

"Yes, if that is what you need to do, then do it. It is the madwoman who Basim wanted to find. It looks as if she found him and came to us to exact her revenge. I would have thought that after what she has done, that it would have been enough for her. You know how greed can affect people, Jamaile. We see this kind of thing every day."

"She denied knowing anything about the explosion. She denied everything. She may have turned into an evil woman after her treatment, Akdemir."

Akdemir reflected sadly, and said, "I cannot imagine her being part of this family, or as my brother's wife, after what we have discovered about her. It may have taken all these years to get to this point, Jamaile."

"I think not, Highness. Her mannerism is evil. Most of the guards will not go near her. They believe the very soul of Shaytan possesses her."

"It is no doubt she and Fariq are responsible for the trouble perpetrated against Ellen and her family through the years. Did you question her about some of those things?"

"Highness, she admits to nothing."

"They must have unlimited funds to travel back and forth undetected – she mentioned Jason was not in Virginia. How would she know that unless she, or her associates, were there?"

"She will hunt Jason until she finds him. Once she finds him, she said she would make him pay for what his father could not prevent, the death of her unborn child."

"That is disturbing; did you not tell me that the child was stillborn?"

"Yes. From what I have been able to find out, your father's guards were only instructed to turn her away from the Royal Palace. After she met with your father, King Basim, months passed when news came the baby boy she carried had died. There are no other details about the birth, except for those. We had assumed she had gone away."

Akdemir rose from his chair and started to walk the perimeter of the large room, pausing periodically to touch the spine of a book. "Those who would know are likely dead now. It would be hard to know the truth in light of that." He turned toward Jamaile, and asked, "Are we sure there is no one we can ask that knew about this incident?"

Jamaile shook his head, and then glanced up quickly. "I may know of someone who was here at that time. Please excuse me, Highness. I will return as soon as possible."

Akdemir walked toward the big man, "That can wait, Jamaile. Will you stay to talk with me, have something to eat before you go? I eat alone most days and could use your company. The others want favors, or something else. It is always about money." Akdemir sat down, then pulled off a domed lid to examine the contents.

"I will stay for a while." Jamaile sat in the chair opposite Akdemir and took the plate offered.

"I do not see you often, Jamaile. I miss our conversations."

"I cannot get away. There is always something that needs attention. I can only rely on certain men now. Their numbers have dwindled since Khalifa is no longer here."

"I regret what happened my brother. We cannot go back and change anything. We must be strong for what lies ahead. I do not think our troubles are over. If this Solana woman has turned up, anything is possible."

"The latest rumors are that your other half-brothers will band together to oppose you. They are likely behind this, and it could be Fariq's sons."

"Ah, yes, you may be correct. In fact, the ministers received news that several tribes are unhappy with how the Royal Palace has responded to some of their demands. More likely they are unhappy with me. Perhaps it is the fact that nothing is divided equally between the families of my father's children," Akdemir replied.

"This could be a diversion to make us look the other way while something takes place," Jamaile said thoughtfully. "It could be what the warring factions hoped for all along."

Akdemir let out a heavy sigh. "Will there ever be a time when peace prevails here?"

Jamaile stared at his half-brother a moment. "It does not appear to be possible; we live in troubled times, Highness. We have always had this rift. For as long as I can remember, it has been a part of our lives and our history."

"It is good to talk with an old friend. I have so few here. At least when you were away, Jason was here, and Turlock was at my side to lend his expertise in state matters. Since they have been gone, I truly miss them both and feel so alone. There is no one to take their place."

"Things will eventually go back to the way they were, Akdemir. It takes time for it to do so," Jamaile added.

"No Jamaile, we have lost our opportunity to be with Basim's family. There is no heir now. It is what saddens me the most. Now the process will begin to choose a new one. It is a daunting task and one I do not look forward to."

"You should consider going away, Akdemir. It might help you cope with all the other things that are troubling you."

"Running away from my problems will solve nothing, my friend. Where would I go? I cannot go to Ellen's as much as I want to. Where would I go that trouble would not follow?"

"I must leave now to take care of that matter we spoke about earlier, Highness. I will return as swiftly as possible. Perhaps you would like to come with us the next time the Blue and Silver have a show."

"I am attached to the Royal Palace now, whether I like it or not. I'm beginning to understand why Basim felt he needed to leave. Do you often feel that you are trapped, Jamaile?"

"No, Akdemir, as I once told you, I have never wanted to be where you are now, leading the people as you do. I am happy in the capacity I already serve."

"May good luck be with you, old friend."

As Jamaile slipped out of the library, Akdemir resigned himself to show the world he was in control, even though he felt as if he was not. Then he decided to consult with the Royal Physician since Turlock was no longer his consultant and Jamaile was too busy with other things. No one could help him with these types of matters, most notably his increased anxiety.

"Your Highness, people wait in the outer room to meet with you," Jamaile said quietly, waiting for the King to answer.

Akdemir turned in his chair to greet him. "Do you know what day it is today, Jamaile?"

"Yes, Highness. It is the day young Jason would have become Crown Prince Jason Obagur, our heir to the throne."

"I cannot meet with anyone today. I must cancel everything."

"Jason would want you to go on with your life, Akdemir. He knew how important your work is to you."

"I am not so sure of that. Jason is not here, and it saddens me. I want to call Miss Ellen. I know that she will not talk to me. I want to send them gifts, and she sends them back. I wanted them as my family, and she will not allow it."

"Miss Ellen has made her wishes known to me. Many times and loud." Jamaile responded.

"I have lost all except you, my trusted friend, and loyal brother. Have we exhausted all information and ties with Mr. Adrian's team? We have heard nothing from them for a long time. It has been since the incident about Mr. Levi, and the child went to live there. Do you think they blame us for his death?"

"I am certain they blame the Royal Palace for not keeping Mr. Levi safe. When I call the number for their headquarters, they route the call to a machine. I leave messages. No one returns my calls. I have given this up."

"We must go on, Jamaile. Our people need us to lead them with good decisions no matter what has befallen us. We must keep our tempers in check and stay the course, no matter how difficult it is. You have selected a new captain for the team, I assume, or you would not be here."

"He is a trusted person and member of my team. He is doing well, not as well as Jason. He is adequate."

"You think that Jason did a good job with the horses? That is a funny thing, Jamaile. Before he disappeared, he told me you raised your voice and embarrassed him in front of *his* men."

Jamaile tried to recall the incident. "I told Jason that he needs to guard you. It was a difficult time then. Much was going on with you and the Royal Family."

"If my memory is correct, I believe you told him that he should be guarding me and not playing with the horses. I had to keep from laughing. He was quite upset over it. When I told him that you did that to both his father and me, he was surprised."

"Yes, I do recall this."

Akdemir grew silent as his face registered sadness. "What do you suppose happened to him, Jamaile? Do you believe that Fariq's men got to him and he is dead?"

"I do not know, Akdemir. We questioned Fariq's men, those that we did find, and no one could give us any good answers. Fariq did little talking. We questioned him before his head rolled from his shoulders. He maintained he had nothing to do with Prince Jason's disappearance."

"And you believed him?"

"It was a deathbed confession, Akdemir. The Royal Ministers who were present said he was extremely hostile, demanding his place at the Royal Table to take your place. He maintained he and his men had nothing to do with Jason's death."

"Was Mr. Adrian informed about Solana?"

Jamaile shook his big head. "That was one of the calls I made. I am unsure if the message got to him. They needed to know that she escaped."

"I understand. Perhaps we shall never know. Any news about what might have happened during that woman's birthing the dead child?"

"The person you had in mind has been dead for many years. We have gone out several times, and there is no one we talked with who has any memories of that time."

"I know that you tried your best, Jamaile. Perhaps we are not to know what happened during that time. This Solana is the only other person who knows the truth of that. Should Jason miraculously reappear, Miss Ellen would most likely never tell me. How did things go so wrong, Jamaile? How could we have gone from this happy household to the one we have now?"

"Maybe Miss Ellen was right. We need a crystal ball to see what is happening, so we can avoid trouble if it is bad."

A chuckle escaped Akdemir's throat. They both laughed to realize how absurdly funny it was that Jamaile was quoting a phrase that Miss Ellen mentioned to them so long ago.

"Highness, will you come now? People wait in the formal room to meet with you. The Royal Ministers say there is much to discuss today."

"We will debate who will take young Jason's place. Many are clamoring for the role. It is not an easy decision. For now, we will put this out of our thoughts. We must let this rest, Jamaile. Someday someone will let us know. For now, we will get on with the business before us."

"Yes, Akdemir, if you are ready, people are anxious to meet with you."

Akdemir realized for the first time in a long while that he had no control over what happened to the Royal Family. When Basim left, he took a piece of them with him, and it continued to deteriorate, until the death of his father, King Basim. He tried to rebuild the family with Turlock, Sheyanna, and their children. It looked promising when Jason agreed to become the Crown Prince. But when Fariq ordered Turlock, and his family's murder, and then Jason went missing, Akdemir suffered an irreversible setback.

The beheading of Fariq gave restitution for what he inflicted during the siege of the Royal Palace. It did little to lessen the pain for the search for another heir to the throne, or the fact that Solana escaped. Will she show herself at the Royal Palace again?

Jamaile said that would never happen. He could not account for how she managed to overcome two strong warriors, nor how she left the palace when she was guarded so carefully.

Miss Ellen's crystal ball would have come in handy. A magic carpet to fly him out of the window would have worked too! Alas, it was not a fairy tale. Akdemir's reality of leading his people to make good decisions of commerce, along with his guidance for the merchants, was what he knew and what he could do well.

In time, he hoped to find solace.

Perhaps in time, Miss Ellen would learn to forgive him.

Although the newspaper headlines and weather broadcasts had settled down about the disaster in the Pacific Ocean, the rescue effort continued. Basic emergency rations were being provided to evacuees after military aircraft from New Caledonia, Australia and New Zealand concluded their aerial assessments of the damage from Cyclone Billy.

A spokesman, from the U.N. Office for the Coordination of Humanitarian Affairs, said this included water, and other items. As the cleanup of Vanuatu continued, the damaged airport in the Capital City of Port Vila reopened, which allowed some aid and relief flights to reach the country.

Radio and telephone communications with outer islands were now almost fully restored after what the country's president calls a monster storm. The city's hospitals were so full that they had to put hospital beds into the parking lot. Once overwhelmed with patients, they are now open for new arrivals. Every available working vehicle was in service to help with the cleanup.

The aid agency, UNICEF, was on-site to provide temporary shelters for those who had nowhere else to go. Emergency crews from many parts of the world continued to work day and night to reestablish communications for the local police; however, things were far from business as usual.

Officer Kensi surveyed the police station office that had transformed. He turned on his new office computer and moved to the cupboard where they kept the coffee. He fiddled with the filter, dumped in two scoops of coffee, filled the reservoir with water, and then pressed the start button. He went back to look over the day's roster, shaking his head at the number of cases that he would either work on or file today.

Officer Laput had not come into the station yet, so he switched to the dispatch radio to listen in on what was happening around the other islands. Many unfortunate things happened because of that cyclone; one of them was that tourists were far and few between, and the crime rate had more than doubled. It's probably due to the lack of services not yet restored, and looting was rampant. In the last few months, Kensi had come up against several gangs and thugs who had appeared out of nowhere.

The relief effort was slow due to the many scattered islands, the lack of boat-power, and people relegated to it. Many boats not securely moored at the Marina before the storm blew through were swept away, along with some of the pilings. Boats that didn't float out to sea were found either stranded on sandbars, sunk, or went missing altogether.

The insurance companies were in a quandary as to whether some of the claims were authentic and sought the police department's help in dealing with it. It was Kensi's job to wade through the quagmire. He suspected that those who knew about the storm confiscated boats that had plenty of fuel. Then they hightailed it toward Australia. The list of damaged or missing marine craft was endless, as were the calls to investigate other missing items--some of them legitimate, most others were not.

Kensi offered to help during his free time, except his superior, Officer Laput, told him the police station needed him more. With so much destruction and so few funds to do the cleanup and help those in need, it's been challenging to keep the peace.

The damage to the police station was minimal compared to other buildings in Port Vila. At least it was still standing, and the file cabinets were found mostly intact. It did smash the coffee maker and destroyed the computers and telephones. Those were found floating in a pool of muddy water outside the building.

The computer pinged that a message was waiting and Kensi roused himself to see that it was an incoming email from someone who had attached a photo of a young man. He didn't understand the message. Even though it was in English, it was not the Bislama-English version of English he knew. How would he handle this dilemma? It could dredge up the Brian-Andru case of a few years ago. Then he wondered why that memory surfaced.

Kensi also wondered how they would communicate. Laput told him to stand down from that case a long time ago. Could this be the clue they need to resolve it? Staring at the screen, he tried to pull something else from his memory. Then he suddenly recalled the list and box of other things he took home when Laput told him to stop investigating that case.

Laput startled Kensi as he walked through the door, "Gud moning, Kensi," a booming voice said as the station door closed.

"Gud moning, Laput," Kensi said in response.

Laput threw his hat on the repaired hat rack and moved toward his paper-laden desk. Then he sniffed the air and went to the coffee station to pour himself a mug of coffee. He looked over at Kensi, noticed that he didn't have a cup, and proceeded to pour one for him.

"What are you working on today?" Laput plunked down his mug with a thud.

"An email came from someone asking something in English-English. It's not the Bislama-English I understand, and I cannot figure it out." Kensi said, staring at the screen. "Thanks for the coffee, sir."

Laput laughed. "Can you send it through our interpreter?"

Kensi looked at his superior. "We do not have one of those. What are you saying Laput?"

"The new computer came with an upgrade," he nodded, sipping his coffee. "It is right here," Laput said as he took Kensi's mouse and moved it to a drop-down bar along the top of the screen.

Suddenly, the knowing light of understanding shone in Kensi's eyes as he reached for the mouse to click on *translation*. "I did not know this was here. I will try it. How do you know of this, sir?"

Laput laughed again. "You do not want to know."

Some hours later, Kensi was able to translate his Bislama language into English the other person knew as their English, even though the words were not entirely correct. Then he printed the attachment and sent back a reply. He waited for a response, and when it didn't come, he looked at the clock and decided he would quit for the day.

Kensi knew his wife, Gor'gena, was working late at the hospital tonight. When he arrived at their apartment, he started to think about the box that held the list, the map of the oil tankers, and the photos of John Doe/Andru/Brian that he put into the hall closet before the storm. Perhaps he should take it back to the station, in case they needed it for reference.

When Gor'gena came home, she questioned why the box was sitting near the front door. Kensi said he thought that it should go back to the station. Figuring it's a police matter, she took a moment to remember Andru-Brian and wondered how he was doing, hoping that his leg and arm healed adequately.

It's the next morning when Kensi fit the fragments together. He placed a piece of paper over the bottom part of each photo to cover them from the nose down, and he compared the eyebrows and hairline on each one against the new one he just received.

"There is too much puffiness to see what this young man looks like," Kensi said out loud. "The possibility exists that this is the same person. It is hard to say; the swelling is too great."

Kensi studied the list of oil tankers, but nothing jumped out at him, so he folded it up and put it back into the box. Something shiny caught his attention, and he reached into the box to pull out an old notebook along with a small camera that he kept for police work.

It came in handy many times for crime scenes, or traffic violations. Opening it to find a canister of exposed film, he questioned how long it had been there, perhaps as long ago as a year? Maybe longer? Gor'gena bought him a new digital camera for his birthday, so he no longer had to wait for the development of the film.

On his break, Kensi took the film canister to the pharmacy where the store clerk told him that he would have to wait for the photos. Their old machine was found a block away, damaged beyond repair when the cyclone whipped through town and, apparently, through this building by way of the back door. Their new machine should arrive within the next few weeks.

"Tangkyu, call me when they be ready," Kensi said politely.

As he left the store to head back to the police station to immerse himself into the next case file, he turned his head to see a craggy, disheveled man who was about to swing something toward a shop window.

"Stop right there!" Kensi's booming voice said as he ran toward the startled man.

Kensi was not fast enough as the window shattered, and the man fell forward. He noticed a truck passing as he glanced down to unhook his gun from his holster. In that split second, Kensi looked up to see the man straighten as he started to run away.

"Stop!" Kensi shouted, "Do not make me use my gun!"

The man was still moving, so Kensi muttered that he didn't want trouble. He stopped to aim for the man's leg and pulled the trigger. To Kensi's amazement, the man fell, did a somersault, got up, and started to run again.

"I told you to STOP!" Kensi aimed again and pulled the trigger a second time. This time the man went down. Kensi approached him cautiously, "You… don't I know you?"

"No!" the man answered quickly. "You shot me! Get medical attention! You shot me! I'm bleeding!" he wailed.

"I told you to stop. Let me see your wound. Where have I seen you before?" Kensi pulled the man up by the collar and practically dragged him back to the storefront.

By this time, the store proprietor was standing on the sidewalk waving his arms and yelling at the top of his lungs. "You imbecile! It will take forever to have that window replaced!" he bellowed.

Kensi released the man, who fell to the sidewalk, screaming out in pain. Kensi depressed the device at his shoulder to contact dispatch. "Badge 224, Officer Kensi. Summon an ambulance, man down, needs immediate medical attention, pistol wound. The address is 790 Main Street." He then turned his attention to the store owner. "Calm down, Mr. Legget. You will need to wait while I talk to him."

"I need medical… oh, such pain. Why did you shoot me?"

"I called for an ambulance; now tell me who you are!" Kensi asked.

"Ask him why he did this?" the proprietor screamed at the man.

Kensi turned toward the store owner. "I know you're upset, Mr. Legget." He took out his little notepad and pen, then asked the man on the sidewalk to start talking.

"He stole…OH, he stole the necklace!" Legget started to beat his fists against the building, as the glass crunched under his shoes.

Kensi stopped writing. "Mr. Legget, be quiet while I ask this man some questions." Turning his attention back to the man, he asked, "What is your name?"

"Tambor. My name is Drexel Tambor. That's right. My name is Drexel Tambor."

"Spell your name," Kensi demanded.

"D-R-E-X-E-L and T-A-M-B-O-R," the man howled again when Mr. Legget touched him with the broom handle. "Get him away from me!"

"He stole the most important thing I owned!" Legget spewed. "And I want it back!"

An exasperated Kensi asked, "Tambor, what did you steal from that window?"

"I saw my sister's necklace. You have no right to have it. Someone stole it from her during the storm. We've been looking for it for a very long time. It is most valuable, and we could sell it to have money to eat."

Kensi and Mr. Legget exchanged glances. By the looks of the man, they doubt very much that his sister owned a necklace valuable enough for him to smash a storefront window. Perhaps he should have the benefit of the doubt, as looks can be deceiving. So many people lost so much that maybe he's wearing borrowed clothes and he is who he says he is.

Legget could not contain his fury as he leaned down to get his point across. "Yes, it was valuable – you are an idiot! It was not from your sister, you stupid man! You were here to steal it!"

Kensi pushed at Mr. Legget's chest to get him to move away, then turned toward Tambor, who was now sitting up. "Why didn't you go inside and ask the owner? Did you have to smash a perfectly good window that broke during the storm and took him months to replace? Did you have to do that? Where is the necklace now? Hand it over."

"I… I don't have it. When you shot me, it flew out of my hands and into a passing truck."

"He's lying!" Legget screamed. "He grabbed the necklace and threw it purposely into the truck! I saw him! It was before you shot him!"

Kensi remembered a passing truck but has no recollection of seeing a flying necklace.

"No, I swear that when this man shot me, it startled me. I wanted to touch it. How would I know a truck would pass by at that time? Hum?" Tambor sputtered.

A siren grew louder as it approached. When it stopped near the group on the sidewalk, two paramedics jumped out to attend to Mr. Tambor and converse with Kensi, gently pushing an indignant Mr. Legget out of the way. Meanwhile, Mr. Legget went to stand in front of his gaping window. His shoulders began to jerk when he started to sweep up the glass.

"Mr. Legget, can you tell me about this necklace?" Kensi asked the distraught man.

"It came from a wealthy woman who left the islands before the cyclone hit. She said her house was in the direct path of the storm and she and her husband were leaving. They had a yacht and came to the mainland after they heard the first warning. I bought the necklace from her so that she could leave. It was in my safe until a few days ago. It does not belong to that despicable man!"

"I will need the names of the original owners of the jewelry and what the necklace was worth, Mr. Legget."

"Of course Officer, I can get that for you. There was a ring attached to it. This man is lying to you! I put it on the necklace yesterday. I think that man, Tambor, was lurking somewhere when I did it. He had it in his head to steal it!"

"You were warned about looters. Why did you put it into your window?" Kensi questioned.

"I thought it was safe. I saw that wretched man use his cane to break the window and then he reached in and grabbed the necklace. He turned and threw it to the truck that was passing, as I heard shots. When I came out, you were running after him. I thought that, after all this time, it would be safe here," Legget said out of breath.

"I did not steal anything. How could I? I am an old man with a cane." Tambor said, as the paramedics cleaned his wound and bandaged his leg.

"We'll get everyone's statement, and we'll see about that," Kensi said to the man, then turned to the proprietor. "You saw the necklace fly into the window of the truck? Did you get a look at the driver?"

"The window was open, but it happened so fast, all I could see was the man's hands on the wheel," Legget said sadly. "It was too fast!"

"Did you get the license plate number of the truck?" Kensi asked.

"No! I was trying to stop this crazy person; how would I have time to see who was passing by, or get a license number?"

Kensi poised with his pen. "How much would you say this stolen necklace and ring are worth, Mr. Legget?"

"I could not give the woman what it was worth because I did not have that much. By then the banks were closed. It's worth close to $1,600 U.S. Dollars. What I am most angry about is the fact that the ring I slipped through the necklace yesterday… is worth over $5,000!" Legget sniffed.

"Oh," Kensi said under his breath, "that is unfortunate. You do have insurance, I hope."

Mr. Legget turned toward the building and started to sob unabashedly, banging his fists against the brick. Kensi could only put a hand on his shoulder, as a way to offer his condolences for his loss.

The paramedics were about to close the door on the ambulance when Kensi stopped them. "Let me see your identification, Mr. Tambor," he said, holding out his hand.

Tambor grumbled, patted his top pockets and then his pants, and said, "I seem to have lost my wallet, Officer."

"We need to get him to the hospital," one of the paramedics said quickly. "You can talk with him there. The wound is not bad; it looks like you only grazed him. They will probably want an X-ray to make sure it did not hit a bone. You did not want to hurt him, did you?"

"No, if I wanted to hurt him, I would have aimed much higher." Kensi stared at Mr. Tambor when he said this, yet it had little effect on him. "I will see you at the hospital. Do not take your eyes off this man. Do not trust him."

In the time it took for Kensi to complete his report, twenty minutes had passed. By the time he got to the hospital, no one knew where a Mr. Drexel Tambor was, and it was apparent that after the paramedics watched a team take him to triage room three, they left on another call and failed to let the staff know to keep an eye on him.

The hospital owned two portable X-ray machines that moved from triage to triage. One was on loan to an oil tanker and had not been returned. A new one was coming, along with the photo machine for the drug store in town; however, no one knew precisely when that would be, so they had to wait for the remaining one to become available. Since Tambor's wound was not life-threatening, there was no need to transport him to the X-ray department in the basement.

Tambor took advantage of the chaos that erupted when two ambulances came into the ER, and all available staff went to triage rooms one and two. When the X-ray technician arrived in triage room three, Tambor was gone.

"Laput will not be happy with this," Kensi mumbled to himself angrily. "Where have I seen that man before? Why does he look so familiar? And I know that name!"

Kensi drove back to the station to file his report and then waited for Laput to come back from his lunch break. His mind would not let go of why he might know this Mr. Tambor. Perhaps this was not his real name. It's odd that his ID was not on him.

How could he disappear from the hospital without anyone seeing him leave? Did he know the value of the necklace with the ring attached to it? Was he lurking around as Mr. Legget alleged? Was he walking by and decided to smash the window and grabbed it as so many looters did when they faced hunger and despair?

Laput walked in and threw his hat on the rack. He headed to the cupboard to get a coffee cup, took a look at Kensi and asked, "Kensi, you look lost in thought. What happened? I heard the commotion from the diner. Since you did not ask for backup, did everything go okay? Did you fire your weapon?"

Kensi glanced at his superior. "Yes, sir. I missed him the first time, then got him with the second. Can I ask you something?"

"Sure, Kensi, you can ask me anything, you know that."

"How many men have you killed in the line of duty, sir, if you don't mind me asking?"

Laput pondered this question. "Three. I have had to kill three men in the line of duty, and to this day, it bothers me. Did you kill that man today? Is that why you are sullen?"

"No, only grazed him. The man looked familiar to me, but not his name. I cannot shake the feeling that we have met before. He gave me this name of Drexel Tambor, and I can't find a file on him."

"Drexel Tambor…" Laput said slowly, leaning back in his chair. "Can't say off the top of my head. Tell me what happened. Did you look in these books?"

Laput turned to a shelf behind his chair, pulled two of them out, and plopped them on his desk, where he opened one to a previously marked page. They were photos of known suspects, those who this station had booked along with several others from outlying islands.

Kensi went into detail about the man. Then they sat in silence for some time when Laput started to laugh. "What is so funny, Laput?"

"You are not going to believe this; I think I know who this man is. Do you remember the man who got away during that police operation we were involved in where the red cigarette boat was shot to hell?"

Kensi dredged up a memory of some time ago. "Of course I do. Mr. Zucker has no love for us. Gor'gena has to pay our boat slip bill using her maiden name. Somehow, he knows when I come there to take my boat out. He locks the door and will not talk to me. He has never forgiven us for what we did to that boat."

"There were several incidents before that one, and it had to do with some stolen items. I do not expect you to know about this, it was many years ago, but it could explain some of what happens here. Do you remember the old angler who caught John Doe in his net, even though the hole was so big anything would have gone right through it?"

Kensi winkled his forehead and shook his head in disbelief. "Yes, I remember the old angler, but wasn't his name Cornwall something? How is this related to what happened today? Do you think it is him? He looked like a bum, unclean and he smelled bad, too."

Laput got up to lumber over to a large file cabinet, rummaged around, and pulled out a tattered folder marked *John Doe*. "I believe he is the same person, Kensi."

"No! That man was small and had baggy clothes with a scraggly beard. Let's look in the wanted book again."

"There is no need. It is Rexley Mansale. Here is his picture. After John Doe went home, I ran across some information that linked him to several other incidents. He is a man of many disguises, Kensi, and it looks like we've been had, again." Laput slammed his hand down on the desk so hard that piles of papers scattered in the air and floated to the floor.

"You never mentioned the connection between this Rexley person and the boat before. Do you think he lied about Brian? He probably didn't pay off the hospital charges. Did someone go after him?"

"I think you were getting married when the information came through, Kensi. The hospital sent a representative to visit with Brian's family. They noted that Mrs. Mansale had no money to pay them. She was fuming mad at her brother-in-law for taking Brian from the hospital. She didn't think he was healing right. She was paying small amounts each month. That's when they stopped proceeding with a lien on the family business. When the storm came and demolished everything, they no longer could make a living there, so that was the end of that."

"They did not try to find them after that?" Kensi asked.

"They were probably evacuated and relocated with many others at the time, no doubt. I wonder where they are now and if they have had contact with this mysterious Uncle Rexley," Laput said.

"We could search to try to find them," Kensi offered.

"The survivors are all over the other islands that would take them. We do not have the workforce to search for him, Kensi. We have many other cases to concentrate on now."

"We need to catch this thief, sir. Wait a minute; he said a truck passed by, as he threw the necklace and ring into an open window. That means he had an accomplice."

"That is right, son. He's a slick one, and he will be tripped-up one day, and we will get him. Crooks always think they can get away with it, until they get lazy and stupid and that's when we will get him, Kensi, mark my words. It will not be the last we see of him."

"What was he doing here at Port Vila? Was he not relocated when those outer islands were damaged?"

"He might not have been there when the storm went through. Keep that up, young man. You ask good detective questions. They will come in handy someday. I hope you are writing them down. But take heed, our other cases must come first."

"I understand, Laput. I am taking notes. You never know when they will come in handy. I will do this on my off-hours. Do you think I should look into the rescue effort, maybe see if this Rexley-Drexel person was on one of the oil tankers that took evacuees to other islands?"

"By all means, check that out. You know of three disguises so far, real uncle to Brian, old fishing angler, the bum one, and there may be more. Oh yes, there is one more; boat captain."

Kensi raised his eyebrows, "What if there are more than those?"

"Then you will dig them out, because you are good at your job, Kensi."

"I take that as a compliment, sir. I will never give up on this. I will find him one day, and he will pay for his indiscretions."

"Of that, I have no doubt, Kensi. We have a mountain of other things that take up our time now, so let us dig into that first. If you have spare time, then look into the rescue data."

"Yes, sir. Do you think he had anything to do with that merman story and that watch that lit up?"

Laput threw his head back to laugh. "He could, Kensi, he could. I would put nothing past this character!"

"I would not call him that, sir."

Rexley Mansale (real uncle to Kalima Mansale's children), aka Drexel Tambor (the thief), aka Abram Cornwall (the old fishing angler), aka Shuster Crumble (the bum), aka Captain Silos Beam (the boat captain), slipped out of the hospital triage through a side door into a waiting truck. He couldn't believe his luck! Those stupid hospital people would lose their mother! Two times, he had come to this hospital, and two times, he had walked away scot-free.

Rexley's accomplice was waiting in the parking lot to retrieve him as planned. After Rexley smashed the store window, he was to wait long enough for the proprietor to strike him. He would fall to feign an injury, thus necessitating a trip to the hospital. Then he would collect on the proprietor's insurance policy, and kill two birds with one stone.

He hadn't bargained for a bullet to his leg, nor was the proprietor supposed to see him take the jewelry. He changed his plan to linger near the broken window long enough to make it look as if the broken glass had maimed him. After the officer shot him, the paramedics really did take him to the emergency room for treatment.

Rexley had been lurking in the background for nearly a week while he and his accomplice practiced the deed. When the big police officer showed up without warning, he had to readjust his plans; right down to the timing of throwing the necklace and ring into the open window of the truck as it passed.

After Rexley left the hospital, via a side door, he signaled to the truck driver as two ambulances pulled under the portico near the emergency room entrance. There was such a frenzy of activity that he knew they could flee without anyone noticing. He told the driver to step on it, as he yanked at his fake sideburns with one hand, and peeled off his nasty wig with the other. He stuffed all that along with his jacket into a bag and threw it behind his seat. Then he unbuckled his pants to yank off the cut up grungy pants, throwing them out the window along with the rest of his clothes. Behind the driver's seat was a clean pair of pants, a jacket, a pair of leather shoes, and a hat.

"Ha, we did it again, my friend," Rexley laughed.

The truck driver turned to him, and roughly asked, "When do I get paid, Rexley? You always take too long to pay up. I won't wait that long again."

"You get paid when I do!" Rexley snarled in response.

In truth, as in most of Rexley's misadventures, once they are off the island, it would be highly unlikely the truck driver would ever receive payment and most assuredly would lose his life. He knew that a smart man never made mistakes, and if he weren't careful, he would inevitably be caught one day when he least expected it. He did not intend for that to happen until he found his nephew because Brian held the key to his success.

Rexley began to worry. What if Brian figured things out, or worse, what if someone found his precious bundles and took them before he could retrieve them? Those bundles were going to fund his retirement. He even had a place he fancied as his, except that crazy storm took all that away. Perhaps he should keep the necklace and ring for now and worry about retrieving his other loot later.

Kensi was busy with a problem he wanted to solve. "I have a hunch, Laput," he said the day after the necklace and ring incident. "I asked for information from that large tanker that picked people up after the cyclone. They said they would look into the names of the people who were on the islands, and any other information they think we might need. The only problem is that there was a small fire in the data room and some of the information might be missing."

Laput sighed heavily. "It will be what it will be Kensi. Keep up the good work. Some of these things might relate to the pirates who roam the ocean and this fugitive Rexley, aka Cornwall, or Tambor and it could be part of it. Keep digging; you are bound to find something useful."

Kensi was thoughtful. "Do you think that it's possible that Brian could have done the awful things his uncle did?"

"I believe that his misfortune was in knowing his thieving uncle. His uncle could have coerced him into helping him, but I do not think that he did the crazy things his uncle has done. That, my friend, is solely on Rexley Mansale."

Laput lapsed into a long-forgotten memory, but this time it wasn't about the red cigarette boat, but a much earlier recollection. It had to do with a large heist that took place near Australia--way before Kensi came to work at the station. It was a few years after he graduated from the Police Academy in Port Vila.

Priceless art and valuable objects bound for a museum in the United States never arrived at their destination. A wide-ranging hunt never turned up one piece of substantial evidence; therefore, no one person, or outfit, was ever linked to this extraordinary theft. The word out of Australia was that it was one of the most mysterious and slickest heists in history. Could this have been where Mansale honed his skills?

"We will dig a little deeper. I have an idea," Laput said finally.

"Where do we start, Laput?"

"We will start with Australia. We will go back about fifteen years, or so…no, make that about twenty-two years ago. I, too, used to say I would never give up." Laput said resolutely.

"Do you still feel that way?"

"Yes, I do, son. And it makes me proud to work with you."

"That makes two of us." Kensi smiled. There are now possibly three people who would never give up in their quest for justice.

"The will to win, the desire to succeed,
the urge to reach your full potential,
these are the keys that will unlock the door
to personal excellence."
~ Confucius

Chapter Eight

The Will to Win

Ashwood Stables is in the limelight, because our driver, Roland T. (Mack) McMillan, has done so fantastic that the media has approached him to do an article. Someone made repeated calls to Channel 5, encouraging them to do a feature story. And why wouldn't they, he's an eligible bachelor, has an amazing record of accomplishment at nearby Billingsworth Racetrack, and been linked to at least one country music singer.

Most of us have narrowed this down to two young women who live within our midst. One of them is Curlie (the girl now known as Tina), and the other is none other than Terre's daughter, Lindy. The newspaper articles have run various stories about Mack jumping ship to work at other stables, but so far, he has declined the offers and squelched any rumors.

Danny keeps plugging along, bringing *Lester* up in class, as Mack does with *Raindrop*, and it's obvious he's itching to show him up. He's broached the subject more than once that he should train with *Peanut Brittle*. Since Reed is *Peanut's* trainer, he will have the last word on this subject.

Mother says Amala and BJ fit in with our eclectic way of doing things. Her obvious delight in their presence pales in comparison to how the girls fawn over the little boy. It's to the point that he screams for more! They take turns playing with him after they complete their kitchen chores and before he goes to bed. The rumble is audible as they run across the hardwood floors above us when they chase him. We don't mind a bit, as its joyful noise once again.

BJ is a loving child with a sweet disposition and reminds me of Jason when he was that age; friendly with us, shy around strangers, he's a little precocious, but a delight to have around. When the girls have other activities, either Mother or I, read to him most evenings. It's the highlight of my day.

Rosie follows him around to keep him out of trouble, woofs when he ventures near potential danger, herding him away from it with her snout. He seems to sense that she's there and slows enough for her to keep up with him. Adrian often takes both Rosie and BJ out to the little brook to throw stones or wade in the shallow water. None of us think he's big enough to handle being on a horse, although Adrian occasionally places him on *Shoo Fly Pie* but he never takes his hands away.

Amala studies her English lessons with a vengeance, as she's determined to eradicate her accent. While she teaches us Arabic words, we, teach her our language. She carves time out each day to do this when BJ has his quiet time each afternoon or leaves him with me to play in my office. Somehow we have worked out a schedule where she helps Nancy in the kitchen and Mona with her baking, giving Mother a little break.

I awake one morning, after having a dream about Amala and Jason. Realizing that we never talked about what happened in Saudi, I've purposely held back questions, in the hope that she would volunteer the information. Her diction has improved so much that it might be the right time to pursue this.

We are in the laundry room folding clothes. "Amala, may I ask you some questions?"

"Yes, Mama T." Amala stops folding to smile at me. "You may ask whatever you wish."

"I hope this will not sound like I'm probing, because that's not my intention."

Amala's eyes widen, and for a brief second her face begins to register fear. "Are you sending us back?" Her bottom lip starts to quiver. "Are you sending me back and keeping BJ? Please do not do that. I would not survive. We could not survive there! They would find me. They would kill us!"

"Oh, no, sweetheart, we would never do that!" I reach to pull her into an embrace. "Amala, you are one of us now. We will never send either one of you back. Here, sit down. I want to ask you some questions. They're about when you first met Jason."

"Oh," Amala says, with a sigh of relieve. "What do you wish to know?"

"How did you get into Jason's room without anyone seeing you?"

Amala lowers her head. Adrian did the standard CIA debriefing with her, but that was after her arrival with BJ, (and what became the trip from hell). He has neither spoken with her after this time nor shared most of what happened, as Levi's death took over his thoughts. It was, after all – a secret mission and I don't have the right to pry into that.

"If you can recall some of the details, it would help me understand what happened. Are you willing to help me?"

Amala lifts her head as tears roll down her face. "Do not be angry with me." Amala pleads. She sniffs, grabbing one of Mother's handkerchiefs from a pile on the counter to wipe her eyes and nose.

"I will not be angry with you, Amala. I need to ask you some questions. Go ahead, when you're ready."

"My father gives me order. He does (she stops to correct herself), he did that many times to me. He said to find out where important documents are and to keep my eyes on Prince Jason."

"We knew that your father wanted his hands on the ancient documents. Tell me how you were able to get into Jason's room and go there without anyone knowing."

"My father knows ways to get in and out of Royal Palace. He said to get Prince Jason to… I am sorry, my father is awful man!" Amala begins to weep openly, and I hug her.

"I'm sorry that this is bringing back this horror for you. It might help us to find Jason, do you understand?"

She shakes her head and tries to compose herself. "My father tell me to go to Jason so he will tell me things. I did not know I will fall in love with him. Jason is a loving man. I forget why I came." Amala stops to wipe at her face again. "I did not ask him anything, and that is what I fail my father."

Dr. Laurel's voice begins to echo in my mind. I'm hoping that by releasing this pent-up information, that it will free her. "Take your time; I know this is hard for you. How long had you been going into Jason's room?" I know the answer to that, yet it would help to confirm my suspicions.

Amala says, "Almost one year. Then the King give Jason a life guard to be with him forever. My father knows of this person, Khalifa, and he grabs me when I come out of Jason's room! He locks me somewhere. It smells bad. It was not a good place. He gives me food and blankets, some clothes. Khalifa comes and asks a question every day for a long time. I tell him nothing. I know nothing."

"How long were you kept there by your father?"

"It is many months. My belly begins to swell with a baby. I have to warn Jason to get out of the palace. I know something is wrong. Some of the guards talk very loud. My father plans terrible thing for him and other royals. If King knows I am with Jason in his room, or if they catch me there, I know I am dead. I have to warn him!"

Amala sobs uncontrollably as she covers her face with her hands. All I can do is try to comfort her, as she relives her last moments with Jason. "I'm so sorry you went through that, Amala. Please don't think that this is all your fault because it isn't. Things were in motion you had no control over."

As I try to console her, I'm wondering where Jam-ale might have been during this. Where were his army of guards? Is this when Fariq commandeered the palace?

"It is my fault," she hiccups the words out. "If I have not gone to Jason, I will be dead, and he will live. I do not know what happened after that. I never saw him again."

"How did you get out of the locked room?"

"That is a strange thing, Mama T. The day I see Jason for last time, a guard came to give me food and did not lock the door. They never do that before."

"That is odd. Who came to give you your food?"

"Same guard as always."

"So you went to Jason's room to warn him when you discovered the door was unlocked?"

"Yes. It took a long time to get there, so many guards, it was hard to sneak into his room. He was not there, so I hide in the bathroom. When he comes in, I call to him, and we talk. That is when I tell him of the baby."

Jason knew about the baby; do I have the timeline completely wrong? Has Adrian told me everything? "Please go on, Amala."

"He tells me not to go. He says we can go together. We told each we love. I get angry and tell him he must get out of the palace, there is a danger. I cannot stay. I tell him my father is Fariq and he is angry. He let go when I tell him baby will live if I go before they catch me. Khalifa is waiting in the hallway. He takes me to my father. My father is angry and he screams at me that I shame my family and I must die."

Amala cries again to remember the rough treatment inflicted upon her and her unborn child. She is understandably bitter about the injustice of her father's wrath and what she thought was undoubtedly the end of her and her unborn child's life.

"My father order guards to take me out to the desert. They leave me no water, no food, no shelter, no weapon. They laugh at me. One puts a gun to my head. I was terrified. They joke that animals will feast on my meaty flesh. They threw rocks at me when they left."

"I had no idea this happened to you." I'm appalled at this treatment, and it's no wonder she didn't want to re-experience this time. "Can you talk about what else happened?"

"I gather stones to throw at animals to kill for food and found a stick to dig in the sand. Not long after my father's men leave, other men came. I think my father send his men back. These are different men. They do not jump down from horse and grab me; they came close and slow and starts to talk with me. They said they are friends and will take me to safety. There is no other way to survive, so I go with them."

"That must have been awful for you, Amala."

"The people I live with take good care of us, and I help in the household. The woman tells me she lost her daughter and I am welcome as her own. BJ is born, and we think we will stay there. Mr. Levi and Papa T came one day, and you know rest of story."

"You don't know what happened to Jason, do you?"

"No, I could not ask. Before I left the palace for last time, no person, or guard, will look at me and no one talks to me. They will not let me see my family. No one came to visit before they take me to die in the desert. They will not let me see my mother. All I want to do is go away from there. At least, I talk to Jason, and he knows of danger from my…"

"Do you know what happened to Khalifa?" Adrian told me the day King Dimmy came for Jason's memorial that Jam-ale had him removed, but he did not elaborate.

Amala shakes her head. "After he took me to library, my father scream for him to leave. He is not there when my father shout at me that I will die in the desert. He is not part of men that take me out of the palace. I do not know what happens to him."

"Did you know any of the Royal Family, Sheyanna, maybe one of their daughters?"

"No. My family not allowed to enter without my father and he would never take any of us. I know of her and her daughters. We never speak. No one of my family is allowed into inner parts as they are. My sister and me sneak around in secret hallways."

"Did you know a person named Jam-ale?"

"My father talks loud about this man. He is First-In-command to the King. I do not know him. The man who takes me to safety is Maheer. He sometimes will come to ask questions, look at BJ, give him play toys, give us coins. He did not stay long. Wait – he asks if I know where Jason is. I tell him I do not know, he asks, if I am sure. Are these important things?"

"It's all part of the puzzle, Amala. We did know about your care. That must have been a terrible time for you. We never have to speak of this again unless you want to. I am sorry for your loss, sweetheart."

"I am happy to be here, Mama T! You and all the rest are my families now. BJ family, Jason family!"

"We are happy that you and BJ are here, too."

It seems that the will to live is as strong as the will to win.

Mother has a grayish hue to her skin. When I mention it, she dismisses it as needing time in the sun. Mother also seems a bit off her game and quickly changes the subject when I catch her looking confused. When she puts her hand to her chest, I know something's up and suggest she see her doctor.

Mother says not to take notice; she's okay. She has seen her doctor, and he prescribed a new medication, it's merely the side effect is all. When I ask her pointedly what kind of drug it is, she sidesteps my question. None of us are to worry, she is all right, and that's that!

I'm tempted to call her doctor myself!

It's a bright sunny Sunday morning, as Terre and I sit on the bench outside the kitchen waiting for the household to wake up. It's too early to get ready for church, and it's the perfect time to discuss what's on our minds.

"I love this time of the morning, don't you Ellen?"

"Yes, I do. Terre. Jason and I started this tradition when we first came here. My, that was a long time ago."

"I know you miss him, Ellie."

"Do you think Mother is ill? She doesn't look right to me. I know her doctor put her on new medication recently. She won't talk about it."

Terre tilts her head. "Now that you mention it, she's not in the kitchen helping with breakfast this morning, and she's usually the first one down to the kitchen. She hasn't been down at all, and that's not like her."

"With everything that goes on here, we all get wrapped up in ourselves, don't we? She's a little quieter than normal. Ever since we came back from Langley and Levi's funeral, she and I haven't talked much. I thought she was tired from chasing BJ around. I know I am."

"It might be more than that, Ellie. I've noticed she isn't eating all that much, either. Do you think she's depressed? Maybe I better go check on her."

"No, I think it's something altogether different. I'm no nurse, but that grey color to her skin might mean something might be wrong. I tried to ask her about it but she told me she was fine and needed a little more time in the sun. I think one of us should call her doctor."

Terre sips her coffee, then says, "I'm no nurse either, but what do you mean she looks grey?"

"She told me that she went to see her doctor. He gave her new medication. She wouldn't tell me what it was and I assumed she didn't want me to know what it was. And she has a grey color to her skin–I don't know like she isn't getting enough oxygen or something?"

When you think you have everything worked out, life has a way of intervening. Mona pushes the back door open and screams so loud it startles us. We are to come quickly, she doesn't say what; she merely motions with her hand, as tears run down her face.

"It's Francesca!" Glen opens the screen door wide so we can pass. "Upstairs, she's upstairs. I already called 911," he shouts. "GO!"

Terre and I take the back stairs moving as fast as we can and nearly mow Amala and BJ down as they stand in the hallway near their rooms. Mother is lying on her big bed; eyes closed, the side table light illuminating her pale face. Terre and I glance at each other; it doesn't look as if she's breathing. When her chest moves up and down slightly, we move closer.

"Mother, are you alright?"

"No, Ellie... I'm not. My arm hurts, and I can't seem to get out of bed today."

"That's okay, you don't have to get up if you don't want to," Terre says quietly. "There's nothing that needs your attention. You should rest today."

A siren grows louder, reminding me of Mr. Lassiter's Murder Mystery Party. "Help is on the way, Mother; they'll be here in a minute."

"I don't...want you girls to...fuss, do you...hear...me?" she whispers.

Sitting down on one side of the bed, Terre sits on the other as we each take one of her hands. She gently squeezes, but there is little strength in them. We can now hear footfalls on the front staircase that slowly stop near Mother's bedroom, followed by the familiar thump and whirl sound of the elevator as it comes to rest on the second floor.

A paramedic steps into the room and asks us to move aside, as he starts to question us about Mother's health. He's in blue scrubs, has a matter-of-fact demeanor, and his name tag identifies him as Roger. He takes her vitals as another young man, who must have come up in the elevator, pushes a wheelchair to the end of the bed. He puts a cube-like object on Mother's finger. He is in green scrubs; his name tag identifies him as Michael.

"What does this mean?" Terre asks in a concerned voice. "Are you taking her to the hospital?"

Roger doesn't answer as he pulls the stethoscope from around his neck, placing it on various parts of Mother's chest and neck. Michael takes the cube-like object off Mother's finger and steps back to fiddle with a unit that looks like a small radio. Its apparent Mother is in pain when her mouth clamps together, and she stiffens.

Michael quietly gives Roger numbers that start to appear on the screen of an apparatus that is about the size of my hand. It's attached to a disc on Mother's chest, which is held there by tiny wires and a sticky disk. They glance at each other, then Roger motions to Terre and me to go out in the hallway, presumably to talk.

By now, most of our household is standing in the upstairs hallway. The clock bongs eight times. I feel the universe tilt as the words come out of Roger's mouth in slow motion. "The cardiologist is standing by," he says calmly. "We need to get your mother to the hospital ASAP. Does she have a DNR in place? And we will need you to bring her will, too."

"You need a what?" I say in disbelief.

Terre has her hand on my shoulder.

Roger says blandly, "It's a DNR; do not resuscitate order. It's standard procedure, Ma'am, when this type of emergency comes up."

"We have those," Terre says. "They're in with Mother's papers. You put them away after the lawyer gave them to you, remember Ellie?"

"Why would you need all that?" I ask Roger.

"Because, they will ask for that stuff when you get to the hospital anyway, and they will want to see the paperwork if they have to do surgery. If you have one, you must find it, or we'll do everything within our power to keep your mother alive, even if she doesn't want us to. I'm sorry, Ma'am. That piece of paper binds us." Roger moves away to return to Mother's room.

Terre and I reach for each other, and for a split second, we are little girls again. When was the last time we felt like this? Was it the time we nearly lost her? Mother's appendix almost burst, and Daddy made the wise decision to drive her to the hospital.

As Michael takes Mother down in the tiny elevator with the IV bag swaying on the pole attached to the wheelchair, Roger gathers his equipment. He looks up at me and says, "Do you have the DNR?" When I don't answer, he says, "We'll meet you at the hospital."

Terre shakes my arm, "Ellen, go find the papers. I'm going with them in the ambulance. Come on, Ellen, snap out of it."

Adrian gently pushes me toward our room as he tries to explain what is happening. Curlie protests that she needs to come with us, but Adrian says that we don't know very much yet and to please stay home, as she needs to call Melanie. There is little any of them can do, except pray. He promises to give them updates when we know more.

With Mother's DNR papers and her will in my hand, Adrian drives us to the hospital. I'm numb and can't speak, so he reaches over to hold my hand. Later, we will talk about this as if we were in a slow-motion movie, as it felt so much like that. It reminded me of a distant memory–and the reasons why I don't like hospitals. It's what transpires there. I had three children at the hospital, and that was a pleasant experience; however, the two bad experiences that stick in my mind are when

Mother had her appendix removed, and when Daddy had his heart attack.

Daddy spent two weeks in intensive care before he died and it was the longest two weeks of my life. I cried every time I left his room because it was such a frightening sight. He was hooked up to monitors while tape and needles stuck in his arms and hands. There was a tube down his throat that prevented him from talking, so all he could do was blink. We communicated by writing yes and no questions.

We knew he was in pain. We also knew he was going to die. I don't want this to happen to Mother. Please God, don't let this happen to Mother! If you have to take her, please don't let her suffer!

Life is not like a bowl of cherries, and it most certainly is not a box of chocolates!

Terre, Adrian, and I are in a little room, down the hall from ICU waiting for someone to give us information. After about two hours, a doctor comes to talk with us, introducing himself as Mother's cardiologist.

The doctor knows we may not understand the medical terms and keeps it simple. He tells us that Mother has a form of heart disease that occurs when valves malfunction and won't allow blood to flow in the right direction. The unfortunate part is that it's been happening for a while. If Mother refuses the surgery to repair the valves, she will not live. Our job, he says, is to convince her that she needs this, now.

Terre and I open the double doors of the ICU and stand outside Mother's room to stare at her through the glass window. Our family is anxious to know how things are going here, so Adrian stays behind to call home and give them an update. Mother looks so fragile in that bed. The staff traded her nightgown for a soft floral hospital gown; her slight body is tucked neatly into white sheets. An IV tube is sticking out of one of her pale hands, as monitors tick around her.

Terre and I sit down on either side and reach for her hands. Mother smiles briefly and opens her eyes when she feels the bed move. How can we tell her that she must have surgery, or she will die?

"It will be okay, girls," she whispers. "I know what's going on. There will be no operation. I'm ready to go." She struggles for breath and weakly tries to squeeze our hands. "You have to let me go."

"What if we're not ready to do that?" Terre whispers as tears run down her face.

"Don't cry for me, Argentina. I will always be with you girls."

"Humor 'til the end. Did you ever meet Eva Peron, Mother?"

"Why would you ask her something like that," Terre snipes, then gives me her best stare-down.

"I did see her once. It was before she died. My adoptive family brought us to Buenos Aries to rally for her husband and show support. She seemed so far away; I didn't see much."

"Did you see the movie, *Evita*?"

"Really, Ellen, you're talking about movies at a time like this?" Terre seems to have run out of patience with me and the conversation.

"It's alright, girls," she says opening her eyes. "I'll haunt you… if you don't remember me, that is. I don't want you to mourn for me. I want you to have a party. Both of you are settled and have wonderful families. I know that you will be taken care of and I want you to miss me." Mother closes her eyes again.

"You want us to dance on your grave?" I question.

Terre has reached her limit. "Ellen, will you stop!"

"Lighten up Terre. Your sister knows what I mean. It's in the papers. You know the ones I mean, Ellie." Mother smiles at something and closes her eyes again.

A nurse comes into the room, fidgets with a dial on the wall, and I ask her to get Adrian. When he comes in, Mother opens her eyes again, smiles at him when he sits down gently behind me. He places his hand on her leg, as slow tears run down Terre's cheeks.

"You take good care of her, Adrian."

"I will Francesca," he whispers.

"They are both strong women," she says.

"That they are, Francesca."

It feels like an eternity before she speaks again. "You have both been through many of life's trials… and I am so very proud of you both."

"Try to conserve your energy, Mother," Terre says.

"You, Ellie, more than most, have been through--never give up on your dream. If you think Jason is out there, even if it's only a whisper, you must follow it, Ellie. You could be right."

Mother closes her eyes again. After several minutes, there is a loud sound and the nurse moves to the panel near the bed, and the noise stops. The doctor has stepped into the room, and we also realize that Mother has stopped breathing. Adrian stands up as a hand touches my shoulder. I turn toward him. It's the cardiologist, not Adrian. He says, "it's over."

OVER - what's over?

As the word slowly sinks in, a loud wail assails my ears as Terre starts to sob, then another as I become conscious, that it's coming from me.

Looking into the mirror, it makes me wonder how we ever made it through the last few days. "I hate this dress, Adrian. I've worn it three times now, and it's time to burn it!"

"Is that one of your family's superstitions?" Adrian asks.

"Yeah, it's like that thing Daddy used to say about three on a match."

Adrian is thoughtful. "I think it's a military thing when the soldiers were in a trench. The first soldier who lit a match passed it on to the second one, and then the third one was shot because the enemy saw the flame?"

"Yeah, it's something like that. I want to burn this blasted dress, so I don't have to wear it again! Mother bought it for me when you all had Jason's…"

Why am I not crying?

"Do you think there's something wrong with me? I didn't cry at the funeral home last night. Am I a bad daughter?"

Adrian comes to hug me. "No, Ellie. You're the best daughter ever, the best wife and mother, too. You will cry when you need to, hopefully not in church. I know how you hate that, especially when they start singing those hymns."

"Adrian, what I hate are funerals. It's the way the church smells of flowers, or it's the smell of the incense. Maybe it's the hymns."

In all honesty, Mother's funeral was merely elegant. She didn't want us to fuss, and she sure didn't want us to mourn her death, it wouldn't matter to her; she would be dead. What she wanted was for us to love her when she was alive…and I'm very sure we did that.

Were we so wrapped up in our issues that we didn't know she was ill until it was too late to insist she seek help? It was after she died that we discovered she had gone to see a doctor nearly a year ago. He told her then that she needed surgery. Mother was adamant there would be no such operation. It was her choice after all, not ours.

In my opinion, funerals are for the living, and they're for people to feel like the last thing they can do for the deceased person is to give them a proper sendoff to the *other side*. Mother had a grand farewell, as each of her eldest grandchildren stood up in the church to say what she meant to them.

It was especially heartwarming when Curlie and Melanie told how their Grandmother Francesca gave them little tidbits of advice that would turn into lengthy lectures, and we all chuckled over that—because she did that to most of us.

Their grandmother would preface these lectures by saying it was only her opinion and we could do with it what we wanted. We knew she was trying to help us through life's little tribulations. Amala's poignant statement made us all teary-eyed. She thanked us for welcoming her into our household and giving her joy, clothes, gifts, food, shelter, and people to love. Mother never hesitated to embrace her and BJ. She asked no questions, choosing to shower them with hugs and affection, and most importantly no criticism. It was pure love.

It's times like this that I miss Jason the most.

Our family has one less person at the dining room table. We will miss Mother the most as her humor, compassion, and honesty gave us the strength to carry on. She would often say, 'that life is for the living, so live it!'

I don't know why her words keep popping into my mind at odd times. I'll want to tell her something, then stop myself, only to remember she's no longer here. When will the empty feeling go away? Without Mother, it's difficult to do our subject discussions at dinner. We sit in gloomy silence, each lost in our thoughts until Adrian stands to announce a solution.

"From now on, we'll do what Francesca asked us to do, carry on. Tonight, we will pick a subject, no matter how ridiculous it is, and we'll pretend we are Francesca. Each of us will have to think and speak as she would. As usual, we'll take turns going back and forth across the table, until everyone has a turn."

No one objects, then again, no one says anything either.

"Oh, come on. Don't be so gloomy. I'll pick the first phrase. Stand up." Adrian says. "I don't mean to stand up literally; the subject for tonight will be to stand up, or any derivative of the word, or words, you know how this works."

"Can you give us an example," Terre asks. "Use it in a sentence, or something, so we get the meaning?"

"Who's gonna be Grandma Francesca first?" Curlie inquires.

"We'll go around the table; I'll start as it was my idea." Changing his voice to a higher pitch, Adrian sounds like Julia Childs when she had her cooking program on TV, which makes us all laugh. "I think all of you should be on a stage because you're a bunch of *standup* comedians."

I'm questioning Adrian's rationale at this. "I would have thought she'd say *stand up* for your rights."

"Okay then, why don't you go next, Ellie."

"I just did. I'll repeat it. I want all of you to *stand up* for your rights, tag you're it, Curlie."

Curlie doesn't seem amused. "I'm Tina now, Mother. I have to *stand up* and go to the bathroom."

"Is that really what Francesca would have said?" Adrian inquires. "Would you like to try it again?"

"No, I like that one. I'll stick with that, your turn Ginny." Curlie/Tina says, taking her plate to the roll-cart.

Ginny blinks. She is holding her finger in the air and says in a put-on voice, "I'm gonna *stand up* and walk out of this place."

Danny chortles, saying, "And you'll see me *standing up* in heaven."

Terre adds, "I'm *standing up* in heaven, right next to that funny old man *standing* next to God."

"Who is that funny old man *standing* next to me *standing up* next to God, right next to me?" Dennis adds with a laugh.

"I'm not following this line of thinking," Mack remarks. He's mentioned, on more than one occasion, that it's weird what we do at the end of most dinners. Lucky for Nathan, he's already left the table to take care of the horses.

Mack looks as if he's about to bolt for the door with Danny close behind him when he opens his mouth to say, "I'm *standing* in the midst of my wonderful family, and I want them to know that nothing can stack up against them."

Everyone in the dining room is silent, an odd occurrence given this crowd. During one of my sessions with Dr. Laurel, she said what my family does is a strange thing to do. I told her it often helps us to work out a difficult problem and we don't realize it.

"I can't top that!" Glen sighs loudly, reaching for his glass to take a gulp.

"You don't have to, Glen. I think my Mother, aka Grandma, aka, Great Grandma, aka Francesca, would be pleased to know she is so wonderfully remembered."

Terre says with a heavy sigh, "She did say she'd haunt us if we didn't remember her."

Shaking my head, I add, "She did say that, didn't she?"

"Is she one of our resident ghosts now, Mom?" Curlie/Tina inquires. "I wouldn't mind if she is. Why does this have to happen? Everyone I love goes away."

"I hope she is, sweetheart; I hope she does come back to sit with Mrs. Ashwood in the nursery. Honey, there are some things we have no control over. It's part of life, sweetheart."

Amala begins to cry. She had so little time with her new grandmother, and it must create memories long suppressed of a country so far removed from her now, that it's difficult for her to digest.

"Who wants dessert?" Mona startles us when she pushes a cart into the quiet dining room. "Why all the long faces? I thought we were gonna be cheerful for Francesca! Come on, *stand up* and dig in."

"Cheerful for Francesca. Of course, we'll be cheerful for Francesca." Terre says happily. "She would want us to get on with the business of living even though we don't want to. Even if our hearts are breaking, because people we love go away. We'll somehow find the strength to be cheerful."

I now miss Mother almost as much as I miss Jason and wonder when the pain of their loss will go away. Most evenings, the girls feed BJ earlier so that we can eat, without a two-and-a-half-year-old to deal with at the table. But tonight, Lindy chases BJ, as he runs into the dining room, with Rosie close behind.

"Zert fo Bee Jay," he announces loudly.

"Zert for everyone," Adrian declares. And we all laugh as Mother would have said those same words.

Adrian and I are in my office. He is sitting on the sofa reading the newspaper while I turn on the small TV. A blurb flashes about a weather documentary put together about the devastation that occurred nearly a year ago. It was when a rare super cyclone named Billy blew through the South Pacific destroying a chain of islands.

"When did you start becoming interested in the news again?" Adrian says absently. "I haven't seen you read the paper, or put the news on for a while."

Pausing to stare at him, replying, "There was too much bad news, and it made me depressed, so I stopped for a while."

"There's other news that isn't bad, Ellie. Look at the comics, or how about the section on clothes and stuff like that?"

"You know, this looks familiar." Turning back to the TV screen, the odd thing about this storm is that it reminds me of when Adrian and Levi went to Saudi to extract Amala and BJ. I'm almost afraid to mention this as Adrian still hasn't talked about that time.

This obscure set of islands is now getting as much, if not more, publicity than Hurricanes Andrew, Katrina, and Sandy combined. They are about to go down in the annals of history because they will need billions of dollars in relief funds.

Clicking the PAUSE button, saying, "Adrian, do you remember that terrible storm while you were gone?"

"Which storm are you referring to, the cyclone? If you recall, I tried to talk to you about it. You weren't interested in current events at the time." Adrian absently glances at the TV and then back to his paper. "It was a cyclone."

"I wonder how they're doing now."

Adrian puts the paper down to stare at me. "Don't say it, Ellie; I know what you're going to say."

"Do you Adrian? Maybe we should go over there and help them. We could use a vacation."

"I was afraid you were going to say that. Are you serious? Their hotels are all flooded or damaged beyond repair. It's almost as bad as that tsunami thing a few years back. You'd have to bring your own tent and sleeping bag with you, and supplies. NO, we're not going there. Pick somewhere where they serve us not where we have to serve them."

"Some Good Samaritan you are. If we can't go there, maybe we can send money to the relief fund?"

Adrian ignores me and says excitedly, "Ellie, take a look at this!" Pushing the sports section into my hands, saying, "*Peanut Brittle's* former owner back in Kentucky made the headlines. One of his horses won the big Championship."

"Let me see that." As I read the article, Adrian is mumbling something, and I ignore him to turn the page. "What were you saying?"

"Wouldn't you like it if Ashwood won a Championship?" he says, smiling sheepishly.

"Sure, can I finish the story first? It's almost time for *Peanut Brittle* to make a show of things. When we hinted that Reed should train as a driver, however, Dr. Jess put her foot down and won't let him past the owner's box."

I suddenly have an epiphany and start to reconstruct the bench seat on the race bike. Up until now, it has been in the barn, after it collapsed with me on it. Is it possible to change the bench to angle it in a different configuration and perhaps have it welded differently? If we change that awkward position I have to sit in, most of the pain in my derrière will go away. Maybe the doctor will authorize shots in that place again. Why didn't we think of this sooner?

"Adrian, you're a genius! That's an excellent suggestion. It could work."

"Thanks. How is it you know what I'm suggesting when I haven't said it out loud?"

"We need to step up our training with *Peanut,* or we need more horses to train. We'll need another driver."

"Yes, are you thinking what I'm thinking!" Adrian grins, "I mean, I didn't think you would even consider it. I'd be happy, no--I would be proud as a polar bear to wear Ashwood Stables colors," he says with a flourish.

I'm stunned. "Oh hell no, I wasn't thinking of you, I thought that I could try this again. You know, if we angle the seat down more, it might work."

Adrian is suddenly sullen. "I thought my idea was a good one, Ellie. You don't want me to do it. You're always shooting down my suggestions. At least Levi would hear me out. You don't even do that."

"I'm sorry, Adrian, I didn't mean to upset you. If I've hurt your feelings, I'm very sorry. Here, maybe we can both train. I'm sure Glen and Reed won't have a problem with that. What do you say?"

Adrian shakes his head. "No, Ellie, I know what I'm good at, and I know what you're good at, so you do it. I'll support you any way I can, besides they want me back at Langley next week for some training or seminar thing." He stands abruptly and walks out of my office.

"Wait a minute, don't go. Are you sure this doesn't bother you?"

Adrian turns around and then shakes his head. He's not been the same since Levi died. He's more reserved, less playful. I miss that about him, along with losing the other members of my family. Maybe life got in his way and took the wind out of his sails, as it once did to me. Laurel said we have to wait. Time does heal all wounds, most of them anyway.

When did Adrian become so sensitive? When did he stop clowning around with me?

BJ bounces into my office as an out of breath Amala follows him. She sits down on the sofa as BJ goes straight to his shelf. Objects that used to catch his attention are now higher up. We taught him not to touch anything that was not on his shelf. So far, he's demonstrated restraint, but still, it's only a matter of time before he figures out that he can climb up to touch other things.

"Do you need anything from town, Mama T?" Amala asks sweetly. "Miss Mona and I are going soon." She practices speaking English as often as she can, as it helps to erase her origins. Her diction sounds better all the time, and she understands the *I* and *me* grammar correctly now.

"Yes. I wrote some things down for you. Give me a minute to find it. It's here somewhere."

"Thank you for being so good to me and BJ. I do not know how we would have survived without your help. It would not have been good if we stayed in Saudi." Amala doesn't often talk about her past, and I wonder why she's bringing it up now. She must have something on her mind.

"Are you trying to ask me something, Amala?"

"Yes, I do not know how to say it. I am a young woman. You are going to be upset with me no matter how is said." Amala stares at her hands.

"Say it Amala. We have a saying; 'don't beat around the bush.'"

"This has nothing to do with a bush," Amala blinks. "I am a young woman. There is a young man at the shopping place…"

"Oh, I know where this is going. You want to know if I will approve of a relationship with someone. You want to know if I will allow you to date, is that it?"

"Yes," Amala says. She closes her eyes and drops her head, so I can't see her face.

"I would be the last one to hold you back from being happy, Amala. You do know that Jason may still be alive, don't you? It's only a matter of time before we find him."

Amala doesn't say anything for a moment. "You and Papa T are head of household. I will do what you ask of me."

"Let's clear something up, Amala. There is no head of a royal household here. That would be my mother." I pause to think about that. "Okay, I'm head of household now. I say that if you feel you want to do this, perhaps you should, but know this, you'll have to live with the fact you think Jason's not coming back."

"You think Jason is alive? What does *go for it* mean?"

I start to laugh at her innocence. "It means that you should try it."

"I will not try it if you think Jason will come back. I will wait for him."

"As long as you know that it's your decision and not mine, then we can move on to BJ's birthday party. How can he be three already?"

Amala smiles sweetly, wiping the tears from her face as BJ smiles when he hears his name mentioned.

"Me tree," he says and goes back to the trucks and cars he has going in two directions on the floor mat we purchased.

I think how proud Jason would be to see him, as would Ravi, and of course, Daddy.

Where are you, Jason? Please come home. I've had enough of this. We all have!

"If you don't design your own life plan,
Chances are you'll fall into someone else's plan.
And guess what they have planned for you? Not much."
~ Jim Rohn

Chapter Nine

Life Plans

I have renewed enthusiasm for training with the horses again, yet Adrian doesn't seem to care one way or the other. Reed and Glen say that training must start all over again, as too much time has elapsed. I'm so exhausted most evenings that trips to the spa are infrequent, as my large bathtub is as spacious and enjoyable as the one down by the pool.

Adrian did agree to go back with me into the wilds of Kentucky to search for the right horse. It wasn't as romantic as the last time, and I'm beginning to understand that his attitude may mean that he's restless. Does he regret staying with us here at Ashwood? Would he be happier doing what he loves back at Langley? Has my melancholia rubbed off on him? He flatly refuses to see Dr. Stevens, no matter how much I try to convince him that it will help.

Danny and Mack continue to practice with *Lester* and *Raindrop*, as these horses will never go on to do more than race at the local track. We have heard rumors that we need to put them into claiming races and there have been several inquiries about selling them. So far, their trainers have not decided about that.

Adrian goes about his day, checking emails, talking on his cellphone to those connections he still has with his friends at the CIA. The problem is, he's aloof, distant, and snipes at me for no reason. I've asked Dr. Laurel repeatedly how we can convince him to see her, or anyone; he's as stubborn as I was a while ago. She says to give him some space, reminding me that there is no time limit on grief.

Grumpy Old Glen is not at all happy with the idea of me racing again. I'm as close to a daughter (besides his daughters-in-law) that he has and he worries about stuff much like an old mother hen. He often mutters under his breath (loud enough for me to hear him) that Francesca would never allow her daughter to race again. It was dangerous before, and it's still dangerous now. He doesn't hesitate to say things were going along fine until I threw a monkey wrench into things.

Reed is taking this in stride, as long as he doesn't have to sit on the race bike, and we think that Dr. Jess has him a little brainwashed in this department. When Adrian and I returned with *Double the Trouble* and *The Desert Prince* (both two-year-olds), Reed's comment gave me pause. He said that I purchased *Prince* so I could make restitution by way of making him a winner, unlike the one across the pond.

Restitution my foot, if I wanted that, I would have renamed The Desert Prince--Ellen's Revenge!

When I first saw *Prince*, he picked up his head and perked his ears and stared at me. I approached slowly to offer him a carrot, and he shook his head *no,* then he merely trotted away. That's what made me want him at Ashwood. A stubborn horse could be an asset or a liability. Maybe the right name for him is *Ellen's Revenge!*

Adrian wanted to know what my motive was for buying this horse. Did I sniff at him when he wasn't looking? The owner laughed, then asked if we were going to leave him out in the pasture, to add horses to our farm, as that one was too wild and undisciplined for racing. It made me chuckle, as I recalled that I'd been there and done that a few times. We decided not to linger to explain. After all, no one can follow my system of winning.

Our racing teams decided to allow Danny and Mack to take turns training with *Double* and *Peanut*, as they have similar movements and personalities. We never know how long it will take to train a horse, though having seasoned ones out on the practice track helps, as it gives us a sense of what a full track would be like when we race. Our goal is to indoctrinate *Double* and *Prince* into Billingsworth Racetrack. That is, when and if the teams agree.

In the meantime, Danny and Mack will also train with *Lester* and *Raindrop,* while I am the sole driver to train with *Prince.* When *Prince* first caught my eye, there was something magical about him. The very first time Reed hooked up the jog cart, and I sat on the new modified bench, *Prince* needed no encouragement to move into the favorite's position.

He did a quick look back at me, and it unnerved me, but now it assures me that we're a team and he considers me a pal. It still makes me laugh that we purchased a horse named *The Desert Prince*. As much as I'd like to, I will not change his name to Prince Dimmy. Was it the way he looked at me and shook his head NO? Adrian thinks I'm bonkers. I think it's funny that we have a prince in the family and he's a real horse!

Now if he'll do this at the racetrack, we'll be in business.

The day has come to test my theory about *Prince*. We're out on the practice track and nearly halfway around it when Glen's voice (in my headset) says to go slow, he wants to try something. Mack opens the gate to let *Lester* and *Raindrop* in without drivers, or jog carts. It becomes evident that Glen and Reed have conspired to test *Prince*. Up until this point, we've been out here alone and without distraction.

Nathan leads our other new horse *Double* from the barn and waits beside Danny, who has *Buttercup* on a lead rope. *Double* nudges Danny's back in a playful gesture. "Hey, watch it!" Danny turns to see Nathan laugh, and then leans down to pet Rosie's head.

"Okay, stop that right now," Reed interjects, when he sees the commotion.

Glen's voice says, "Hey, Missy, are ya day-dreamin? Watch your flank, *Lester's* comin up behind ya."

"Oh please, they don't have drivers or carts attached. It's easy for them to pass us."

Mack's voice says in my headset, "Is that a challenge, Miss Ellen?" He's coming out of the barn with *Peanut*.

"What do you think, Mr. Mack?" Glen's voice crackles before I can say anything. "We're tryin somethin. Let *Buttercup* in, and then *Peanut* in after that. Now let *Double* out."

I'm not following their logic today. "Are you kidding? How are you going to get them to the fence when we're done practicing? I thought Rosie didn't round them up anymore."

"Not ta worry, that's what we got a round-up dog for, and b'sides, when they get hungry enough, they'll be standin at the gate waitin ta get let out," Glen bellows in my ear. Now keep goin around the track till *Prince* gets tired."

Reed adds, "Miss Ellen, keep your head up, arms close to your sides, eyes left and right. Now try not to look so stiff."

"I keep forgetting the small stuff guys."

"It'll come back to you. It's like riding a bicycle. Once you know how to do that, it comes back," Reed replies.

"Okay, but I never learned how to ride a bicycle." Laughter rings in my ear. "I was busy with horses, you know. I didn't do standard childhood things."

It must be funny to everyone, as there is more laughter. "We know, Miss Ellen, we know."

After our practice is over, Danny opens the gate to let us out as a blur of fur runs past us. It's not like Rosie to ignore me. And what has Glen been feeding her, she looks very spry. Nathan is on hand to unhook the practice cart as I jump off, clicking the lead rope to *Prince's* halter. Rosie is waiting near the back door.

"That's your surprise, Miss Ellen," Mack says laughing.

Glen's beaming face says it all. "We're all gettin on, and Rosie's got her snout busy watchin little BJ, so we thought we'd surprise ya and that there is Gus. He's a border collie like Rosie, so we're trainin him to do her job. Give her a rest so's she can watch BJ."

"That was a good call on your part. Rosie must be tired of running after that child."

"Darn tootin young lady."

Sure enough, as Glen predicted, once the horses go around a few more times, they stop to munch at grass sticking through the fence. Eventually, they gravitate to the gate, where Gus is waiting.

Mother wanted us to be positive and carry on with our lives. Even though her loss leaves a huge gap, life slowly returns to our regular training which gives me a new direction and purpose.

Her words often come to me when I start to think of her.

"The will to win is strong in human nature, and the yearning to succeed is even stronger." She also said to follow my dreams, and I distinctly remember telling this to Jason, but can't recall when I told it to Melanie. Was it during her graduation from high school, or was it when she went away to college?

Adrian saunters into my office and flops down on the sofa, then gets up to look out the window. "How did training go today? Did *Prince* perform the way you thought he would?"

"I'm going to be a little sore tomorrow, but it went okay. I thought you would come to watch us, Adrian."

"Naw, you don't need me there. I had a call from Headquarters today," Adrian says fiddling with the shade pull.

"And they what, want you to go to D.C.? They want you to go to Rome, Istanbul maybe?"

Adrian turns to face me. "Not to Rome, Istanbul, or any place exotic. They do want me to help with some training back at their facility. What do you think? Should I do it?"

"You don't look very enthusiastic about it. Is it something you want to do? Did you tell them no?"

"No, I told them yes. Now I'm having second thoughts about it. I don't know if I should leave Ashwood, or maybe, I should go. Is there something I should be doing here? Maybe it's not a good time to be away."

"When did the strong CIA man I married turn into a person who can't make up his mind? The old Adrian would have jumped at the chance. He would have run for his car the minute that call came in."

"The old Adrian, as you call him, has had his fill of…" He stops mid-sentence, turning toward the window again, and becomes unusually quiet. "I don't want to talk about that."

"I was in your shoes not too long ago. I think you're ready to talk to Dr. Stevens, Adrian. You insisted I talk with her and I felt better after I did. Won't you give it a try?"

"And how much have you benefited from your sessions with her, huh, Ellen? Do you feel that you can move on with your life now that you have come to terms with Jason's death?"

"I never said I came to terms with Jason's death. I did say that I feel better when I share things with Dr. Stevens. I never said I don't think he's alive, ever."

"Even though you know in your heart that he's dead you expect me to do the same. You want me to see Dr. Stevens so she can help me. I can never undo what I've seen. I also can never forgive what happened to Levi and the circumstances that brought us to that!"

"What I know in my heart is that Jason might still be alive. No one will ever take that away from me, not you, not Dr. Stevens, NO ONE! You blame yourself, don't you, about Levi? Isn't that why you haven't let this go yet? Adrian, after what we've been through, out of all the people in the world, I, of all people, understand what you're going through now. I know what it's like to lose people you love! I also understand that you loved Levi. There was an unfortunate accident that you could not prevent. It happened. You need to deal with it and let it go."

"Really? That's coming out of your mouth? Ellen, I do understand what it's like to lose people you love; you loved Jason. There was an unfortunate accident that you could not prevent. It happened. You need to deal with it and let it go."

Sucking in a breath, I reply, "Adrian, that's an awful thing to say. Are you trying to make me feel bad?"

"I'm giving you a little of your own medicine, that's all. You don't have a certificate to psychoanalyze me. You're regurgitating what Dr. Stevens has been filling your head with for the last few years."

"Where is this coming from, Adrian? You're the one who told me to go to her in the first place. If you think you can manipulate me into thinking that Jason is dead, you are very much mistaken! You should know by now that I'm not easily swayed. And I'm certainly not trying to psychoanalyze you. Why are you saying hurtful things? I also lost my mother. That's three people that have gone out of my life, in a short amount of time."

"I LOST THEM TOO, YOU KNOW!" Adrian shouts.

Adrian walks out in a huff. Minutes later, the back screen door squeaks, and then slams shut. We do not fight, we banter back and forth, but we do not ordinarily have shouting matches. His outburst stuns me; it is so not like him. As Adrian left the library, BJ and Amala were coming down the front staircase. BJ runs straight to me.

"Is Papa T okay?" Amala asks.

"We're having a little disagreement, that's all."

As I bend to pick BJ up, he puts his little arms around my neck, and I kiss him until he starts to protest and pull away. We have become friends at last.

Now that Amala is one of us, BJ can no longer hide behind her skirt, as we asked her to dress differently. The jeans and top look great, as does her long dark hair that is braided down her back.

"We are going for a walk, Mama T. I have finished in the kitchen now. Would you care to join us?" Amala says in perfect English.

"Yes, I would like that very much. Come on BJ, let's go look at the horses."

"Bee Jay lo hors," he shouts. Amala corrects him. He giggles and runs toward the kitchen when he squirms out of my grasp.

"A package came for you and Aunt Terre," Amala says. "Nancy put it on the counter in the kitchen. We will meet you at the back door."

Out of curiosity, I pick up the package. To my surprise, the label is in Mother's handwriting, addressed to Terre and me. Could it be something Mother ordered before she died? Good thing I found it first or Terre would have torn into it as soon as she saw it. It's about the size of two shoe boxes, and I'm mentally making notes about what might be inside it. Why would this mysterious box come to our house now? Maybe it isn't even from Mother.

BJ calls from the mudroom, and I absently put the package back down on the counter to deal with later, thinking that Terre has as much right to tear into it as I do. Maybe it will give her a good laugh. "Want to see the horses, BJ?"

"Bee Jay, lo hors!" He jerks his body as if he's riding one and Amala and I laugh at the way he does this.

"Don't you want to open the box before we go outside? We can wait," Amala asks.

My thoughts go back to the box. What is in this mystery box? "No. It can wait."

At dinner that night, most of our regular companions are out doing other things, and there are few at the table. Adrian wasn't hungry, Terre and Dennis went to a banking function, and Ginny and Lindy ate leftovers in the kitchen because the twins have gone back to school to plan for some event that's happening next week. Reed and Dr. Jessica are out on a rare dinner date while Curlie babysits their children at the Carriage House.

We don't seem to have a subject to discuss tonight.

"You're lookin good out there on the track, Missy," Glen says, breaking the silence. "Missy, you still here?" There's a loud clunk as Glen's fork hits his plate. Mona walks in carrying a bowl and quietly sits down next to him.

"Why did ya do that? Maybe she don't wanna talk to ya, ever think a that?" Mona says under her breath. "Here I made this for ya." Mona starts to scoop pudding into a little cup then passes it to Glen's waiting hands. "Want some, Miss Ellen? It's your Mother's favorite, tapioca puddin, made it special taday."

"I'm sorry, Mona. Did you make pudding? Yes, I'll have a little, thanks."

Glen poises with his spoon in the air. "Somethin botherin you, Missy? Ya wanna talk about it?"

"No, everything is fine. Why do you ask?"

"B'cause ole Adrian never misses his dinner unless he's not home. I saw him go inta the pool house. You two have a fight or somethin?"

"No, a little misunderstanding. He'll be okay in a day, or two. At least I hope he will. Can we practice again tomorrow, Glen? I'm a little rusty and need some extra practice time."

"Sure, whatever ya want. You're not one ta say you'll do somethin and then pull back, so I guess you're gonna want as much time out on that track as possible. Cleared my schedule for ya, no problem."

"I have a good feeling about *The Desert Prince*, Glen. I think this is the one who will take us all the way to the…"

"Don't say it, Missy. Then you'll jinx it. I know what you're sayin, don't say it, okay?"

That was easy. Adrian didn't take my racing aspirations that well. Why is Glen okay with this? Does he finally realize how serious I am about winning?

Are the planets finally aligning? Will our difficulties melt away so we can go on with our planned life?

Wouldn't it be nice if parents received a set of instructions with each child when they were born? That way, they would know how to steer them in the right direction and avoid all kinds of complications and heartache. Or, what if we had a map to guide us through that process, we'd know if we were making mistakes ahead of time. In fact, we could avoid the pitfalls of making bad decisions altogether!

Mother had a plan for Terre and me from the moment we were born. In the French she seldom spoke, called strict vérité, (which translates into English as meaning plain truth) we were to have three elements present throughout our lifetime: one, we are healthy, two, we are well-adjusted, and three, we are self-sufficient.

They didn't have to happen all at the same time. Mother wanted us to have them fit somewhere in our lives. She also made it her mission to guide us to decisions when she thought we were deviating from her plan that also included, college, marriage, and, of course, grandchildren.

She never specified how long it would take us to reach each goal. She never said no when I tried to ride horses, and she didn't bat an eye when I wanted to study equine studies or interior design. The only negative comment received was that under no circumstances could I train to be a jockey, other than that, she always said to follow my dreams. Terre will agree that she said those things to her too.

There isn't a day that goes by that I don't think of Mother, Daddy, and Jason.

We are together as a family, gathered on a rare Sunday where Reed and Dr. Jessica are with us for dinner. We hope to regain our sense of humor and camaraderie around the dinner table. We don't launch into ridiculous topics of conversations much anymore, as it doesn't seem suitable with so many people missing; however, that's all the more reason to get together.

Tonight, we'll discuss life plans and try to guess what's in the mystery box that Mother addressed to Terre and me. We managed to avoid it for weeks. Nancy moved it to the pantry when I didn't take it off the counter. Mona found it and moved it to the buffet in the Morning Room. Adrian saw it and placed it on the long library table. And although it's difficult for any of us to believe, Terre mentioned she saw it in the mudroom and took it to the table in the front hallway. It somehow made its way into my office, although no one owned up to moving it there.

As a child, Terre would unwrap the Christmas presents that were under the tree, taking a peek inside them, and then taunt me with the knowledge of their contents for days on end. Mother's package is too well-wrapped for her to do this without calling attention to the deed.

Although she's demonstrated restraint, I know she's anxious to know what's in the package.

"Terre, do you want to start us off?"

My sister moves to the sideboard, picking up small notepads and pencils to pass out to each of us. She explains it's not a test but a place to write our thoughts.

"You all know that Ellie and I received this mysterious box addressed to us by our Mother. We have speculated what might be in it, but then we also thought we'd save it for a time when we're all together. That way, you can share what we find. It might even contain something for one of you."

"Maybe Grandma put something embarrassing in it," Danny remarks.

"And maybe it's something special," Terre says. "Aren't you the least bit curious?"

"Grandma sent the box to you, Mom. She already gave me Grandpa's ring," Danny adds.

"Really, when did she do that?" Terre wants to know.

Nathan starts to push himself away from the table. "Miss Ellen, I think I best be gettin on back to the barn now. Thanks for dinner. It was good, as usual. I don't need dessert tonight, please excuse me."

Motioning for him to sit down, saying, "Why don't you stay, Nathan. Whether you like it or not, you are part of this family. No one gets out of this tonight. You might be pleasantly surprised to find out something not only about yourself, maybe learn a little something about us, too."

Nathan stays where he is, but doesn't pull himself back to the table, glancing at Mack and Danny as they sink down into their chairs, looking a bit glum.

"Aren't any of you the least bit curious?" I pick up the mystery box on the buffet table, and shake it, then put it on the table within arm's reach. "Don't look like I've stuck you all with a branding iron. We're going to go around the table, as we used to. The exception is that we're going to guess what's in the mystery box Francesca sent us while telling us what your life plan is."

It becomes apparent that the crowd is skeptical. Terre starts to explain. "Take a few minutes to think about your life. Numbering one to ten, list your goals on one side of the paper, and on the other yes, or no, whether you achieved it or not."

"If you don't feel comfortable saying it out loud, then say pass, right Terre?"

"Yes. Okay, let's give everyone a few minutes to compose their list," Terre says, reaching for a spoon to dig into her fruit parfait.

As I glance around the table, it looks as if this is having an unusual effect on everyone as they write things down on their pads. It will be interesting to hear what they've come up with for this challenge.

After about ten minutes, Terre says, "Ellie, why don't you start since this was your idea."

"Sure. First of all, our Mother was a unique person. She was born in France, as you know, and left there to live in Argentina. She came with an anomalous sense of humor, along with an idea of how Terre and I should conduct our lives, from adolescence to adulthood."

"It never occurred to either of us that we should question her about it, it seemed normal to us," Terre says quietly.

"That's right. We don't know exactly when your Grandmother acquired this set of rules. I can't believe I'm saying this, but it's much like Uncle Dimmy's royal household rules, except hers centered on our life plans."

"I get it, it's like your bucket list," Danny says, nodding his head.

Amala seems confused. "I do not know this word, Mama T. What is buck it list?"

"Danny is correct. A bucket list is a list of things you want to accomplish in your life before you kick-the-bucket. In your case, Amala, what do you want to do on your journey through life? We already know that you wanted to learn a new language; you did that. Write down what you always wanted to do and if you got to do that, it's that simple."

Amala shakes her head to acknowledge her understanding and then starts to write as BJ, Mandy, and Little Reed (Dr. Jess & Reed's children), play quietly on the floor near us.

Terre adds, "We have a few rules before we start. We are to allow each person their right to say what they feel, without criticism or sarcasm. Then guess what's in the mystery box. There will be no gesturing, sniggering, and most certainly no complaints. Ellie, do you want to start?"

"Yes, I would. If you don't feel at all comfortable saying any part of your list out loud, keep it to yourself, and we'll move on. Are you ready? My plan started when I was eight years old. I knew where I was going. I have either done or nearly done them and am working on a few that I can say yes to in the future."

"What's on your list, Mom?" Tina asks.

"My dream was to become a jockey, then it changed to an equestrian, attend college, own an interior design business, get married, have at least three children, own a horse farm, and do lots of traveling."

Goal	Yes or No
1. Be a jockey	No
2. Be an equestrian	mostly
3. Go to college	Yes
4. Interior design business	Yes
5. Get married	Yes
6. Have children	Yes
7. Own a horse farm	Yes
8. Travel/spend a month in Paris	No
9. Win the championship	?
10. Find Jason	?

"You really had a horse farm on your list?" Tina asks. "What do you think is in the box, Mom?"

"Yes, your father and I talked about it before our lives got so busy. I think Grandma put a lot of thought into this mystery box. I'll bet she's sending us to Paris."

Adrian looks surprised. Through the years, although we never mentioned it, I've secretly wanted to go to Paris, to experience all those wonderful things we planned and didn't get to do.

Tina shares her list, although it's mostly about clothes and material things. "I want to go to college to study art, not music. I've met half of my goals, one being the owner of a baby grand piano thanks to Grandma. I want a fancy car, and I think Grandma left you and Aunt Terre your baby shoes--and maybe some money."

As twins, Ginny and Lindy have always wanted to act. They want to use their talents for any show available at school productions. Terre and Dennis agreed they could join our local theater guild. It's no surprise when they announce that they've auditioned and they have accepted parts of Tweedle Dee and Tweedle Dum in the next production of *Alice and the Looking Glass*.

"That's manners!" they say together, laughing. "We agree with Tina, but we think that Grandma gave you each something of value that only you can appreciate," Lindy offers. "We don't think there's anything in that box for us. She already gave us stuff to put away."

Terre motions to Nathan, as he seems eager to join in tonight. "I don't have a big list," Nathan says. "At one time, I wanted to be a rodeo clown. But I always wanted to belong to a big family, and I sure do have that! I want to thank Reed for asking me to come here in the first place. I think your Mama gave you jewelry, maybe something special."

"I'll drink to that," Dennis says, taking a sip from his glass. "My turn. I had a bucket list, and it was quickly thrown out the window when I met Miss Terre here. Once she introduced me to her family, Francesca helped me rearrange my priorities to include her daughter. I've achieved most of my goals except one. Is anyone up to go skydiving with me?"

We all react to this and then break into laughter. It's good to hear it again around our large table, we've been too serious lately.

Adrian comically puts his hand up to signal he wants to say something. "How many times do you plan on jumping, Dennis? I'd like to go with you."

"Great, let's make a plan. I think Francesca put a wishbone in the box."

Danny shakes his head. "A wishbone, really Dad? What would they do with that?"

"No criticizing, young man," Terre says to her son. "Go ahead, Danny. It's your turn."

"Sorry, my list is not very long. I wanted to become a famous racecar driver, and I changed to racing horses instead. I'd like to travel, maybe get married, and have children someday. I think Grandma put a special handkerchief in the box, one for each of you. She always had one as I remember, stuffed into her sweater or apron. She'd retrieve it when she saw us sniff."

"Yeah, she did that to us, too," Terre points her finger at Mack. "You're up next."

"I always wanted to make my Mom proud of me. From the eighth grade on, I wanted to do something with horses, either train them, or ride them, not breed them. I think my bucket list is short because that's the only thing on it and I'm doing it."

"Meredith would be very proud of you, if she were here, Mack."

"Thanks, Miss Ellen, I think Miss Francesca left you two a book of recipes. I know you have one already, but she left you the ones she wanted to experiment on, and then didn't for whatever reason."

Dr. Jessica was writing as others were talking and raises her head, smiling as we hold our breaths. "My turn? My list is extensive, as some of you might guess. My bucket list never included a husband and children. It changed the day I met Reed. I knew exactly where and what I wanted to do with my life by the time I was eighteen. My parents stood by my decisions and agreed with all except for one. I believe that Francesca would want you each to have a lock of your hair. That's what I think is in the box, correctly and tastefully displayed and engraved with each of your names."

"What was the one thing your parents didn't let you do, Jess?" Reed inquires.

"I'll tell you later, dear. Not in front of everyone," Dr. Jess says sweetly. "Your turn, sweetheart."

Reed absently scratches his head. "Okay, I had a long list and had to cut out lots of stuff. Some I tried, they either didn't work, or they didn't matter at the time. I wanted to go out west and become a rodeo star after I got my Olympic medal. A broken leg side railed me, but I've always wanted kids, and I got them. I've always wanted a sole-mate, and I got that too." With adoring affection, he smiles at his wife. "The only thing I have not done is…" Reed turns to whisper in Dr. Jess's ear. She puts her hand up to her mouth to stifle a laugh.

"Hey, that's not fair. Aren't you going to tell us?" Mack inquires.

"No, son, we're gonna keep that between us. I think that Francesca put a challenge in that box. I think it's something you have to do to win something."

Adrian looks thoughtful. "You mean a quest, Reed?"

"Yeah, she's gonna send you two on a quest. Adrian, it's your turn."

Adrian looks down at his list. "My bucket list consisted of wanting to help people, like comic book heroes and live an exciting life and travel the world. I found the CIA early and pretty much have everything I've ever wanted. I think Francesca left you two a poem, correctly and tastefully displayed and engraved with each of your names."

"You're funny, Adrian," Dr. Jess says in his direction.

Looking down the table, I see the twinkle in an old man's eyes. "Glen, what's on your list that you want to share with us?"

"Missy, I've been thinkin, and there might be a few things I never did and planned ta do, but they don't seem so important when you're livin a good life, after livin a bad one. I've told ya more than once our little story about tryin ta survive here. Without ya, Mona and me would have starved ta death. and we want ta say thanks for that. I've always wanted ta take care of horses, find a good woman ta live out my days. We raised some good kids who gave us some grandchildren, and we get ta see 'em sometimes. I think Miss Francesca left ya girls her wedding rings."

"I never thought of that one," Terre says, "Mona, how about you?"

"I never had a list. When ya said ta write 'em down, they came tumblin out. I've always wanted ta be a real chef in a restaurant, or pastry chef, get married and have children. I love ta bake and make up new recipes. Francesca spent hours makin lists, and we'd have the best time tryin ta find the ingredients and experimentin with food. I'm gonna say that she sent ya ingredients. But not any ingredients, hard ta find ones."

"That leaves you, Terre."

"I used to think that the goals Mother set for us were unrealistic. Somehow, her vision had a purpose. My dream was to become a teacher, get married, have children, then maybe write a book or two, the usual. I've done more than half of them, and a few that I hadn't planned on, but overall, Mother made sure we met our goals, one way, or another. She'd give little hints about the kids, maybe something I might do for Dennis. She did that to you, too, Ellen. I think we're all right; Mother would have given us every one of the things you each mentioned. I don't think we should open the box at all. I think we should leave it as a mystery and put it in the attic."

I know how curious my sister is; she isn't fooling me. "You found a way to open the box, didn't you? You already know what's in it and you're either very clever or very devious sister dear."

"I don't know what you're talking about, Ellen. I would never do such a thing," Terre says a little miffed.

"Is that your final answer? I say we're going to open it now."

I stand up to reach for the box but Adrian gets to it first. He begins to run around the table as Dennis stands up to bump it out of his hands and it tumbles into Dr. Jess's lap. She picks it up, puts it to her ear, shakes it a little, and then declares the contents now rattles.

Then she tosses it to a surprised Reed who throws it quickly to Danny, who catches it with both hands. He looks around as Terre pushes her chair away from the table to move toward him as he tosses it to Tina.

Tina tosses the box across the table to Ginny, and she and Lindy toss it between each other, until Terre says to **STOP,** as Ginny throws it across to Mack. Mack sees the tortured look on my sister's face and hands it gently to Nathan. Nathan knows better than to sail it across the table again and stands up to put the box in front of me.

"Miss Ellen, I have to go out to the barn now, can I please be excused from this madness?" Nathan says soberly.

At this point, Terre comes to stand next to me, making no further attempt to take the box. "I did not open it. If it's tickets to France, you should know about it before they expire."

"How about if we open it together!"

Terre turns to her husband. "Wait a minute, Dennis do you know anything about this?"

"Francesca made me swear not to tell you. She left that box with me. She made me promise to send it within a given time frame after her death. There's a note inside to explain the contents."

"Read the note, Mom," Tina says.

> *My Dearest Ellen and Terre,*
>
> *Your father and I have only wanted what was best for you. You have surpassed our wildest goals, and you should know how very proud we are of both of you. And I am equally as proud of each of my grandchildren as well, including Amala and BJ.*
>
> *I pondered a long time about what I wanted to give each of you. These are my treasures, some of them you know about, and others you have never seen. Share them between you. It's a time capsule of some sorts. The snow globe – was given to me by your father when I became pregnant with you Ellen, a Venetian vase – given to me by your father when I became pregnant with you Terre.*
>
> *A locket for each of you, and photos of my birth parents. My wedding rings – which you could make two pieces of jewelry to share the stones. The shoes I wore when I went to Argentina. Locks of hair and small photos of when you each had your first haircuts. And the Serenity Prayer – laminated on two bookmarks; one for each of you.*
>
> *Always remember that I love all of you forever.*
>
> *Mother, AKA Grandma Francesca*

Terre slits the top of the mystery box as I hold it. When she folds back the flaps, she sets each wrapped item down in front of me and stands back. Her hand immediately goes to her mouth, where she lets out a small cry as I unwrap each piece.

Tears are next when she touches an old snow globe that Mother purchased in Switzerland, the water is a sickly yellow now, despite that, the snow still moves within it. Next, Terre lifts a Venetian vase to admire it.

"Where did that come from?" Ginny asks. "I don't remember seeing that before."

Terre starts to laugh. "I remember some of this stuff. I didn't know she still had this. I thought it all vanished with those two dimwits," she whispers.

"Neither did I. Mother left us things we would want and cherish. They are things that remind us of who we are and where we came from, Terre. Did we reach our goals? I think what Mother was trying to convey is that what matters most is that we have goals. When we reach a goal, we succeed in life. That's what she meant by having life goals. We need to try at least, don't we?"

"Do the lockets open, Mom?" Tina asks.

"I think so."

A delicate locket with a tiny clasp opens to two miniature photos. On one side is a picture of me sitting on *Trinidad*, the other is of my children. Terre opens her locket to a photo of her wedding to Dennis on one side, her children on the other. She reaches to pick up a small double frame with pictures we have never seen.

"Let's see who they are." When we pull out the photos and turn them over, we are startled to discover that they are Mother's parents. "We resemble her Mother, Terre. Don't you think? Grandmother Monique was beautiful."

Tina jumps up to take the little frame out of my hand to show the others. "You do!" she exclaims.

Lindy adds, "I've never seen these pictures before either! Wow, that makes them our great-grandparents."

"Francesca wanted all of us to have a goal. She wanted us to make the most of our lives. As we went around the table, it was clear that either most of us have achieved them, or we still have to try to reach them. She would never allow us to drop out of a club or stop what we begged her to let us do, without giving it our all. That's what this all means. It isn't a box full of mystery; it's a box full of memories."

For several moments, no one moves until Terre says, "You can all go now, thanks for participating."

Adrian hangs back to help me clear the rest of the stuff off the table, and then leans in to whisper something in my ear. "Are you disappointed that tickets to Paris weren't in the box? We could still do that, you know."

"I don't feel bad about that. I know we could plan to go there at any time. It's no longer a priority."

"You wrote down more than you shared, Ellie. What were the other items on your list?"

"I'll tell you if you promise not to laugh, or get angry."

Adrian's expression changes, "I promise."

"I wrote that I'd like to win the Championship."

Adrian sits down at the table. "Are you thinking of doing that this year? What horse are you thinking of doing it with, *Prince*? Do you think he'll be ready?"

"I think *Prince* might be a long shot. If the training team decides he's ready, it'll take extra work. It may not even be this season, but it could be."

Adrian shakes his head. "Isn't that a little out of your league? Wouldn't *Peanut* be a better choice with one of the boys doing the driving?"

"Since when have you started to question me about horse stuff? I want to win it all, and I don't think *Peanut* can do it for us."

Adrian seems skeptical, reaching for the salt and pepper shakers, he turns to place them on the sideboard. "I thought you said you have it all."

"No silly, there are always one or two goals that I still want to achieve. Isn't there still something on your list that you want to do?"

"What's the other one?" he asks.

"I don't know if I should share that one with you. Don't bite my head off but you haven't been very receptive to things lately."

"Okay, don't share it. I've told you everything. If you want to keep it a secret, keep it a secret. I'll see you later."

"You promised not to get mad or angry. That's an odd response, Adrian. What do you mean you'll see me later?"

"I'm going for a walk."

"Wait and I'll go with you."

"No. I prefer to be alone."

Something is bothering Adrian, and he hasn't opened up to me about it. He's sharp-tongued where once he was smooth talking and funny. He was always in tune with me, then again, since Mother and Levi are no longer with us, he's become uncharacteristically moody, aloof, and distant. Dr. Laurel says to give him some space, but really, how much more space does he need?

As I look at my list again, I planned to own a stable and ride for as long as I wanted. The plan took a detour when I went to college, and then it changed again when I met Ravi. He shared my goals which by then were a distant dream. As life got in the way; children came, and then we needed a bigger house, a new car, braces for the children, a new dining room table, and the other items on my list didn't materialize.

Despite the best laid plans, plans change. You can try to map out your life, but it's the decisions and choices you make along the way that ultimately make things change.

Unclasping the necklace Adrian gave me the first time we met, I slip the locket through the chain, and put it back around my neck. They are now my new treasures and will stay close to my heart.

On one of Terre's rare Saturdays off, we are sitting outside to welcome a new day. "That was a good idea putting that shadowbox together with Mother's precious items, Ellie."

"Now everyone can see and enjoy them. I still can't get over the photos of our grandparents. Wonder where she had them hidden all these years?"

"I have no idea. Speaking of Mother, we need to tackle her room at some point, you know," Terre sighs heavily. "Maybe if we go up there and do it today, it won't take long." What she doesn't say is that I should do this to Jason's room. Danny might be feeling a little cramped in there.

"We could redecorate it, so it's more to Amala's liking."

"Why don't we get it over with? I'll see if she's done in the kitchen. She might want to help us," Terre says.

"Okay, I'll get some boxes and meet you up there."

We have put this off for months. There isn't much to do, as Mother had given each of her grandchildren something way before we knew about her heart, a figurine here, a vase or picture frame there until she scaled back her possessions and the furniture that moved here with her when she came to Virginia.

Maybe it's time to move Jason's items up to the attic where his box of swords, the blue and silver costume, and his riding boots reside. Adrian took them up there to get them out of my line of vision. I still can't go to the attic without getting a funny feeling in the pit of my stomach. I don't think of him as joining our resident ghosts, but I can't help wonder if they know where he is.

At one point, the attic was empty. It has slowly filled with stacked boxes of green wreaths with red bows, plastic containers of twinkle lights, and boxes of ornaments. It also has discarded items from each of us that we merely cannot part with, items from Terre's move here, a toy chest filled with dress-up clothes Tina and the twins used to play with, plastic bins full of seasonal clothing, and Adrian's odds and ends from his old apartment.

I've located some empty boxes that Reed had in his office that he didn't mind giving us. I'm on my way up the front staircase when dizziness suddenly overtakes me.

Shutting my eyes, I sit on a step, letting the boxes tumble toward the floor. Without warning, the sensation washes over me that I'm standing in a jungle-like setting. Strange bird-like sounds are passing overhead, but they aren't African Jungle sounds, or monkeys as they screech jumping from branch to branch.

"Come on, Ellie, what's taking you so long? Ellie, are you okay? What are you doing down there? Did you fall down the stairs?" Terre's voice seems far away as if the world is turning without me. I'm vaguely aware that people are talking.

"Ellie, its Adrian. Where are you? Are you alright? Amala, please get a glass of water. Did you fall down the stairs?"

Amala says, "I will get water, need anything else?"

"Yes, a cold washcloth," Terre says as she thunders down the stairs toward me. She then reaches down to pluck BJ off the stairs.

"Gamma," BJ's small voice calls. "Gamma, Gamma!"

"Ellen, come back to us, okay?" Adrian's voice talks me back to the staircase. "Open your eyes and stay with us. We're getting you a glass of water."

Amala is back with the glass and Adrian hands it to me, saying to drink as he places a washcloth around my neck. Sipping the water, I suddenly feel self-conscious. "Why are you all staring at me?"

Mona and Nancy are standing to the side of Terre, as she hands BJ back to Amala.

"Gamma," BJ says, holding out his arms to me. "Gamma, Gamma!"

Adrian takes the glass from my hand. "Let's give her a little room, okay? Everyone, go back to what you were doing, she'll be fine."

Mona and Nancy leave as Terre steers Amala and BJ up the stairs with the boxes. "Go on up, and I'll be with you in a moment." Terre sits down on a step near me. "I'll call Dr. Stevens," she says. "She might want to know what's happening. I'm concerned about you. How often do you have these things, Ellie? Do you have chest pains?"

"No, there are no chest pains," I manage to say.

"Then maybe we should do this at another time, unless you want Amala and me to go ahead and do it without you."

Adrian stares at Terre. "What were you going to do?"

"We were going to take Mother's stuff out of her room; maybe move down to Jason's to do the same thing."

Adrian stands up and hands the glass to Terre. "That explains it. Ellen, you need to be honest with your sister. You don't have to invent a seizure to get out of it. I'm going for a ride. See you later." Moments later we hear the screen door slam.

"That was insensitive!" Terre observes. "What the heck is wrong with him, Ellie?"

"He's been through a lot. I can't get him to talk with anyone. Some of the things he says are wacko, and he was never like that."

"People change, Ellie. You said so yourself the other day. Are you feeling better? You look a little pale."

"Yes, I got dizzy there for a second."

Why is Adrian acting this way?

Terre motions to Amala who is standing at the second-floor railing holding the boxes. "I'll be up in a moment. Start with the bedding, okay?" Terre turns back to me, saying, "Alright, Ellen, let's have it."

"I might as well tell you, Terre; I see things. I see Jason, and periodically, I see me, and I'm always trying to find him, always. I don't know how to explain it to you."

Terre hugs me. "That makes sense. Isn't that the meditation thing you and Dr. Stevens worked on? Maybe you can do that, and you don't know it."

"I wish Mother had bequeathed us a crystal ball instead of a snow globe."

"That's funny, Ellie. Don't you think that life would be rather dull if we knew what was coming?"

"No. I honestly wish I had a crystal ball! I do want to know what's coming, or where certain people are."

"We don't have to do this now. It can wait for another day." Terre stands and reaches down for my hand. "We don't have to do Jason's room for that matter either."

"Yes, let's save Jason's for another day, but I'm okay to do Mother's room."

Once we clear everything out, we'll paint and decorate it with Amala so that she will feel more comfortable here. We'll even take her to select new furniture, as I've promised Gerald Tillman Mother's bedroom suite will come to his antique shop. The original sticker on the cheval mirror dates it to 1920, and we realize that she and Daddy were careful collectors.

They were selective with what they purchased and only considered pieces that would blend in with our house and way of life. The furniture needed to be functional, tasteful, as well as useful. None of our children wanted them or had a use for them, so we decided to sell her bedroom furniture along with some of the pieces that were in the sitting area.

Are we giving up a piece of her when we do this? Sara Ashwood didn't part with much of what she brought into this house. The generations who came after her kept most everything. We're sure Mother would want Amala to have her room now that she isn't here. She'd want her to feel welcome and part of our family.

The next week, I'm at my weekly therapy appointment. Dr. Laurel and I exchange greetings, and as usual, she suggests that I either sit or lie down on the sofa. It is what she has done for every session I have ever had with her. She seems brusque today, not her usual even-tempered self. I'm not in a good mood either.

"How have you been, Ellen? You missed your last session."

"Sorry I missed it. We were trying to go through Mother's belongings. Didn't Adrian call you to say I wasn't coming?"

Dr. Laurel tilts her head and looks thoughtful. "Yes, yes he did, and your sister Terre also called. They seemed concerned, especially Adrian. He thinks that you've been hallucinating about Jason."

"Did he really use that term?"

"Yes, he did."

"You know that meditation thing you taught me? I think it's backfiring."

"I didn't know it worked that way, Ellen. Can you tell me why you feel that way?"

I take in a lungful of air and slowly expel it. "Why, you won't believe me. Adrian doesn't believe me, and I'm not sure Terre does either. The only other person who halfway believed me was Mother, and she's gone. What's got your dander up?"

"My Dear Ellen..."

"I don't believe you're using that phrase. I truly don't wish to hear those words, ever again."

"Ellen, you seem overly sensitive today yourself. Perhaps we should explore what it is."

"His Most Royal King-pain-in-the-ass used to preface most of his sentences with 'My Dear Ellen.' I guess it still bothers me when I hear it. I never thought it would come out of your mouth!"

"Alright, let's try this again, shall we?"

"No, I've had enough. I'm not coming back. You see, unless I have proof that Jason is dead, you and everyone else in this town think I'm looney tunes. So, we're going to stop now. I'm going back to racing, and that's where I'm going to put my energy and dollars. As for my family, they can come and talk to you all they want. Thanks for all your help. Have a nice day."

"Ellen, please, don't leave like this."

I'm about to slam her door when she comes to the doorway. "I don't know how to control the pent-up anger I'm feeling. Maybe I'm irritated with Adrian for dissing me last week, or maybe I'm pissed at Terre for calling you and discussing me, and maybe, maybe I'm irritated that no one believes Jason is still alive."

"Please come back into my office, Ellen. We shouldn't leave things like this."

"No, I'm done here. Send the bill to Adrian. I'm sorry Dr. Laurel, I don't think you can help me anymore."

On my way home, the sudden urge to flee is uppermost in my mind. What would happen if I packed a bag and traveled around the areas that Jason might have gone? Am I going crazy as everyone thinks? Have I already gone over the edge?

When I get back to my office, the house is quiet. A light humming emanates from the overhead fan that reminds me of another time. The way I see it, there are two possible choices; I can throw myself into racing again next season, or I can go and search for Jason.

Which one should I do first? If I wait until next year to search for Jason, are the chances of finding him slimmer as time passes? On the other hand, do I concentrate on racing while I still have the energy?

Tough decisions are hard to make if you don't have someone to talk with who sympathizes with your point of view. My solution is to flip an old 1971 silver dollar that I keep in my desk drawer. It will decide for me.

If the coin lands with President Eisenhower's face, my energy will go into racing. If the coin falls on the eagle, then the search for Jason will commence, and racing will wait for another year. If we don't win the races that will take us to our goal this season, the logical, methodical, and thoroughly thought-out search for Jason will still take place. However, this time, I'll travel that journey to find him myself.

I feel the pull to go in two different directions, and it's getting stronger.

Tossing the coin into the air, I'm slightly disappointed when it lands heads up. With the tough decision made, racing will take top priority for the next six to nine months, where the goal is to win the Championship. Whatever happens, when the racing season ends, I will go for the eagle side of the coin.

Our present horse trailers will not be able to withstand the rigorous travel to the important races we might want to attend this season. After contacting a manufacturer that does custom trailers, we are starting the process to enhance a new one that will serve a multitude of purposes. It will be both functional and ground-breaking.

The trailer company was skeptical when I showed them my ideas. Our new trailer will be able to double as a shelter should the need arise. Most trailers have a door at the end, but my design includes two doors on both sides, with an accordion type door to separate the compartments. That way, two horses can fit comfortably inside with room for storage to stow our gear, clothes, and coolers.

We have ramps that hook on rails that slide and store securely under the trailer when not in use. We can then open all the doors and pull the horses forward when loading them, pulling them ahead when taking them out. That way we don't have to coax them into a dark space. Once the new trailer is here, Reed will put *Prince* into it to see how he likes it.

I'm able to tolerate the race bike seat, as the doctor agreed to pain management injections over a period of several months. He said it should do the trick if I don't fall again.

Only one issue remains; The *Prince*'s tail is longer than most, and I practically inhale it when we pace flat-out on the track, which throws me further back on the seat trying to dodge it.

"Glen, do you think I can trim a small amount from *Prince's* tail? It's difficult to avoid it when he's moving fast."

Glen shakes his head at my request. "Have ya totally lost your mind woman? Ya need ta get a grip on reality, b'cause if ya don't, the men in little white coats will be callin on ya."

"So you don't think I should do this, even if it gets in my mouth? It's a little trim, Glen. How could that hurt? He's not Sampson. He won't lose his strength if I cut it!"

Glen laughs when I turn to leave with a pair of scissors. When I return, handing him a fist-full of dark brown horsehair, all he can do is take off his hat and scratch his head.

There, problem solved.

"Courage doesn't always roar. Sometimes courage is the little voice at the end of the day that says I'll try again tomorrow."
~Mary Anne Radmacher

Chapter Ten

The Courage to Change the Things We Can

As the weather changes, the mood reflects that change at the Manor House. We gear up to celebrate Christmas, but it's more subdued than usual. It's not the same without Grandma Francesca, and we all agree that her little tidbits of wisdom so freely offered, are what we miss the most.

Those who come for the *Magic of Christmas* also feel Mother's absence as she used to hand out cookies and hot chocolate when guests came into the house to warm themselves by the fireplace. Reed mentions that in light of our present mood, and the ever-present existence of thick mud and absence of snow, that we should suspend it early this year.

The once extravagant gifts from King Dimmy have finally stopped arriving. I merely refused delivery and marked the packages 'return to sender.' We no longer want to keep up pretenses that we are his family and have severed all ties with him.

Melanie came home from college to announce that she switched her major (again) to Art History. Her goal is to one day own an art gallery. Then she returned to school after the holidays, to switch her major back to Performing Arts. Tina couldn't resist a chuckle at that one.

We've speculated that if Mother were here, she would have talked with Melanie about the nonsense of vacillating between majors. Then the thought occurred to me that no, she would smile and say to follow your dreams. If you want to own an art gallery or be on the stage performing, then do it! But don't keep going back and forth, because it's too costly.

When spring came early to Virginia, we were all glad as that meant we could start practicing and going to the racetrack sooner than anticipated. It is where the teams feel *Prince* will hone his skills. If he does well (provided there are no injuries, the modified bench stays intact, and the injections keep working in the tailbone area), the intention will be to take him to several other tracks to see if my hunch is correct.

All of our racehorses did a great job last season, including *Peanut Brittle*. But, I'm still favoring *Prince* as our Champion. He's now a three-year-old who has developed a real liking for being out on the track when we practice. Let's hope he can do that when we go to the racetrack. He does a look-back at me before we start, except now I find it reassuring.

As I turn my five-year calendar to a new month and see a date circled, I suddenly get a pain in my chest, and my eyes begin to water. It would have been Jason's big celebration. The entire family would have been in Saudi as he became a crown prince.

Has Dimmy found a replacement for his missing heir to his precious throne? Do I even care?

The remnants of our mild winter mud have slowly dried, which allowed us the opportunity to move forward with training and racing. Mack and Danny already have many wins to their credit. It seems to be a winning season for all of us.

No one took me seriously at first when we brought home a wild, untrained horse that was decidedly head-strong. They were even more shocked when I declared that I would race again until we started to win.

When *Prince* won several races in a row, the U.S. Trotting Association, which covers both trotting and pacing, named him, 'The Horse of the Month.' It is, thanks in part, to the modified race bike seat and my tolerance to withstand the rigors of sitting on it.

Glen tried his usual contrary reasoning on me. He mentioned the nuttiness of doing this, except we both knew that Mother would have encouraged me, not tried to talk me out of it. He's watching out for me as any father would and doesn't want me to get hurt.

He thought there would be enough abuse going around the practice track and figured that would be the end of it. He changed his tune soon enough after we went to Billingsworth a few times. Then I pointed to a horse and told him to place a *winner takes all* wager, which left him smiling and patting his pocket.

Throwing myself into training and racing again, it's noticeable that Adrian is pulling away even more. Although he has more space near the window in the library, he lacks an official office with a door. He spends more and more time on his laptop computer squirreled away in the Guest House out by the pool, or riding by himself.

Does he wish he were back at CIA Headquarters in Langley? Does he feel guilty about Levi's death? Or, does he feel inadequate somehow?

Adrian no longer comes to the racetrack when we go. It seems that he has given up all hope of ever winning wagers on his own. That connection is what I dearly miss. His answer is always the same, that he's okay. He's not as interested in it as the rest of us are.

CIA superiors continually ask Adrian if he wants to take Levi's place. Knowing what that entails, he flatly refused. He doesn't feel qualified to lead teams into what could culminate in their deaths. It could be the underlying meaning of his issues. When I mention Langley, he becomes partly unreceptive, saying to mind my affairs.

Isn't he my affair?

It's early February and time to get a jump on the forms for the upcoming racing season. These are the out of the state races that are a must for us to win. Then there are the entrance and stable fees, for the week of elimination races. Research also includes racetracks and casinos that run races from May to August, with purses of at least five hundred thousand.

Besides the race fees, there will be hotel rooms, food, feed, and supplies for *Prince*, and gas for the truck. It's on top of extra costs for security for the stable. We'll subtract any winnings, and that's our profit. The hope is that *The Desert Prince* will be our winner, and if we don't win big, we'll be happy to break even.

Choosing racetracks that will give *Prince* the best chance to win, a search on Standardbred horses turns up several items. One is *The Hamiltonian Society* that puts out a list each year that has most, if not all, the races we might want to attend this season. Their Combined Payment Form is confusing.

It lists nineteen possible races along with the entrance fees for early closing events. During a call to a representative, he rattled on about proper paperwork to substantiate whether *Prince* is a Standardbred horse. Aside from the usual fees, an owner needs to nominate his horse and pay an additional fee. We can still enter *Prince* even if they declare him ineligible, and after exhaustive research, the fee for this is astronomical.

Who in their right mind would do this?

On a notepad, I start a list of the races that are possibilities. At some point, our ambitious agenda will need adjustment. We'll narrow down the races that will gain us the most probable wins. Certain races seem like sure bets; however, we'll see how it goes during the Grand Circuit Tour.

Since Adrian doesn't show interest, Reed will step in to help. He doesn't want surprises. Given our track record, I don't either, but, there is no guarantee we won't have a few.

RACES TO CONSIDER:
1. John Simpson Memorial Stakes: April 27 - May 3rd
   (don't think we can do this one)
2. Max Hempt Memorial Stake: May 17 - May 27th
   $47,035, $500K, and 740.0 miles
3. Art Rooney Pace: May 17 - May 31st
   $55,500, $300K, 918.0 miles
4. Landmark Stakes: June 27 - July 4th
   no overnight boarding/do not consider this one
5. The North American Cup at Mohawk: June 6 - June 15th
   $65,050, $ 1.5 mil, 1,155.0 miles

6. Meadowlands Pace: July 4 - July 12th
    $ 48,500, $ 600K, 882.0 miles
7. The Del Miller Adios: July 22 - July 30th
    $ 47,050, $600K, 675 miles
8. Tompkins Memorial & Geers Stakes: Aug 8 - Aug 16th
    too close to Battle
9. Battle of the Brandywine: Aug 16 - Aug 23rd
    $ 47,900, $2.2 mil, 646.0 miles

If we get through these, then we'll consider continuing, but it looks as if we'll have to make a compromise with the first three races on the list. The John Simpson Memorial Stakes, the Art Rooney Pace, and the Max Hempt are all too close together with the Simpson and Hempt races running on the same weekend.

CONTINUE ON TO THE TRIPLE CROWN OF PACERS
10. Cane Pace:
    Sept 3 - Sept 10th, $ 51,300, $800K, 846.0 miles
11. Little Brown Jug:
    Sept 15-Sept 20th, $ 49,300, $ 526K, 830.0 miles
12. Messenger Stakes:
    Nov 7 – Nov 14, $46,000, $750K, 524.0 miles
13. Breeders Crown:
    Nov 14 - Nov 21, $ 54,500, $ 500K - $5 mil,
    882.0 miles
14. Cleveland Classic:
    on Dec 5 – Dec 12th,
    (not needed, too close to Christmas)

It's essential that our selections are as detailed as possible. The first decision is to skip the first race, as there's no way we can physically get from one track to another so quickly.

After discussing this with Reed, we'll start with the Max Hempt Memorial for three-year-old pacers that is traditionally run on Memorial Day weekend at Pocono Downs.

It could be a long drive from Ashwood Stables, with six to eight hours of drive time, including brief stops. If we leave early in the morning, we could be there by dinnertime. I'll have to come up with a solution for sitting that long in the truck. Maybe I can find a unique cushion!

Many racetracks have a purse-distribution format that helps owners consider what races they want to attend. Even if we came in fifth position, we would still get a piece of the prize. We need to place at least third, as it will give us anywhere from 11–13% of the total purse money, which allows us to break even.

The fourth race on the list is the Landmark Stakes that has no overnight boarding. We rule this out right away, as it would be difficult to trust others to care for *Prince* at an unknown farm.

The fifth race is the North American Cup that runs at a track in Ontario, Canada. We will not pursue this one, as the miles add up to over twelve hours of drive time alone. We most certainly would have to overnight somewhere as it's too long of a drive and too close to the Max Hempt Memorial race. The purse for this race is a whopping $1,500,000! Someday, we may want to revisit this, but not on our first Grand Circuit Tour. The large purse is attractive, but it isn't our primary objective.

They hold the Meadowlands Pace after the Fourth of July weekend. Located in New Jersey, it could be a seven to eight-hour drive from Ashwood. With time tacked on for stops and such, it could work.

Stopping to discuss the possibilities with Reed, he assures me that the list of races is doable, and then he questions whether we will be in top form to race the eliminators. He also suggests that we may want to work in a little vacation during this time. One of the girls might want to come, and we could go earlier than we need to. Or, maybe we can entice Adrian to join us once in a while.

Going back to my office, I continue down the list to the next race. The Delvin Miller Adios Stake Race is on July 30 at a casino in Washington, PA. It will take six to eight hours of drive time, the exception here is that there is a bevy of things to do along the way. Maybe this would be the opportunity to coerce the girls into coming with us. We could stop at a quaint bed and breakfast place that could stable *Prince* for a night.

The form turns up another race called the Battle of the Brandywine, which is in the historic City of Philadelphia. Again, the criteria for the races are about the same, and they include large purses. The purse amount can fluctuate as it depends on the number of horses that are nominated, and where we place at the end of the race.

Some of these racetracks are near historical battlefields. Is it a mockery for racing and betting to take place so close to where people died? Will the ghosts of the past be on our side? Perhaps a chat with one of our resident spirits will help. Maybe one of them can put in a good word for us.

Going through my usual routine of rules of observation, I write down who our competition might be. How many races have these horses won? Who are the owners and trainers? What do we stand to gain/lose? This thought pattern leads me to conclude that the competition will be fierce. We'll be up against drivers and trainers who merely don't lose. Ashwood Stables is unknown in the harness racing world, as we've only raced in Virginia. Will this be a disadvantage?

Do we have the fortitude and the courage to move forward?

If the stars align for us after the first four races, and the universe is in its zenith, can we possibly move forward to the other three races that will take us to our ultimate win? If it does, we can drop other races such as the Breeders Crown and the Cleveland Classic, since they are both too close to Thanksgiving and Christmas. Besides that, I'm confident that we will have had our fill of traveling by then.

Writing checks for the fees, it occurs to me that if we place anywhere from first to third in the first race, we could win an estimated purse worth between $100k - $300k! It is a definite win-win situation if we win and an expensive learning experience if we don't.

The Serenity Prayer pops into my head. '*God, grant me the serenity to accept the things I cannot change, the courage to change the things I can, and wisdom to know the difference.*'

Is there enough courage to do it all over again next season, or the season after that, until I reach my goal? Or will wisdom fail me, if we don't do well?

Adrian is not interested in our plans. He goes through the motions of daily life and doesn't joke with us much. We haven't spoken in a while, not even about silly things. He rises before me most mornings and is out either in the barn, riding a border's horse, or out in the Guest House where he seems more comfortable using it as his office. The only one he does pay any attention to is BJ.

As we sip our coffee, in our usual place out on the picnic table, Terre sighs heavily. "Ellie, why don't you call Agent Sara? Maybe she can talk some sense into Adrian. I don't see this getting any better without professional help. If he doesn't want to see Dr. Stevens, then you need to talk to someone else."

"That's a good idea, Terre. You've noticed, too, hum?"

"With a household as large as this one, you notice when someone is about to step off the edge."

Sara was happy to hear from me and wondered how we lasted this long without support. She suggested that I contact her superior, who is Adrian's former partner, our friend Larry. After a lengthy conversation about our families, we got around to the real reason I called, Adrian's state of mind.

Larry said he would do anything for Adrian. He read the obligatory report that Adrian filed when the incident first happened where Levi lost his life. He figured Adrian needed some space, and as time passed, he intended to do a follow-up. When nothing more was mentioned, he assumed that Adrian was okay.

Larry went on to explain that Adrian had his debriefing session with a superior and a psychologist who evaluated his behavior and mental state. Larry also mentioned that notes in his file point to symptoms that may not manifest right away, and in Adrian's case, not talking about what happened, made it worse for him.

A few days later, Adrian announced that he would go to Langley for a training session, but what he doesn't know is that it's a small respite. His closest friends will attempt to help him regain a sense of who he once was. Larry called before Adrian left and said that Josh and Jake would also help our Adrian to restore the person we all know and love.

Our plans for keeping up with our racing schedule for the Grand Circuit Tour will not include Glen, as he must stay behind with Danny and Mack. Since Adrian is not part of the equation, Reed says it will all work out, then reminds me of our strong faith and trust. Fortitude helps a little, too.

Before attempting our rigorous racing schedule, Reed and Glen agree that *Prince* and his driver need preparation for what it entails. It's time to put our money where our mouth is.

From February through April, *Prince* will go to Billingsworth along with *Lester* and *Raindrop,* using *Peanut* as an alternate. Danny and Mack will race three times a week, while *Prince* only runs one day a week. Reed feels that we need to take it slow and easy, as practice will be enough.

It will tell us whether we have a snowball's chance in hell to win, or if my theory will hold up. I expected confrontation the first time we took *Prince* into the barn at Billingsworth, but Jockey Jerry and the others who became our friends the day the bullies surrounded me, made sure we were welcome.

As the months flew by, the racing teams made several decisions. *Prince* will not race at Billingsworth for the rest of this season, as Dr. Jess felt that we might be pushing him too hard. If we're going to participate in our ambitious agenda, he needs to conserve his energy.

Glen and Reed also pointed out that if I want to adhere to our Grand Circuit racing schedule, we need to get through mandatory elimination events which are strenuous enough.

Reed taped our schedule to the inside door of our new trailer:

Racing Schedule for The Desert Prince/Ashwood Stables

1. Billingsworth, Virginia; ~~February-April~~
2. Max Hempt Memorial Stake No. 59, for 3-Year-OldPacers. [6-8-hour drive time] POCONO DOWNS, WILLKES-BARRE, PA; DATES: leave Ashwood May 17; May 27 actual race date.
3. Meadowlands Pace. Rutherford NJ at the Meadows Racetrack. [7-9-hour drive time] DATES: leave Ashwood July 4; July 12 actual race.
4. Delvin Miller Adios Stake No. 47. Raced at: Washington PA, at the MEADOWS Racetrack. [6-8-hour drive time] DATES: leave Ashwood July 22; July 30 actual race.
5. Battle of the Brandywine. Harrah's Philadelphia Racetrack and Casino PA. [6-8-hour drive time] DATES: leave Ashwood Aug.12$_{th}$; Aug. 20 actual race date.
6. Cane Pace. Tioga Downs Racetrack & Casino, Nichols, New York. [8-10-hour drive] DATES: leave Ashwood Aug. 27; Sept. 10 actual race date.
7. Little Brown Jug. Raced at: County Fairgrounds, Delaware, OH. [6-8-hour drive time] DATES: leave Ashwood Sept. 12; Sept. 19 actual race date.
8. Messenger Stakes. Raced at: Harrington Raceway, Delaware [6-8-hour drive time] DATES: leave Ashwood Nov. 4; Nov. 12 actual race date.

In the event that we win certain races, we'll be on our way to winning the Triple Crown of Harness Pacers. This is not said within earshot of Glen, because I know what he'd say. He's been sulking these last few weeks anyway, because he has to stay behind to manage the stables, but more importantly, take the boys to the racetrack.

If this doesn't work out for us, we don't need Mr. Negative to tell us 'I told you so.' It's important that the senior of the trainers be on hand for the bulk of the training and guidance. If *Prince* does well, then we can move on to the second important race. The Meadowlands Pace is close to the 4th of July, and it will be a long drive. It's the wealthiest pacing race in the United States because the reward is a cool $1 million purse.

It's hard to speculate with unknown factors; we'll be happy with a well-placed anything.

Terre and Dennis assured us that everything would be under control at Ashwood. They'll keep their eyes peeled for trouble and call Adrian at the slightest concern, or resort to calling Sheriff Rocky. We are to go and have a good time. They'll handle what comes their way, and besides, the girls have summer jobs, and everyone is busy. Amala has her hands full with BJ, Mandy, and Little Reed, and Nancy is stepping in to help Mona with her baking.

Can life get any better than this?

After a grueling day of practice, I'm sitting at my computer when the familiar ping signals an incoming email. In the subject box are the words: *responding to an inquiry from an Officer Kensi*. I remember a while back that someone contacted me when I sent out the first photo of Lance (my pseudonym for Jason), and several inquiries also came in around that time. Some were strange responses, some were encouraging, and still, others I had to delete quickly.

My original inquiry was: Has anyone seen this person? His name is Lance. I included some statistics, and when this Officer Kensi finally replied, he used a type of English variation that I couldn't understand. When he didn't respond to my return email, I finally gave up.

It is so odd as the date of this email is nearly three years old. It looks as if it's in response to that original email, except that it seems different. This person must have tried to translate my text into his native language and regurgitated it back in almost my version of English again, but it's still difficult to read. This time, he has attached two items. I open the attachments and gasp at the photos!

The first picture is of a severely injured man with two swollen eyes and a smashed face. The other photo looks like the same person taken months later. My heart does a flip/flop. Am I staring at a beat-up Jason?

Or, could this possibly be the suspected pirate, who had Jason's watch?

It's times such as these that I miss Mother the most. She would know what to say and at the right time. And if Adrian were here and in his right mind, he would try to make me laugh, and do silly things.

Waiting for the photos to print, and swinging the magnifying glass attached to the drawing board to take a closer look, it's difficult to distinguish whether the images are Jason. My return reply requests additional information. Where is this officer located? What is his badge number? (He could be impersonating an officer, and this could be a trap.)

When there is no fast response, I abandon this to put my energy into racing. I can't pursue this now anyway; the flipped coin fell on heads. When racing season is over, it will have my fullest attention. As Adrian needs to get over his sadness, I too must focus on other things.

We have a small window of time to prepare for the first important race. *Prince* has done well in the last few months and has almost as many wins as *Raindrop* and *Lester* their first year racing with us. However, *Peanut* is holding his own and gaining quickly on those wins.

A car horn makes me jump.

Glancing out the front windows toward the garages, Amala is sitting in the front seat of our beat up old clunker, but it's BJ that's behind the wheel. It brings back the memory of Jason driving Tina and Mel to school. Mel had it briefly until she purchased her red convertible. Tina uses it now to get to and from her activities.

"Hello there, you two."

BJ looks up at me and says, "Hi Gamma, me divin a car."

"So you are. Where are you going, young man?"

He's trying to look through the opening of the steering wheel as he sits on his legs. "I'm goin to stow to buy goseries, wanna come?" The locked wheel prevents movement. "Ugh, move!"

"Don't you think you're a little young to be driving? Can you reach the gas pedal? Amala, are you waiting for Tina?" The realization hits me that perhaps she should learn how to drive.

"I am waiting for her to take us to the store," she says sweetly.

An out of breath Tina runs out the back door, saying, "Sorry Mom, gotta get going so I can get back for my piano lesson. Do you need anything?" She opens the car door, helps BJ back into his seat while Amala fastens him into the seatbelt, then looks at her cellphone to declare, "Oh, we're never gonna make it back in time. Can we do this tomorrow, Amala?"

"Why don't you go back in the house and take a deep breath before your teacher gets here. I'll take them to the store."

Tina looks at Amala and grabs for her purse. "You'd do that? Thanks, Mom!"

"Okay you two, let's use my car."

Amala tugs on the hooks to get the latch clips to unlock the car seat. BJ has changed so much since he's come here to live with us. He's no longer the baby with the dark wavy hair, he's a toddler who speaks two languages, (almost anyway), often mixing words from both languages in the same sentence. We don't always know what he's saying. It's a little like playing charades when he asks for something. Somehow, he gets his point across in spite of this.

"Get into your big boy seat, please."

After Amala straps BJ into his car seat, she settles in the front passenger side. "Thank you for taking us to the store, Mama T," she says.

"No problem, Amala. I have an idea. Would you like to learn how to drive?"

"I wanna dive, Gamma!" BJ hollers from the back seat. "I wanna dive, where Papa spesal?"

"Was that English for the word special or Arabic for something else?"

"I do not know," Amala says, shaking her head.

"You can drive when you're the right age, mister, and when you can reach the gas and brake pedals," I say laughing.

"You mean to drive a car?" Amala inquires.

"Yes, unless you want to drive a tractor around the yard to cut the grass."

BJ chimes in, "Me cut gas Gamma, beep, beep."

"You would let me do this? What if I cannot control the car and I crash into something?"

My brain screams that I can't understand why she thinks this way, then remember that she had a suppressed and extremely controlled life until she came here. Habits are hard to break. Even where they are deeply ingrained, it takes patience to help convince a person that they can make decisions for themselves. What would Mother say?

"Yes, you can do this."

"What if I hurt someone?" she says innocently.

"Gamma me dive… beep, beep, beep, outta way, beep, beep!"

"Who taught him to say that? You won't hurt anyone if you have the proper training. If you study as hard as you did for our language, you'll have no trouble with the test. Besides, if you fail the test, then you can retake it. We'll get you a training manual. If you pass that and get a temporary license, a driver training company will come and pick you up and drop you off. We'll figure out a schedule, so it doesn't interfere with your jobs or BJ. How does that sound to you?"

"I will try this training car, if you think I can do it," Amala says with a smile.

"Me too," BJ says from the back seat. "BJ dives, outta way, beeeeeeep."

"You can drive the cart at the store, BJ."

"Okey dokey," he says, and we laugh.

Later that night, Adrian calls to say his friends have done an intervention, and he's been talking with a professional. So far, there hasn't been any great revelations, but being back with his old team and friends have made him realize how much he's missed his job with the CIA.

Are there undertones of regret? Adrian assured me that although he might miss it, he can still be a part of it for specialized training of teams, they can come to Ashwood and camp out as they once did, and then he might feel like he belongs somewhere again.

So that's it, he doesn't feel as if he belongs with us? Where does he think he belongs, on Mars?

Wanting to ask a hundred questions, he's bitten my head off by my asking if he wants another cup of coffee. "Adrian, I think it's time for Amala to learn how to drive, what do you think?"

"Are you planning on putting her on a race cart, Ellie? I don't think that's a good idea."

"No, silly, I think it's time for her to learn how to drive a car."

Adrian seems distracted. "Oh… that's a good idea. Tina's been the one to take her to the store and things, yeah, that's a good idea."

"BJ keeps asking for you. He wants to know where you are. I told him you were doing something special, so he's been calling for Papa special. Are you doing something special, Adrian? I miss you."

"Tell him for me that Papa misses him, and I'll be back soon."

"I'll tell him. Did you look over that list I sent you about the races?"

He's quiet for several seconds. "No, honestly Ellie, I've been swamped. When did you send it?"

"I sent it last week. It's for the races that Reed and I think we should take the *Prince* to that will help us move into position for the Grand Circuit Tour."

"Oh Ellie, I haven't even turned on my computer for the last four days. I've been distracted with stuff here. Can't you give me the skinny version?"

"I'll resend it to you. It's not a big deal Adrian, there's too much information for me to regurgitate it now and I can't remember all the dates. Find the email with the list. All I'm asking is that you look at it and see if you want to join us, that is if we win and move forward. If we don't win or place in the top, there will be nothing to celebrate."

"Alright Ellie, I'll take a look at it the second I have some time, but they have me extremely busy here. It might be hard to get away."

"I hope you can get away sometimes, Adrian. People miss you, besides BJ."

"All I can say is that I'll try, okay?"

"You sound tired, Adrian, are you getting enough rest?" I regret the words as they leave my mouth. "Did I say that?"

"Yes, Mother Francesca, I'm fine. I miss her too, you know."

"At times, I think she lives inside my head. I find myself saying things she would say. When did I become my Mother?"

"She was a big part of your life, Ellie, as Levi was a big part of mine. I loved him like. … I have to go now; I love you."

The phone clicks before I can reply. Did I say something wrong? Emailing the list to him again, it makes me sad he's going through this without me, then still, I'm grateful he's not alone and surrounded by people who love him.

I stare out the front window and think of Adrian, wondering why he hasn't called the last few days. Jake said he would keep him busy and let me know if things didn't go well. Has the world according to Adrian finally fallen sideways and he's succumbed to the icy fingers of depression?

The house phone rings. That sound used to make me jump out of my skin every time the phone rang because it could have been Jason calling. The caller ID identifies the number as being somewhere in Saudi, Arabia. It might be either Dimmy or Jam-ale. Whatever they have to say, they can tell it to someone else. That whole part of my life is over, and there is no wish to open that assortment of problems for anyone. It stops ringing, and I'm relieved there is no light flashing to indicate a message is waiting.

Then, my cellphone rings twice. The number flashes so quickly that it doesn't catch it. Perhaps the number is already blocked. I check the log, but the number does not show up. It looks a little suspicious. Does someone have my old cellphone that has never turned up?

With the uncertainty that Adrian will join us, and past events threatening to overcome me, my thoughts segue into how we have come so far and yet not moved forward with certain things. Have we played a part on life's stage? Will the play end well? Are we small and insignificant creatures doomed to gloom? As this cloud of depression hangs above me, BJ bounces into my office holding a plaque.

NEVER, NEVER, NEVER, GIVE UP
By Winston Churchill

I take it from his little hands and he giggles. Jason's face shows up when BJ smiles. Holding out my arms, he gladly complies, and I hug him tightly.

It is what life is all about. What was I thinking? Looking around my office at the many sayings in frames and inscriptions that were given to me at intervals throughout the past few years, the *Serenity Prayer* stands out. Saying each word out loud, BJ tries to imitate the words, and then we give each other kisses.

Amala comes through the library door and BJ tries to hide behind my legs. As she reaches around to grab his arm, Reed knocks on the doorjamb. He wants to know if we can make a change in our schedule to include a side trip. He wants to surprise Dr. Jessica.

"What do you have in mind, Reed?"

"You know how we haven't been away since our honey... I mean trip to Mexico."

"You can say honeymoon, Reed. I promise not to go ballistic on you."

Reed hands me a brochure, saying, "Okay, I was thinking that if we left a day early, we could go to this place. What do you think of this one?"

"What will we do with the *Prince* while we're otherwise occupied? You don't mean for me to stay with *Prince* in the trailer while you and the good doctor have a special fling, do you?"

"No, open it up. It's a fancy place that has a special bed and breakfast, and it's done up in the Victorian Period. They cater to people like us who travel up and down the racing circuit. Most of the owners take their wives there. It has a reputation for some pretty darn good food. I'm thinking Jess might think that it's romantic. And you know how hard it is to be romantic when you have little kids."

"It sounds great. Where is it and does it need a deposit?"

"The cutoff date is today. The website's on the brochure. Can you do it for me, so Jess doesn't find out? We can all stay there; they seem to have as big a place as Ashwood. It looks like a hotel. The *Desert Prince* will be treated like a real Prince!" Reed laughs, "Really, probably better than us."

"Hum, I wonder if he would get that same treatment if he were named *Ellen's Revenge?*"

"You're not still thinking of changing his name, are you Miss Ellen?" Reed's face loses all expression. "That would be bad luck to do that!"

"Why is it bad luck? Is that why they name ships after women?" My mind suddenly clicks back to my list of oil tankers for some reason.

"Miss Ellen, are we still talking about the trip?" Reed touches my arm, and I stare at him. "You okay?"

"I'll look up that website and register us for the night before we have to get to our first race."

Right after I do that, I'm going to look into something else.

After making the reservations, and going over the details of our upcoming trip, I pull out all my notes and drawings, along with anything that pertains to Jason's vanishing act.

Since Adrian is not here to talk me out of this, and everything is copasetic, it can't hurt to delve into that list of oil tankers again. We might have missed something.

I take a closer look at the map, comparing the list of oil tankers in the Persian Gulf with other tankers that might have moved in and around the South Pacific, either getting crude oil or taking it to refineries. Then use a methodical process where I put them into relevant categories.

What direction could the oil tankers have taken after they came *out* of the Persian Gulf? Did they go west to refineries or did they go south to Australia? All of the information seems to point *away* from the Gulf, yet not to a specific or particular port.

If Jason made it out of Saudi and down the Persian Gulf, where could he have gone from there? Was it out through the Gulf of Oman and into the Arabian Sea? Where could he have traveled from there? What ship could he have been on when it passed through there? Did he go through the Gulf of Aden, or did he go the other direction to the Bay of Bengal, around India?

Then again, did Jason go south through the Indian Ocean and head toward Australia or an island somewhere near there? Isn't that where that awful tsunami hit a few years ago? Didn't the latest cyclone blow through there? Searching through the saved emails, the house phone rings, as I drop the pile and everything scatters across the floor.

The caller ID identifies Adrian's cellphone. "Hello, how are you?"

"I'm okay. Thought I'd give you a call before I turn in for the night."

"That's thoughtful. Did you get a call from Dimmy or Jam-ale today?"

Adrian doesn't answer right away. "No, why do you ask?"

"Oh nothing, the house phone rang, and the caller ID was the same as Dimmy's, or somewhere close by him."

He sounds annoyed. "Why didn't you answer it? It could have been important."

"If it was important, those certain people whom I don't wish to talk to could have left a message, now couldn't they? Then there was a call on my cellphone, but they blocked the number. I thought my new number was not given out?"

"You know how clever people are when they want to bug you. By the way, I looked over your list of races, and there might be one or two I can join you for, provided you win, that is."

"We can still go to the last three even if we don't win first at the early ones. I'd love that. Which races are you thinking?"

"Can't say yet, maybe I can surprise you. Would you like that?"

"You bet I would! It's been a long time since you surprised me. Oh my God, it is not eleven thirty!"

"Yeah, it is. I was going to ask what you're working on at this hour. You don't usually stay up past ten o'clock."

"Then why did you call if you thought I was sleeping?"

Adrian laughs, "A little birdie told me that you were still up."

Glancing out the front window toward the Carriage House, the light winks out in Reed and Dr. Jess's bedroom. "That little birdie wouldn't happen to be a man named Reed, would it?"

It's comforting to know they're in communication.

"Good night, sweetheart, I love you."

"Good night, Adrian. I love you, too."

Surveying the piles of paperwork, it makes sense to postpone this until tomorrow after a good night's rest. On my way up the front staircase, my thoughts seem scattered, and insecurity starts to creep in. Is there enough courage to let this go if there's no new information? Or, will there be enough courage to put it aside, if there isn't?

What is there to lose by trying?

Both Reed and Adrian agree that my little Glock should come along on our trip. It is unknown territory for us, and anything can happen. We don't intend to shoot our competition. It's a little fail-safe.

"You remind me of Annie Oakley, Ellie." Reed startles me, as I'm about to reload.

"You goofy man! Don't you know that you're not supposed to sneak up on someone holding a gun?"

"Hey, I was going to say something nice to you, but now I won't," Reed says.

"Pardon my dust, mister. What's got your knickers in a twist?"

Reed looks as if he's lost his best friend. "Jess can't come with us. I was going to surprise her, and now she says she has too much to do and can't get out of it. She also said that Mona might need extra help with her baking and Amala can't take care of the children so, she's not coming. I guess you made those reservations for nothing."

"Don't write this off yet, Reed. I'm sure I can fix this, don't you worry, okay?"

"Thanks, Miss Ellen. What are you going to say to her?"

"Leave it with me. I haven't figured it out yet, but I'm sure she'll come with us on the trip, you can bet on it."

After Jess hears what trouble Reed went through to surprise her, and I assure her that Amala is capable of taking charge of a whole nursery of kids, she agreed on one condition, that we would not tell Reed.

Who says she doesn't have a sense of humor?

Since we do not have training today, and nothing is on the schedule, I return to study the oil tankers and the shipping lines list. This exercise brings up information that I must have missed during previous researches.

Taking the list of oil tankers first, I make a grid with the information noting the name and data known about them. I figure that the more I know, the likelihood of understanding how they move around will help determine which ship was moored and who was going into or out of the Gulf. I don't have much yet, but a pattern begins to emerge.

I'm impressed by the amount of information that is available for these ships and even more so with the fact that I can Google almost anything I want to research. One idea takes me to one website, where I spend time reading everything that is available, then I think of something else, and it takes me in another direction.

It's lunchtime when I stop to stare blankly at the clock. I've been at this for hours and have only scratched the surface of the first two ships. Deciding that I will stop, for now, I'll come back at this after a little break, hoping that someone will have received my emails by now.

Unfortunately, there have been no responses, but I forge ahead anyway. Cutting small pieces of cardboard to represent the oil tankers, I use my finger to move them around on the made-up map grid. It gives me a sense of where the oil tankers might have gone

Where could they have ended up in specific countries and refineries? The outcome is a total surprise when compared to the original oil tanker list. It takes nearly all day to finish the shipping grid that includes ocean currents, and other pertinent information.

Tucking it under the desk blotter, I take myself up to bed and then can't get this out of my mind. It needs to stop, as racing is about to get underway and we leave the day after tomorrow; packing hasn't even begun yet!

PERSIAN GULF/INFORMATION - OIL TANKERS	
❖ CRUDE- transports unrefined oil from oil fields	
• Product – transports smaller amounts to other locations	
1. Apollo's Universe	Moored – normal shipping lines
2. Alhambra	Moored – normal shipping lines
3. Hellespont	Going out-went south, then east- Normal shipping lines
4. Giant – ultra carrier	In the South Pacific area – too large to fit into the Gulf
5. Seawise	Moored – normal shipping lines
6. no name – where is this?	Usually goes around Australia several times
PERTINENT DETAILS	
CREW INFORMATION Names Country of origin	SHIP INFORMATION • Origin of nation
Manifests Types of cargo Crude Set for refinery other	Dates of travel Inland Or port Piped from ship Ocean currents Time of year/storms miscellaneous

Journey of a Thousand Steps

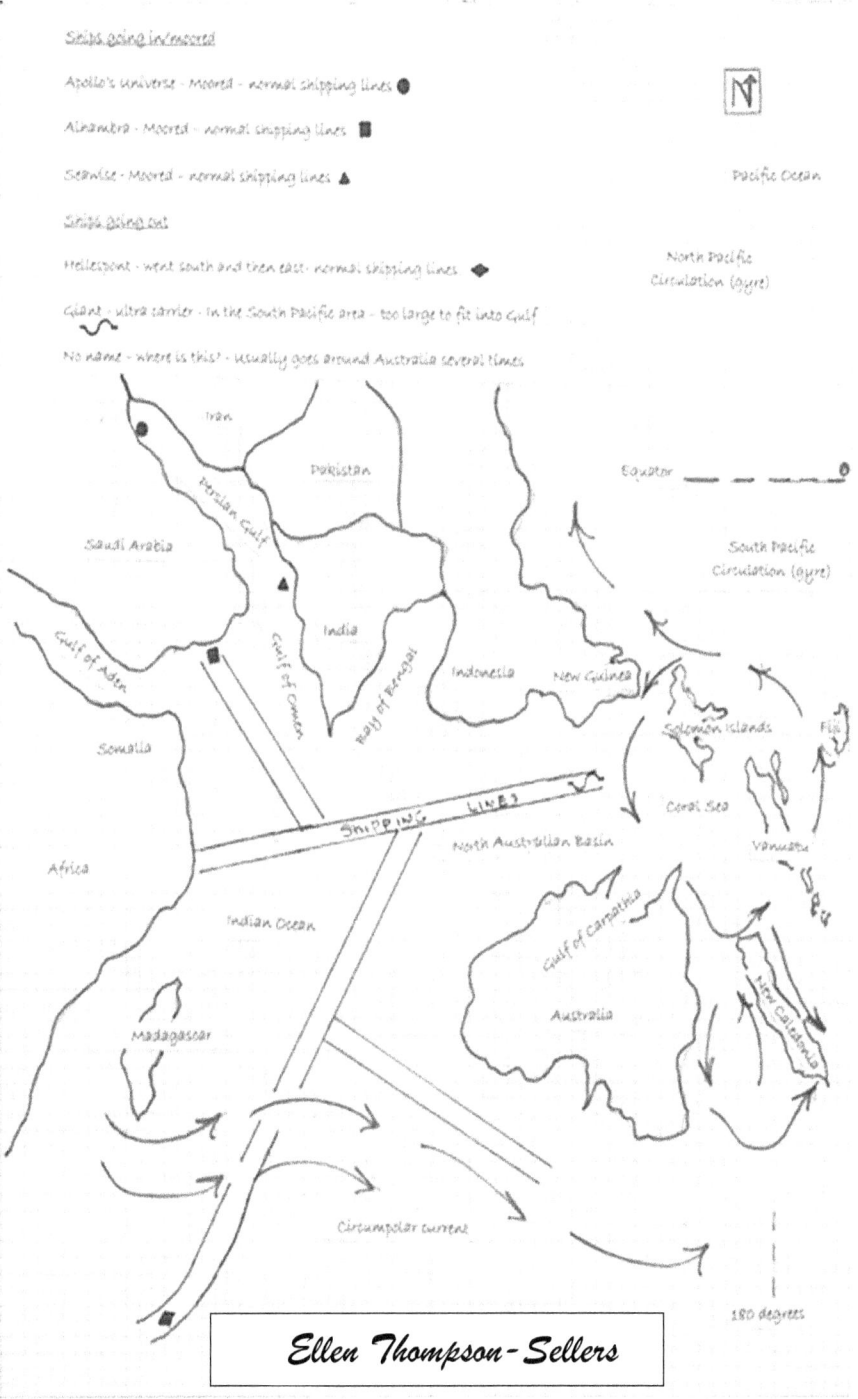

"Our greatest weakness lies in giving up.
The most certain way to succeed is always
Try just one more time."
~ Thomas Edison

Chapter Eleven

Challenges and Fierce Competition

The morning of our departure finally arrives. It is the start of our journey into the unknown world of circuit racing. Reed expertly guides *Prince* into our custom trailer, while Glen shuts the door, pushing the ramp up and under to secure it. He hasn't said much; it may mean he's still miffed he's not coming.

He surprises me with a big hug, then whispers, "I want ya ta know how proud we are of ya. I'm not mad. Do me proud." Glen steps back as Mona hands me a tin of her little cookies. She leans in to say that Old Mr. Grumpy Pants wants me to be careful.

Dr. Jess slips into the front seat unnoticed, as Reed bends down to hug his children.

"Gamma me come. Gamma!" BJ hollers when he sees me open the extended door on the truck to throw my stuff inside. "Gamma!" He has launched himself at me and wrapped himself around my legs, so I pick him up to hug him.

"I'm coming home BJ. We talked about this yesterday. Mama needs you to help her with Amanda and Little Reed. You promised you would help her, didn't you?"

"Yes," he says sadly, wiping his nose. "Me wanna come too," he wails.

"You can't come this time. Maybe another time. I'll bring something back for you if Mama says you're good, okay?"

"Okey dokey, I be good, hug Gamma."

"I love you, BJ."

"Luv yu, I be good," BJ says, wriggling out of my arms.

By this time, Reed has discovered Dr. Jess in the front seat and lets out a whoop people in the next county can hear. We say our goodbyes and head down the dusty road that eventually joins the two-lane highway on our foray into the unfamiliar.

Once we're on the road for an hour, my cellphone chirps but I'm not fast enough to slide the arrow to the right. It stops ringing and there is no message. I find this very annoying. It could be that we're not near a cell tower, or it could be a telemarketer. However, when I check, it's another blocked number.

We knew there would be challenges along the way. The racing teams held several meetings to discuss different scenarios, yet doubts are beginning to seep into my mind. Could the odds of winning be insurmountable? Could natural consequences take over? The simple truth is; if we win we continue, if we lose, we go home.

Can I accept that, or continue to do this each year, until we do win the Championship?

The quest for this Championship and the one to find Jason is waging a battle inside my head. If I don't attempt this now, the opportunity to reach my goal may slip through my fingers, and then I can concentrate on Jason again. On the other hand, could the chance of finding Jason fade away while we're trying to gain the Championship?

A few hours later, we're on a slight detour from the familiar path of the freeway to a farm in northern Virginia. It not only specializes in pampering horses; their owners get the same treatment. The website and brochure did not do this place justice. Lovely majestic oak trees and tall Douglas firs line the driveway, which reminds me of *Gone With the Wind.* At the entrance gate of an old Victorian mansion, there is a warm glow from within that beckons us, weary travelers. Adrian would have liked this.

"We're here, Miss Ellen, look at this place!" Reed says, rousing me from my self-inflicted conflict.

A man in livery is approaching our vehicle, directing Reed toward the barn that has an opening much as a drive-through beverage store. He takes our luggage to a waiting horse and buggy as two men drive our truck away. Once we're in the carriage, it makes a slow circuit around the barn, until we end up at the elaborate front portico of the mansion. He then escorts us into the parlor where he introduces a woman named Miss Agatha. She's wearing a costume and offers us a cold drink. It instantly brings back the memory of Lassiter's house and the Murder Mystery Party.

When the large grandfather clock in the hallway chimes, Jessica leans toward me, saying, "Does this place remind you of a certain party, Ellen? Barring any odd things that might happen here, I don't think murder is planned for our entertainment this evening."

Reed starts to laugh as he signs the guest book. Jess mumbles something and then turns her head so I can't see her face, "I've heard this place might be haunted."

"Yeah, like I'm falling for that one, Lady."

"Don't look at me, I never said it was haunted," Reed says, handing the pen to me. "It would be an awful start to our racing circuit."

"You're right," Jess says. "That would not bode well for the first time out."

Miss Agatha takes us up the curving staircase to the second floor while she talks on and on, not unlike Gladys did years ago when we toured Ashwood for the first time. She tells us about the history of the house, who once lived here, and intersperses quaint antidotes.

We talk a bit about the antiques that are everywhere, and I gently segue into asking if there are any resident ghosts in the house. She doesn't answer at first until I explain that we have a few at our place. She then launches into a story that we may, or may not, encounter the man who once lived here, and we may, or may not, encounter the daughter who murdered him.

Guests can have their evening meal in several areas of the house; the large dining room for those who wish to mingle with other guests, or a couple can choose to dine alone in the front parlor, and still, one can eat in the music room.

After freshening up and a small lie-down, Reed knocks on my door to say they're going downstairs for dinner. Reed and Dr. Jess move toward the front parlor where they will have their meal, as I walk toward the music room. The liveried man is there to open the door for me. He smiles, then closes the door behind me, without saying a word.

The old piano draws my attention. Curlie/Tina would undoubtedly appreciate the exquisite artistry, the old oak, and the original ivory keys. A dimly lit built-in cabinet holds porcelain figurines in muted colors, colorful Depression-era glass plates, and small boxes along with an impressive collection of sheet music.

When the piano starts to play a lovely melody, it hadn't occurred to me that it was a player piano. Perhaps it has a new kind of mechanism that's on a timer somewhere hidden inside. Or, maybe the ghost who dwells within this room started it. A female presence usually creates a cool breeze or scent of flowers. Since these are not present, it could signify a male presence. What would it hurt to ask?

"Hello, my name is Ellen Thompson dash Sellers. Are you the owner of this great piano? It sounds splendid." My cellphone rings and the music stops. The screen ID's the cellphone number of Curlie along with her 8th-grade picture.

"Hi sweetheart, how's it going?"

"Hi Mom, did you try to call me?" Tina asks. "Are you there yet? Did you win?"

"No, I didn't call you, but I was thinking about you. We stopped for the night, and we're about to have our dinner. There's a lovely player piano here."

"Okay. We have a surprise for you. I'll send you the pictures. We had to Photoshop some of them so you can't see Lindy's hands where she held BJ in place. Have a good time. Everyone's fine here, love ya. Bye."

Minutes later, my phone beeps as several messages arrive with photos of BJ wearing outfits the girls bought him. Ginny, Lindy, and Tina posed him and then took the pictures. The first one is BJ sitting on *Shoo Fly Pie*. He's wearing chaps, a plaid shirt, cowboy hat, a holster with guns, and cowboy boots.

The next photo has him dressed as an astronaut, followed by a lion, and the last one is BJ in a firefighter's suit, complete with fire hydrant, hose, and a plush Dalmatian dog. Adrian and Jason would most assuredly get a kick out of these.

The piano starts to play a lively ragtime tune. The music stops when the liveried man opens the door for Miss Agatha, who has my dinner on a tray. When I ask about the player piano, she says it plays by itself. She and her husband, the liveried man named Hank, spent several thousand dollars to get it to work correctly. It has a mind of its own, and no amount of money could prove there was anything wrong with it.

The music starts again when Hank closes the door behind Miss Agatha. I'm betting it has a great sense of humor too, and it doesn't like Miss Agatha. Perhaps he's the murdered man, and she reminds him of his dreadful daughter. This time it's a melancholy-ish romantic melody that sounds familiar.

"You don't have to tell me who you are, but I'm enjoying your music. By the way, do you know a woman named, Francesca? How about a woman named Sara Ashwood or a little girl from Virginia?"

There is no answer.

The piano plays until the door opens again and Agatha comes in to clear away the dishes. The music immediately starts again when the door closes. Reclining on the lounge chair to enjoy the music, a thought surfaces. Is it possible for ghosts to travel? Many people swear they've had encounters with ghosts who came with their antiques. Are spirits able to move within a realm that no one can see? Should I ask if this ghost knows Jason?

"Thank you again for the music. I'm going to my room now, good night to you." Maybe staying up late the last two nights is responsible for making me talk to a piano that plays by itself.

Hope the piano-ghost doesn't take that as an invitation.

After a surprisingly restful (and uneventful) night, we're up early to enjoy a traditional Victorian breakfast set out in buffet-style that consists of artery-clogging crisp bacon, sausages, fluffy scrambled eggs, grilled tomatoes, assorted bread, gooey along with puff pastry, and fried potatoes. It's a good thing Adrian isn't here, or he'd wipe out the entire basket.

While Reed and Dr. Jess coo over the delicious spread, taking small plates to sit at the table, I grab a biscuit and stuff a piece of bacon into it. "I'll get a coffee to go and meet you at the truck, okay?"

"Sure, we're ahead of schedule. We aren't leaving until nine, and it's only eight fifteen," Reed says, as he stuffs his mouth with a fork full of potatoes.

Today, we will travel five to six hours for our first week of elimination races. When Reed added last night to our timetable, it was an opportunity for them to get away for a short while, and there's no need to rush them.

Instead of flying out after we settle in *Prince*, they suggested they stay to help me this first time. It's a little strange without Adrian here with us, yet it's a welcome surprise and extremely generous that they would do this for me.

Amala is perfectly capable of caring for BJ, Mandy, and Little Reed. Tina, Lindy, and Ginny will help her at night when they're home. None of them wanted to abandon their summer jobs to come with us on our racing circuit. There would be no shopping available as we are going to casinos and racetracks, and they lost interest fairly quickly. And with everyone either in school or working, none of them will be able to come to watch us race either.

Mother left a void when she died. She did so many things so effortlessly and knew just how much baking supplies and ingredients Mona needed each week. Mona, most of all, is having the hardest time coping with her loss. Terre says that she's very close to calling it quits with the bakery since it doesn't seem like fun anymore, especially without her pal Francesca by her side.

We've planned things down to the wire for our racing trips. We are taking what we cannot possibly live without and only essentials. Since we also need to keep in touch with our families, we've opted to bring small devices that will help us stay on top of important issues. I can pay bills easily online anywhere there's Wi-Fi and Glen will let Reed or me know, if he needs funds for the barn.

About two hours after we leave, Reed declares a pit stop. We take breaks about every two hours or so, as *Prince* needs a chance to stretch his legs. We choose rest stops that don't serve food to keep the curious public from approaching us and spooking him. It's odd how a horse trailer attracts attention, especially when the horse is out of it. It's bad enough people yell out their car windows when they pass us; a practice that seems ludicrous to me.

Reed stops where Wi-Fi is available. I switch on my device to check emails. Many of them automatically go into the spam folder, so I check that one too. There's one from Melanie, but the date throws me off, as it's nearly two weeks old. She'll be graduating from college soon, and we haven't talked about her plans for the future. Is she excited about coming home this summer? Will she find a job in our area or will she opt to go elsewhere?

My cellphone rings and Melanie's unmistakable voice starts to yell, "Why are you ignoring me, Mother?"

"Hello, Mel, I wasn't aware that I was ignoring you. I was thinking of you."

Melanie is exceptionally curt, "Sure you were. Why haven't you called me?"

"I've been a little distracted, sweetie. We're driving to our first race outside Virginia. You don't have to be snarky, Mel, what's going on?"

Mel breathes heavily into the phone. "I sent you tons of emails and called and left you hundreds of messages. Are you ignoring me as you always do? My graduation is what's going on! I have to know when you and Adrian are coming! I've planned a whole weekend of stuff for us to do and it'll be ruined if you're not here."

BJ might be responsible for the missing messages on the house phone, or at least some of them. I left him to play while I stepped out of my office to look at information strewn on the library table. On two occasions, the phone rang, and when I came back in, he looked a little guilty. He kept playing with his toy car and shook his head when I asked him about the red flashing light. It would have been easy for him to press the button that erases messages. If it's someone we don't wish to speak with, we're all guilty of that infraction.

"When is the date of your graduation, Mel?" I silently pray it isn't on the day of our first race.

"It's May 30th. You forgot, didn't you? I knew it. You won't be here, and now there won't be any of my family here for my graduation. And I'm graduating with honors! All that stuff I planned will go out the window!"

Reaching for the list of races, I already know we're in trouble. If we get through the eliminators, we'll be racing on May 27th. Doing a mental calculation, Reed and Dr. Jess could drive home alone with *Prince*, and I could jump on a plane. Maybe the pot could be sweetened by having them stay at the Victorian mansion again on the way back home.

"Mel, get a grip, will you? I'm sure we can work something out."

"Mom, its May 18th today! How will you work this out, if you haven't planned for it yet?"

"Why didn't your sister say anything about this? Aren't you two talking to each other?"

Mel sniffs into the phone, "You must be referring to that snobby child of yours called Tina."

"What's going on, Mel? You can tell me."

Mel sniffles in the background. "Oh, you mean besides my family not being here for my graduation? No, I can't tell you anything.

Grandma was the only one I could talk to because you were always too busy, but she always… I wish she was here! I wish Grandma was here, Mom!"

"I wish she was here, too, sweetheart. We have to learn how to get along without her."

"Is that psychobabble necessary, Mom? Don't you think I know that?"

Reed and Jess are back, and they know something's wrong when I shrug my shoulders and mouth the word MEL.

"I wanted you and Adrian here. Kenny wanted to talk with him. He's majored in criminal science, and he wants to be either an FBI or CIA Agent."

"Who is Kenny, Mel?"

"I've only been dating him for three months, Mom; I told you all about him the last time I was home! See--you do ignore me. Are you coming, or not? The hotels are filling up, and you can't stay with me. Where are you anyway, the phone keeps cutting in and out."

"We're on our way to Wilkes-Barre with the *Prince* for our first race."

"Where's Wills Bear?" Mel asks.

"It's Wilkes-Barre, and it's in Pennsylvania. We're going to a racetrack at Pocono Downs. I told you we were thinking of doing this, Mel. You don't listen to me, either."

"I've had a lot on my mind with finals and everything! Tell me you're coming and bringing Adrian. I'd appreciate it if some of my family members are here."

"You've all grown up when I blinked my eyes, Mel. I love you."

"Yeah, yeah, yeah, just make your reservations soon, before they all disappear. I have ta go, bye I love you, too." Click! The phone call terminates.

Reed looks into the rear view mirror to ask if I'm okay, as tears obscure my vision. "Maybe this wasn't such a good idea, after all. If my Mother were here, she'd know what to say. Mel thinks I've let her down, and I'm about to make another blunder if I don't get us to her graduation on time."

"When does she graduate?" Reed asks.

"May 30th. I don't think it's physically possible to be in two places at once. If we win or lose, it won't make any difference, if Mel has no family there when she graduates."

Reed carefully maneuvers the truck and trailer back on the highway. "We'll work it out, Miss Ellen. We'll see to it that you get to her graduation on time, right Jess?"

"Of course," Dr. Jess says sweetly. "We'd do anything for you, Ellen--we're family."

Staring at the buttons on my phone, and trying to ignore the pain in my heart, it's challenging because it's right next to Jason and Mother. It's going to be a big deal for us to get to Mel's graduation. It has to come together for her sake.

Do my children feel that I've ignored them? Maybe my head was in the sand when things started to go wrong. Still, I'm there for the big stuff. Why did Mel pick this, of all times, to tell me how she feels?

Adrian's cellphone goes straight to his voicemail. My brief message about Melanie's upcoming graduation should get him to call me tonight.

As we approach the South Franklin Street historical district of Wilkes-Barre, the shop windows show how quaint this town is. It's much like others we've driven through when we ventured off the highway to sample the cuisine and absorb the local color.

Reed decides that we need to work out *Prince's* lodgings before we head to our hotel. He'll stay with him if he feels there might be hanky-panky in the barn. However, when the stable manager informs us that they have a strict policy, it assures us there's plenty of security. We paid dearly for this service, yet we agree it will be worth it as none of us want to sleep with the horses, least of all me.

After we check into the Casino Hotel and have dinner in the restaurant attached to the casino, I feel like a third wheel without Adrian. I excuse myself to play catch-up with the many details that still need finalization of the races that will take place later this summer. Glossing over the unsolicited emails, when nothing stands out, I press the delete button to run a search for a hotel close to Melanie's college.

There is still no word from Adrian.

The next morning, as we walk toward the stable area, a familiar voice shouts in our direction. When our friend, Jockey Jerry, said he would see us soon, it meant that he would see us here. He's been around a while longer than we have and will give us a run for our money.

"Hello Jerry, I didn't know you were going to be here."

"Howdy, Missus Thompson-Sellers," Jerry says politely. "I knew you'd be here."

"Oh really? And how did you know that? Did a little white-haired bird tell you?"

"We weren't planning to go anywhere else except Billingsworth, but Mr. Landers thought it would be a good idea if we try this because he thought you might up-him one. He said we needed to get in the same game," Jerry grins.

"It seems a little awkward for you to say my name like that. May I suggest you call me Miss Ellen?"

"That would be fine with me, calling you Miss Ellen."

"I'll bet a certain man named Glen Murdock's been talking to you! What do you think, Reed? Or was it you?"

"It wasn't me, Miss Ellen. It had to be Glen." Reed and I glance at each other while Dr. Jess goes into the stall to check on *Prince*.

Jockey Jerry takes off his helmet and throws his gloves in it. "Yeah, Glen mighta mentioned that you was coming to the Memorial Day Race here. And he mighta said that your horse, *Prince,* was gonna be a tough one to beat. So's I figured that Mr. Landers ought to know, and here we are."

"If the competition is you then I don't mind one bit. Have you done this before Jerry? I mean have you been to the other racetracks and done the Grand Circuit Tour thing?"

"Long time ago, I rode for a Mr. James out of Stoneville. We did a few of the ones on the circuit, but we never really ran many of the races, since we didn't qualify to move forward. Which race are you talking about?" Jerry asks.

"Will you be going to the Adios or the Battle of the Brandywine?" Thinking that if we qualify and move on, Jerry and I can talk horse stuff and pal around while Reed isn't with us.

"Oh, those races, I don't rightly know. It'll depend on where we place after the eliminators. If we do win, then Mr. Landers will decide the next step. He already told me that we have to come in second, or third, to break even with the expenses and stuff."

Reed shakes his head in agreement. "Miss Ellen and I discussed that stuff too."

"There should be purse distributions even if we come in fourth, or fifth, did you know that?" I add.

"Yeah, I heard they changed that, but that won't pay for our keep, Miss Ellen. We have to win bigger than that, or go home."

"You're right, Jerry," Reed says moving away from us. "We need to win big, or go home. It's that simple. I'm going to see what Jess is doing. You two stay out of trouble. I mean mostly you, Miss Ellen."

"It would be great if we could train and race together. Reed is only here for the first one and will drive the truck and trailer back and forth. He won't stay for the elimination races next time. I'll be mostly on my own."

Jerry's eyes grow wide. "Then you need me, don't you? I don't see Mr. Adrian. He's not here with you, is he?"

"Not this time, Jerry. He's back working again doing a little training with a new group. He'll show up when he needs to. Now tell me what you know about these elimination races."

Reed pops his head out of the stall and Jerry motions for him to join us. Jerry says he's bunking with several other drivers and they were kind enough to give the rookie some advice that he's glad to pass on to us. We're welcome to join the group for drinks and dinner later tonight if we feel like it.

We're doing things a little differently, as I entered as the trainer and owner. Reed's presence is neither required during elimination races nor does he have to spend precious time here, when he could be back at Ashwood. This first week, Reed and Dr. Jess will be sitting in the grandstands to watch.

As the time approaches, we are ready for the first elimination heat. I haven't been this nervous since my first race at Billingsworth. I'm hoping I won't make any stupid mistakes today, as statistics will show that injuries occur when you are not careful. Going through my usual ritual of praying that there are no injuries to any of us drivers, or horses, my mind starts to wander.

I'm shaking, or more accurately, quaking in my boots. Can Adrian's absence be affecting me? I must stop to psych myself up for what's coming. Is it fear of the unknown, or is it just plain fear? Glen or Reed is usually with me before we go out on the track back home. It's a little strange not having either one of them here with me.

Wouldn't Glen be surprised if he heard me say that?

The grandstands are not usually full for these types of elimination heats as there is no betting, or wagering going on yet (legal ones anyway). That happens during the actual races.

The announcer's voice comes over the sound system and goes through the usual information about the eliminators, etc. Even though Jerry told me all that he knew, there are things I have to experience for myself.

"Are you ready, Miss Ellen?" Jerry asks. "Good luck, then."

"Good luck to you too, Jerry."

We are waiting for the parade to start. I've placed my cellphone on the strips of Velcro on the seat beside me, and when it vibrates, a message pops up. The text reads: **Good luck. Love you. A**. Now I can get down to business because Adrian does care and he's responded in the only way he can.

Jerry gives the thumbs up to signal we should get on our race bikes. I've added something to my ritual, besides holding the locket when I say my prayer, I lean in to whisper something to *Prince*, and then pat his neck.

I'm a little apprehensive going into the first eliminator, as the competition is keen. The object today is *not* to be eliminated, so it isn't as important where we place yet. When *Prince* does his look back, it tells me that he's ready. We follow Jerry and take our position behind the retractable arm. It feels like a typical day at Billingsworth. The track is dry, the horses and drivers are moving beside each other as they usually do there, and the race bikes are moving along nicely.

Except for one significant difference; there is little aggression. Are the drivers restraining their horses for what might come later this week? Did *Prince* hold back as well? It's indeed something to ask Jerry about. Did the horses chat amongst themselves in the stables last night? Did they come up with this strategy to throw us off?

With the first day of elimination races over, and the lucky survivors gear up to repeat it tomorrow, we settle *Prince* in for the night and stop to get a cold drink. Jerry introduces us to Mr. Landers, several owners, and their wives, along with a room full of trainers and drivers. For the first time since putting on a racing helmet, there's no confrontation, no harsh words, no snarling, and no threats.

Do we all live on the same planet?

After a hard day at the track, everyone goes to the casino bar before dinner. It's where we trade stories and share tidbits of information, in what I can only describe as a camaraderie that our teams never experienced in Virginia.

We also say goodbye to those who are going home. It's not for good, as we'll likely see these drivers and owners again at one of the other races. Elimination doesn't mean it's the end of the road; it means you don't qualify to run this particular race.

Adrian does not call, and an astute Reed says to give him time.

We've raced without him before, but I genuinely miss Adrian's presence. Are my nerves failing me? Telling myself not to get distracted, this week of eliminators is critical, and concentration is of the utmost. Mother and her words echo in my head. 'Get a grip! You can do anything you set your mind to, Ellen,' she would say. 'Take your rightful place on that track and do your best!'

The third night, I beg off the casino thing, too exhausted to do anything except take a hot shower. I need to organize and prepare for the real reason we're here, the race on May 27th. Then I can worry about Mel's graduation.

As we work our way through the rest of the grueling week of elimination heats, Reed remarks that if *Prince* can keep this up and we stay in the game, then we'll be ready for the real race.

Day after day, heat after heat, we place either third, second, or fourth, with the race heats getting more aggressive as the week progresses. When Pocono Downs lists Ashwood Stables as contenders for the Max Hempt Memorial Race, we are elated!

Many races will take place today, starting with the one-year-old Open, and then the Filly Division, with ours later this afternoon. As usual, all drivers must meet with the racing secretary and receive their assigned numbers. *Prince* has number 12; it could be our new lucky number. We met with the chief steward, and he's satisfied that we qualify and know the rules and regulations for racing today.

Leaning to whisper into his ear, *Prince* reacts by shaking his head, which makes me laugh. We have rehearsed possible scenarios, and Reed is confident to leave me with *Prince* to sit with Dr. Jess in the grandstands. It's a well-attended event with a full house today. In a booming voice that startles me for a second, the announcer gives the information about the first race.

Jerry puts a hand on my arm. "We're gonna do okay, today, right Miss Ellen?"

"I hope so, Jerry. I'm not ready to go home a loser."

Before Reed and Jess left to sit in the grandstands, he told me to enjoy the journey. He also said not to be disappointed if things don't go as planned. Then Dr. Jess warned me to take it easy on *Prince,* as his temperament is similar to *Peanut*. He often pushed forward with a burst of speed, without as much as a wiggle of encouragement. She doesn't want him to overdo things today.

We knew the first time we let him go around the practice track, and again when we took him to Billingsworth that *Prince* loved to race. How can he be held back? He probably wouldn't let me anyway.

Jerry and I will race side by side today. That could be a good thing, or it could be a bad thing. The racing secretary positioned us on the outside, not an especially favorable place to be in to win. We've been here before, and it's made no difference in where we've placed at the end of the race.

Jerry nods his helmet in my direction, as I nod back to him. As Mr. Landers unclips the lead rope on Jerry's horse, I wiggle *Prince's* reins. As we move out to take our positions behind the retractable arm, I glance into the grandstands, hoping that Adrian is sitting with Reed and Dr. Jess.

There have been no texts from him since yesterday.

Prince is doing his little dance, which tells me he's ready. His coat is shimmering with excitement, and I'm as comfortable as possible, hanging on to the crop and reins. As the arm slowly swings toward the vehicle, the strongest of six horses move forward quickly, and luckily, *Prince* is one of them.

Prince glides across the turf in smooth movements trying to avoid other horses. Without the irksome juggling, or vying for position, the air seems to flicker around us. What an incredible feeling! When Jerry's smiling face whizzes past us, *Prince* moves to slide into the number two position right behind him comfortably.

Before I know it, the race is over. It was pure power and determination on *Prince's* part. With this second place win, we'll go home happy, knowing we've done our best, and our winnings aren't bad either!

"You gave them a run for their money, Miss Ellen," Jerry says, as Reed takes *Prince* back to the barn. "No one could catch him until I passed you. What did you say to him before the race started?"

"I gave him a little pep talk, Jerry. The rest he did all on his own. What did you do to your horse to win first?"

Jerry laughs, "I can't tell you that, then you'd know my secret."

Proud doesn't begin to cover what we feel right now. Did *Prince* overdo it? Dr. Jess reported that although he ran hard, he's of good stock. She suggested that I hold him back a little longer, before sending him to the front again. Is it my naiveté that surfaces, as Glen taught me to use restraint where needed and let the horse run when it wants to?

Dr. Jess is in the stall with *Prince*. "May I ask you a question, Jess?"

"Sure, Ellen, ask away."

"It's been my experience, in the short time I've done this, that most drivers accelerate during the last quarter. The rationalization is that they don't want to strain their horse before they need to. Should I keep *Prince* back, until they all pass us?"

"No. Don't misconstrue what I told you, Ellen. All I meant was that you should use restraint where needed."

"If you could see what I see. You and I both know we could all get tangled up in trying to get to that coveted first position. Are you saying that I should keep *Prince* back until then, as the other drivers do? Then push him to get to the finish line, as they do?"

"Look, Ellen, I'll give it to you straight since you asked me. It's my job to make sure *Prince* doesn't strain himself. We don't want him to bleed from the nose, because that could mean pressure is building up inside his head. So far, *Prince* seems fine. I want to caution you that you could do him harm if you continue to push him the way you did today."

"Thank you. I appreciate that advice. I will certainly keep this in mind the next time we race."

Dr. Jess puts a hand on my shoulder and, for a split second, she smiles and hugs me, then moves out of the barn. Reed pokes his head around the corner. "That was uncharacteristically nice of her."

He's laughing as people start to mill around to congratulate us. We're asked to join them at the casino for our last night to celebrate our wins and put the race to rest in the form of a post-mortem party.

My cellphone vibrates that a message has arrived, it says: **U done good kid. C U @ M's grad!** How did he know? Of course, Reed must have told him.

Since we only have a few days between this race and Melanie's graduation, Reed and Dr. Jess agree to drive *Prince* back to Ashwood while I jump on a plane bound for home. In gratitude, I gave them the gift of a second night at the Victorian mansion in Virginia, and they graciously accepted.

It gives me time to get us ready to jump back on another plane bound for Melanie's college. If we time things right, Adrian will meet us at the airport. I look forward to seeing Adrian and can't wait to meet Kenny.

Tina seems distracted, acting as if I've made her come on this boring trip based solely upon guilt.

When will she snap out of this? What happened to my little Curlie? We are settling into our seats on the plane. "Did Mel mention a person named Kenny to you?" I ask.

Tina glances at me and winces. "That's so yesterday, Mom. Mel's back with Jered."

"When did that happen?"

"A week ago maybe, don't you talk to her?" Tina says in an exaggerated voice.

"Yes, but she didn't say anything about him. Why didn't you tell me?"

"It's not me who's engaged one minute and not the next. It's Mel!"

"Okay, you don't have to bite my head off."

"Mom, I'm sorry. I wish," my little Curlie says. "I wish things were different. I wish Daddy was here and Jason. I love Adrian, but he's gone too. Why do things like this happen? Everyone I love keeps going away. First, it was Grandpa. Then you and Daddy didn't come back, then you did come back, then Jason left, Mel went to college, Grandma died, and now Adrian doesn't want to come home."

Tina starts to cry, and I reach to comfort her. She is right in that we don't talk. Like Mel, she only spoke to her grandmother. "Oh Curlie, it's the cycle of life, sweetheart."

Laughing, she says, "You mean the circle of life. Adrian would have said that."

"Have I ignored you?"

"No, Mom, I'm a teenager and we teenagers have issues. Most of them are about our parents and what they won't let us do, or stuff Grandma would help me through. Mom, you don't listen, and then I have to repeat it, and it drives me nuts."

Then Tina agrees to allow me to call her Curlie again. And she's back – for a while at least. "For the rest of the time we're together, I will make it a point to listen."

"Thanks, Mom."

Mel and Jered are at the airport to pick us up, and while we wait for Adrian's plane to arrive, we make a deal to put our differences aside (no matter how big they might seem) to concentrate on enjoying each other's company this weekend.

Mel admitted (confidentially) that she played Kenny against Jered. He finally realized that Mel was his one true love. Everything is back on track as Jered is once again her fiancé.

Jered's parents are somewhere in the south of France vacationing and will miss graduation. He seems unaffected by this and mentions he wants to get a job that will take him away from his incredibly snobby parents.

After the long graduation ceremony, and a brief reception for the students and their guests, we return to our hotel suite for dinner. We are delighted that Adrian is here, as it means so much for Mel to have at least part of her family to celebrate her milestone. She is a little miffed that Aunt Terre and Amala didn't come, then I remind her that school is still in session. She got over it, especially when she opened their gifts.

Adrian and I are alone as Jered, Melanie, and Curlie have gone off to parties around campus. "Mel's graduated from college, and she has a ring on her finger. Wow," he says. "Thanks for giving me the heads up about the guys, Ellie. I honestly thought she was still dating a person named Kenny."

"I'm glad you're here, Adrian. It means a lot to all of us. And as Curlie says, that's so yesterday."

"This is one of those milestones you can't miss. Besides, I heard Francesca's voice somewhere in my head saying I better be here this weekend, or else."

"You did not."

Adrian laughs, "It was Mel's voice. She left me a message that said she'd disown me if I didn't try to get here this weekend. She sounded like your mother."

"She would say that. She told me I ignored her while she was growing up and could only talk to her grandmother. I also found out what Curlie was cranky about during an unusually deep discussion yesterday. She thinks that everyone she loves has gone away, including you. Maybe she feels that if she's not nice to us, she won't miss us so much."

"It's not always about her. Does that make you feel bad, Ellie?"

"At first it did, then I realized there might be some truth in what the girls told me, so I started to examine my life and came to one conclusion."

Adrian looks at me in that adorable way he used to, and I melt into him. "And what is that, pray tell?"

"Since they didn't come with a set of instructions when they were born, I did the best I could to raise them. I don't know if I would have, or could have, done things any differently."

"That's a good answer, Ellie. I've missed you. We need to talk about what might be coming down the road. I'd like to help get this new team up and running for Larry. Can you do without me for a little while longer? I know Reed has things under control and takes good care of you guys when you're gone. What I mean is, are you able to race without me for a while?"

"Sure, Adrian, I never meant for you to drop your career to stay with us. When you did, I knew you wouldn't be happy being away from it. I now release you from that. Go forth and be whomever you need to be Adrian B. Thompson dash Sellers. Make us all proud."

"Gee Ellie, I didn't know you'd say that!"

"What did you want me to say? That no you can't go? Or worse?"

"You are an extraordinary person Ellen Diller Thompson dash Sellers. I'll come to where you're racing as often as I can get away, okay?"

"It's Dillon, not Diller, and look, the bottom line is, it gives me time to concentrate on the elimination races and put all my energy into the big ones. We're staying at some fancy casino hotels with some awesome amenities, so it would be nice to have you there if we qualify and we make it through the eliminations. But let's face it, Adrian, you would be an enormous distraction to me."

"I understand. And I thought it was Diller, as in Phyllis."

"She's way funnier than I am. Come home when you're done, okay? I love you very much."

Our next race is not until early July. In the meantime, we anxiously await Melanie's return home from college next week. All we have heard since her graduation is that she's coming back to look for a job; however, there is no mention of Jered.

Over the last several weeks, Adrian has been home a total of four days. His involvement with a new team requires maneuvers out of range (he means out of touch). We aren't to worry, as a Mr. Kelvin Ingles will keep us informed from now on. Another restructure within the CIA's Clandestine Unit has him as our new contact.

Adrian's one-time partner, Larry, has assumed the role of *anchorman*. Created specifically for him, he opted not to join Adrian working with new teams, because he prefers to stay stateside with his family. Are we to understand that this new team does not train on our soil? No one can answer that, as it's on a need to know basis.

Throwing myself into our next destination that will take place in New Jersey, we're already expecting some difficulties, as it will be a long trip for us. However, the rewards will be many should we win. Reed will drive us there, check us in at the stables, and fly out the next day. Should we get through the week without being eliminated, he will return the day before the race to help and support us. No one will be with me during this time unless Adrian shows up to surprise me.

After a relatively uneventful drive through some beautiful country, we pull into the town of Rutherford. As we near the racetrack, there are familiar trucks and trailers. Spotting *Landers Highland Stables* written on the side of a horse trailer means that Jockey Jerry is here along with some of the other members of the racing circuit. He waves to us as Reed guides our truck and trailer into our assigned slot.

It's unseasonably warm for July, and everyone seems a bit on edge. Even the horses stomp their hoofs and refuse to comply when motioned out on the track for practice. Maybe this wasn't such a good idea, as the heat didn't enter my equation for winning the races.

As is their custom, it's the end of a dusty, dry day, and most of the drivers, trainers, and owners are at the bar in the casino. I've wanted to ask Jerry about something that has troubled me from the first day we started to race.

"Jerry, do you get the jitters when you get on the track? What I mean is, I get the shakes right before the arm retracts and the horses come out of the gate. Does that happen to you?"

Jerry chuckles. "Yeah, that happens to me every so often. I get nervous like everyone else. Guess it's like stage fright. It goes away right quick after we get going, though."

"How did you get into racing, Jerry? And how did you get the name, Jockey Jerry?"

"Miss Ellen, one of my friends started calling me that, and it just stuck. I originally trained as a jockey, then I grew too much and couldn't keep my weight down enough, so they told me to find another career. It so happened that a harness race owner was looking for a driver about that time. Changed careers in about a week and never looked back. I still keep in touch with most of my jockey friends and on occasion, see them at racetracks, but mostly, they look down upon us lowly drivers."

"You make more money than a regular jockey, do they know that?"

"That's the funny part, Miss Ellen. I tried to tell them that, but they laughed at me. I'd rather be taller and able to eat what I want than have to go through what they do to stay up on that saddle."

"Me too Jerry. I wanted to be a jockey, but Mother and Daddy said no to that idea. Height and weight had nothing to do with my career path. They tried to steer me elsewhere, but I came back to horses eventually."

"We all got a story, don't we? Maybe some of the other fellas would like to hear that. They all thought you was an arrogant owner until I set them straight. It don't have to be a bad sport if people would be nice and let us do our jobs, right?"

"I agree. You have a big heart, Jerry, and you've got a good head on your shoulders. I'm glad to be racing with you. Thanks for putting in a good word for me. I never felt this comfortable around the stables back home."

"There won't be anyone to dispute how you and Ashwood did this season, with your drivers Danny and Mack," Jerry says, patting me on the shoulder. "And there won't be no disputing you, neither, by the time the circuit's over!"

Reed flew in last night, and he's not at all surprised we got through the eliminators this week without a hitch. After he fills me in on what's happening back in Virginia, he mentions that Amala passed her driver's test. As a family, we chipped in and purchased a car for her. She cried when Terre presented her with the keys at dinner the other night.

It's essential for Reed to be here the night before the actual race as the trainers and owners discuss strategies. None of us expect difficulties, and you never know when something important might be said. Although Reed is an excellent trainer and trusted friend, I wish Adrian was here, too.

The next morning, after Jerry and I go through our usual pre-race rituals, Mr. Landers unclips Jerry's horse as the pick of the draw has them ahead of us in the line going out to the track. I hang back two race bikes to wait for our turn.

When the Meadowlands Pace is over in a flash, I wonder if *Prince* is chuckling when he moves ahead of everyone. He's an amazing animal, and I thank God for this incredible experience. Our win means that we'll move forward to the next race on the circuit and bid *adieu* to our friends, knowing we'll see them again.

Most will be at the next race in Pennsylvania at the end of July. We hope that we can continue along our winning path. The rigors of training has been especially hard on my bottom area, and unfortunately, it's slowly getting worse.

On the way home, Reed and I discuss our options, wondering whether we should buy a portable spa. He thinks we should install it in the horse trailer under the cot, or somehow lay it into the truck bed. Then again, maybe we could put it on the roof of the horse trailer, so it looks like a cupola. Then we got silly and came up with a child's swimming pool with a submersible motor that swirls the water.

Melanie is home from college and stressing unnecessarily over the fact she doesn't have a job. Everyone else is busy with his or her own life and tries to avoid her.

Amala seems content to look after the three children in her charge, grateful that she can now take herself out in her new used car. Reed casually left some brochures on the hall table in the hope that someone would like to join our racing team for our next race. To our surprise, Mel expressed an interest in the Miss Adios Contest while Curlie declared that the Adios Hat Competition looked like fun. How much time do they have to get ready?

Are they serious? No one expected this type of enthusiasm.

As we start out on our trip to Pennsylvania, the girls chatter away in the back seat. Reed will stay with us the entire time as Dr. Jess took the kids to see her family and he would have been alone anyway.

When we get to the racetrack, a carnival atmosphere greets us as we turn into the big parking lot. The aroma of onions and sausage are making my mouth water, as the girls start planning their activities.

Reed settles *Prince* into his assigned stall as we head toward the hotel. The girls seem excited to get away from their usual routine, and it will give us a little mother/daughter bonding much as we used to have before things changed--and they grew up and out of it.

After we have a nice dinner in the hotel dining room, we retire to our rooms. We've already laid out our expectations for the girls. While Reed is busy helping me get through the week of eliminators, the girls will busy themselves with the things that attract kids to a carnival.

They are to be extremely careful and stay out of trouble. Reed mentions that Melanie is flirting with a carny kid—so it comes as no surprise when the winner of the Miss Adios Contest is none other than Mel!

Oh boy, there will be no living with her now! Her flirting garnered her votes. Curlie didn't win the hat contest; however, she quickly informed us that she would enter the beauty contest next year as she'll be eighteen by then.

Yikes, what have we created?

Do they want to come back here? After the shock of this latest development, I'm not so sure there will be a next time. Even though we did manage to place fourth, it was difficult to concentrate on the race fully. It still means money in our pocket, although not as much as what Jockey Jerry received as a bonus for winning first--again!

August rolls around and Adrian is home a few times, then slips back to Langley to train another team. His absences don't bother me, as long as he remembers we're still a part of his life.

Our next race is near Philadelphia. Dr. Jess will again travel with us on our journey. None of the girls wanted to come, and we merely attributed this to their busy schedules of movies, and nonsense, along with shopping at the newly built outlet stores that opened near the interstate.

Our fourth important race is the Battle of the Brandywine. All the advertisements give it a high rating, due to their top-notch entertainment, and open gambling. Reed and Dr. Jess will stay a few days to see if we qualify to move forward. Checking in at the front desk, Reed and Dr. Jess's room is ready, but mine is not.

We've come from the stables and haven't changed our traveling clothes, so they head up on the elevator, as I wander around the hotel looking for a café. I'm about to pass the obnoxious light-blinking doorway into the casino when someone seated at a blackjack table suddenly yells in my direction.

Good God, maybe if I hurry he won't notice me.

"Ellen!" a voice yells. "Ellen Thompson, is that you?"

Too late, Mr. C has seen me. When he catches up to me, he pulls me into a firm embrace. "I thought that was you, Ellen. How have you been? How's that family of yours?"

"I'm fine; we're all fine, thanks for asking. What are you doing here? Don't you have a gambling problem?"

He turns to signal the casino dealer, saying, "Guess I'm done here, Nick. Say, why don't we get a drink or something? I have plenty of time before my show starts. We have a lot to catch up on, don't we? I've been here about three weeks now; a little one-act play."

Mr. C has my arm in a tight grip pulling me toward the sliding exit doors, where the bright light temporarily blinds us. Trying to shield my eyes, I reach for my sunglasses, then remember I left them in my helmet in the trailer.

"Thanks, we drove in today, and I'm exhausted. I'd like to go to my room. Can I have a rain check?"

"You look great, Ellen. How many years has it been; five, six years now?"

"It's about eight or nine, but who's counting?"

"Has it been that long?" Mr. C says, scrunching up his face.

"Yeah, it's been that long. I came from the barn. I'm here to race the Battle of the Brandywine and I was going up to my room to change and get a little rest before dinner."

"I'd love to talk to you about that. Let's grab a cup of coffee or a cold drink so we can catch up with what we've been doing. Aren't you curious about what happened?"

"Am I curious about what happened? You bet I am!" Since there's no room to go to, this might be my only chance to ask him questions, such as, what the blazes was he thinking when he promised to send money, and he didn't?

Going back into the building, he steers me to the little coffee shop located within the hotel. I try to answer Mr. C's questions, and when he asks about Jason, I merely say that he's fine. I stick to generalities or racing. I don't know what he knows, or doesn't know, and it seems prudent not to say much about that end of things.

"Enough about me, tell me what happened to you."

"I meant to send you money, Ellen, honestly I did. You don't know what pressure that man in the booth put on me. He said not to send you any money. He said you owed him, not the other way around. He was waiting for you to make a mistake. He never thought you'd sell the antiques. When he found out, it made him crazy. He was sure you had some old money. I never understood what that was all about, but he was distraught with you."

"And you believed his cockamamie story?"

"Quite honestly, Ellen, he paid off my gambling debts, so yes, I believed him." Mr. C looks down at his cup. "When my lawyers discovered he was the one behind the tax evasion charge, and he was living in my guest house while I was otherwise disposed, that was the last straw. I live a clean life now, and I'm happy to say I'm also debt free." He notices the ring on my finger and reaches for my hand.

"Yes, I'm married now. My husband should be here soon."

"My only regret in life is that I never had a family of my own. I'm truly sorry about how the silent partners went about procuring the horse farm and how things went so wrong, Ellen. I feel duped, too, and somewhat feel responsible for not warning you sooner."

"You have no idea how much that screwed up our lives, or how much we counted on your support. We managed to muddle through it and moved on with our lives. We can't go back and fix it."

Am I laying it on too thick?

"I always admired the way you took charge of your life and family, Ellen. You are a better person than I am, that's for sure. Can you find it in your heart to forgive me?"

Is that really regret, or his ability to act?

"I'll think about it. I really must be going." Something is inherently sad about him. He lived his life the way he wanted, with no regard for anyone else, and I'm too tired to hear any more. As I stand up to leave, he grabs my hand.

"Have a good race, Ellen. Hey, why don't we get together after my last show? We could catch a late supper? You and your husband?" Mr. C asks.

"What time is your last show?"

"Usually about one or so, is that too late for you?"

"Are you serious? If you're talking about one o'clock in the morning, I'll be asleep by nine. We're out on the practice track very early. It appears that we still live in two different time zones. Sorry, that won't be possible."

Mr. C stands up, kisses my cheek, and says, "Maybe next time then, good luck to you Ellen, and say hello to your family for me."

Now it's my turn to act.

"I'll do that. It was so nice to see you again."

"When your horse follows you without being asked,
when he rubs his head on yours,
and when you look at him and feel a tingle down your spine
you know you are loved."
~ John Lyons

Chapter Twelve

The Road to the Championship

During the last eliminator, as we were coming into the home stretch, a race bike flipped about four horses behind us. The driver was later pronounced dead. It has been one of my greatest fears from the moment we started to race. Glen and Reed instilled in us drivers how potentially dangerous it is out there on the track. Accidents happen when you least expect them.

It brings back the memory of my beautiful *Trinidad* and the accident that made me quit riding. I tried to explain to everyone that this was my quest. It's the last-ditch effort to bring Ashwood Stables back to its former glory; no one else can do this for me. If, after giving it my best and we don't win, then we'll have at least tried.

Is the road to the Championship paved with doubt or is it paved with hope? Did the incident happen as a wake-up call, or did it happen as a warning to stop this nonsense, as Glen so aptly puts it? Is it time to go back to my duties as wife, mother, and grandmother without ever knowing our potential?

Reed flew in the day before the race to bring me news of the home front. Melanie announced at dinner last night that she's serious about a Christmas wedding. She wants everyone to pitch in, so it's perfect. It will include a large church wedding and a reception to match. She and Jered haven't decided on the theme for the wedding, or where it will take place.

Oh Dear Lord--she wants a wedding at Christmas!

What on earth does she have in mind when she says wedding theme? It has to take a back seat until we get through the next few races! Already eliminated are some of the best drivers and horses. Will we be next?

Apprehension begins to overtake my thoughts, as these drivers had more experience than I have. When Jerry and the rest of us gather for our evening group strategies meeting after dinner, he offers some very sound advice.

"Miss Ellen, keep alert and enjoy the ride, but don't get too cocky. Stay the course."

It sounds simple enough, but it's good to know we're all in this together. Many of the drivers stay to chat, but then most nights I'm too exhausted and go directly to my room to avoid the pitfalls that entice those who remain too close to a casino.

When race day comes, all strategies fly out the window when *Prince* does his look back seconds before his coat ripples. Somehow, miracle upon miracle, we place third and move forward to cross another milestone race off our list.

Next up will be our fifth race that will be a significant hurdle--it's the Cane Pace, at Tioga Downs Racetrack and Casino. I must gather all my energy to concentrate on this one, as it's the first of three races that will kick off the Triple Crown series of harness racing. It will make or break what we've set out to do thus far. During our latest debriefing session, we discussed that this set of eliminators are especially harrowing.

Jockey Jerry and I get into a discussion about why we race in the first place; is it prestige? Is it for the money? Do the men do it to attract women? Knowing the female side of things; it isn't all glamor!

"I got a question for you, Miss Ellen. You mentioned you wanted to be a jockey and your parents wouldn't let you, right? They said it was too dangerous. Do you know how many times jockeys--and I mean seasoned, well-trained jockeys fall off their horse?"

"No, I hadn't given that much thought. After we saw Henshaw taken to the hospital, I thought that flipping my race bike was the worst thing that could happen."

"Yeah, that's a concern, too, but there's another thing that might put you out of the game. We all fell off our horse at one time or another. Most of us suffered concussions when we hit the deck, and it didn't matter whether we had a helmet on, or not! I saw it many times, Miss Ellen, sometimes the guys didn't pull through, and they died right in front of us."

"I hadn't thought about that aspect of things. I worried when Jason played sports. The coaches warned about possible concussions. Are you saying that to scare me? Come to think about it, Jerry, I've fallen off my horse." Then I remember what happened to *Trinidad* and my eyes suddenly tear up. "Horses get hurt, too."

"I'm saying it to help you realize that racing ain't all glory. It takes stamina, guts, and training to stay up on that horse. Your parents were right in not letting you race that way. It's a better way for you to win. Just so you know, there's been plenty of accidents with race bikes like we saw this week, too. Every one of us drivers used to be jockeys." Jerry stands to address the group. "Hey! How many of you jockey brats fell off your horse onto your noggin? Raise your hand if you did."

As we look around the room, nearly all drivers and their trainers raise their hands, including Jerry and me. Jerry shakes his head. "How many of you got a concussion from it, or broke some bones?"

Nearly everyone, except the owner's wives, raises their hands again.

"Okay, how many of you guys had more than one concussion in your years of racing and passed out when you did?"

Everyone looks at each other, then very slowly, every one of the jockeys raises their hands.

"There you have it, Miss Ellen; we've all fallen off our horses, and we've all gotten hit on the noggin and passed out. Some of us became confused, and doctors told us it's part of the concussion thing. I think it's that our brains get slammed around in our head when we hit the dirt."

"I don't know what to say, Jerry. I hadn't thought of racing this way, and I sure owe my Mother… boy, do I owe her an apology. Maybe she knew she was right, after all, I only broke my tailbone."

"Is that why you sit on that funny seat, Miss Ellen?" Jerry says, laughing.

"Yes. You can laugh all you want, but it works for me."

"Some of us are different when we wake up, Miss Ellen. Take Stevie there. He had a bad fall three years ago, and even though the doctor told him not to race anymore, he does it anyway. One morning we found him in the barn eating oats with his horse. He does some pretty strange things."

My thoughts go straight to Jason. Initially, we surmised that when he went missing, he might have been rendered unconscious. Maybe he couldn't recall who he was, and that's why he couldn't contact us.

A jockey named Jackson interrupts, saying, "Hey Jerry, did ya tell Miss Ellen here about that fella that was thrown from his horse and died right on the track? They took his body away, and when the doctor went in to check on him, he wasn't where he left him. He was seen walking around the betting window. He told everyone he was okay, and he was getting on his horse, which he did."

"That can't be true."

"It most certainly is, Ma'am, ask anyone in this room. They call it brain injury. Some of them have what's called traumatic brain injury. You know, our veterans get it when a bomb goes off too close to them. I heard they don't ever come back the same as they went. World War Two Vets called it shell shock.'"

"You're a computer person, ain't you Miss Ellen? Just search on brain injury. It'll give you lots of information," Jerry says, sipping his beer.

I don't know whether to be grateful for the information Jerry and his cronies have provided or mortified that they've told me this terrifying news.

The Battle of the Brandywine is only a week away from the qualifying races at the Cane Pace; however, it's too close to the Little Brown Jug. If we qualify and win to move forward, it will be too stressful for us to go back and forth to Virginia.

We have opted to have Reed drive us directly to Tioga Downs. Should we qualify to move forward from there, we could drive straight to Delaware, Ohio.

Even though Reed seldom complains, I guess that he's a little tired of all this driving and hauling and that he'd like to stop all this nonsense and stay home. Has Glen's negativity finally rubbed off on us? Some days it feels like nonsense to me too, especially the grueling and exhausting part that makes me fall fast asleep each night. At the back of my mind, the worry of injury is ever-present. Another horrible accident happened yesterday as a race bike flipped. Unlike Henshaw, he's still in ICU fighting for his life.

The entire time we were gone, Melanie bombarded me with emails. She sent at least forty-five pictures of wedding dresses, samples of invitations, gaudy flower arrangements, crazy linens, extravagant decorations, and brochures of exotic destinations. Then Mel nagged that no one was home to help her decide on these things. She couldn't rely on her family when she needed them the most.

Mel has no clue where she and Jared will live once they're married, although she has hinted a few times that Ashwood Manor (as Melanie calls it now) is large enough to house them. Then she stressed about Jared, who still hadn't decided on his career path. He was now spending more time with his parents, than with her lately.

Although she is trying to put up a brave front, the main thing is that Jared's parents haven't given their blessing upon their union. My suggestions fall on deaf ears as she refuses to postpone her wedding until spring. She's adamant that it will take place when she says it will–the day after Christmas.

Then one day, the email barrage stops, and it seems as if there might be trouble in River City. Mother used to joke when either Terre or I, had a problem with something. Taking a quote from the musical, *The Music Man*, she'd try to speak in a man's voice. "Ya got trouble, my friend, right here, I say, trouble right here in River City." It used to make us laugh, and it would defuse whatever was happening.

Sweet Jesus, how I miss her!

When we got to the hotel, my room had somehow vaporized. Reed will have no problem, as he's flying out tonight. He offered to clean out the horse trailer so that I could stay in it. It isn't half bad for brief periods of rest, but it hardly qualifies as a hotel room.

"I made this reservation months ago; here's the confirmation number! There better be a good explanation for this."

The front desk clerk explains that there is a big convention nearby and there isn't a single room available, anywhere. He called around to check. He's apologetic, but this sort of thing happens on occasion.

Not relishing spending the night in our horse trailer, when we meet up with Jerry, he mentions that Mr. Landers knows someone who might be able to pull some strings to get me a room. The hairs on the back of my neck tell me to be suspicious of rooms in strange hotels that are given by unknown do-gooders.

Before Reed left, he cleaned our trailer, and it doesn't smell as if a horse has been inside, and aside from the lack of electricity, and a proper bathroom, it's not half-bad. Jerry offered to let me use the shower in his room, but I declined as the restrooms at the racetrack are quite modern and updated.

The nights have cooled and the little vents on either side of the compartment open to allow air to flow through. The screen covering keeps the majority of the mosquitoes out. It would never have worked a few months ago when it was so hot. It's a pleasant experience, as there are sounds in the night much like there is back home in Virginia.

Adrian texted a day ago that he's coming to see the race, yet he didn't say when. Reed and Dr. Jess flew in yesterday, and I told them to take my room, as it became available. Until Adrian shows up, or another one is ready, the horse trailer will have to do.

Our discussion with the owners, trainers, and drivers last night after dinner, brought up some interesting topics. They mentioned that it's nearly impossible for an amateur such as myself to win. Some have gone on to win, and I'm here to either prove them wrong or enjoy the journey!

Then someone mentioned *American Pharoah* and how incredibly proud his owner must have been when his prized colt won the Kentucky Derby. Victor Espinoza, the jockey who rode him to victory, is now as famous as Red Pollard, the jockey who rode *Seabiscuit*.

Jerry has as many pre-race rituals as I do, and we laugh at each other when we've completed them. When the familiar sound of the horn taps out the *Call to the Post*, he gives the thumbs up, which signals to move into position.

In the time it takes to blink, *Prince* takes the lead as soon as the arms retract on the pace truck. We pass race bike after race bike as the grandstands go by in a blur. When the checkered flag falls, he keeps going. He's won, and we're doing our victory lap.

How does Prince know he's supposed to do this?

"Nice job, Miss Ellen," Jerry says when we come into the barn.

"Thanks. Didn't you come in second?"

"Yeah, Mr. Landers' right proud of *Little Anthony Two Shoes* here and me. You know, I think you've been good luck for us. Mr. Landers figured we'd be heading home after the third race. I told him flat-out that we could both make some money if we stuck to it like you and *The Prince* here. Guess he believed me."

"I don't think we had anything to do with it, Jerry, you're a good driver, and he's a good owner and trainer. It makes a big difference in the racing world, doesn't it?"

"Sure does, Miss Ellen. He sure has respect for you and your man, Reed. In fact, he asked if you could join us for dinner tonight."

"Oh, sorry, Jerry, Reed's wife is here, and they've planned a night out, or in. And I'm half expecting my husband to show up. Please extend our thanks to Mr. Landers. Maybe we can do it again sometime very soon."

I'm a little bummed that Adrian's latest text message says he's tied up and can't get away. I fight the impulse to leave a snarky text message. Is he literally tied to a chair? Or is he busy with something he can't talk about because of its sensitive nature?

We are on our way to Delaware, Ohio, for the second of the Triple Crown series called the Little Brown Jug. It takes place on September 19th, and it still amazes me that we're even here. Wasn't it a few short years ago that we came to Ashwood? And wasn't it Glen who mentioned the previous owner took his horse all the way to this very race? He called the other day to say how proud he is of us and it gave me a good feeling.

I'm relaxing in the trailer, about to eat a sandwich before the next elimination race. I'm debating whether I should answer it or let it go to voicemail. Deciding to answer it, Melanie begins to scream into my ear.

"I loved him, Mom, I really did!"

"What's happened, Mel? I'm not following you."

Between sobs, she says, "We talked about where we were going. We talked about what Jered wanted to do with his life! I thought I knew him!"

"Did something happen, sweetheart?"

"Mom, we were going to get married the day after Christmas! I never expected this, never!" Mel screams into the phone. "You told me to let him go, and I did! He did come back, and then he changed his mind!"

"I'm sorry Mel, maybe it wasn't meant to be, sweetie." Oh boy, what should I say? "It will get better sweetheart. I know your heart is breaking now, but it will get better."

"When? How did you ever get over Daddy?"

"I didn't. I might be angry with your Daddy for what he did, but he's still in my heart. He's right there with Jason and Grandma. Maybe you don't have to get over him. Maybe he'll always have a place in your heart."

"He's ripped it out you mean! It was so sudden! One day he was talking to me, the next he was leaving! I feel so used. His parents never liked me, you know. They're so stuck up I can't stand it. They have him so brainwashed, it's ridiculous."

Mel launches into a staccato-type sob mumbling something inaudible. Wishing now, that I was at the County Fair across the way, I'm instead listening to my daughter go on and on about how her fiancé dumped her for a girl of his parents' choosing. It's going to be a challenge to stay calm and focused for this next important race.

"Sweetheart, I'm going to have to call you back."

"Sure, go take care of your little horse and don't mind me, your own daughter. See, you're ignoring me again. You should be home with your family! Goodbye, I love you." Click. The phone call terminates.

Grabbing my laptop to search on a saying about the word love, it might help Mel to realize that now and then, we have to let go of things so that we can move on with our lives. Deciding that an email will have to do, for now, a few minutes later, she calls to apologize for her rudeness and tells me to have a good race. She will try to be better by the time we get home.

With the last elimination race complete for the day, it's easier to rest in the trailer for a few hours, rather than walk back to our hotel. We purchased a little scooter to help us get us around quickly when our hotels, stables, and trailer are not located close together.

Delicious aromas of cotton candy, sausage, and onions, or funnel cakes is assailing my nostrils. Reed took the scooter, and I'll bet he's out there right now getting a treat.

There's a knock on the trailer door. The small peephole only allows me to see the top of a cowboy hat. Opening the door cautiously, asking, "Who's there?"

When I open the door, a voice says, "Going somewhere little girl?"

I'm so happy to see Adrian that I jump on him, nearly knocking him to the ground! "Hello, cowboy, where in the heck did you come from?"

"Take it easy there, little filly, where are you headed in such a hurry?" Adrian sniffs the air and says, "Never mind, it's fair-food! Let's go."

"When did you get here? I'm so glad to see you. Reed took the scooter, so we can walk toward whatever you smell. How long are you staying? How did you know I was here? Did you see Reed? Did you check in at the hotel? Did you hear about Mel and Jared?"

"Ellie, let's take one question at a time, okay? One, I'm staying forever, two, I tracked you here, three, I didn't see Reed, four, I did check in at the hotel, five, I know all about Mel and Jered slash Kenny slash Jered and his fall from grace."

"Wow, have you been practicing memory games? That was amazing. I couldn't follow it, and I asked the questions!"

"It was also deductive reasoning. Reed told me you come to the trailer to take rests between races. I wasn't paying attention, but I'll be here from now on, okay?"

"What's changed? Did you give up the you know what? And I only come to the trailer when it's too far to go back to the hotel."

"A new director and a restructure of the you know what and Larry and I decided to retire. It's changed, Ellie, from a few years ago. It's changed so much, and since Levi isn't with us, neither one of us has that ambition anymore."

"I'm sorry, Adrian. That was your vocation in life."

"I want to be with you and the rest of the crazy clan called Thompson dash Sellers. I don't need that you know what thing all the time, but I do need you."

"Hey, what do you mean you tracked me here?"

Reed pulls up on the little scooter that looks like a toy under his big body. "Adrian! You old son-of-a-gun! When did you get here? And how long are you staying?"

As they talk, Reed slides the little scooter into the trailer, leaning it against the wall, locking it in place with the braces welded to hold it when we travel. It's lightweight so that anyone can roll it in and out without difficulty. It certainly made more sense to opt for the scooter instead of a golf cart.

Since we had space, we added a pull-down bunk bed and a little toilet room large enough to sit on a portable camping toilet. Everyone chides me about it at every opportunity. They merely don't understand what it's like out in the middle of a parking lot miles from a restroom!

When we first arrived, there were Little Brown Jug posters plastered on every telephone pole within the fairgrounds. It's amazing how many people had already gathered for this event. It has a long and prestigious record, for being one of the two most coveted races for Standardbred horses. Named in honor of the horse *Little Brown Jug*, he won nine consecutive races to become a United States Thoroughbred Association Hall of Fame Immortal in 1975.

Aside from all the excitement this second (of three) races promises, and unlike the previous elimination races, they consist of two heats. The first heat is split into several divisions. If we win in our division, then we return for the runoff heats. If we win both heats, then we could win the whole enchilada!

With Adrian here with us, Reed graciously bowed out of his duties and is on his way back to Virginia. I've decided that Adrian is precisely what I need to keep going.

We are in the barn to groom *Prince* when Adrian steps away to take a call. Patting his nose and moving toward his rump, there is a small package wrapped in brown paper on top of a bale of hay near the wall. Instinct and distrust kick in, as that's an odd place for Adrian to leave a gift.

"Houston, we may have a problem," he says, coming around the corner of the stall. "Security at the racetrack went RED. A call came into the Racing Secretary's Office about an hour ago, and it seems that a story is circulating about racehorses that are randomly killed before they're about to race. It sounded a little familiar."

"We may have another problem. Did you put that little package here to surprise me?"

Adrian instinctively pushes me behind him and knows better than to pick up the package. Instead, he bends to sniff the wrapper, poking it with his pen.

"Looks like someone left you a little gift."

"Who would do that, Adrian?"

"An admirer, perhaps? Let's let the racetrack people know, and they can x-ray it." Adrian places a call to racetrack security.

Within minutes, two people dressed in full bright yellow HAZMAT suits drive up in a yellow golf cart. As one person takes off the lid on an oversized, dark grey box, the other carefully places the small package inside, and they drive away.

"What do you think this is all about, Adrian?"

"I'll show you why security is nervous. You'll understand it better if you see it." Adrian opens his laptop, pressing a button, the screen fills with photos of *Didgeridoo* and *Truly Yours*. "This is what they're showing on Channel 9."

I'm dumbfounded! When the audio part comes on, it says that this was the first and second in a string of horse killings that plagued the south for more than a decade.

"Not this crap again."

"We don't know how the photos even got to the national level, Ellie. I talked to Sheriff Rocky, and he filed it away years ago. We can't understand what the purpose is for bringing it out now, do you? Did you royally upset someone, Ellen?"

"Not that I know of, but do you think they will disqualify us? Is this that fickle finger of fate thing coming back to haunt us?"

"Beats me." Adrian's cellphone rings and he steps away to answer it. When he comes back, he says, "Racetrack security says that the package is safe to open. The X-ray shows no bomb. It appears that it's a gift an admirer left. They opened it to make sure and will deliver it back to us in a few minutes."

Curiosity is getting to me, "What's in it?"

"They didn't say. We'll find out when the hazmat team gives it back to us." Adrian makes another call. He's still talking when racetrack security rolls up in their tricked out, streamlined, bright red golf cart. One of the men places the package in my hand.

"It's okay, Ma'am. There's no bomb or harmful substance in it. We had to open it, to be sure, and there's no way of knowing how it got here. We couldn't see much. Someone inadvertently erased our security footage. We're sorry for any inconvenience. Have a nice day."

Adrian ends his call. "Did you look inside?"

"What is this ridiculous nonsense about *Didge* and *Truly Yours*? Then the package shows up out of the blue."

"Do you want me to open it?" Adrian asks.

"Yes, mister smarty pants, you open it."

Adrian picks up the package and puts it near his ear, shaking it. We are surprised when it not only rattles, but there is a faint tinkle of bells. Opening the lid, he pulls out a square, silver box tied with a sloppy blue ribbon. "Care to guess what it is, Ellie?"

"What else have we seen that looks like that? They could have tied the bow better. It can only be one thing. I'm betting its tiny silver bells, Adrian."

He proceeds to pull off the ribbon and removes the box lid. He pushes the tissue paper aside and reaches in, and suddenly, he starts to shake his hand as if something has grabbed it. "Oh, it's got me!"

"Sure, and I'm the boogeyman. I've missed you, you know. Let me see it, please."

Adrian wrinkles his forehead. "How did you know it wasn't something awful?"

"The security guys would have told me." As Adrian pulls out the contents of the box, I'm speechless. "That's the same cluster I saw in Lassiter's barn, Adrian. You know the one I mean. It's the one that disappeared along with my cellphone! Is my cellphone in there, too?"

He rummages around in the box, then shakes his head. "How do you know it's the same cluster? I'll bet you can buy these online, Ellie. You do have a point. Don't let this throw you off today, okay? You've worked too hard to get where you are, so don't cave now. We'll get the teams on this, and we'll get this resolved. Let's go on about our business and keep our eyes open for anything strange."

"We all know how you bet, Adrian. I want you to be right about this. Would you talk to the track officials? It would make me feel better."

"Sure, be right back."

After Adrian has a chat with the track officials, they agreed that it would be business as usual, however, if they feel we're placing others' in jeopardy, or cause undue stress to anyone, our only option will be to withdraw from the heats and races. They also mention that we will have nothing to say about it.

What is the purpose behind the taunt of the tiny silver bells?

Adrian and I agree that something doesn't add up. Until we can get a better handle on it, we've decided to carry on. We'll stay vigilant, and keep a sharp eye on *Prince*. We will also bring our little pistols with us and complete what we came here to do.

For added insurance, Adrian called Josh and Jake, who are on their way to the race track. They will check the video footage, or find out what happened to the missing minutes, along with contacting companies who might have delivered packages this morning.

After our interesting afternoon, during our usual get together with the others, Jockey Jerry and I expound on what might come out of tomorrow's elimination heat runoffs.

We will both be working against some outstanding horses, and the competition will be aggressive. While I talk with Jerry, Adrian works the room asking discreet questions; however, no one can explain how the news studio acquired the damning photos.

After Josh and Jake arrived, they went to speak with the station manager at Studio 9. He merely told them that the photos were left in his cubby two days ago. He figured he'd look into the matter and felt that it was a newsworthy story.

When Josh and Jake view the security video with the station manager, they confirm that there are nineteen missing minutes. That's ample time for someone to sneak in and out of the building without detection. Adrian surmises that it might have been someone working at the station--someone bribed a handsome amount to risk their job there. No one knows who might be responsible.

How could two different video cameras go down at nearly the same time?

The voice inside my head screams that this incident is not enough to worry about right now. Things happen on a daily basis that we have no control over. Only yesterday, a horse was found dead behind one of the barns. Racetrack officials absolved all of us of any involvement and had the animal removed. What bothered me the most was that it was casually side-stepped. If someone is trying to mess with my head, they're doing an excellent job of it!

Adrian reminded me that 'united we stand, divided we fall,' which snapped me back to reality. I'm certainly not in total control of how *Prince* runs his race any more than Jerry is with his *Little Anthony Two Shoes*. We do agree that our *'silent code of conduct'* that drivers adhere to is what we need to concentrate upon; proper training equals good drivers, careful drivers equal no accidents, no accidents equal wins.

Keeping our race bikes from colliding with one another, or reining in our horse after we encourage them could be disastrous if it isn't done at the proper time. But the real power comes from the horses themselves. They are the ones who deserve most of the credit.

And when the moment of truth comes, we line up for the last heat as Jerry nods in my direction. It is the race that will determine whether we go on to the last one on our list. When *Prince* does his look back and his coat glistens in anticipation, I know he's ready.

Today, something is different. It's an exhilarating and liberating feeling when the pace truck moves forward, and the race bike begins to move. When the arm swings toward the sides of the truck, *Prince* is in his glory as he swiftly glides across the turf passing other drivers and race bikes with ease. As the grandstands go by in a blur, this reminds me of how grateful I am for this experience.

I try to remember all the things that Glen and Reed taught me, then give up and hang on. When the checkered flag waves, it signals that the race is over, but *Prince* keeps going around the track. He only starts to slow down when he sees Adrian and the guys near the fence.

Once again, *Prince* performed like a seasoned veteran. He left everyone behind long before I knew what was happening. He didn't hesitate from the start and never wavered, or slowed down, even when I tried to rein him in. Our magic word 'whoa' did not affect him, even when I tried to shout it in his direction. Glen would be so proud if he were here to see this, he'd be taking some of the credit for our success, and rightfully so.

At a celebratory dinner, we congratulate each other and show appreciation for our incredible teams. Everyone is here, owners, trainers, drivers, their significant others, as well as Adrian, Josh, and Jake. It's so noisy we can't hear what people are saying. They're all smiling and joking, sloshing their beer, smacking their glasses because they're so proud of what they have accomplished. Adrian is at my side since there is no way he's getting away from me.

One more win and one more race to get through. It's the reason for all the training, worry, and sacrifices that brought us to this point. Can we do it? Can all the distractions be put on hold or driven out of my mind long enough to concentrate? Are we able to take it to the end? Adrian assures me that we can and will. He's also promised not to leave my side. Win or no win, after this season, I'm hanging up my spurs for good. The demands are too high, and the pain is becoming intolerable.

We have a good long break before the eighth race in the series called the Messenger Stakes, so we try to adjust to being in each other's way again. Adrian suggests that we reconfigure the library to allow him more space and it works perfectly as his new office area.

Before Josh and Jake left for Langley, Adrian gave them the tiny silver bells so Jewels can examine them. Then, they will delve into the mystery of who might have sent them and get to the bottom of the pictures of our dead horses. These photos made national news, and when our family asks about it, Adrian says that the CIA is investigating the incident, and asks that it never be mentioned again.

After we settle back into life at Ashwood Manor, we resurrect our nonsensical topics of discussion around the dinner table. Since there are many of us together tonight, it makes it even more special.

"Tonight's word is *hyper*. The rules are that you can use it in a sentence, try to figure out a new word using it, or make something up using it as a derivative. It was Mack's idea, so it's his turn first, and as usual, we will not allow criticism from the crowd. The difference is that we can go around the table more than once."

"Thanks, Miss Ellen. I got a hyperactive horse," Mack says.

"That horse named *Prince* is hyper," Nathan says excusing himself, picking up his plate as he moves quickly toward the kitchen. "Thanks for dinner. I'm gonna skip dessert tonight. Night everyone."

We're all still thinking when Terre says, "You have to hyper-extend your neck to see into the fishbowl."

"The hypermedia has been hounding me lately," Danny declares.

Mack shakes his head, rolling his eyes, he says, "That's a bunch of hype, Danny."

"This is a diabolical hyper-boil," Dennis declares.

Lindy frowns, and then says, "That's not a word, Daddy. You have to use a real word."

"Then you come up with a better one," Dennis retorts.

"Okay, the child is hyperactive, like Little Reed." Lindy stands up to reach for the salt and pepper shakers. "Next."

Amala smiles, saying, "I think there is a thing called hyper-market."

"Don't be hypercritical of my sentences when I speak," Mona adds.

Curlie jumps in with, "Way to go, Miss Mona. Wait a minute. That hyper boil thing is real, but it's hyperbolic. I'm going to put the meat in the hyperbolic chamber to give it oxygen."

Adrian waves his napkin around his head. "Hyperbolic chamber, I've heard of that. It's used to treat people with the bends. My sentence is, I'm going to make a list with my hype, um, hyperbolic paraboloid."

Dr. Jess shakes her head in his direction. "That would be a hyperbaric chamber, Adrian. You can't make up words."

"I think you mean diabolical paraboloid," Reed offers. "That's my sentence. I think you mean diabolical paraboloid. Wait, it didn't have hyper in it. Let me try that again. You have to use a hyper-paranoid to make a building."

"No," Ginny says. "it's a math thing. I think that hyper-diabolical-paraboloid thing is a math equation."

"No, I say my teeth are hyperacid," Lindy replies.

"No, I say you need to be hyper-aggressive about getting a good summer job," Curlie announces.

"No, I think it has something to do with science," Melanie says with conviction. "Or maybe it's architecture. The hyper-sided building is leaning."

"You're all wrong, Danny says jumping in. "It means something different. I say you should be hyper ready for what life throws at you."

Glen throws a card on the table the size of a business card which reads: FREE PASS in bold letters. "I have no idea what you people are talkin about, so I'm gonna use my pass card."

When we began these shenanigans, we gave each person a free pass card to use. Up until now, no one has had to use it, and Glen has always been able to keep up. However, we all agree that this one is difficult, even for those of us who know what to do with the word.

Feeling the need to step into this, I offer, "Some of you were on the right track, and Ginny was right about it being a math equation, it's a geometry thing, such as lines going in different directions. I'll try to give you the short version. It's too complicated to describe elliptical paraboloids, used in architecture."

Terre starts to laugh. "I forgot you studied architecture, Ellie."

"The correct term is a hyperbolic paraboloid," I begin. "It's a saddle-shaped quadric surface that has hyperbolas and parabolas. Hyperbolas run parallel to two other coordinate planes called parabolas. Then you go into proper orientation, axes, and it's used to get those intersecting ceiling lines in cathedrals."

"Oh!" everyone exclaims at the same time.

"Yep, you're right, it's way too complicated for this group," Adrian says snickering.

After Melanie returned home from college, she secured a research-type job with the city, except she was never happy with it. Then a new museum opened in town, delighted that her Fine Arts Degree came in handy, as she accepted a job with the Crawford Museum.

Their exhibition of antique to modern doll houses, rare porcelain dolls and figurines, and stuffed bears is right up her alley. A bonus to having Mel home now is that she and Curlie are chummy once again, having mended their fences. In fact, all the girls go to town together, to either a movie or other activities. Curlie's fascination with Mack has waned, but to our chagrin, has picked up speed with Melanie.

BJ is the highlight of my life. I take him out to the paddock to pet the horses, and he squeals with delight. Since our talk about Jason, Amala has distanced herself from men. Did I make her feel that she should stay true to him? Adrian assures me that one day, she, too, will find love again.

I've pushed everything out of my mind to keep focused for the last and most important race that's coming up at the beginning of November. To my surprise, everyone wants to come. Since the race is on Veteran's Day and there isn't school, we agreed to allow the girls to go with us, but only if accompanied by an adult. Melanie becomes overly dramatic as usual. She reminded me that she was a college graduate and perfectly capable of getting them to the airport and back with no problem. Didn't I trust her to rent a car?

When the day arrives for us to leave with *Prince*, Reed and Dr. Jess tell me that the girls will fly with them two days before the actual race. The rental car companies have a strict policy that prohibits drivers under the age of twenty-five from renting vehicles.

Isn't it odd how things work themselves out?

Harrington Raceway is in Delaware, Ohio and it will take us longer to get there from Virginia. If a hotel room is not available, then we'll stay in the trailer. It's been modified to sleep two comfortably, a mini-sink was added, along with a small generator Reed and Adrian installed.

This race is making me more nervous than all the other races put together, as there's so much riding on it. As with the Little Brown Jug, the Messenger Stakes honors a horse named *Messenger*. He was born in England and later brought to the United States. Virtually all harness horses here can trace their lineage back to him.

The twist for the Messenger Stakes is that we have to win an elimination heat *and* the final heat on the same day to declare us the winner. If we survive the week of eliminators, we'll be in a good position. However, sporadic rainfall might eclipse the entire thing. Downpours dumped inches of water on the track in places where it was a muddy mess for days, closing down the racetrack for several hours.

We put so much time and effort into this, a little rain is no significant obstacle for us. To go home now, without winning, will mean failure. If we don't win, no amount of energy or stamina will help me to try again year after year. It's now or never.

Day after day, rain or shine, we somehow survive the week of eliminators and are waiting for the last heat that will determine who the winner will be. Mona stayed behind with Amala and the smaller children while my cheering section is in the grandstands. Glen, Terre, Dennis, Danny, and Mack surprised us yesterday when they walked in before dinner. We stood in a circle and prayed for a safe race, as we lifted our glasses to Jason, dedicating the race to him. They are all standing along the fence while Adrian is in the owner's box with Melanie and Curlie.

Jerry was sure he would ride beside me, but he was eliminated yesterday, which left his owner scratching his head. Instead, he's here to unclip the lead rope and give me last-minute advice. Putting his hand on my shoulder, he leans in to whisper that everyone is cheering for me, even Mr. Landers. Relax and enjoy the ride.

When the *Call to the Post* sounds, my body starts to shake before *Prince* does his look back, as he must feel the vibration. Whispering something in his direction, he moves forward when it's our turn to take our place in the parade out to the track. *Prince's* coat is glistening in anticipation, as if he's cold, except that I know from experience that he's full of energy. Does he know how important this race is to Ashwood Stables?

Are we expecting too much from him?

As the truck moves away, *The Prince* takes to the track in a burst of speed, and all I can do is hang on for dear life. I don't dare move from the awkward position this throws me into and wedge my boots through the footholds to stay on the bench. Hoping that *Prince* will slow a little, he doesn't, and it's impossible to turn my head, or pull back, as he will most certainly flip us at this speed.

As the other race bikes and grandstands fly by in a blur, there's no telling where we are, until the checkered flag appears. No one is next to us, and there's no one ahead of us. *Prince* slows down a little, and it's clear from that point on that we are the only ones left on the track.

"Whoa!" It's the signal he understands to mean he should slow down, but it doesn't always work when he's running flat-out. Pulling back on the reins slightly, he finally slows when a racetrack rider grabs his bridle. As he whispers to *Prince*, I try to straighten myself out. The young man eventually steers us toward the winner's circle.

Adrian cleverly adapted a contraption for my cellphone so that I could see incoming messages. It flashes: **U DONE GOOD KID** as drops of rain hit the screen. No one can see my joyful tears, as the rain starts to pelt us. It's a perfect day to win. I think how proud Daddy would have been to see this. Mother would be rejoicing, but Jason would be the most impressed.

The photographer captured a hilarious photograph of a soggy driver, as an equally pleased, but dripping owner held an umbrella over *The Desert Prince's* head. The second photograph was of our family as they gathered around us with their umbrellas. It's a most gratifying moment for Ashwood Stables and our grey, red, and black colors. Glen got so emotional that he hugged me. When he finally released me, there were tears in his eyes which he said were raindrops.

My silks are ruined.
It matters not, because I won't be wearing them after today.

The same dream keeps repeating itself almost every other night and each time I wake up screaming unintelligible words. We've been home less than a week, and Adrian's already tired of this, and frankly, it's getting a little old and exhausting for me too. I have an unshakeable feeling that someone is trying to whisper something to me. It isn't Mrs. Ashwood's spirit, nor is it Old Miss Abigail. The only other person it could be is Mother, or maybe it's Jason.

Mother has come to me in dreams. She helps to guide me when there's a perplexing problem, or we need a solution for something. Adrian's not receptive to stuff like this. If I tell him about it, he'll question my sanity and pull away from me again. What should the course of action be? Should we consult a medium, find a crystal ball or, how about using a Ouija board this time?

"Ellie, it's four o'clock in the morning. Stay here, and I'll get you some juice. Happy Anniversary, sweetheart!"

Is that today? How could I forget an important day like that?

Adrian comes back with a little glass. "We're out of juice, so I got you some wine. Try to go back to sleep, okay?"

"Happy Anniversary, Adrian, I completely forgot."

"Well, I didn't. Here, my wonderful-harness-winning-retired-from-horseracing-wife." Adrian hands me a little gold box tied with a red ribbon. "You made a new office for me in the library, so what more could I want?"

"It's wonderful having you home again. Adrian, this is beautiful."

"It's a locket. I know you already have one, but this one is different, see? Open it; all your children are in it, including me, although I'm not one of your children, I am important like one. After Levi died, it wasn't the same without him. I realize now that I can't change what happened and my life is here with you and everyone else. I'll take you warts and all."

"Thank you, how did you get the pictures so tiny?"

"I had help. I love you, Mrs. Ellen Thompson dash Sellers."

"I love you too, Mr. Adrian Benson Thompson dash Sellers."

"Now that racing is over, at least for you anyway, the thing that needs attention is Christmas. You can make up for this with a nice Christmas gift, okay?"

"Oh Lord, Adrian, Thanksgiving is mere weeks away, and Christmas will be here before we know it! I have some serious shopping to get to."

"It can wait until tomorrow. Come here, my little snickerdoodle."

When we were on our way back home, we took time to reflect on how much we missed each other. Adrian's absence left a gap, much as when Jason went missing, and then when Mother died. We were all affected by the departure of family members. We each had to figure out how to cope with that. He felt that no one understood what he was going through, then realized that we were only trying to help him.

As Adrian journeyed through the void that Levi left, I needed time to concentrate and travel with *Prince*. We achieved an unbelievable goal. The results of all our hard work will continue to pay off for a long time to come, as Ashwood Stables receives recognition as a prestigious and notable stable.

In fact, several magazines approached us for stories, which we've put off until after December, so we can also include the *Magic of Christmas.* It will also be an excellent way to promote Reed's new fund called the 'Jason Wish Foundation.' He wanted to honor Jason's memory and give children who need special prosthetics a means to have them for no cost.

Reed also wanted the child, and his/her parents to stay at the local bed and breakfast, during a weeklong equestrian experience. This year requests are triple the usual number.

BJ bounces into my office and goes straight to his shelf to pull items down to his truck mat. He didn't like the fact that Grandma wasn't here and he sure didn't like see my face on a video call. He was not allowed into my office while I was gone, so the message fiasco didn't happen again. Then Adrian moved the answering machine to a higher shelf in the library, so anyone can press the button and take messages. So far, this system is working fine, except that his little fingers have found the TV remote. As it clicks on, a smiling BJ plops down on the floor to watch the weather, of all things.

"Let's turn on something more appropriate. How about this?"

I press the buttons to change channels until a PBS station that has Big Bird reciting the alphabet comes onto the screen. He sits quietly, as I reach for the stack of mail to separate the envelopes from the magazines.

BJ sneaks up to take the remote off the side of the desk, as I make a grab for it and miss. He laughs and presses a button. While I'm trying to convince him to give it back to me, he aims it at the TV.

Disaster fills the screen. We are both so captivated by it that we sit down on the floor to watch. It must be an old recording of something. Then I notice last year's date. "Did I record this, or did you BJ?"

A young woman talks as the camera pans slowly to the right, then to the left. She begins by saying, *"Steve Danbury is our camera operator. I am Janice Danbury, who is the Producer of this Documentary: The Island of Kakae Luna, After the Storm."*

Hitting the PAUSE button, he looks up at me and starts to protest. "Where have I heard that before BJ?" He tries to grab the remote, but I hold it high above his head to think. "Now I remember; this *is* from last year. I must have pushed the wrong button."

Was this a mistake, or meant to happen? Adrian had come into my office and sat on the sofa. It was right after he brought Amala and BJ home. He asked me to turn it off because Levi was dead.

Pressing the PLAY button on the remote again, we continue to watch as the young woman talks about the destruction that followed a massive storm called Cyclone Billy. Footage taken days before the storm show pristine beaches and beautiful azure blue water. Mesmerized by what we are seeing, the camera slowly pans left and right to display the cabanas at the White Sands Resort.

As Janice interviews people, my phone rings. Hitting PAUSE and placing the remote on a high shelf, Amala comes in to announce that it's lunchtime. Temporarily distracted from the program again, this stays out of my mind, until after lunch.

When the red light begins to flash on the TV, it reminds me of the program. Pressing PLAY to rewind to the beginning, I'm interrupted twice more, so I abandon it once again. By now, it's time to celebrate with Adrian, as he's made reservations for our anniversary dinner.

Although Adrian and I are experiencing an extravagantly perfect meal, that documentary won't stay out of my mind. Adrian questions what is distracting me. I'm not ready to tell him yet. But I am determined to watch the entire thing very soon, and this time I'll pay closer attention.

> *"No man ever steps in the same river twice, for it's not the same river and he's not the same man."*
>
> ~ Heraclitus

Chapter Thirteen

Journey of a Thousand Steps

A delicious aroma wafts from the kitchen all the way to my office. Nancy is preparing our Thanksgiving dinner. Is she blowing the turkey aroma down the hallway? Mona is at the Gate House preparing her usual delectable pies, made from the pumpkins she grew this past summer in her garden.

Thanksgiving is not until tomorrow, and we don't want to keep Nancy from her own family, so she's fixing four small turkeys for us today. She figures there will be ample legs for those who like that part of the bird! The only problem is that we have to hide them so they won't disappear before dinner tomorrow.

Thanksgiving comes and goes, and I'm finally able to watch the program that has preoccupied my thoughts for the last several days. Shutting my office door, to signal no disruptions, I turn on the TV and click on the pre-recorded program.

Armed with a pad and pen, I'm determined to find out where to send funds. Scrolling through the program, I find where the young woman comes to the part about the small island. A chill runs up my spine, as it sounds familiar. I press PLAY and sit back to watch.

"We are a journalistic and adventurous couple who likes to visit out of the ordinary places before they become so popular you can't get a room. We specialize in volcanoes and obscure island retreats."

As the young woman continues, she says that she and her husband were on their honeymoon in the seaside village of Nakeilen, on the Island of Kakae Luna. It's part of the chain of islands that consist of the archipelago of The Republic of Vanuatu. The camera shifts to show a pretty woman dressed in white capris pants and a halter top. Her blond-streaked hair, tied back to keep the wind from blowing it into her face, is talking to the camera. I realize it's the same young woman who introduced the documentary.

It brings back the memory of all the newscasts of what happened when a cyclone blew through the South Pacific. It was around the same time Levi and Adrian were gone. Wasn't this close to Australia? And didn't an oil tanker move out of its path? As the camera changes scenes to the beach, I realize why it looks so familiar. It has captured the exact scene that has played out in my nightmares–and my heart skips a beat.

I press the PAUSE button to get Adrian. "Can you come in here and look at this program with me?" Moving swiftly into his space, I take his hand to pull him into my office.

"What is it, Ellie? You look like you've seen a ghost. What am I supposed to look at, the foaming water?" he says. "It's a tropical island! That's nice. You dragged me in here to see this?"

"It's what I see in my nightmares, Adrian. That's exactly what I've seen in my dreams!"

Adrian looks a bit stern. When he wrinkles his face in this type of expression, I know all too well what it means. He either thinks I'm exaggerating, or I'm telling him something that can't possibly be true.

"Ellie, when was this program recorded? That was a while ago, right?"

"Yes."

"Then you've seen it before. It must have stuck in your head, and you merely dreamt it. Doesn't Dr. Stevens have a name for this? It's a subconscious thing, isn't it?"

"Yes, it must have been recorded a while ago, but what has that got to do with anything? I never saw this part, until now."

"Are you sure? It was on the weather channel at least a hundred times, and it was plastered in every newspaper and newscast for months. You must have seen it, and it stuck in your head, and it came out as a nightmare. I learned a lot when I was back at Langley. I had nightmares too, about Levi, and about what happened. Once I worked through all that the dreams stopped. It was a huge relief to let go of it. When you work out whatever it is, it'll go away."

"Then I want to go there."

"Go where? To that obscure place that has no electricity and where the destruction was so bad that the boats couldn't drop off supplies? They can't even get near it. No, Ellie. I don't want you to go. Wait a minute. I remember this place. You wanted to help, and you wanted us to go there. I think I talked you out of it and you decided to send them money. Did you ever do that?"

"I have a sliver of recall about sending money to a relief effort, but no, something must have happened, and I never sent them anything. Those people probably still need help. I always felt that we should have helped the Hurricane Katrina victims."

"Ellie, leave it to agencies and organizations that know more about how to take care of this kind of thing. They don't need people like us who might get in their way. Why don't we send them money as you suggested?"

"Okay, let's do that. I'll find out where to send it."

Adrian goes back to his office space in the library, as I go back to the program to watch it in its entirety. Rewinding to when the young woman in the capris pants started to talk, I press PLAY.

"What you are about to see is actual footage taken a day before the storm blew over the island. Some dialogue will be from the actual footage we shot when we were there to celebrate our honeymoon. Other commentaries will be back at our studio."

The screen filled with a pristine landscape with beautiful skies and fluffy clouds. The ocean was calm, and the beach was empty except for a few seagulls that flew down to investigate an empty bag.

Janice said, *"It was a peaceful place, a place to enjoy the surf, do a little snorkeling, take a dip in the ocean, and lose yourself for a while."*

The camera wiggled slightly. *"I'm Steve Danbury. From this height, you can see out to the ocean where mountain ranges look like dark globules. My new bride and I came up to investigate the caves carved into the volcano's side. These volcanos are responsible for the birth of this island. As with other tourists, it's what draws people to the area as they can climb up here to explore the caves that someone dug many years ago. In the background, you can see some of the more than eighty-five such islands that make up the Archipelago of Vanuatu. Only sixty-five of these islands are inhabited."*

Janice took over the story from here. *"The White Sands Resort is run by a woman named Kalima Mansale. She was born and raised here. It is where she married and raised her four children. They all help her to maintain their resort and are very polite people who attempt to meet our every expectation. You will see how delightful the children are later in the program."*

In the next scene, Janice introduced a rather robust woman who was the proprietress of the White Sands Resort. She had an odd accent, and at first, it was difficult to understand what she was saying.

Janice turned toward Steve's camera, and said, *"I know what you're thinking, but the language is merely delightful once you understand it. It's a mixture of Hawaiian and Cajun, and you can pick it up quite easily, as I have."*

In the next scene, Janice was wearing shorts and a colorful t-shirt. She waved to the camera as it spanned the resort grounds and small round buildings came into view. Janice continued her commentary from the original video, and said, *"This is our little Cabana Number 3; it's our home for the next week. It's our honeymoon suite. Step inside; it's cozy and comfortable. Every morning, Mrs. Mansale sends over a tray with food piled so high that we eat it for lunch, too. We often pack a cooler and take it with us on hikes around the island."*

Steve followed his wife up the stairs and into their compact cabana. As he scanned the room, the bathroom door was ajar slightly, and blue ceramic tile was visible. A large bed faced wide plantation-type shuttered windows, and it looked quite cozy. Janice paused near the bed to touch the mosquito netting that was held back with a ribbon. Then she remarked how necessary it was, and made a silly gesture with her hands.

Steve's camera followed Janice back outside where he zoomed in on children playing under a huge tree. Janice began to talk to them, and they glanced at the camera and back to her. *"Hullo, hullo,"* the children said, waving at the camera, giggling.

Steve was now near the pool area, where Janice stopped to wave and acknowledge a thin young man who was holding a pile of towels. Janice walked toward this young man and said, *"Hullo, Brian!"* She turned back to wave at Steve, as his camera stayed focused on his wife. Brian's face was too far away to see until Steve zoomed in. As Janice got closer, he handed her a towel. Brian then turned toward the camera to wave at Steve.

Janice then said, *"Tank yu tumas, tata now."* Janice turned toward the camera and started to walk toward Steve. *"As you can surmise, the language is fun once you get the hang of it. Brian takes care of the pool area and is the eldest son of the widowed proprietress. The view from here is spectacular."*

The young woman stopped here, and the next scene is back in their studio. A large map was set up, and Janice Danbury started to expound on the unpredictable weather patterns that the world was experiencing. She talked about what the experts had to say about tsunamis, killer waves, cyclones, hurricanes, and typhoons. Then she mentioned how she lost her brother when he happened to be on Sumatra the day a killer wave came ashore.

"Here is a map of the South Pacific. You can see this is Australia and northeast of this are the islands in The Republic of Vanuatu chain. The storm of the century, called Cyclone Billy took this path, as you can see here." (Janice used a laser pen to illustrate and trace the path). *"These are the islands affected by the monster cyclone. Here is where the oil tanker had to move out of the area and later came back to rescue us and evacuate the surrounding islands."*

Janice continued speaking, adding her observations, and the proximation to Fiji from the Island of Kakae Luna. She talked about other areas affected by known storms and then mentioned how millibars are calculated. Then she segued into how the next videos might be disturbing to some people, apologizing for the graphic nature of them.

After a short pause, Janice said solemnly, *"We had a weather-band radio that alerted us to the potential danger, and we heard the first shrill alarm siren go off about eight hours before the storm hit. Steve was outside when he noticed people were boarding up their windows and moving about more quickly than usual.*

When the second alarm went off, it was Mrs. Mansale who took us to safety. She came to tell us to gather our things and follow her up to the caves. The same one we explored, the day before. What you are about to hear is the actual sound of that storm as we hunkered down inside the cave."

The screen faded from a serene beach scene to one that was completely black, as if Steve had left the lens cap on the camera. Then there was a strange howling sound. Steve's voice half-whispered while the audio played out in real-time.

"What you are hearing is the actual sound of the storm as it rages outside our cave. The storm sounds like a freight train whizzing past the opening. The water is seeping in a little bit, but the cave has drainage places, so it isn't much, and it drains quickly."

The documentary paused here, and the next scene is back in the studio as Steve continued with his commentary. *"Most of us fell asleep amidst the crashing and howling, as Mrs. Mansale passed out cotton balls. At one point, a tree branch wedged itself in the opening, but it helped to block out some of the rain and noise. It was around six a.m. when it started to lighten inside the cave. It was then that everyone began to venture outside. Again, we apologize for the graphic nature of what you are about to see."*

It is where their video footage started up again. Steve's camera panned slowly from right to left. The young man's voice cracked with emotion as he explained, *"The storm is over now, and people are coming out of other caves to see what remains of their homes and businesses. Oh, my God."* (Background audio picked up faint screams and noise.)

Steve followed Janice with his camera, as she began to speak. *"I have no idea what we'll find down there. I hope no one was hurt. There are no words to describe what we're seeing. Wow, I hope everyone got up to the caves in time."*

The camera jittered as Steve carefully made his way down the trail to the town following behind his wife. *"Steve is filming minutes after Cyclone Billy blew over the Island of Kakae Luna. It's a slippery and muddy mess leading down to the town. The trail is strewn with debris. I can't believe what I see,"* Janice mumbled toward the camera. *"It's indescribable."*

Steve's studio voice explained what his camera recorded as he moved toward the pool area. *"As you can see, the force of the wind blew random objects into the pool. The odd thing about that was it blew most of the water out of it. Janice found her hat sitting on a sofa inside the pool. The inhabitants were in shock when they saw what Cyclone Billy did to their homes and businesses."*

Janice continued her lecture in the studio, as Steve's footage scanned the scene. *"We lost whatever we couldn't carry to the cave that night, yet amidst the rubble, I found a pair of my shoes that looked as if someone stacked them up for a shoe sale. And this is what is remained of the White Sands Resort, and what the island inhabitants found that morning. Tourism had been the sustaining revenue for most of them, and it will take billions of dollars to reconstruct what is ruined. There are twisted signs; wood smashed against, and through things, there's a bicycle embedded in the only tree that still stands on the island, and the rest of it has been leveled and spread out."*

Steve was on the move, capturing the destruction, the large tree, and the bicycle when his camera stopped to catch Mrs. Mansale, as she surveyed the devastation. She was standing with her mouth open as her eldest son, Brian, tried to comfort her. For a moment, I'm dumbfounded.

I press the PREVIOUS button and replay the part where Brian turned his head and smiled at his Mother. It is so shocking to me; it leaves me speechless! Replaying and repeating it over and over again, I finish watching the rest of the program and jot down the names and email address of the people who made the documentary.

My heart is pounding in my chest. Deciding that Adrian should see this, I call out to him. "Adrian, can you come here and watch something with me? I think you should see this person. He looks like Jason."

"Ellie, why are we doing this? We've gone over this a hundred times."

"I know it's a long shot. Can you see that it could be Jason?"

Adrian stands in the doorway, his face reflecting his answer. "Ellie, it's not him."

"Can't you look at this before you make that decision?" Finding that part, I ask Adrian to take a look at it.

"It doesn't look anything like him. That person looks like a native. You have to let this go."

"I can't Adrian. Look at that destruction. Can't I go there to check it out? I know there's a slim chance that he could have gotten there. Maybe he was on an oil tanker, and it was going to Australia. They found him and pushed him overboard."

"Ellen, it's not Jason!" Adrian raises his voice. Adrian never raises his voice, and he almost never calls me Ellen.

"How do you know that? You don't know that for sure. It could be him."

Adrian moves me to the sofa, and pushes me gently to sit down, "It's not Jason. It's not Jason. They found him, Ellie."

"What do you mean they found him? And who are they?"

"It was almost three years ago, Ellie."

I start to rock my body and pull away from him, "What are you saying? Why did you wait until now to tell me? Were you ever going to tell me? I don't believe you!"

"No, Ellie, I wasn't going to tell you, at least not until I had to. All you had was faith, Ellie. I couldn't take that away from you. It's what kept you going." Adrian looks sad.

"Tell me now. There's more, isn't there? Tell me everything you know and don't leave anything out."

"I don't really want to."

"Do it anyway. I need these nightmares to stop, Adrian. How can they stop if there's no closure?"

"Okay, but you have to promise you won't go ballistic."

"I can't promise that. Tell me, Adrian!"

Taking a few moments to compose himself, he starts to pace the room, then says, "A signal came from the watch you gave Jason. It came from somewhere near the vicinity of those islands, so Levi gave the okay, and we sent someone there to investigate. The team was there for nearly two weeks, and they combed the area. They never found out where the signal originated. Then they went to the main inhabited islands to ask if they knew anything about a strange wristwatch and showed them a photo of Jason. That's when a police officer by the name of, I can't remember his name now."

"Really, the man who practices numbers, names, and places can't remember an important detail like that?"

"I remember important information. I drop it if it isn't something we need to know. I don't remember the guy's name. Don't you forget stuff once in a while? He did say there was a rash of unsolved murders around that time. It probably had to do with pirating or smuggling. A person matching Jason's description washed ashore with others who had no identification. They found Jason's watch on one of the bodies."

"Did they show this officer a picture of Jason?"

"Yes, they did, and they showed our team a picture of a John Doe injured at that time, and they were not a match."

"But one of them could have been Jason. Did you compare fingerprints, DNA, his dental records? What was this John Doe's name?"

Adrian seems impatient. "Ellie, the team may have noted that in their report, but the bottom line is that they couldn't confirm that the people who washed up on the beach were matches for Jason."

"How many people washed up on the beach at that time? Did they at least compare dental records or fingerprints? I gave that stuff to you and Levi right from when he went missing. Didn't the team use it?"

"Ellie, they would have told us otherwise. You have to let this go now. He's gone. Jason is gone, and he's not coming back. You have to get that into your thick head that he's dead!"

Adrian is so overwhelmed that he slams my office door behind him. Momentarily stunned by his reaction, determination takes over as the need to uncover the source of my nightmares starts to take shape. One way or another, there will be closure. It's time to flip the other side of the coin and finish with this once and for all.

Taking the paper chart from under my desk blotter, I go back over the emails from the people who responded from the oil tankers, making notes of where they are in approximation to the small islands in the South Pacific. Then I compose an email to the young couple that made the documentary of before and after Cyclone Billy hit, hoping against all hope that they will respond quickly.

The sheer number of islands that consist of The Republic of Vanuatu is impressive. Searching through the colossal information will take time. I decide to send emails to both the Vanuatu Police Force and the paramilitary wing, the Vanuatu Mobile Force. If photos of this John Doe person matches the one sent to me around the time Jason went missing, it could be the same person.

Luganville and Port Vila have main police commands. Perhaps one of them will have something to share with me, even though it might be a remote possibility, it's still an option. The information about Vanuatu is extensive. Digging a little deeper to see if there's anyone else to contact, there's a list of secondary police stations and eight police posts. That's not much coverage for so many islands, so I dismiss these, as they probably don't have telephone lines.

A website designated explicitly for islands hardest hit provides the name of a contact person. I email to offer my help, thinking this might track down more information because there's a great force pulling me in that direction. After an hour goes by without a response from anyone, it dawns on me that they are in a different time zone.

It's four o'clock in the morning, and I'm wide awake. I tiptoe downstairs to turn on my laptop. I'm disappointed when there are no new emails. Picking up a book to read as a distraction, I fall asleep on my office sofa. Rosie nudges the door open to wake me and I glance at the clock; it reads six. It will give me an early start on what needs to get done today.

Adrian has left me alone most of the day, and I've lingered in my office making Christmas gift lists and ordering things online. I'm sticking close to my computer hoping that by now, someone out there will respond to my emails.

It's well past dinner when a ping sounds. It's from the woman from the documentary. Unfortunately, it says that Janice and Steve Danbury are unavailable to take any emails at this time. She and her husband are out of the country on assignment and will not return, until January 10th of the new year. Sorry for any inconvenience, and have a lovely holiday! That's a fine howdy you do!

Was it supposed to be easy? Is anything ever that easy?

Everyone seems to have called it an early night as the house is quiet. "Come on, Rosie, let's go for a walk." Putting on a light jacket, we walk along the fence. *Prince* picks up his head when we get near. He slowly moves toward us, as he knows there's a carrot in my hand.

Rosie ambles toward the barn as Glen and Nathan push the door open. When Gus runs out, he makes a beeline toward us, barks loudly, and *Prince* pokes his head over the rail, as the dog jumps up. It always surprises me when they get so close their noses touch. The first time they did this, Glen said it's something that happens between animals that no one can explain.

"Time ta go home," Glen says. "Night, Missy. Come on, Gus, Mona's waitin on us."

Gus trots off to walk with Glen, as Rosie stays near me. Nathan reaches up to gently coax *Prince* to move along so that he can put him into the barn for the night.

"This horse don't like stayin in the barn, Miss Ellen. I open the door, and he thinks it's an invitation to leave."

"Did he let himself out again?"

He waves absently in my direction, and says, "Yeah, no matter what I do, he figures out how to get out unless we lock the door. He's smarter than some humans I know."

Chuckling to remember that *Didge* used to do that, too, I turn to watch Glen move slowly down the driveway toward the Gate House. He has aged in the decade we've known him. Still quick to give advice but slow to move. How much longer will he be able to keep up with the grueling schedule of maintaining our stables and training with the boys?

My mission is clear.

I know what my next move should be. When I come into the library, Adrian is facing the window overlooking the southern pasture talking on his cellphone, and doesn't notice me. Heading to my office to research when the next available flight to Port Vila is, I'm noting the only direct flight starts in Texas and ends in Sydney. Either way, it'll be an unbelievably long adventure. If I can sleep through most of it, there will be less pain from sitting so long.

Diving into Christmas plans, when everything's in order, I start to second-guess myself. What if I'm wrong about this and my theory won't hold up? What is my gut telling me to do? And why would this be okay with Adrian?

If I'm wrong, he may never trust me again. When I don't listen to my gut, that's when we get into trouble! I feel compelled to follow the whispered dreams, as there has to be something to this. My nightmares keep playing and replaying in my sleep every other night. The dreams have not slowly faded away as Dr. Laurel and Adrian said they would, they have become more frequent.

It's December 4th, and I make my big announcement at breakfast the next morning, saying, "Adrian, you know that spa we saw advertised when we went racing? I've decided to go there. Then I'll get down to some serious shopping. And I don't want to find any tampering with the boxes that are being sent home, understand?"

"Can I come too?" Curlie asks. "I could use a break from school."

An indignant Melanie says, "You're not going shopping without me!"

"Take me, take me, oh please take me away from the end of the grading period!" Terre laments. "Come on girls, let's get going or we'll be late!"

"No one's coming with me. I'm going shopping in town first and will send them home. Don't go snooping. None of you can keep secrets."

Adrian eyes me suspiciously. "What kind of secrets?"

"Christmas presents kind of secrets. I'll be sending some home, so I don't have to lug them all with me. Put them in my closet and no snooping, so that means DON'T open them! I'll know if you so much as sniff at them."

As the girls complain, Adrian says, "Remember, Santa is watching, so you better watch out."

"Yeah, yeah, yeah, you're blowing a perfectly good opportunity to have me as your stylist," Mel says. "I'm sure Mrs. Clemons will give me a few days off to help you."

"No one's coming with me. Have a good day, girls."

The grumbling starts as they all move out of the Morning Room, gather their coats and lunches as they leave for school and work. That was the end of that discussion, except Adrian isn't entirely satisfied. He leans toward me with an odd expression on his face, saying, "Where is this spa you're going to, my darling Clementine?"

"It's that one in Pennsylvania we kept passing. You remember the one they advertised everywhere the entire time we went out-of-state? We must have seen it at least a dozen times when we drove up through there when we raced. I told you I'd like to go there. You probably don't remember, since you were driving. Maybe that was Reed, anyway, I've made reservations, so don't disturb me for at least three days, okay? Then I'm going shopping."

Adrian drops the newspaper to pick up his cup, then looks at me over the rim. "Ellie, what are you really up to?"

"Whatever do you mean, Adrian? Don't you trust me?"

"Are you playing coy with me? You're not going to do anything stupid, are you? Are you planning on driving there, or shall I drive you to the airport?"

"What do you think I'm up to, darling? No, you don't need to drive me to the airport. That's all arranged."

Adrian raises his eyebrows. "Could you be going somewhere you shouldn't be going?"

"I don't know what you mean, Adrian. I'm going shopping right here in town first and expect some packages, but don't open them! Brenda said she would take me to the airport. She has someone coming in to stay at the Inn right about when I go out. It's all settled."

"I thought you said you were going shopping *after* you go to the spa?"

"You must have misunderstood me, darling CIA man. What I said was I'm going shopping in town first. Then I'm going to the spa to get into shape to do some marathon shopping. I'll be sending some stuff home. Don't peek at them. Stop trying to trip me up."

"If you're trying to stay in shape, why don't you take your thingy-doodle you purchased a while back that helps you keep track of your steps? I've heard that it encourages you to walk more. I'm just saying."

"Okay. I'll do that and thanks for reminding me."

Kissing Adrian's head and curious how many steps it will take to find Jason, I'm calculating that it will be at least a thousand, perhaps a hundred thousand, or maybe it'll be an epic journey of a million steps. Then Mother's words rumble in my head that I must follow my dreams. Did she mean that literally or figuratively? Was Mother referring to my dream to find Jason, or my quest to find peace and closure?

Adrian must decide to let it go. No one else knows about the documentary or cares much about what's happening so far from their lives. They won't even miss me.

I've deleted any incriminating emails that Adrian might figure out quickly. The part about Brenda is correct, as she'll take me to the airport. She also has instructions to put an envelope into the mail should I not return home by December 21st. It explains everything. And I did make reservations. But the truth is, my intention is not to go to the spa, but in a completely different direction.

I don't have much time before the flight leaves. I swore Brenda to secrecy should Adrian or my family ask questions. Packages will arrive within a few days, and the spa and shopping story should buy me at least a three days' head start. The only thing left to worry about is navigating through unfamiliar airports and time zones.

Trying to travel as light as possible, I've packed all necessary items into one suitcase including flattened cushions that can quickly inflate. A carry-on doesn't leave room for much else, besides my laptop, but I've managed to bring several thousand dollars and a prepaid cellphone that Brenda gave me. I have a credit card in Mother's name that Adrian doesn't know about, and it should throw him off for a while. The CIA man in him will pursue me relentlessly, should he figure this out.

Absently attaching the step counter to a belt loop on my jeans, anxiety threatens to overtake me. Australia is a country we wanted to visit at some point. Without a companion, it's making me a little nervous. Not keeping a journal of my earlier travels has always been one of my regrets, so I've taken to writing things down in a notebook.

When it's time to board the plane for the two-and-a-half-hour flight to Dallas-Fort Worth, an elderly couple sits down next to me and starts to chat, but I'm in no mood to do this and politely say I have a headache.

The step-counter already reads 6,675 steps, for a total of 3.47 miles. I'm trying not to stress over the fifteen, or so, hours that I'll be sitting in a seat, so I'm walking as much as possible. The two-hour layover in Sydney will give me time to walk before boarding the short flight to Port Vila. I intend to trick Adrian into thinking that I'm exercising at the spa.

Eating a salad as I walk, I absently look at my cellphone; there are no messages. Then chuckle, as no one knows the number. Flipping through my notebook, I now have several pages of written text that are mostly observations of the weather, architecture of the buildings, anything that is unusual plant wise, and how many steps calculated for each day.

After purchasing two paperbacks at a kiosk, I stand near the gate bound for Sydney. I usually can't sit for more than two hours without discomfort, but if I'm ever going to find closure, a little pain shouldn't stop me. I paid dearly for first-class tickets, so here's hoping they're worth it.

After reading for a while, my thoughts go to Officer Kensi. His Bislama-English improved after we started to correspond. My intuition tells me that Kensi knows something and he's unable to articulate it in his emails. Maybe by being there in person, we can connect better, that's the plan anyway.

Hardening myself for the long flight, I take a sleeping aid after dinner. When the cabin lights dim, I get as comfortable as possible, hoping my items stay inflated. Sleep comes quickly, and when the first vestiges of light peek through the windows, I'm pleasantly surprised there's relatively no pain, but I'm far from rested.

As I navigate through the Sydney airport, I walk as much as possible waiting for the short flight to Port Vila. Once I'm on the plane, I occupy my mind with possible strategies. From the air, the islands look clustered, some close to each other, others far apart.

My prayer is that my mission is quick and without incident. No matter what, this is an adventure. Information gathered thus far about what we know about Jason's disappearance is traveling with me. When something occurs to me, I write it down in my notebook immediately, before it vanishes.

After the plane lands and I retrieve my bag, I leave the tiny airport to find a taxi. Since there will be obstacles with our languages, I've printed the address on a piece of paper, which I hand over to an eager driver.

"Welkam yu," he chirps, opening the rear door reaching for my bag. He then nods his head and flips down the meter counter when he gets into the front seat. After a twenty-minute ride, the taxi comes to a stop, and the driver points to an unassuming red brick building. He gets out of the vehicle and comes around to my side where he opens the door, shakes his head and says, "Yu stesen polis!"

Maybe the sign blew away during the cyclone, and they haven't replaced it. Is this where Officer Kensi is? Suddenly, a large man wearing a uniform opens the door and walks toward us.

"Welkam. Gud aftenun, Misis. Mi polis Ofisa Kensi," he says, smiling broadly, trying to shake my hand.

Kensi helps with my suitcase, then says something to the taxi driver. I don't know how much the fare might be, so I fan some bills hoping he will help. "How much is the taxi ride? I mean, ha mas is taksi?"

Officer Kensi pulls out three bills and hands it to the driver. The taxi driver smiles, and he says something to him, and they both nod politely to each other. As the taxi drives away, Kensi grabs the handle on my suitcase, taking my arm to escort me inside the building.

"Wanem nem blong yu, mi polis Kensi," he smiles, then points to a chair next to a desk piled high with papers. The stale smell of coffee assails my nostrils, which reminds me of Glen and his never-ending pot of java.

Kensi is asking my name in what he thinks is my English, or is it his? He must have told me his name again. Before I left, I printed a quick A to Z reference sheet along with some phrases to help in understanding the Bislama language. It's not clear whether it will prepare me for the fact that people who inhabit these islands speak 113 languages. As if by magic, he produces a small pamphlet called *A Guide to Understanding the Bislama Language*, which he hands to me.

Turning the pages, I attempt to communicate with him. "Nem blog mi Fran Pe ters."

It's a little like playing charades in that Officer Kensi says something, and then I try to figure out what he means. We're tooling right along until he says something that I can't understand at all. He takes the book gently out of my hands, and thumbs through it, until he finds the right phrase.

"Pik in in i," he says slowly. "Lukum yu pikinini."

The translation means child. "Pikinini, yes, yes, I'm looking for my Pikinini Jason!"

"Bigfala pikinini," Kensi says proudly, and then laughs.

Shaking my head yes, I laugh too, because he must mean big child. Reaching into my bag to pull out the latest photo I have of Jason, he shakes his head to signal his understanding. Kensi then pulls a picture off his desk, and we look at them together. Pointing to the word translator that means *match* (or same), he shakes his head, NO.

Oh crap. It'll be a long few days if we can't communicate.

"Kolwater Misis?" he asks politely.

What is the word for yes, besides nodding my head and looking like a parrot imitating a word? I thumb furiously through the book to find the meaning is cold water. "Yes, I would like Kolwater."

Kensi nods his head and walks over to the little refrigerator under the cupboard where there is a nasty looking pot of coffee. He pulls out a bottle of water and then hands it to me as I find the correct phrase to say thank you, grateful he didn't ask if I wanted coffee.

"Tangkyu, tumas."

Kensi smiles, then starts to laugh. Am I saying thank you to Thomas, or does it mean thank you so much? Then he launches into a litany of words that have absolutely no meaning to me, stopping when I put my hand up to say, "Me no savee."

Officer Kensi laughs again. He takes the book to search on something, then reaches under his desk blotter to pull out a sheet of paper. He puts it into my hands to watch my reaction. I can read the left side of the page, but not the right side.

However, his list is impressive. I reach into my bag for my laptop, turn it on – then spot a printer, gesturing that I'd like to print something. Officer Kensi shakes his head NO, and points to my computer and then at his printer and it dawns on me that it will be difficult to print, without the proper codes or software.

Kensi says, "sendum postem," then points to his computer and then to mine. Of course, I can email it to him, and then he can print it. When my paper prints, he takes both papers and proclaims, "Lukum, sam. Sam ting, Misis!"

The door opens noisily as a man in the same type of uniform as Kensi comes in and expertly tosses his hat onto a coat rack. Kensi introduces him as, "Mi polis Ofisa Laput, nem blog Fran Pe ters."

"Hullo, Ofisa La put, sir."

Nem Oel Sip	Impoten Infomesen
Seawise	Kru infomesen
Alhambra	Blong Beginning Kantri
Hellespont II	Listim/Kago Oel Narafala saplae
Apollo's Universe	Frenem Kem
Giant	Frenem Livim
Mont Bagarap	Drag Bisnes Stilman Pirit sips
Leader of the Universe	Presen sip Ona
Hellespont I	Seves/aot seves
Praevet Selbot – Bottom	No trabole
Sip MO Nem	Narafala

PERSIAN GULF/INFORMATION - OIL TANKERS	
❖ CRUDE- transports unrefined oil from oil fields	
• Product – transports smaller amounts to other locations	
1. Apollo's Universe	Moored – normal shipping lines
2. Alhambra	Moored – normal shipping lines
3. Hellespont	Going out-went south, then east- Normal shipping lines
4. Giant – ultra carrier	In the South Pacific area – too large to fit into the Gulf
5. Seawise	Moored – normal shipping lines
6. no name – where is this?	Usually goes around Australia several times
PERTINENT DETAILS	
CREW INFORMATION Names Country of origin	SHIP INFORMATION • Origin of nation
Manifests Types of cargo Crude Set for refinery other	Dates of travel Inland Or port Piped from ship Ocean currents Time of year/storms miscellaneous

Kensi's Ships and Lines

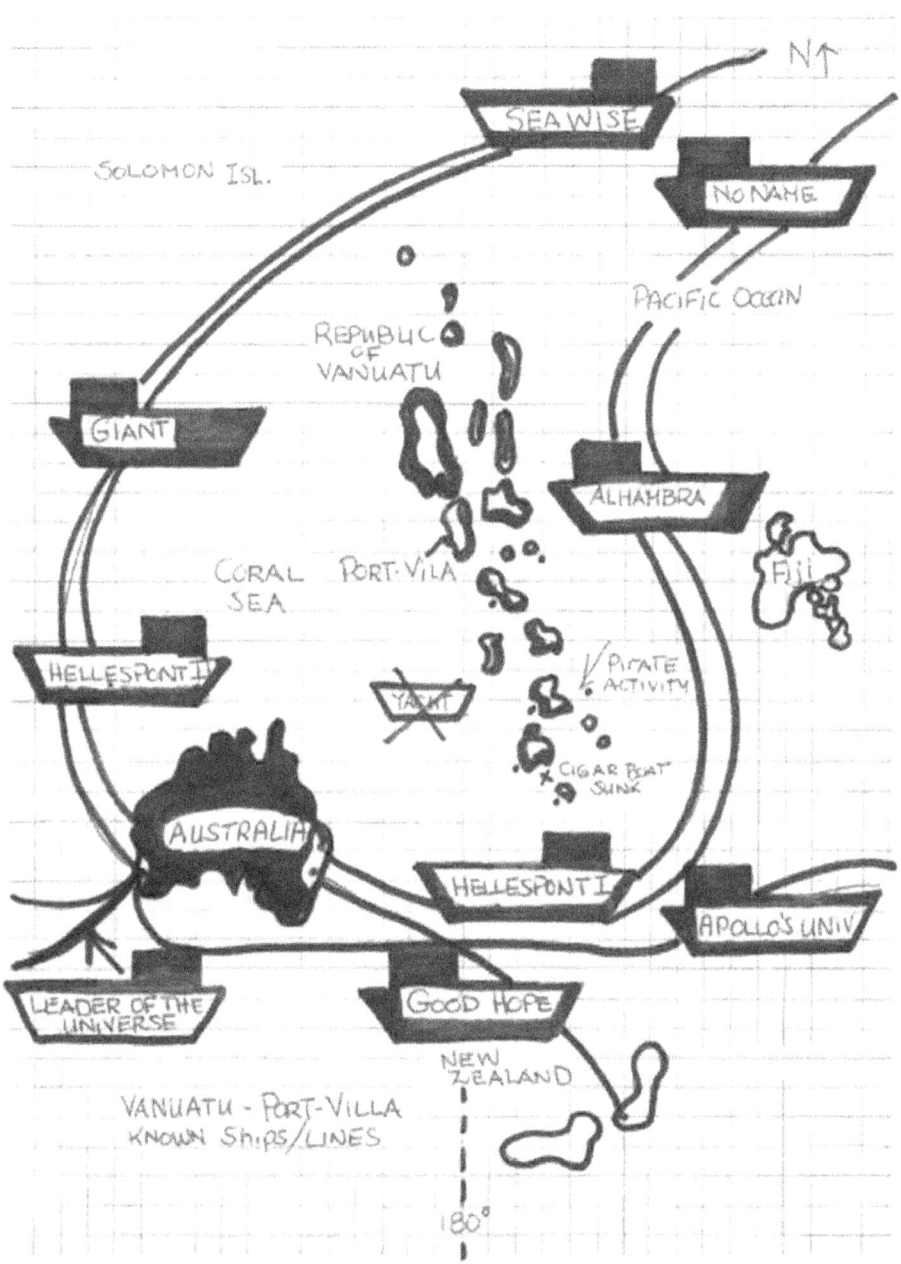

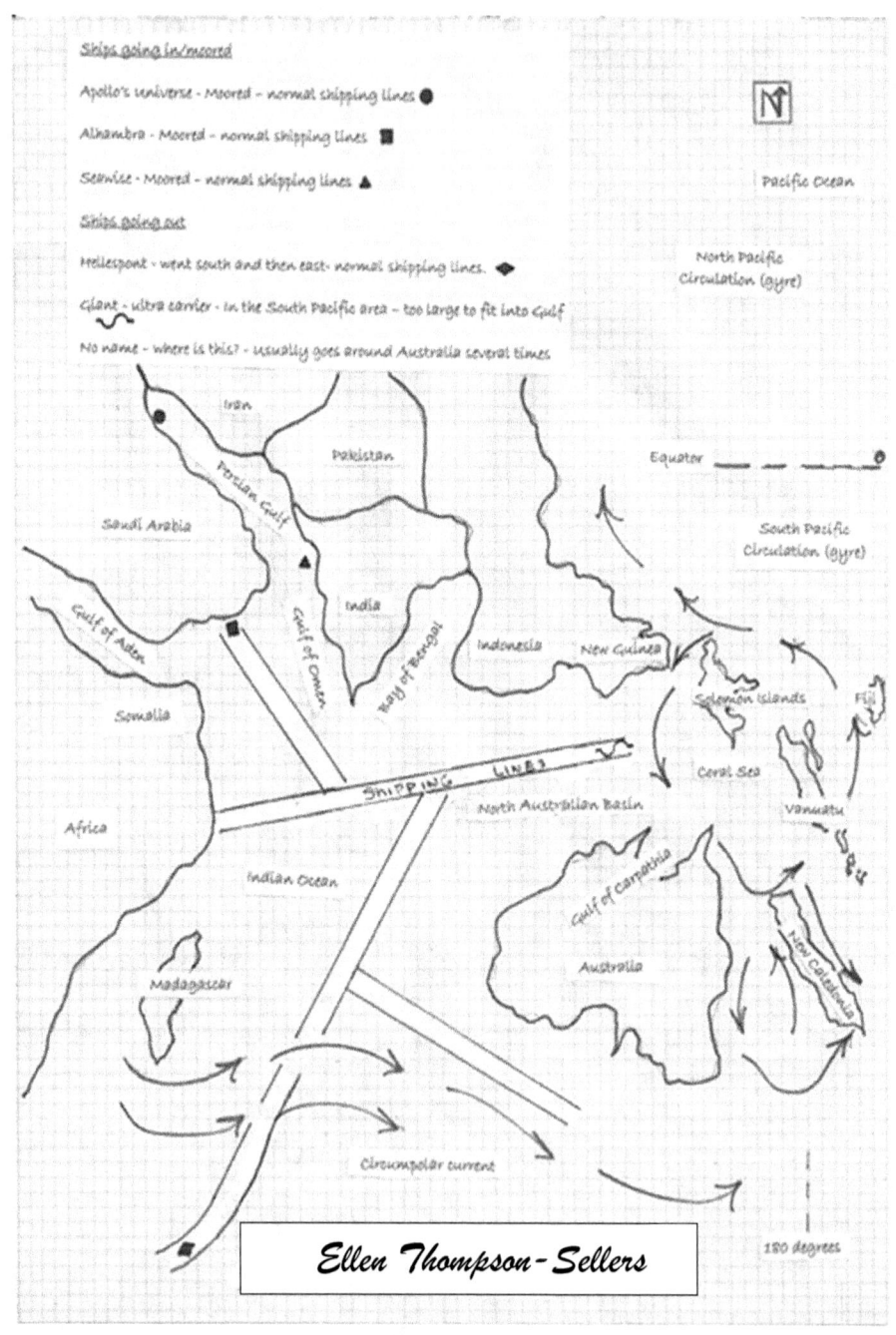

How will I communicate with these people without sounding stupid, or condescending?

Kensi takes both lists to show Officer Laput. They stare at each other for a few seconds. We have managed to narrow down several of the same oil tankers with almost the same criteria. The older officer shakes his head, mumbling something, and then throws his head back to laugh. Then Kensi starts to laugh, as they both look at me and smile.

"Nambawan!" The officer named Laput exclaims.

I rummage through the book to find the translation, which means best or excellent. "Nam ba wan, yes. You are saying it's a good thing. Nambawan!" Repeating the word several times will help me to remember it.

Officer Kensi proudly states, "Sam ting."

Then he reaches under the table to pull out a large piece of paper that has little cardboard pieces, where he points to the oil tankers, and then at his list. He then waits for the information to come on my laptop screen. We sit and look at each other in astonishment. It looks as though we have worked on the same theory!

"Lukum, there is more." I hand him my map of the oil tankers.

Officer Laput's pronunciation is harder to understand, so Kensi points to his map, then to mine. Officer Laput scratches his head and starts to laugh again. Is he laughing more at our remarkably similar maps or the idea that halfway around the world we have connected in a common bond to solve a mystery?

Putting the CD of the documentary about the White Sands Resort into the slot on my computer, I'm pointing to the Island of Kakae Luna. When Janice Danbury starts her narration, I stop it when she gets to the pool area, where I point to the person she says is Brian.

"Brian. Is this your John Doe?"

"Andru mo Brian," Kensi says.

Then I ask where everyone went after the cyclone blew through. However, either the language barrier or my tiredness is catching up with me.

From the information I was able to gather, there are several known facts about the residents and their extraction, yet what interests me is where the inhabitants went *after* the Red Cross tanker took them away. In my humble estimation, it could lead us to the person named Brian. As we put our heads together and try to communicate, we study the oil tankers. We've narrowed it down to two ships; the ***Hellespont***, and the one that eluded both of us that we finally found called the ***Sea Nymph***.

Kensi has one more surprise. He hands me a photo and then launches into an animated gesture by taking his camera out of his desk drawer, pretending to take a picture of me, then pantomimes opening the back to take out the film, walks to the door, and points down the street to the drug store.

All I get out of that was that he went to the drug store down the street to get his film developed. Perhaps he forgot he had the film, as the date stamped on the bottom of the photo is from nearly three years ago. He then hands me two pictures of a young man in a hospital gown. One I'd seen before; the other one is new. Kensi touches the back of the photo, nods his head, and raises his eyebrows, "Brian, Misis, tat Brian, yu pikinini?"

I'm shaking my head when he takes a sheet of paper to cover the bottom of both photos, showing the noses to the forehead, and then does the same thing from the opposite direction. "It could be, tangyu tumas."

Kensi smiles, pointing at me and then at himself walking his fingers across his desk, he says, "Yu wantem samting long kakae and slip?" Then he switches to pantomime eating with a pretend fork, sleeping by putting his hands together, and then he closes his eyes and makes a snoring sound.

Was that in Bislama English, or my English-English?

Weariness is slowing me down, so I stuff this into my bag along with my laptop, notebook, and the other papers, unsure whether this is or is not Jason. "Yes, mi wan tum go long kaki and sleep."

Officer Kensi takes the handle on my suitcase and says to Officer Laput, "Gud naet, lukim yu." He makes hand gestures and says we're walking to a rentem slip that is not far from the police station. Did he say we're going to a rented slip? Yikes! Not entirely sure where we're going, but when we step into a hotel lobby, it's clean, charming, and colorful.

"Welcome to Port Vila and the Grand Hotel, Madame. How may I assist you?" A cheerful young woman greets us. As it happens, she speaks the King's English, and I nearly jump over the counter to kiss her. Her nametag reads Miss Cindy Gifford, Gloucester, UK. "May I see your identification, please?"

Handing Cindy my passport, ID, and the credit card, Cindy remarks that the photo doesn't do me justice, asks about my new hairstyle, takes the card, and then turns to the register for me to sign.

The ID cards are from Mother's past life that I forgot to shred. Luckily, they haven't expired yet. Her signature was easy to replicate. I look remarkably like Mother, the more so with age, although the hairstyle and color of hair are not the same. The security people had the same reaction, but no one said anything, except a comment or two about the new hairstyle.

Why I kept this stuff is a mystery.

Pulling out the photos Kensi gave me, I ask Cindy for her help. "Can you ask Officer Kensi some questions for me?" Beyond tired, I push myself to stay alert. Kensi needs to know why I'm here and what I need from him.

"Of course," Cindy replies, "ask away."

"How can we find this person named Brian?"

After Cindy understands the question, she translates my request into Bislama-English and then back into English-English for me.

"He says that Brian, or Andru as they called him at first, was claimed by his Uncle Rexley about three maybe four years ago."

"Where does Officer Kensi think this Brian might be right now?"

Cindy translates and then turns toward me. "Kensi thinks that he lived on the Island of Kakae Luna. Unfortunately, the cyclone destroyed it, and he doesn't think anyone went back there to live."

"Okay. Would you ask Kensi if he has any idea where we might find this person named Brian now?"

Miss Cindy turns to speak to Kensi again where they converse for several minutes. "Kensi says that if Brian was part of the relief effort, he could have gone to another island. There's no telling where Brian is now. He sent out photos of Brian a while ago, and no one responded. He hasn't seen him since his uncle took him away."

My heart sinks, it could be a virtual needle in a haystack to track this person down. They both see how distraught I am. Officer Kensi puts a gentle hand on my shoulder.

"Can you ask him if he can help me find this Brian? It might be my son. He's been missing for nearly four years. Perhaps he's seen his picture in the paper a long while back. He was going to be a Saudi Crown Prince."

Miss Cindy starts to explain, and when she gets to the part about the Crown Prince in Saudi, his face lights up. "Kensi says he will help you because he also thinks that this person named Brian could be your son, but you will have to travel around in his small boat, and that will take time."

"Thank him for me, Cindy. I appreciate this gesture."

"Kensi has several days off and knows most of the islands so that he will take you. He's unsure where to look first but he can put a plan together by tomorrow morning. When do you want to leave?"

My eyes fill with tears, as hope returns. Turning to face the big man, saying, "You would do that?"

Cindy adds that it will be his distinct pleasure to help me, as he always knew there was something off about the way the uncle took Brian from the hospital. Something always bothered him about that.

Instinct. It's an odd little word. Does Officer Kensi use this to solve local crimes? He looks as if he could lift two hundred pounds without a struggle. Still, he has a very gentle way of speaking. He gets the point across without being overbearing, as some people his size can. We agree to meet tomorrow morning at around eight.

I'm feeling a bit guilty because of how this came about, but exhilarated at the prospect that there is progress. One whole day and a half are gone. What will Adrian say when he finds out about the spa in Pennsylvania? He'll no doubt find out by his extraordinary deductive reasoning. He was a little suspicious before I left. He might know by now.

(Note in journal: 77,800 steps = 31.12 miles today)

It can't be right! Did the counter capture some of the miles it took to get here?

Now I'll have to concoct something to tell Adrian.

*"And I looked, and behold,
a pale horse, and his name that sat on him was Death, and
Hell followed with him."*

~ King James Version Bible, Revelations 6:8

Chapter Fourteen

Determination, Fortitude, & Resilience

After a good night's rest on a real bed, I'm up early, refreshed, and full of anticipation. Who knows what the day will bring? The possibility exists that we won't find this person named Brian today, but the betting woman in me thinks that the odds are in my favor that we'll find him in the next few days. Did someone whisper that to me during a dream last night?

Did Mother's presence follow me here? Was it her voice or my own?

Resetting the step counter back to zero, I walk toward the lobby as Miss Cindy, and Officer Kensi turn to greet me. He has chosen to wear cutoffs and a shirt with no sleeves, no socks, and off-white tennis shoes.

Pulling the ball cap off his head, he cheerfully says, "Gud moning, Misis Pe ters."

"Good morning, Officer Kensi, you're up bright and early."

"Mo eli," he says shaking his head, laughing.

It's a good start anyway. Miss Cindy needs to deliver information to Officer Kensi before we leave. We need a clear understanding of why and what I expect of him. A handsome reward for the safe return of my son is what I'm offering him.

As she relates this, she suddenly remembers reading about a John Doe who was snagged by a local angler and taken to the hospital. She and Kensi talk back and forth, and she mentions there were several unsolved murders at the time.

Dead men seemed to show up on the beach. Everyone thought that it had to do with pirating or smuggling. It almost destroyed tourism at that time, and then Cyclone Billy took the headlines. Over time, everyone forgot about the murders, as the relief effort took center stage.

It feels like the right place to start the search for Jason. In the short time we have, my goal is that it won't take a thousand steps to find him. Kensi seems good at what he does, and his efforts will be well-rewarded.

As we walk through the lobby on the first day of our adventure, we'll have to get around by pointing and making due, as the booklet can't come up with all the things we want to say, or apparently, what Kensi intends to convey. He knows the skinny version of my mission, and we'll rely on his good judgment in matters that only he knows are lawful.

"Nes Gor'gena mo dokta Malas ospital," Kensi says smiling.

I understand that to mean that our first stop will be the hospital to visit with his wife and Dr. Malas, as Cindy explained before we left, as they were on hand the day Andru/Brian came into the emergency room. They tended to him throughout his recuperation, before his uncle took him away. The language barrier might be difficult, yet it's an obstacle we must somehow overcome.

Kensi pulls a small tattered notepad from his pocket, saying, "Andru mo Brian." He told me earlier that it's the one he used to make notes on the day he first came to question John Doe/Andru/Brian. Then he taps his finger on the pad and says something else I don't comprehend.

We walk down the hospital corridor, as the green color jumps out at me, reminding me of my dislike of hospitals. Kensi stops to talk with the woman at the front desk who is talking on the phone, glances up at the unlikely duo, then points down the hall to her left.

A female voice greets Kensi, and we turn to see a beautiful young woman in white scrubs who Kensi says is his "waef Gor'gena." She smiles, taking my hand to squeeze it, and we walk down the hall to wait for Dr. Malas.

While the two of them converse, there is a window facing the ocean. What a lovely setting it is with the mountain range behind it. Did Jason see this same thing? Realizing how unwise this line of thinking is, it reminds me of the cruises we've taken. Most islands look the same from a distance. It's when you get up close that the differences make themselves known. Brightly colored buildings are indistinguishable until you're nearly on top of them.

Several minutes later, a man in a white lab coat comes into the room with a folder whom Gor'gena introduces as Dr. Malas. "Alo, Mrs. Peters. I am happy to meet you."

We won't have to play guessing words to understand each other since Dr. Malas is an educated man who attended the Oxford School of Medicine. He takes my hand and asks what he can do for me.

"Dr. Malas, thank you for taking the time to meet me. I'll be as brief as possible. My son disappeared a few years ago, and I know in my gut and my heart that he might still be alive. It's a rather long story. Officer Kensi and I believe that the Andru-Brian person who was here at your hospital may be my son, Jason."

Taking the photos that Kensi and I brought to show the doctor, I fan them all out across his desk. Dr. Malas pulls out a magnifying glass to scrutinize them.

"Do you think it's possible that these are the same person?"

He stares at me for a moment. "Anything is possible Mrs. Peters. I must tell you that we had no photograph of the young man. We had no frame of reference before surgery. His cheekbones were, I am sorry; this must be so difficult for you. You have come a long way."

"Please go on. I must know all of it."

"This young man needed several surgeries. His cheekbones were such that he had trouble breathing. We assumed he was native to the islands, because of his skin tone. We had no idea what his face looked like without relatives to supply photographs. His appearance, well, it was difficult, so we tried to reconstruct what we thought was his normal features. I see from this photograph that your son's nose is more refined. I am sorry, we did the best we could."

"Dr. Malas, a doctor who tries to save a person's life never needs to apologize. You did what you thought was right. I appreciate what you did for him. Even if it turns out that he isn't *my* son, you gave a mother back *her* son."

"Thank you for your kindness, Mrs. Peters. He may have additional surgery to comply more with his normal nose should you find him, and he is your son. After he left the hospital, no other doctor saw him. I checked with all the other clinics. It didn't seem right that the uncle took him away like that. Nurse Gor'gena tried to contact me when the uncle came to collect Andru; however, I was unavailable. We assumed that it was his real uncle that took him home to his mother. Months later, I believe the hospital sent someone to look for the uncle. He ran off and left a large hospital bill."

I open my notebook to thumb through the pages, asking, "What about the other bodies that came in at the same time? Is it possible they are connected to what happened to this Brian? If Brian is not my son, could one of the other unidentified bodies be him? I need to know."

"Yes," Dr. Malas blinks and sits back in his chair. "I believe two more men were also brought here at the same time. They are most likely in a crypt for unmarked persons. There were more after that, too." Dr. Malas glances at Kensi, says something to him, then Kensi shakes his head, yes.

"And did anyone check their fingerprints? How about dental records? Were those checked?"

The doctor looks thoughtful, turning to Kensi to speak again, except this time he looks at the floor. Kensi launches into a string of words, but he's talking so fast, that my little translation booklet is useless.

"Officer Kensi says that they did not take Andru's fingerprints, as Officer Laput and he thought one, or the other had already done this, but it turns out that neither one of them did it."

I then pull out Jason's dental records, a card with his fingerprints, and a sample of his DNA, saying, "Then let's start here, shall we?" I point to my teeth and then at the tips of my fingers and everyone responds with, "Ahhhhhh."

"You have come prepared, I see," Dr. Malas smiles. "We will need to consult with the authorities to have the bodies exhumed for testing. It may take time to do this with the holidays coming up, but I will try to push this through as quickly as possible."

"I'm on a tight deadline. I only have until December 19th, and then I have to go back home." (tick-tock is rumbling in my head) "Is there any way you can get this done sooner?"

"We will do the best we can with the samples you brought, Mrs. Peters. Perhaps we can move this along a little quicker."

"Here is my cellphone number. Please call me if you have information that will help to find my son."

"I shall," he says, patting my hand. "I hope and pray for your success in finding your son before you have to go home. I also hope that you will not be disappointed if it is not your son."

"Thank you, Dr. Malas, I appreciate that." Another thought surfaces; if we find Brian and it turns out to be Jason, I'll be dealing with either an irate or a hysterical mother.

Gor'gena says something to the doctor. They converse back and forth for several minutes, and then he turns toward me to explain. "Gor'gena would like you to know that she and Kensi were quite fond of Andru-Brian as was I. They sat with him many nights to read to him. He didn't always respond with words, especially the first few months he was with us. They tried to be as kind to him as they could."

"Please tell them both that I appreciate everything all of you did for him. If it turns out not to be my Jason, in my book, you are all kind and wonderful people."

Dr. Malas adds, "I also want to caution you that if it is your son, you need to prepare yourself for a shock. His CT scans showed some brain damage along the left frontal lobe, and he may not be able to speak or remember who you are due to his amnesia. Traumatic brain injuries are different than other injuries. It is not like a broken bone that heals in a certain amount of time."

I did some research on what a blunt force trauma could do to a person's brain when Jason played sports. And then recall what Jockey Jerry and his friends went through when they suffered concussions. Severe head injuries can leave the person in a vegetative or unresponsive state, or the person can lose all or parts of their memory. I've maintained all along, that if someone hit Jason on the head, threw him overboard, and he now suffers from amnesia, he might not remember who he is. And this is the reason he has not called us.

Thanking Dr. Malas, I put my hand out and he pulls me into a hug instead. "What a brave person you are to come all this way on a hunch. I hope you find your son quickly. A miracle for Christmas," he whispers near my ear. "That is what the doctor orders for you."

Before we leave Gor'gena at the front entrance, she reaches out to hug me. She is somehow attached to this Andru-Brian person and wants closure to this madness called life, as I do.

Kensi stops at a little café to plan our next move. He spreads a map of The Republic of Vanuatu on the table and points to the islands south of Port Vila that he has already marked as possibilities.

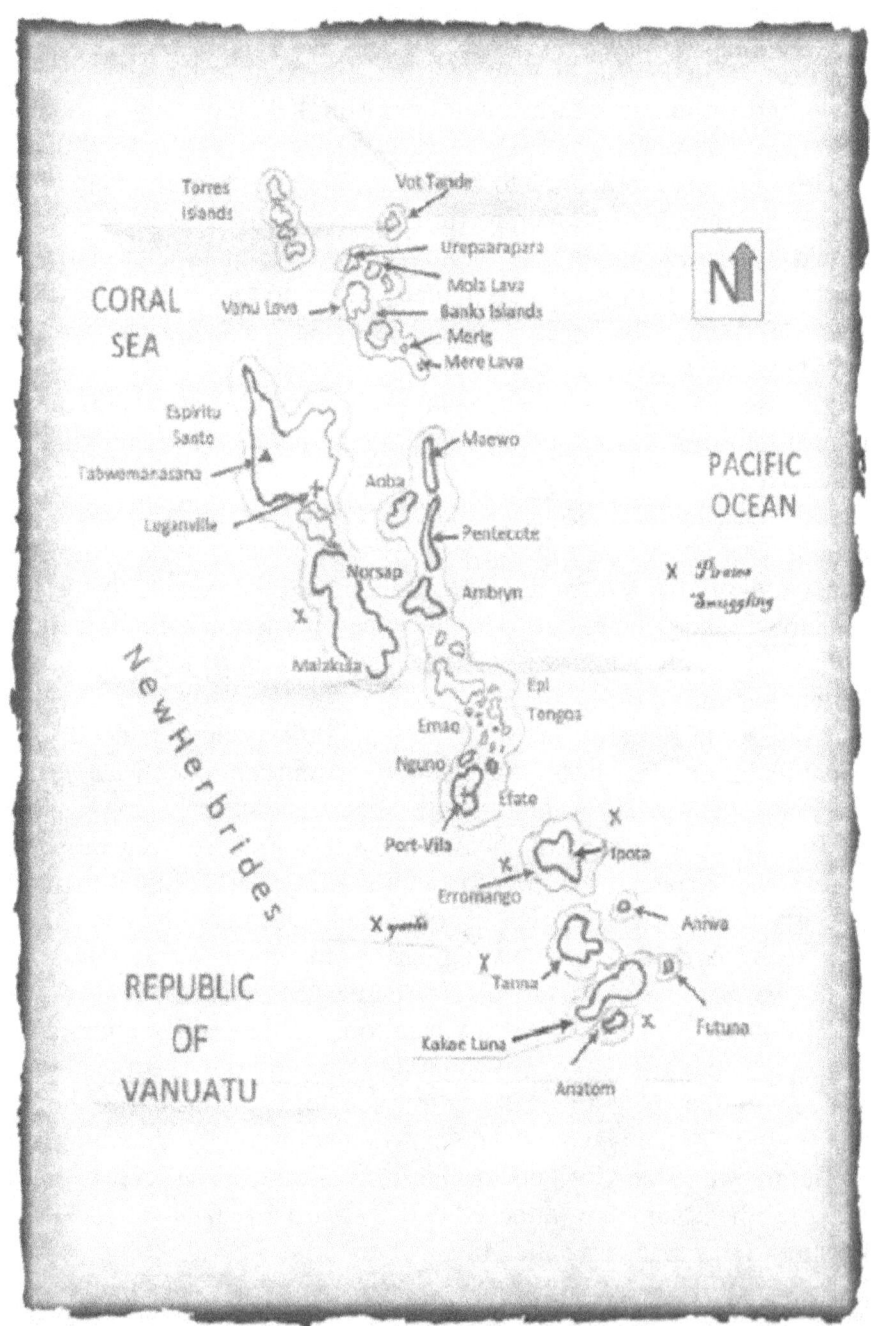

During lunch, we agree to start at the Port of Erromango. We will need supplies, so Kensi takes us to several stores adding this to the items he carries in the trunk of his old vehicle, most notably; life preservers, a paddle, and a first aid kit.

Opening a duffle bag, he points to it, then pinches his top, and shorts, gesturing that this goes into the bag, too. Ah, he wants me to pack a bag as we may have to overnight it between islands.

Kensi takes me back to the hotel to pick up my clothes. When I return to the lobby, I find him outside with the map on the hood of his car. He has circled where we agreed to start first, Erromango. He has already called ahead to the police station there. We will move out from Erromango to the island of Kakae Luna, where Brian was last known to have stayed.

We are near the Zucker Marina where Kensi says (in animated gestures) he has a boat. When he points at what is little more than an outboard motor mounted on a canoe, shivers run down my spine. It looks old and unstable.

"We're going to need a bigger boat, Kensi." Shaking my head at him, I point to the door marked: SALES. "Be right back."

I do not intend to set foot in what Kensi calls a boat. After negotiating a quick sale with the marina owner, we come outside so he can personally take me to a more suitable replacement. Kensi is fiddling with the stuff on the pier. When he slowly turns around, Mr. Zucker takes one look at him, and his face begins to take on a rather odd shade of red. He mutters something unintelligible, slams the keys into my waiting hands, and runs back into the marina.

I don't know what all that is about, and we don't have time for explanations, so I motion for Kensi to follow me as we stand next to a used forty-foot boat called a Downeast Cruiser. Kensi smiles, then puts his hand out for the key.

Mr. Zucker told me that the cruiser was initially brought over from New England by a couple that wanted to start a small fishing charter business here on the mainland. Then the husband won the lottery. They abandoned that idea, sold the boat to Zucker Marine, then high-tailed it to a private island somewhere out in the Caribbean.

"Hoa kwick bot, Misis Pe ters?"

Putting up two fingers tells Kensi that it will take two minutes to find this information for him, so he wanders back to his wreck of a car to gather the rest of our gear while I go back inside to ask Mr. Zucker.

When I come through the door, whatever triggered his reaction when he saw Kensi, has him backing away from me.

"Please leave. If I had known you were with that man I would have never sold you that boat. You have what you need. Please go away," he says, shaking his head.

"I don't know what happened between you two, and I don't much care right now. I want to know how fast the boat will go!"

Mr. Zucker closes his eyes and holds on to the countertop and doesn't speak.

"How fast will the boat go, Mr. Zucker?"

Zucker opens his eyes, takes in a deep breath, and starts to talk very slowly. "It has a maximum speed of 64 knots."

I'm running out of patience. "I'm not a boat person. How fast is 64 knots?"

"You have engines that have three hundred and fifteen horsepower motors each, and there are two of them, plus the added weight of the boat itself, and a fuel tank that can hold twelve hundred liters. It will go about seventy, or so, miles per hour. You need a faster boat?"

"No, that will be fast enough, thank you."

I pray that Kensi will use common sense and not put us, or the boat, through such speeds. Mr. Zucker did say that the boat had a complete overhaul recently. It's gassed up and ready to go. It looks comfortable enough. It can sleep six people, has a head, which is little more than a closet with a port-a-potty, and a large canopy for shade. And two fish coolers used as seats near the outboard motors are plenty large enough for whatever we catch.

As we load the gear from Kensi's car, his head comes up when he hears a familiar motor and horn honk. When Dr. Malas overheard Gor'gena talking about our possible trip to the surrounding islands, he insisted that she take the next two days off to come with us. Kensi reaches for her bag and helps her board the boat.

Mr. Zucker said there were six life preservers; there are only three. The ones Kensi brought smell as bad as his stale pot of coffee back at his station. We can't spare the time to go back and haggle about it, so these will do for now. We'll get more at a later time should we need them.

We fully expect to move beyond Erromango, past Tanna to the Island of Kakae Luna. We don't know what to expect beyond this, but we will keep our minds open to whatever might come. I'm grateful that Gor'gena is with us, as she can help with the language issue.

"Hoa kwick bot?" Kensi asks as he turns the key in the ignition.

"Fast," I answer, hoping he doesn't want real numbers.

"Hoa kwick?" Kensi laughs as the mighty engines roar to life, and he glances at me to grin.

"It's going to go a lot faster than your little boat."

As Gor'gena interprets, he throws his head back to laugh. "Hoa kwick bot, Misis Pe ters?"

There will be no fooling him. "About seventy-five miles per hour, Kensi, is that fast enough for you?"

Kensi laughs again. "Kwik naf!" he declares. "Gud dai to Port Vila."

He is an able captain who happily sips on a cola. Officer Laput agreed to allow Kensi time off on one condition, which is already in the works. Gor'gena grabs my arm to pull me down on the bench seat, as we slowly move away from the pier.

What will it be like to find this Andru-Brian person? If it is Jason, will he know me? If Jason is the injured man in the photo Kensi gave me, was he so injured that his brain no longer functions, as Dr. Malas says it might? I push these thoughts out of my mind. Time will tell if my hunch is correct.

Kensi is packing heat. I assumed he carried it for police business. After he saw my gun permit, he allowed me to bring mine in an inside vest pocket. He questioned why I chose the little Glock, then started to laugh because his is so much bigger. Am I going to kill fish with it? I tried to tell him that with my luck, there is always a surprise lurking somewhere.

Gor'gena burst into laughter when she saw our pistols side by side. "Kensi tinks you can kul fish with yurs."

"Tanks, Gor'gena, I understood what he said."

And it is funny when we compare them. Just how much damage could I do with my little pop gun, anyway? Here's hoping we never have to find out.

Our first stop takes us to the east side of the Island of Erromango, to the Port City of Ipota where a police officer named Laevo greets us. He speaks better Bislama-English than Kensi, yet not as well as Dr. Malas.

Gor'gena is a quick study and tries to interpret catching on to the conversation. We show Laevo the photos of Jason and the ones that Kensi gave me, and he says that although he remembers the one of John Doe that circulated a few years ago, he doesn't think this person is on this island, as few refugees came here after the cyclone.

Gor'gena says, "Kensi is asking Ofisa Laevo if bodies wash up on beechs as they did in Port Vila when Andru-Brian did. He says one bodi kam on beech tat week, two bodis afta tat."

As Gor'gena interprets for us, I ask Laevo and Kensi if they know anything about an odd-looking wristwatch found either on Andru-Brian, or on another body that washed up on the beaches at the same time. Pulling out my necklace to show them, not intending to press it, when Gor'gena stops to hold the lockets, opening them to admire the photos.

Kensi looks surprised and pulls out his old tattered notepad to flip the pages back and forth. "Trabol wetem fisaman mo mista. Fisaman sun, net Andru, bikos it baot hemia, mo fisman, sili stori."

Gor'gena starts to laugh when Kensi mentions a 'mer mista story' that I don't get, not even with her interpretation. Flipping through more pages, he shows us the sketch of a watch he drew from a description someone gave him.

My heart skips a beat. "May I see that?" Sure enough, it looks similar to Jason's watch. "What happened to it?"

"Not on any bodi on beech afta Brian," Gor'gena says.

Kensi is sure that it wasn't on any of the bodies that came into the morgue that day in Port Vila because he checked. I distinctly recall that Adrian said that they found Jason on the beach, along with two other men. One of them was wearing the watch. Could someone have mistaken Jason for this Brian person? Could someone have stolen Jason's watch before the bodies went to the morgue?

Officer Laevo pulls out a file to look for anything that might help our search. He shows us the sheet with the calls that alerted the islanders as there was another murder a month earlier near the Island of Anatom. He seems to recall that it had to do with smuggling daeman, staka mo penting, which Gor'gena says were many jewels and paintings, but no evidence surfaced. As with most things, it was forgotten and put aside as other cases took over their attention.

Opening my laptop to show Laevo the documentary, he slowly shakes his head at the young newlyweds. As Gor'gena explains, she tells him that they took videos of the Island of Kakae Luna, specifically the town of Nakeilen, before and after the storm. It is the first time Gor'gena has seen it. She puts a hand over her mouth to stifle a cry when Brian's face is visible when he is talking with his mother.

"Tat Andru/Brian!" she screams.

Pausing the CD, "I think so too. Where do you suppose the people went after the cyclone hit that island?"

Officer Laevo seems thoughtful for a moment. "Afta saeklon, olgeta pepoles spred out in bots as they cud and takem pepoles as de cud. Rilif pepoles cum on big oel bot mo aelan to aelan. Staka kam bak afta gun sikis manis, be doti had trabol klinium. No saplaes, staka bagarap, no towenty ded."

Gor'gena merely says, "After the cyclone, all peoples spread out in boats and took peoples to other islands. Rilif came on big oil boat. Many came bak, so much rubbish, no way to clean up. No supply materials to buy. Some rilif got true, but he does not know how much. Gud ting is that peoples knew what to do and there was twenty or so dead," she concludes.

Officer Laevo vows to dig back into the files again to see if they might have forgotten something. I'm thankful for what information we have gathered so far. I ask Kensi to take us to a nearby hotel, one that has Wi-Fi. Then we can sift through whatever might be available about who was responsible for the relief effort. It might shed some light on that island, maybe prevent us from wasting precious time and resources going from island to island on a wild goose chase.

Maybe we'll get lucky. Perhaps that miracle Dr. Malas mentioned will happen!

Kensi and Gor'gena wait in the lobby for me to join them for dinner in the lovely, redecorated dining room attached to the hotel. Somehow, we manage to communicate that Dr. Malas ordered the bodies of the young men exhumed to check their teeth, take fingerprints, and a DNA sample so that the lab can run the necessary tests against the records they now have. The only sticking point is that it might take a good week to do this.

TICK-TOCK! Will there be enough time for that?

In the meantime, Kensi sends the pair of photos he has along with the two I brought to the eight outposts on the other islands. They ask about my husband, and I try to make a joke, saying he'll be here as soon as he figures out where I am. They think I'm trying to be funny, yet in reality, that's what Adrian has to do, exactly.

Since we have the paper copies of our lists and maps of the oil tankers, we discuss which ones might have been in the vicinity during or after the storm. Kensi says the oil tanker **Sea Nymph** that was in the vicinity during Jason's disappearance has merely vanished. "**Sea Nuph** mo bagarap," he says. Gor'gena says he means destroyed or gone.

Questions swirl around in my mind. The **Sea Nymph** is too big to hide. How can a big thing like that vanish? Could it be related to the smuggling and treasure thing he talked about earlier? Could it hide during the day and do their dastardly pirating at night? Was this Brian person caught up in that drama, and Jason happened along right about then?

Maybe it's the wine, perhaps it's the time difference that finally catches up to me, but my eyes will not stay open. Vanuatu is fifteen hours ahead of my home time zone. I've had only one night of decent sleep since I arrived. My appetite has me eating antacids, instead of dinner as the ocean was a little rough coming to the island. Excusing myself, I say, good night to Kensi and Gor'gena.

Sipping on ginger ale lounging in the fluffy white bathrobe provided by the hotel, I'm checking for messages, as the familiar foghorn signals that Adrian is calling. Looking at the screen to see the date is December 8th, noting the time is seven p.m. Vanuatu time. Adrian's face fills the screen as I press the green button.

"Hello, darling. What are you doing up at this hour?" If my calculations are correct, it's four a.m. back in Virginia.

"I thought you were going to call after three days, Ellen. It's December 7th, and you didn't call when you said you would!"

"Has it been three days already? My how time flies. I'm having the best time, sweetie."

"Cut the crap, Ellen. Where are you?"

"I've been busy. I got my nails done, see?" I wiggle my hands close to the screen, so he thinks I had a manicure when in actuality, I painted them a minute ago.

Adrian puts his face close to the screen. "How many miles have you traveled, Ellie? What does your step counter read?"

"How do you know I took it with me, Adrian?"

He looks thoughtful and then repeats the question. "How many miles have you walked since you left, Ellie?"

"If you must know, let me get my notes, and I'll tell you." Reaching for the notebook, I thumb through the last few pages. "Okay, here it is. I walked 9,752 steps for a total of 5.07 miles." I can't tell Adrian the real numbers, or he'll be suspicious.

"When was that, yesterday?" he asks, shaking his head at the screen.

"You don't think I walked five miles? Maybe it's not working. Is there a battery in this thing?"

"No, it has a mechanism inside it, like a pedometer. Nice try. Where are you, Ellie? Why didn't you tell me what you were really up to, hum? We've all been trying to call you. Melanie called you. Curlie called you.

Even Mona tried to call you. We're all a little concerned about you, darling."

"I called everyone. And I left everyone messages. What did Mona want? Didn't you check the machine? I'm on a mission, and I'm making progress."

"Oh, my darling Ellie, what are you talking about?"

"Don't worry, Adrian; I'll be home for Christmas. No one there needs me now, so I'm taking a needed rest. Did the boxes of stuff get there yet?"

"What do you mean you'll be home for Christmas? Do you intend to be gone that long? Where are you, Ellie? I called every spa in the state of Pennsylvania, and the only one that knew of you, said that you never showed up! Don't you trust me, Ellie?"

"Of course I trust you. I told you, I'm on a mission. It's a fact-finding mission. So far, I've uncovered several key pieces of evidence. I need more time to scrutinize and analyze it before I figure out how to solve this mystery."

Adrian looks exasperated, and runs a hand over his face, then stares longingly at the screen. "Mystery? Now I get it. You're wasting your time, sweetie. Would you please give it up and come home?"

"How do you know I'm wasting my time? You don't believe in me, Adrian. No one does except the people I'm here to see."

"Ellie, come home. Please let this go. Jason is gone."

"There is significant evidence to suggest otherwise, my dear, sweet CIA man."

Adrian looks confused. "What are you talking about?"

"I'm talking about what you told me when they found Jason's super watch."

Adrian cocks his head to the side. "Please refresh my memory, sweet cheeks. What did I say?"

"You told me that the body they found on the beach was wearing Jason's special wristwatch. You said that person was dead. What you don't know is that it might not have been Jason's body. Did anyone check his dental records? How about his DNA and fingerprints? Did anyone think to look at those? I gave all of that to you when you went with Levi to Saudi three years ago. What did you do with it, hum, can you explain that?"

I watch Adrian's facial expression change from concern to worry, and then to thoughtfulness. "Where are you, Ellie, I want to help."

"Sure you do. You'll try to talk me into coming home. Why this sudden change of heart, my dear, sweet husband? Why would I even need your help when you don't believe me?"

"Because I love you, damn it, and you shouldn't be where you are without me. You're having fun somewhere exotic without me. Weren't we supposed to go on an exotic vacation together? Besides, you might be on to something. Honestly, I can help you. Tell me where you are."

"How do you know I'm somewhere exotic? You're going to have to do better than that, Mr. CIA man. I dare you to find me."

Not expecting what he does next, Adrian purses his lips and shakes his head. He's taking this as a challenge, as he starts to laugh. "Challenge accepted Mrs. Smarty Pants. You have a head start on me. I'll see you in a few days. And Ellie, if you're wrong about this, tick-tock, Ellen May Thompson dash Sellers, we'll have to abandon it."

It amazes me that we have used the same expression, but I won't let it unnerve me. "What if I'm right Adrian, so what? We'll have had a good time on an exotic island. If we don't achieve what we set out to do, then we will have at least tried. We both go home and have a nice Christmas with the family. I did go shopping, you know."

"Yeah, I know, the packages started to arrive a few days ago. Your credit card must be smokin, Lady. The deal is, that we go home on December 21st, Ellie. If we are, or are not, successful, do you agree? And where did you say you are again?"

"Very funny, as if I'd tell you. Catch me if you can, Adrian B. Thompson dash Sellers. Let's see what kind of CIA man you really are. Bye for now."

Adrian smiles that goofy grin of his as I wave goodbye. Pressing the red button terminates the call. It blows me away to think he's changed his attitude! He would have tried to talk me out of it, had he known what I was up to these last few days. What changed his mind? Was it the part about Jason's wristwatch, or the part about spending time on an exotic island?

Now the pressure's off, and there will be no more deception. We'll be working toward the same goal; finding Jason.

Tick-Tock indeed!

It is now December 9th. It feels good to have a solid twelve hours of rest. Has Adrian figured out where I am yet? After a light breakfast, we check out of the hotel and walk to the marina. Kensi has already refreshed the coolers, and we climb into the Downeast Cruiser and set a course for the Island of Tanna.

Laevo called ahead to the local police outpost. Several people came to that island after the cyclone, but they don't exactly know where or who they are. We are indeed welcome to come to look for them.

Kensi somehow conveys that it will take a good two hours to get to Tanna, if the sea behaves, four if it doesn't. The sea bands are on my wrists this morning to make sure I'm ready for rough seas.

We hug the shoreline as much as possible, always on the lookout for potential danger. I understand this to mean pirates or looters. Kensi starts to snarl and puts on a funny raspy voice, saying, "Arrhh, guv mi yur mane, meit, ur mi katem yur trot."

My mind wanders to the movies in which a hilarious pirate named Captain Jack outsmarts the British Navy as the Island of Tanna comes into view. In the distance is a dark shape that Kensi says is Kakae Luna. We approach the marina slowly. Boats bob placidly in the water as people stroll near the shops. Tanna seems undisturbed. Could Kakae Luna look like this? As if he's reading my mind, Kensi puts his thumb up and shakes his head YES toward Tanna, then puts his thumb down and shakes his head NO when he points to Kakae Luna.

After a disappointing trip into town in which we met with the local constabulary, they don't know where the people went after the oil tanker dropped them off. One woman was supposedly working at a self-laundry. At the laundry, they told us that she went to work at a restaurant. By now it's nearly lunchtime, so we decide to eat there. It's surprisingly wonderful. As it turns out, that woman wasn't a cyclone victim at all. She was hiding from her husband.

We climb back aboard the boat Kensi has nicknamed Natamata, (which means peace) to continue our mission. An hour-and-a-half later, Kensi slows the boat as we near the cove that used to take tourists into the City of Nakeilen.

Several things strike me at once. We already know that the airport no longer exists here, and the thriving marina that typically would have sailboats large and small along slips as on other islands, is obliterated. The brunt of the cyclone made an unpredictable zigzag across the ocean, as it rounded the last of the islands in the archipelago.

Because of its placement within the chain, the backlash caught the island full-force, smacking everything in its path near the southernmost side. The high volcanic range that runs northeast to southwest is the only thing that saved Tanna and the rest of the northern islands from total annihilation.

It must have been a serene place at one time with its calm, azure blue water, and cloudless sky. The odd thing is the mountains of debris it rests against, and the once pristine beach display the scars of wind so powerful it not only blew over palm trees, it uprooted them to drag their sorry carcasses out to sea. Their remnants are visible as the foaming water washes over them.

As we drift closer into the cove, there is nothing to attach our boat line to, as the piers lost their footing when they succumbed to the cyclone. Kensi drops the anchor as near to shore as he dares. As far as the eye can see, the landscape displays piles of junk and garbage.

Gor'gena puts her arms around me. Does she also think that there is no hope here, as I do? Why would anyone want to come back here when there's nothing left? Birds fly in to pick at the heaps, fly away quickly when Kensi jumps from the boat making a splash. From here, I can see a small blue boat that's bobbing in the water near the beach that appears tied to a fallen tree. Did the tree snag the little boat? I motion to Kensi to look in that direction.

Kensi pulls at the line to secure the front of our boat. He glances behind him, and we nod to each other. It could not have survived the storm. Someone else might be here on the island.

A massive tree is half-way up the side of a hill with a bicycle either wrapped around it or embedded into it. Suddenly, a shadow passes in front of it, but we're too far away to see what it is. I recognize the tree and bicycle from the documentary Janice Danbury and her husband made of the aftermath of the storm. How could this tree have survived what so much did not?

Kensi steadies himself against the side of the cruiser to reach up to help Gor'gena and me out of the boat. What strikes me is that there are no barking dogs, only the sound of the sea, a distant birdcall, and silence.

As we maneuver our way over the massive mounds of debris, it's obvious how utterly impossible it would be for anyone to survive this type of carnage. How would they get along without electricity or proper drinking water?

Standing on what might have been the central section of town, we survey the scene. Where once hotels and cabanas stood, there is only rubble and disarray. Tears sting my eyes as I say a prayer for those touched by this tragedy, asking that they are granted peace.

How could this bad thing happen to so many good people?

Kensi says, "Nating gud ta se, Misis. Taem ta goes, letem go."

"Not yet, Kensi."

As I look to my right, there is a string of large volcanic-type black rocks of various sizes that look as if they rolled in from the sea. They are about two hundred yards away. Drawn in that direction, I try to navigate over a pile of rubble, careful of where to step.

I am standing on the spot where my nightmare-dreams originate. I look up at the sky to see fluffy clouds lazily drift by in an otherwise clear blue sky. The white of the moon is low, and to the right, as it was the day Adrian found me practicing with my pistol. The sea is creating foam as it slams against the black rock with a soft swoosh.

Kensi and Gor'gena make their way over to me, and question why this is so important. They manage to ask how this is helping to find Brian, but I can't explain it, so I don't try. Taking my digital camera from an inside pocket, I take several photos at various angles.

Kensi wades into the water to investigate the little boat, as Gor'gena stands with me. Somehow, by viewing this scene, it gives me a peaceful feeling. Was I here before? Or was it another type of transcendental meditation thing?

Turning toward the big tree, I take a few more shots when I see a shadow move near the tree. Instinct kicks in, and I dive behind the debris, as a crack sounds over my head.

Did someone shoot at us? Was that gunfire?

"Kip doan, Misis," Kensi yells, as he runs toward us, mumbling something to Gor'gena. They flatten themselves out on the beach behind the large rocks.

We hear the crack sound again, as something whizzes past my head, as my hand reaches in for my Glock. I slowly pull my pistol out to point it at the shadow on the hill, while Kensi aims his firearm and pulls the trigger.

Our pistols echo in the stillness, a loud crack from Kensi's, and a soft pop from mine. The shadow moves behind the large tree, then back again quickly. Whatever, or whomever it is, is too far away. When I position my pistol at the shadow again, all I can see is a smoke curl, which must have come from Kensi's gun, because mine would never do that from this distance, even if it hit the target.

"Pirate, Kensi?"

We listen, aim, and fire again. When there is no return fire, Kensi stands up and shakes his head at Gor'gena, saying, "Lego naoia. Misis, jas combus ton, fire wurk."

"Gunfire is not combustion, Kensi. Someone was shooting at us! It's probably the person who owns that little boat."

"Sori tumas, emi naet sun," then motions to me that we leave. "Bot be long taem. Kam, Misis Pe ters."

Those were unquestionably gunshots. Someone was shooting at us. Since Kensi is in charge, if he says we're leaving, we're going. We turn back toward our boat, mindful of where we step. Kensi carries Gor'gena and me back through the water to the cruiser, and it's a solemn trip back to the Island of Erromango.

We will stay at the hotel tonight, as it is hazardous to navigate back to Port Vila at night. Kensi checks with Officer Laevo, and he agrees to join us for dinner. We talk about what we saw today, in the English language we each know is not the same, and discuss the little blue boat. Laevo says that the blue boat we saw could have snagged itself, except I suspect Kensi thinks otherwise.

We raise our glasses in a toast to the decimated Island of Kakae Luna. We hope that the inhabitants are doing well wherever they are. May God have mercy upon their souls and give them peace.

(Note in journal: 11,500 steps today = 4.6 miles. I think the step counter is working again.)

During the night, I have disturbing dreams about debris, black rocks, and a heaving sea. Waking at intervals, I'm trying to figure out the time difference, but staring at the clock doesn't help. If it's six a.m. here, then it's two o'clock in the afternoon in Virginia. If it's December 10th here, then it's still December 9th there.

Determined to continue with my mission, regardless of the outcome, when I try to contact Adrian for a video chat, there is only static. A disturbance in the atmosphere or technical difficulty could be the reason, however, when the calls to Ashwood Manor go straight to the machine, my frustration level rises. After leaving a message there, all other calls to cellphones go straight to voicemail. They must all be working, or in school.

Although the dream last night was disturbing, it's not the usual nightmare. Has seeing the black rock in person somehow resolved that issue? And I don't buy that story about combustion. I'm 99% sure that it was gunfire.

Officer Kensi might not want to admit it, but the possibility exists that we disturbed a smuggler or a pirate. What was that person doing? Was he adding treasure, or digging it up?

I'm checking through the emails, scrolling through the nonsense when I see one from a person named Joan who is from the Red Cross. She was part of the cyclone relief effort and was on the oil tanker named *Alhambra* that moved around the islands. She would be happy to check her records to see if the Mansale family was onboard during the evacuation and will get back to me. Sending her my thanks in a reply, I shut down my laptop and carry it to breakfast so that I can share this news with Kensi and Gor'gena.

After breakfast, we walk to the Ipota Police Station to speak with Officer Laevo. Gor'gena translates as we show him the emails. Then Laevo turns to Kensi, and they start to talk. When Kensi's cellphone rings, he steps out of the office. When he returns, he says Dr. Malas has news. He wants to see us in person and won't discuss whatever it is over the phone.

Laevo also has news. Smiling broadly, he says, "it's ol gud." With Gor'gena's help, she says that the eight outposts are in the process of passing around the latest photos of Andru-Brian, including the screen capture of him from the documentary.

Laevo hopes that I am happy with this news, and pulls me into a hug. Gor'gena says that if Brian is alive and living on one of the other islands, then it's only a matter of time before we find him. I try to express my thanks, but it will never be enough if we indeed find this person named Brian. My only hope is that he's Jason.

Tick-Tock. I hope it's not too late!

Kensi decides that we will go straight to Port Vila to see what Dr. Malas has uncovered. It's a more comfortable trip back, as the waters are calmer today. When we arrive at the hospital, Dr. Malas is in surgery. He will be available sometime in the next three hours. Since its well-past lunchtime, Kensi and Gor'gena drop me off at the hotel, with the understanding they'll return for me when the hospital calls.

When I open my laptop to check emails, there are several voice messages from my family. Each one is similar in that they want to know where I am, except Mel's is different.

"Mom? Where the heck are you? We've been going crazy. Adrian said you aren't where you said you'd be. He left yesterday and said he was going to find you. What the heck are you up to?"

Melanie's message is as dramatic as she usually is in person. I call her back, but it goes straight to her voicemail. I leave her a reply, 'tag, you're it,' and then calculate it's nearly nine p.m. Virginia time.

If Adrian left yesterday, is that his yesterday, or is it my today? The betting woman in me says he's on his way to either Sydney, or New Zealand, and he'll be here soon. Adrian probably knew where I was going from the start.

The telephone on the desk rings and Miss Cindy's voice says a visitor is waiting for me in the hotel lobby. It's doubtful Adrian has found me that quickly. When I get there, a smiling Kensi greets me. Cindy says Gor'gena has gone home, so Kensi is taking me back to his office to wait for Dr. Malas to call again as there was another emergency.

At the station, Kensi hands me a fax that came in less than an hour ago from the relief worker named Joan. It indicates that Brian Mansale was aboard the oil tanker named ***Alhambra*** along with the rest of the Mansale family. They stayed aboard for about two weeks as they dropped people off at other islands on their way north.

After that time, they took the Mansale family to Pentecost Island. It sounds vaguely familiar, so I turn on my laptop and wait for the Wi-Fi to connect.

Kensi has a whiteboard set up with two maps, a large one of The Republic of Vanuatu and a smaller one named Pentecote Island. Arranged around the edges are photos of Brian and the ones I gave him of Jason. He tries to explain the spelling differences, as the island has two names, one French version of Pentecote (Bislama-English), and the English-English translation of Pentecost; they are the same nonetheless.

Pentecost is one of the larger islands of the Vanuatu chain. It received plenty of rain and wind but sustained little damage as the cyclone zig-zagged around it. Joan's information only went as far as to say that the Mansale family went to this island, but doesn't give the specific name of the towns where the people were dropped off.

Glancing at the map, how on earth will we find him under these conditions? Kensi must anticipate this as he hands me the list of possible town names so I can print them on the whiteboard. He laughs when I try to pronounce them, then gives me his Bislama version of what they are, because they're real tongue twisters.

He begins to cross off the settlements away from the coasts, as it's unlikely that the oil tanker dropped them off for several reasons; too much jungle, rainforests, volcanic mountain ranges, and out-of-the-way places, only the island natives would know about.

Kensi gets the point across by using markers to draw trees, vines, and what looks like rain. Are you kidding? Talk about a needle in a haystack! How about an impossible journey through jungle *and* rainforests! The sheer number of cities overwhelms me.

```
                      Pentecote Island
West Side              Middle              East side
Lanoe                                      Nazareth
Lottong                                    Sara Airport
Nambwarangiut                              Atvtbamgga
Namaram                                    Renbura
Bwatnapni              Enaa                Wutsunmwet
Melsiisi                                   Vanrasini
Ranwadi                Fansip              Poinkros
Waterfall
Bwaravel
Lonorore Airport                           Vasare
Hotwata                                    Baie Barrier
Ragusuksu                                  Ranwas
Panas                                      * Bay Martelli
Wali                                       * Lodat Bay
Panngi Pangi                               * Bay Homo
Ranputor                                   Wanur
```

It would take the better part of a year to transverse this area. As if Kensi's reading my mind, he laughs, opening his book translator to find the right words. Using hand gestures, he points to the fax machine and then at the telephone, saying, "Polis gat fakis."

Of course, we can use the fax machine! We can rule some out right away. Kensi points to Laput's vehicle, motions that the villagers have one or two, "four-wil draevem kamiong, or spid bots," holding up the corresponding fingers for effect, walking his fingers across his desk. He then proceeds to feed the photos of Brian into the machine, and we wait to see who might respond.

Just as he puts the last photo through the fax machine, Dr. Malas calls and Kensi says, "Kam ospitol, Misis. Mitim Dokta Malas."

We jump into Kensi's devil of a car and drive to the hospital. Dr. Malas is standing near his office door waiting for us. He hugs me lightly and politely asks us to sit down.

"It is good to see you again, Mrs. Peters. I am not sure that what I am about to tell you will be what you want to hear. Someone from your government came to view the bodies of the young man who matched your son's description."

"Do you know when that was, Dr. Malas?"

"Here are the technician's notes. He was in the morgue at that time, and remembers a man and a woman, roughly in their mid-thirties who looked like American tourists. They asked many questions and requested to see the bodies. They took a few photos, made some notes, thanked the technician, and then they left. He never saw them again after that."

"Did this technician get their names? What were some of the questions they asked? Did the couple ask about dental records, or fingerprints? How about the wristwatch?"

"You must understand that if they were born in remote parts of the other islands, many do not see a dentist. There would be no dental records. The technician failed to ask their names. He did not mention anything about a watch," Dr. Malas offers.

"Don't you have security here? Didn't they have to show identification before they saw the technician? Is there a record of them, a video perhaps?"

"Those are all good questions, Mrs. Peters. I shall pursue this line of thought; however, I must caution you that we are mostly trusting by nature. We do not use sophisticated means, as they do in other areas."

"Wait a minute, go back. Are you saying there are no records for Brian?"

"The same goes for fingerprints." Dr. Malas sits back in his chair. "The technician said the couple seemed satisfied with what they saw and they left. I am pleased to tell you that the people who are in the morgue do not own the fingerprints you brought to us." Dr. Malas smiles while his words sink into my brain. "I managed to pull some strings and told them of the urgency of this and…"

"It's not Jason!" I shout.

"Yes, it looks like they are *not* a match for your son. Neither one of the bodies in the morgue is your son. The DNA does not match either of the other two men who came in after them, as well." Dr. Malas smiles, closing the file.

"So the real possibility exists that one of the bodies who washed up on the beach could be the real Brian. Neither one of the first two dead bodies was Jason! There was no carrot shaped mark under anyone's left arm, near the armpit, and there was no scar on anyone's right thigh?"

Dr. Malas sits on the edge of his desk to grab both of my hands. "The technician certified that no distinguishable marks were on any of the bodies, except for the bullet holes. He is certain the bodies in the morgue are not your son. There is no DNA match. It is most likely the real Brian and another unfortunate soul."

He turned his head to say something to Kensi, and they speak for a few minutes. I'm not paying attention to what they're saying, because it's difficult to follow anyway. My cellphone starts to vibrate. I look down to see a text message come in but I don't retrieve it.

"Now all you have to do is find him," Dr. Malas says.

"I can't thank you enough for what you've done, Dr. Malas. You have no idea what this means to my family."

"I told Officer Kensi what I told you. He thinks that you and he will wait until someone responds to the photos he sent. I suggest you go back to your hotel and rest. I understand that your husband is on his way here to meet you. I hope you have success in locating your son. It will be a Christmas miracle, after all."

"Excuse me? How do you know my husband is on his way here?"

"He contacted me, as I came out of surgery." Dr. Malas smiles, then looks at his vibrating pager. "I must go now. It was lovely to see you again, Mrs. Peters," he winks at me, "and remember the Christmas miracle."

I retrieve the message and listen as Adrian's voice says, "Tag Ellie, you're it. Call me ASAP."

He's getting warmer. How did he know about this cellphone? I'm not about to call him back. That wouldn't be fair! Let's see how good a CIA man he is.

Kensi drops me off at the hotel, gesturing that he'll come back in three hours. We're getting good at sign language. The few words that we do comprehend from each other are starting to become more understandable. Another two weeks and I might speak and appreciate this unique language like a native!

Walking into my hotel room, I grab a bottle of water out of the refrigerator and find a spot near the pool, and get comfortable. Pulling out one of my paperback books, after a few pages, I fall fast asleep. My cellphone vibrates, waking me up. I'm not quick enough, so it goes straight to voicemail.

Again, it's from Adrian; did I get his text? Why didn't I pick up? Why didn't I text him back? Then he accuses me of not playing by the rules! What rules are those, his? How did he trace this phone?

Miss Cindy will join us for dinner tonight as Kensi and Gor'gena have no problem adding her to our little group. I'm grateful that we won't have to play the guessing and gesturing game tonight, as Cindy will interpret for us.

After walking to a local restaurant, Kensi says there's no word from the cities and villages he sent the faxes to, then laughs because we are on 'island time'…which means it takes a while for people to respond. All we can do now is wait for someone to recognize Brian Mansale's photos.

We order drinks that come in large round glasses that remind me of a fishbowl. In fact, they're so large that the fruit pieces that would typically be on a toothpick, are on BBQ skewers. Cindy points out that some things are difficult to replace. After the storm, people had to make do with whatever they had. It is one of those things.

"Here's hoping you find Brian Mansale quickly," Miss Cindy says, raising her glass.

"I'll drink to that!"

As we get to know Cindy, she tells us about her upbringing in Australia and her quest to see the world. Her goal is to see Paris, the Grand Canyon, New York City, and Venice.

"You'll love Venice," I say. "But make sure you go in the cooler months." Out of the corner of my eye, there is a man at the end of the bar that seems to be listening in on our conversation. Was he sitting there all along, or did he move a stool closer?

Raising my eyebrows at Kensi, I move my eyes toward the bar and back quickly. Kensi catches on right away, and stands to excuse himself politely. As we girls continue to chat like we're old friends, the man moves one more stool closer to us. He doesn't look familiar to me, and the girls don't seem to notice what he's doing, so I keep quiet for fear of upsetting them.

The next thing we know, Kensi has rounded the other side of the wall and has the man pinned face down on the bar. He's pulling one of the man's arms behind his back, pushing it up so he can't stand up.

"Yu, yu!" Kensi screams at the man. "Stilman trabol, staka trabol yu!"

Everyone in the dining room stops to stare in our direction. The bartender knows what's going down and steps away from the bar. Kensi says something to the man but doesn't allow him to lift his head to answer.

Gor'gena, Cindy, and I are now standing near the bar. Cindy says, "Kensi is asking the man questions. The man is a fugitive, has many aliases. It is Uncle Rexley; Brian Mansale's Uncle Rexley. He wants, no, he demands to know where Brian is because he heard one of us mention his name."

Perhaps drinking half of the contents of the fishbowl is what gives me the confidence to speak my mind. Getting as close as I dare to the man's face, I say, "If we knew where Brian was, I wouldn't be here, Pal, I'd be taking him home with me. He's probably not your Brian at all. He might be my son, Jason!" Gor'gena puts a gentle hand on my arm to pull me back.

Rexley looks confused. Then screws up his face, as if he's about to shout again, but doesn't. Cindy continues to talk with him and Kensi. After she tells him what I said, he tells her that I am a liar. Brian is Brian, he knows of no one named Jason. I am the one who is wrong.

Kensi can spot a liar a mile away, as I can. He will not let up on his grip until the man convinces him otherwise. They converse back and forth, then Kensi takes out his handcuffs to snap them on the man's wrists. He evidently carries them with his firearm, which he presses against the man's temple.

Kensi pulls Rexley with him, saying he'll be right back, then stops to apologize to the other patrons in the restaurant. To our surprise, they break into applause. As if on cue, Gor'gena, Cindy, and I curtsey. At this point, the three of us decide that we need to finish our drinks.

As the main course arrives, Kensi returns to our table. Miss Cindy translates that he apologizes again for any inconvenience the little show may have caused and hopes that we're all still having a good time.

"They booked Rexley Mansale on conspiracy charges and theft. The police have a large file on him. He doesn't have a lawyer. Kensi hopes that he will stay in their custody, as he gave them the slip a few years ago. He's been on their most wanted list ever since. He also says that they can come up with more reasons to detain him, which he'll deal with tomorrow. Nice work, Mrs. Peters, good eye!"

"Tangkyu Kensi, but you are the de tec tive, not me."

During dinner, Cindy laughs when she interprets for Kensi again. Uncle Rexley admitted he was not on Kakae Luna when the cyclone hit, but he was on an oil tanker. Conveniently, Rexley cannot remember the name of it. When he went back to the island, there was nothing left of the town, including everyone and everything. Rexley's been searching for his sister-in-law and her family ever since.

Could this Rexley person be the shadow who fired at us?

Rexley says it's close to two and a half years since he's seen his brother's family. He was innocently sitting at the end of the bar when he overheard us talking about Brian Mansale. Kensi can't get anything else out of him, except that he thinks there's a connection between Rexley and the suspected pirate ship called the **Sea Nymph**.

My thoughts wander to Adrian. If he made the last flight to Port Vila from Sydney, he would be here any time now. If not, he'll be here early tomorrow.

After we say goodnight to Kensi and Gor'gena, Miss Cindy and I decide to go into the hotel bar for a nightcap. If Adrian were here, he'd be bugging me by now. Then I remember that he can't, as I turned my cellphone off nearly two hours ago.

Cindy is delightful company. The people at corporate thought it might be better and more interesting for the hotel if her name tag read that she came from the UK. Cindy mentions a transfer to another hotel, hoping for Paris, but thinks it'll be somewhere in Spain, preferably Barcelona. We part company saying we should do this again the next time she has a free evening.

When I open the door to my room, a man is reclining on my bed. Adrian has found me.

"Hello there, Mrs. Peters!"

"Why Adrian, you're here."

"Been out socializing without me, I see? I called and called you. Funny, no one by the name of Ellen Thompson dash Sellers checked in at this hotel. They do have a Mrs. Francesca Peters, though." Adrian jumps off the bed. I don't know if he's joking, or if he's angry.

"I was out having some dinner. We had a huge drink in an absol…." His lips are on mine before I can finish my sentence. I know he isn't angry, but happy to see me.

"Why didn't you tell me where you were going?" he asks.

"I'm so glad you could make it."

"Tell me what you found," he asks.

After I fill Adrian in on what the local police and I have discovered so far, he's adamant we keep a low profile. He also knows something about the couple that went missing. He explains that they came to investigate the signal that came from Jason's unique watch. They never returned home, they disappeared, vanished off the face of the earth, and so did a lot of loot.

I show Adrian my notes and information, and he shows me his. We have come to the same conclusion. It has something to do with the mysterious oil tanker, the CIA has designated a pirate ship called the **Sea Nymph**.

(Note in journal: 9,753 steps today = 3.9 miles)

It feels more like 10!

"People will forget what you said,
people will forget what you did,
but people will never forget how you made them feel."
~ Maya Angelou

Chapter Fifteen

Final Absolution

It is now December 11th as we walk to the Port Vila Police Station after a light breakfast at the hotel. Adrian knows everything, right down to the little shooting incident on Kakae Luna.

Kensi is pulling up in his noisy jalopy. We make quick introductions and follow him inside where Laput waves to us, as he talks to the box on his shoulder, moving quickly past us on a call.

A glum Mr. Mansale is sitting on a bunk in the caged area. Kensi puts his finger to his lips. While we finished our dinner at the restaurant last night, a snarling Officer Laput escorted Rexley Mansale to court to face a judge. He'll stay in their cell until officials come to retrieve him, where he will be transferred to a maximum, holding facility in another city.

Because of his suspected piracy antics, he may lead them to a cache of stolen goods. They're hopeful that he'll tell them more about the oil tanker that has eluded them for nearly ten years, named the **Sea Nymph**.

Kensi positions the whiteboard, making sure Rexley can't see it from where he's sitting. While we try to match the faxes that came in during the night with the cities on our list, he takes a marker to cross off more of the cities, because they either don't know who the Mansale's are, or they are sure they couldn't have gone there.

We narrow down three possible locations where the oil tanker ***Alhambra*** could have dropped off the refugees; Lodat Bay, Bay Homo, and Bay Martelli. Each of these has cities that the refugees could have gravitated to, and we quickly become frustrated when they don't seem to match the names on the board.

We already know that most of the towns have two different spellings. I make a feeble attempt to ask a question. "Kensi, defren taetel?" Adrian starts to laugh at me. "Can you do any better at this, Mister Smarty Pants?"

Kensi takes the marker out of my hand and starts to scribble something. Just as Pentecost Island has two names, there are many different names for the same village. Some of the villages are inland and are crossed off already, so we move on to the east side of the island where Kensi says there are, "Tu seraotem." He draws lines through more names, and we stand back to look at the board.

Adrian takes the marker and circles Lonorore Airfield on the map, and then draws a line to it from the city called Lonoror without saying a word. Then I step forward to draw a line through the town called Panngi and then circle the word Pangi.

Once we figure out what goes where, we cross off all but six possibilities. Now, where do we go from here? As the men put their heads together, I try to put myself in Mrs. Mansale's shoes.

If I have six, or so mouths to feed, how will I support them? What would I do if my life revolved around the business of tourists? Would I seek a job near a resort so that I could rebuild my business, or would I work for someone else, because I know how to run a resort?

I begin a search on hotels and resorts on Pentecost Island. Several show up with some fantastic amenities when a thought occurs to me. "Adrian, Kensi, come outside, please." Once we're outside, I point at my screen. "We should concentrate on the largest cities that have resorts and hotels." Turning to Kensi, "Risot and hootels. Maybe Mrs. Mansale found wok em ploy mint and settled there."

"Ellie, in case Rexley can hear us, whisper and point to stuff when we go back inside," Adrian cautions.

"Good idea." Once inside, I point to the northwest side of Pentecost Island at the circle Adrian drew around Lonorore Airfield, Kensi shrugs his shoulders and shakes his head in disagreement.

"If they had a choice, it makes the most sense that the refugees went there. They didn't say where they dropped what families off at what cities. My hunch is that the Mansale's went here." On a pad of paper, I scribble, "that's where most of the tourists come into or out of on their way to somewhere else!"

Adrian is skeptical but allows me to continue. "The other logical place is here," pointing to Pangi. "It's close to a road system."

Kensi has a quizzical expression on his face. Adrian is also unsure, but then again, all other areas are too remote and hilly, for that many people to navigate daily. He finally says, "Prisena Mansale gun sun," then motions with a pretend fork that Adrian and I should go and get something to eat; he'll stay at the station.

Hopefully, more emails will arrive while we're gone, and it might allow us time to digest this latest information. Then we can decide on which city to go to first.

"So, you still think I don't have premonitions, Mr. CIA man?" Pulling my camera out of my bag to thrust into Adrian's hands, "Take a look at this. It's what I've been trying to tell you."

After several minutes of silence, he says, "Okay, suppose you're right, Ellie. Man, I wish Levi were still here to help us. We could get through this gobbledygook so much faster if his teams could handle it. It's no longer a government issue, but a personal one, so I can't ask Kelvin Ingles for help."

"Why not? Didn't you say one of your teams went missing? How is that not a government issue?"

"You're right. I'll get in touch with Kelvin, but he can't stick his nose in where Jason is concerned."

"Again, why not? We're making real progress Adrian. Look how far we've already come? It's only a matter of time before we find him, I know it. And if I know your friends, they'll want a piece of this action, too."

"Ellie, I don't want you to get your hopes so high they come crashing down if we can't find him, or it turns out that this person Brian isn't Jason."

"Adrian, Adrian, Adrian. Where is your faith? Don't you know that I've already thought about that? Don't you know that I won't give up until I'm positive it is, or is not, Jason? Let's look at this as the ultimate challenge? You've already made it over a major one by finding me. Now, how fun was that?"

"You left me a big clue. You didn't take your cellphone. When I went snooping, I found the chart with the oil tankers, and put two and two together." Adrian wrinkles his nose and makes a funny face.

"So you do snoop. How was that a clue? I left it behind on purpose. I honestly thought no one would bother."

"I started to wonder why you didn't take your cellphone. Then I realized you took your tablet and laptop. It was the only logical explanation. You didn't want me to know where you were going, or did you?" he says flatly.

"But I told you where I was going, to the spa. I simply didn't go there first."

"So you intended to go there? The only rational place you would be is, well here, looking for Jason."

"I thought I was clever."

"Oh you are clever, but I know how your mind works, my love, remember?"

My cellphone rings and Kensi asks if we can, "Kam bak, mi gat nius."

Three additional faxes came into the station, and one of them is from Lonorore Airfield. It states that a Brian Mansale worked there approximately six months ago. His mother called him away one day. He never returned, and they do not know of his whereabouts.

The second fax is similar to the first few Kensi received days ago in that they never heard of the Mansale family, but the third one says that someone fitting Brian's description might work at a local hotel. Known as the Barrier Reach Resort, it's about a mile from the Lonorore Airfield.

It goes on to say that women often set up markets near the airport on flight days, so that's the logical place to spread his photo around. The climate on Pentecost Island is suitable for growing vegetables. Many set up little stoves to serve cooked food to tourists either arriving or leaving the airfield. Are we on the right trail to finding this Brian? Will we find him quickly, before our deadline of December 21st?

Today is December 12th. Adrian reminds me that the clock is ticking when a thought surfaces. I haven't had a nightmare or dream about the rocks in the sea for several nights. It's beginning to bother me. Has the connection broken? Since I've seen the real rock and beach of my nightmares, has this somehow resolved this issue?

(Note in journal: 8,900 steps today = 3.56 miles. I'm beginning to dislike this thing.)

We are up early today. Adrian has gone to talk with the technician at the hospital and meet with Dr. Malas. CIA Special Agent Kelvin Ingles instructed him to check into the matter of the couple that went missing, as he has questions and wants answers. Who else, besides Adrian, is trustworthy enough to get the job done?

Stretching across the bed, not wanting to read, or go out to the pool, I'm trying to make sense of the information Kensi shared with us yesterday. Closing my eyes, the next thing I know, Adrian is gently shaking me.

"Ellie? Wake up, you're yelling! Are you okay? You must have fallen asleep. Did you have a bad dream?"

"I don't know what it was."

"I'll get you a cold drink," he says, leaving the room.

As I try to sit up, it's difficult to articulate what happened. Was it a dream? Was it a nightmare? It's so jumbled up, that I can't put it into words. Was this image through my eyes, or was it through another's? It's disconcerting, and my brain has a hard time trying to wrap itself around this idea.

Adrian is back with a cold beverage. "The young woman at the front desk says hello. I think her name is Cindy." He sits on the bed waiting for me to speak.

"She's very nice, Adrian. She's the one that went to dinner with us before you got here."

"Okay, Madam Medium, I know you saw something, so you might as well tell me about it," Adrian says softly. "Come on, give it a try."

"It isn't like any of the other dreams or even the nightmares. This time, the sadness is so overwhelming I can't talk to anyone. No one can understand a word I'm saying. It's also frustrating! I can't understand much of anything anyone says to me either. It's a little complicated."

"Ellie, that's understandable. I think the term for that is projecting. The psychiatrist talked about this. After Levi died, I couldn't cope with stuff. You're feeling a little inadequate because the people here speak a different language, and you don't understand them."

"No, Adrian, that's not it at all."

Adrian sighs. "The language isn't familiar to you. They can't understand me either."

"It's not about me, Adrian. I think it's the other person."

He stares at me. "What do you mean you think it's the other person? What other person are you referring to?"

"I've told you this before, and you didn't believe me."

"Ellie, try me, again."

"I think I was feeling sorry for myself; only it wasn't me. Does that make sense? No, it probably doesn't."

"You were feeling sorry for yourself? But it wasn't you. So it must have been someone else that was feeling sorry for themselves. You maybe saw it through their eyes? Is that what you're trying to say?"

"See, I told you it was complicated. Let's drop it for now. What did you find out from the technician at the hospital?"

"Are you sure you want to drop this? It might help if we talked more about it."

"No. Maybe it'll make sense if I *don't* think about it. What did you find out?"

Adrian sits down on the chair opposite the bed. "I was right in thinking that Kellie and Drew were the ones that were here. I showed the tech a photo of them. He was extremely agitated until I told him that I wasn't there to take him to jail."

"Why would you take him to jail? Oh, never mind, you showed him your badge, didn't you? It kind of looks like you're the sheriff. Who are Kellie and Drew and why do their names sound familiar?"

"They're the ones who were with Jason and Mack in New York. Their names were Jimmy and Sharon then. They were their language professors, remember? They were also the couple that stayed at Ashwood when we went on that Cape Cod vacation. The tech said they asked a lot of questions. When I told him they disappeared, he thought I came to arrest him. Seems that he pilfers items from the bodies that come into the morgue from time to time. When I mentioned a strange-looking wristwatch, and showed him a picture, he nearly ran out of the room."

"Was it Jason's watch?"

"I don't know. When I put a little pressure on this guy, he told me he pawned it. Unfortunately, the cyclone annihilated the pawn shop, along with the contents, or looters took it. By that time, the kid was so scared he couldn't talk, Ellie, so I left him to think about the consequences of his actions. I think he's quite remorseful. I doubt that he'll steal anything ever again."

"How did your office handle this Kelly and Drew disappearance? Didn't they have an alert, so your people could track them?"

"Those are good questions. You know the whiteboard you wanted to start when Jason first went missing?"

"Yes."

"We made one when Jason's signal came in. Levi didn't have much intel then, but it kept going off in many places. I didn't want to alarm you. Many people must have held and played with the face of the watch until it went silent. That was probably when the hospital tech pawned it."

"You followed his signal. Oh, how stupid I am! You tracked me with my necklace. I thought it only gave off a signal if I pressed it, but it was tracking me all along, wasn't it? You knew where I was all the time, Adrian B. Thompson dash Sellers!"

Adrian smiles that sheepish grin of his then reaches to hug me. "You left a little trail of crumbs, Miss Gretel. Didn't you think I would find that poem about being stranded on an island? You hid it in plain sight under your desk blotter. Here, I brought it to you."

"I love this poem. It was telling me to go and search for Jason. Did you read it?"

"Yes, that's what convinced me you were here," Adrian says, handing the poem to me. "and the signal came in loud and clear."

"Wait a minute. This poem doesn't say anything about Vanuatu. I didn't know this place even existed until a few months ago."

"I understand how it would get you to wondering about things, but I still don't see the connection to Jason."

"For someone who makes his living out of obscure information, it's very obvious to me. Don't you see, Adrian? I know you don't believe my theory, but what if someone kidnapped Jason after he left the Royal Palace?"

Adrian picks up the thread. "We don't think he was, but someone could have taken him aboard that oil tanker that seems to have vanished."

"Maybe he somehow got away and landed on one of these islands? I studied the currents, Adrian. It's entirely possible that if he fell overboard, he could have drifted toward Port Vila."

"That might be a possibility, go on," he says.

"Maybe he doesn't know who he is. Say, for instance, he has amnesia as Dr. Malas said he might, or he can't call us. He might not remember our phone number. I had such a bad headache one day that I couldn't remember my Mother's phone number. It's possible, isn't it?"

"Ellie, that's the stuff movies are made out of, sweetheart. It doesn't happen like that in real life."

"Yes, it does! It happens like that in my life, anyway. Hold it, if the CIA is now involved, why can't we ask Mr. Kelvin for some backup to help you find Kelly and Drew? Don't they have family who might want to know where they are?"

"Mr. Ingles gave his okay to share that information about Kellie and Drew and the *Sea Nymph* with Jake, and he's on his way here. He thinks several things are going on that don't add up. We also didn't want to tell you that Andrea Simmons aka Solana slipped out of Dimmy's hands, and has disappeared."

"Oh, Dear Lord, I knew she'd outfox them. What else don't I know?"

"That oil tanker called *Sea Nymph*? We think we know where it is now and how it vanishes. Kensi's right, it's a pirate ship of some sort."

"My hero. Hey, I'm not sharing a room with Jake!"

"He'll be coming in tomorrow morning from Sydney. I got him the room next door. I checked outgoing flights, and we can be on one to Lonoror Airfield tomorrow afternoon."

"Good. I'll pack a bag for us."

"Kensi has to stay in Port Vila, so it's you, me, Jake, and possibly Miss Cindy. Jake spoke to her earlier and invited her along – said we could look like a couple of couples traveling together."

"Why would Kensi stay here, I thought he was at our disposal?"

"He won't fly. Says that he, 'dunt trastem,' and he'll keep the boat gassed up, in case we need it. You know, it was brilliant that you involved the police. Kensi and Laput have been trying to get their hands on whoever absconded with a treasure worth several million dollars for a long time. Some of the smuggling and pirating stuff happened years ago, but a rash of theft and hijackings went on a little before Jason went missing, and they think they're connected."

"I think that sleazy Uncle Rexley has something to do with things. And it's an interesting theory; but what about the missing couple named Kellie and Drew? How do they fit into all this?"

"If they were snooping into the Uncle Rexley, Brian, Andru mystery, they could have gotten a little too close for comfort. Kensi thinks their disappearance might be related to that. It's his piracy-missing treasure theory. It could all tie in together."

"I'm getting a headache."

"You're probably hungry. Let's go and get something to eat. Oh, and you better call home. Your family thinks you've lost your mind."

I'm suddenly sullen. What are the refugees eating right now? How could they go back when everything except that big tree was the only thing standing? What if some of the treasure is buried on the beach there? It might be hiding under the roots of that massive tree with the bicycle wrapped around it. Who would know?

Stranded On The Island Of Life, by Beth Ann

"Life sometimes seems like you're stranded on a desert island
waiting for the ship to come and rescue you.
When no one knows, you're missing so you keep waiting
and hoping they will come for you
not knowing that they don't know you're missing.
They're having so much fun on the yacht
that they won't come back for you.
So you keep hoping that one day they'll come back for you
And not knowing that you're only 5 miles off shore you sit there
and wait not knowing you could swim to shore.
It's only 5 miles away you're so close to shore and you don't even know
it but you keep waiting for them to come back for you.
So years pass, Months pass, Weeks pass, Days pass,
Hours pass, Minutes pass, Seconds pass.
Eventually you give up not knowing you're so close to shore
and all you had to do was swim 5 miles.
There might be some danger in the water but it's worth all that
you go through just to get to the main land where all the other people
are." but it's worth all that you go through just to get to the main land
where all the other people are."

(Note in journal: 12,013 steps today = 4.8 miles)

At this rate, I have to throw my theory out the window of finding Jason in a thousand steps. Added up, the total has already amounted to way over what I originally calculated.)

Kalima Mansale kissed her son's cheek, and said, "I know you try, Brian, but we need to feed your brothers and sisters. Take Alfred with you today. Go out and get as many vegetables as you can for your sisters to cook at the stove. Good luck, son."

She watched as Brian and Alfred left the larger of the two tents that all six of them had shared since the relief people left them on Pentecote Island nearly a year and a half ago.

They gave them tents, bottled water, blankets, and some food, but little else. They came back about six months ago with more supplies, but they had not returned. Aside from what they could carry off the island the day they left Kakae Luna, all they owned was here with them. Had the world given up on them? Kalima glanced around her and realized she would be thankful for what she had, and made up her mind to put on a happy face for her family.

Her eldest sons, Brian and Alfred, knew of several farms that had harvested their crops, where they typically left some under the surface and rarely went back for them. If they went now, they could pick enough root vegetables before they rotted in the ground.

Their sisters, Silvi and Monta, cooked the vegetables at their little stand, near the airport. Dani, her youngest, would stay with them until she returned from town. He sat quietly playing with his only toy, a little truck and the boat his brother Brian carved out of a piece of driftwood. Kalima hugged him and began her walk to work.

After the boys returned with the vegetables, his sisters washed them off in the ocean, as they could not use the lavatory at the airport. He told Alfred (Brian could speak a little better now that time had passed) to stay with the others while he walked into town. His determination might land him a job today.

Their mother gave them a warning before she left, she expected cheerful and appreciative salespeople. Accept what the tourists offered, no matter what it might be. Tourists wanted to sample the local cuisine. They would not hesitate to bargain with them since that was half the fun.

"Bargain a little, but do not let them walk away. It will mean no sales at all," Kalima had said.

If they were lucky, they would have enough to buy items for their dinner that night. Work was scarce, but Kalima had a part-time job at the Barrier Reach Resort. If the airport shuttle had an empty seat, the bus driver allowed her to ride for free and would stop for her to get on as she walked to town. If she had to stay late, she would miss the last shuttle and have to walk the mile and a half back.

Kalima was hopeful that the resort would need Brian to help with pool duties, as there was talk that tourists were starting to return. She did not understand why the airport let Brian go. Even though his salary was small, it helped the family.

"Adrian, hold up. I want to stop in the gift shop to get something to take with us. Can you give me two minutes? You and Jake go ahead and save me a seat."

"Be quick about it. We're on a tight schedule, Ellie. Tick-tock, remember? The bus is coming now, so make it snappy. I simply don't know how to say, 'hold the bus, my wife's not here yet,' in their language."

"Okay, okay, be right back." Ducking into the little shop at the hotel to select several items, I'm hoping it will buy information, or at least put a smile on a child's face today. Maybe we'll get more than one.

Jake pops his head in the doorway. "Bus is here, let's get a move on, Mrs. T."

The hotel provides a shuttle bus to the Port Vila airport. It's bumpy but quick. After we grab our bags, we file into the large one-room open-air building.

"Who are we flying with today, Adrian?"

"That one," he says, pointing to a blue **Wicked Airlines** sign.

A bright yellow background makes the blue stand out. I don't remember seeing it on my way into this building when I arrived, then remember that my back must have been to it when I exited the airport to find a taxi.

"Are you kidding, Adrian?"

"It's a name, Ellie. It has nothing to do with how the plane flies."

Meanwhile, both Jake and Adrian are trying not to laugh.

The man behind the ticket counter is wearing a starched white shirt and is sporting a head of spiky blonde hair. I figure that is what is making the guys laugh. Mikah's diction is perfect. He politely asks to see our passports. When he gets to mine, he says, "Um, drastically changed your hair, Madam, it seems."

"You're a fine one to talk about hair, Mr. Mikah," I say under my breath.

Adrian pulls something out of his pocket. "Sorry, you have the wrong one. Here, this is her passport, must have given you her Mother's by mistake." He turns in my direction, and grins.

"That's quite alright, sir." Mikah looks at me to compare it with the one Adrian handed him, then hands them both back. "Please take a seat. I will call your names when it's time to board. Next in line, if you please."

Adrian pockets both of our passports. "Yours is safe with me, Ellen Thompson dash Sellers," he says.

Something occurs to me, and I turn back to the desk. "Aren't you going to assign us seats?"

Mikah raises his eyebrows. "There's no need for that, Madam."

Interrupting him again, "Aren't you going to take our bags?"

"No need for that, either," Mikah says, smiling. "You'll be taking them with you." He turns to Jake, saying, "May I see your identification, sir?"

As I look out the airport window toward the empty runway, I wonder if there's going to be a delay. "Sorry for the interruption, Jake. Excuse me, Mr. Mikah? Where's the plane? I don't see one."

Mikah is understandably annoyed with my interruptions, and says, "I assure you, Madam, it's out there. Please take a seat in the waiting area." He turns back to Jake, who is now laughing out loud. "Now, where were we, sir?"

Glancing out the window again, the only thing that resembles an airplane is a tiny, twin-engine propeller airplane. "That can't be our plane, it's so small. Where will the luggage go?"

Adrian steers me toward a row of seats. "You'll see," Adrian says, trying not to laugh as Jake turns away to hide his face.

"Why are you two laughing?"

"You'll see," Jake says.

After the few people at the counter are taken care of, Mikah calls our names. We follow him outside where he asks that we stand in a row next to the tiny plane.

"Okay, Mr. Ogden, please take seat number one, and Mrs. Ogden can take seat number two. Leave your luggage over here before you board. By the way, we need a co-pilot, any volunteers?"

Jake says without hesitation, "I'll volunteer."

Mikah nods. "Very good, sir, you are a good weight distribution, for the other side of the plane."

Adrian and Jake exchange glances, then start to chuckle. As Jake moves to join Mikah, he whispers as he passes me, "We're on an adventure, Mrs. Thompson dash Sellers. You were expecting luxury?"

Adrian grins. "This is what you came here for, isn't it? You're not bailing out now, are you?"

"Okay, Mr. Adrian is it? Please take seat number four. Madam (meaning me), are you taking your satchel on-board with you?"

"Yes."

"Then please take seat number three. There are no overhead bins, so you will have to stuff it under your legs, or we can put it with the other luggage. It's your choice."

"Nope, it goes with me, Mr. Mikah."

Mikah then asks that we board with the highest number first. "Number six, please take your seat at the rear of the plane. Number five and so on."

"I haven't had enough Piña Coladas for this. Really, where does the luggage go? Are we honestly taking this thing over water?"

"Mrs. Thompson-Sellers, will you kindly take your seat so we can stay on schedule?"

I'm not thinking good thoughts. "Now I know what Kensi meant when he said he'd rather ride in the boat instead of fly. I should have done that too."

"Quit complaining, Amelia. If she can do it, you can too."

"Seriously, Adrian? You do know what happened to her, don't you?"

"Yes," Adrian whispers near my ear. "They never found her body. Then they had to declare her missing and presumed dead."

"Why are you so morbid, Adrian?"

"It's a gud dei to flae," Jake interjects, as he climbs into the plane.

"Is that why Miss Cindy declined *not* to join us? Was it because she knew we'd have to travel in this thing?"

Jake shakes his head. "No. If you must know, her co-worker didn't show up today. I'm having dinner with her when we get back." Miss Cindy was not at the front desk when we left, so I can't corroborate Jake's story.

A small plastic packet is on each seat that resembles earplugs. "Are these for music?" Adrian has chosen to ignore me. Glancing out the tiny window, Mikah is stuffing our suitcase into an opening on the wing section. "So that's why you two were laughing. That's a clever place to put it."

Once we're all seated and belted in, Mikah pulls up the stairs, shutting and locking the door into place. Then he launches into his spiel.

"Ladies and Gentleman, we at Wicked Airlines ask that you turn off your electronic devices. It will greatly interfere with our equipment. We do not have seats that recline nor tray tables, so we'll dispense with that. Your seat-backs are your flotation devises should the need arise. We will be flying over water, and should one of you get the urge to tell the others that you have spotted something wonderful down in the water, please refrain from getting out of your seat to look through the windows. It will significantly disturb our weight distribution. The flight is short, so we'll dispense with drinks. You have complimentary earplugs on your seat. Hope you enjoy the scenery. Thank you for flying Wicked Airlines."

Mikah is not only the man behind the ticket counter, but he is also the baggage handler and the pilot. He gives a little salute before he goes into the cockpit area, taking the seat opposite Jake. We can see everything from our seats, as there's no door. Mikah hands Jake a headset, as he puts one on his head. He then proceeds to flip switches on the dashboard.

On this particular aircraft, there are six seats on either side of the aisle. Adrian is sitting opposite me. He playfully reaches to touch me. "Why did you mention Amelia? How long after she went missing was she declared, you know. Is this your polite way of reminding me that we might never find Jason's body? I already considered those options. Do you think there are parachutes on this thing they call an airplane?"

Adrian pats my hand, saying, "There, there, my little princess, we'll be there before you know it. You might want to open up that packet and put your earplugs in your ears."

Tearing open the packet, I push the plugs into my ears as the plane sputters to life. The sound immediately becomes deafening. As the little plane lumbers down the short runway, I white-knuckle the seat in front of me because there are no armrests.

The earplugs don't drown out Adrian's laughter completely, and it reminds me of the countless stories he's told of the vehicles, planes, and other oddities he's had to fly in for missions with the CIA.

"It's part of the island's charm, Ellie." Although it's a bit muffled, his voice comes through the earplugs.

On commercial aircraft, the nose comes up first, but on a small plane, the sensation is much different in that we leave the ground, and are in the air all at once. As we start to gain altitude, the little prop-plane slightly wiggles as if the wind is pushing it sideways.

As I look out the tiny window, there are fish swimming about, because we're so close to the water. Adrian tries to keep the mood light and says we won't get too high, in case the pilot has to drop us into the water. Then he leans toward me.

Has Levi's wicked humor rubbed off on him?

"Hey, stay on your side of the plane, buster!" I push him back toward his seat because he might upset the balance. Instead, he laughs, then reaches over to touch my cheek tenderly.

"I hope you're right about all this," Adrian shouts.

"I hope I'm right too. If I'm not, then we'll have at least tried, right?"

Adrian smiles sweetly, "Right, we'll have at least tried."

The flight takes about thirty minutes. When the wheels hit the dirt runway, we brace ourselves, but it's a smooth landing. After Mikah stops flipping the switches on the dashboard, he and Jake unlock the door to push out the stairs.

When we exit the plane, warm air greets us. Mikah is removing our bags, giving Jake and Adrian a little salute, saying, "It's been a pleasure having you on board, please consider flying with Wicked Airlines in the future."

I'm with Kensi; No matter what, I'm going back by boat!

We don't know how long we'll be here, but we each brought extra clothes, our toiletries, and a bathing suit. Adrian says we might as well enjoy our time here, but we also know it could be a wild goose chase.

As we walk out of the front of the building toward the outside entrance to the tiny airport, an aroma of something delicious beckons to us. A blue tarp, stretched over some tables along the side of the building, must act as a sunscreen.

When I finally made a connection with the woman named Joan, she told me that she was the one who was on the oil tanker during the rescue. The information she gathered during that time is sketchy, as there was a small fire in the data room shortly after everyone left the tanker.

Joan did say that candy, especially chocolate bars are what the refugees craved. I bought as much as the little gift shop at the hotel had in stock. We also went by the bank to exchange some twenties for one-dollar bills; another thing the Islanders covet is our American dollars.

Approaching the first table, I give a candy bar to a young girl, asking her name in the Bislama-English that Kensi has taught us. She answers, "Mi Palla."

I show her a picture of Brian, and she shakes her head no. Handing her another bar along with some dollars, she smiles, as tears run down her cheeks.

"Hamas," Adrian asks. He wants to buy what she's selling. The young girl scoops a spoonful of brownish goo into a green leaf and then hands it to him. After he takes a bite, he clamps his mouth together. "Spi see," he manages to say.

"Here. Now, aren't you glad I brought this along?" Adrian unscrews the lid and shakes his head. He thought I was silly when I insisted on bringing bottled water.

At the second table, we do the same thing, but the girl points down the line to the third table. Handing her two bars of chocolate along with several singles, Jake steps forward to ask what she's selling. This is evidently, not spicy and he likes what he's eating.

At the third table, two boys are sitting on a blanket, as two girls stand near a makeshift table. They don't immediately acknowledge me and seem a little timid. The taller of the two girls slowly comes forward. Handing her four bars of chocolate, I show her photos of Brian. She opens her mouth to speak, throws the candy bars on the table and grabs one of the pictures to take a closer look. Then she turns to talk to the others.

When she turns around, I put the picture of Jason in her hands, but she pushes it back pointing to the photo of Brian that was isolated from the documentary where he's holding towels near the pool. The others mill around her as she talks to them. All at once, they move together to form a tight circle.

From the limited knowledge we have of their language, we understand her to say that their brother, Brian, is in trouble and they will not say anything to us. I want to know where their mother might be so we can talk to her. "Brian not in trabol. Where is your Mama? Brian not in trabol, we're lukum for him, and want to talk to him."

Adrian takes some dollars out of my hand and offers it to the eldest girl, saying, "No trabol, mo tok." She does not budge. He takes more bills to add to the pile, again offering it to the girl, "Mi wanna tok wetem Brian. No trabol, jas tok." Adrian smiles, and reaches into my bag for more candy bars, as Jake points to a simmering pot.

"Hoa hamas?" he asks. Then he hands the tallest girl a twenty-dollar bill. She hesitates, shakes her head, but Jake pushes it back to her, then folds her hand around it. "Yu kip it," he says.

"Tangkyu, tumas," she says timidly.

"Where is your Mama?" I ask the girl.

Adrian shakes his head, pulling me aside, saying, "Ellie, she's probably working somewhere, and she had no choice but to leave her children here. The oldest girl looks like she's in charge of things, but the youngest looks relatively safe, let's concentrate on him."

Pulling out pictures of our animals, the youngest child comes forward. From what we can gather, the small boy is Dani, who is eight, Alfred is sixteen, Silvi is fourteen, and Monta is eighteen. Their brother Brian went to find work. They don't know when he will return, probably the same time their Mama comes back.

Jake says, "Mi go long town." It means that he will go into town to explore the area while Adrian and I stay with the children.

I'm dreading the confrontation with Mrs. Mansale. Or maybe it will go smoothly. Either way, we're definitely on the right track in finding this person named Brian. The children are thin and in need of medical attention. "If they had a decent meal once in a while," I say out loud.

Adrian understands my need to help them. "Be right back," he says. As he walks toward the airport building, Jake is already walking down the road toward the nearest town as he has missed the shuttle by about twenty minutes.

Monta nods her head that it's okay for me to come around the table. Sitting down on the blanket, I take out my laptop and place the CD into the slot. It's clear from their expressions that this is new technology to them.

"Big cy clone," I tell them, as the documentary about Cyclone Billy starts to open. I stop at the place where the young couple started their presentation, and they smile when they see the familiar faces of the young couple that stayed at their resort.

They point and giggle when they look at themselves moving about the island. The camera pans the area, and the massive tree comes into focus where several bicycles are leaning against it, as others are chained to a large round tap.

Small stores line the center street, as people go about their day. Children are walking with books, some are lingering near the drug store, while others are loitering along the boardwalk that leads to the marina where boats of all sizes are bobbing in the azure blue water.

Three people have stopped to wave to a couple on a sailboat that's moving out of the cove. The children nudge each other when they see their brother, Dani and his toothless grin. Ice cream is dripping down his chin, and they shove each other affectionately.

I purposely fast-forward the CD to where Steve Danbury is filming the ***Alhambra*** out in the bay, precisely where the camera focuses on the distant image of the oil tanker. When it zooms in to show other Islanders at the railings, the children giggle and smile when they recognize themselves.

It must have been a scary time for them. These children know firsthand what it's like to live through a cyclone. They're the ones who survived the storm and were dumped on this island to fend for themselves. I can certainly relate to that!

The oil tanker must have seemed like a floating city to them. Little Dani's arms fly out around his body in an exaggerated motion, which means the oil tanker was huge, as his siblings laugh at him. How could this tragedy not affect them more?

Then, some scars are not visible.

I stop the CD and retrieve pictures of our stables, our horses, family photos of Jason, Melanie, and Curlie the summer we had our family reunion. I avoid other buildings and Ashwood Manor, so they won't think I'm full of myself.

Monta points to Jason, who is near the fence to pet one of the horses and turns to say something to Silvi. She nods her head and shrugs her shoulders. They both glance at me and then away quickly. A photo of Gus where he is nose to nose with Prince elicits laughter. Monta turns to talk with her siblings again. Was this a bad idea?

Did they lose their pet when the storm went through? I don't know how to ask this in their language.

Adrian returns to say that Jake is near the town and is heading toward the first hotel. He'll canvass the area and show pictures of Brian and Jason around. In the meantime, Adrian asks the children to come into the airport café for a meal, which they gladly accept.

Silvi turns to me and hugs me, "Tangkyu Misis." Hugging her back, I don't know how to say 'you're welcome' in her language, so I pat her head.

The tourists who came in other planes have moved away, and few remain, so the children happily abandon their table to settle into a booth near a window. They can keep an eye on it from here.

They chatter to each other and ask us questions, some are easy to understand, but many are not. We're almost finished eating when Monta glances out the window and her expression changes to shock. The children immediately stop eating to stare at a woman who is standing near their table. It's apparent that she is not happy as her hands are planted on her hips, and her mouth is moving.

Silvi and Monta say something, stand up quickly, and leave the table. The woman's arms and hands are now moving as fast as her mouth. By the way things look from our side of the window, she's probably yelling at them for leaving their table. Alfred and Dani let out a loud moan. Then they wiggle away from the booth, leaving Adrian and me to stare out the window.

"I think the girls are trying to convince the woman to come inside to talk with us," Adrian says.

The children have each grabbed an arm of the unhappy woman, but she's shaking her head, firmly planting her feet in the dirt. Monta points at us, and we don't know what to do, so we wave.

"What have we done, Adrian? That has to be Mrs. Mansale. She'll never help us now. I better go talk with her."

Leaving Adrian at the table, I walk out to confront the woman. When they see me, Monta and Silvi pull me into their circle. They're trying to convince her by saying, "Missis no frum bigfala boat," and "Missis no fuidrong!" As well as, "Misis no tak pikininis."

I do not understand most of this; however, the part of about pikininis comes in loud and clear. It must look comical from Adrian's side of the window, as several others have now gathered around us.

"Mama Mansale?" The woman stops moving when I address her. "Are you Misis Mansale?"

The woman nods her head, then grabs her youngest child to shield him. I hand her Brian's photo and she sucks in a breath, as a moaning sound leaves her throat. Tears slowly roll down her cheeks, and she closes her eyes for a second or two. Then she pushes Dani toward one of the girls, and pulls me into a tight embrace.

Adrian is now outside to watch the growing circus. "Does anyone here speak their language?" he says to the crowd.

As I try to pull away from Mrs. Mansale's grip, an older gentleman steps forward to say he's from Australia on holiday. He can generally understand most of their language, as he's been here so often, so he'll give it a go. He begins to speak with her, and she repeats something back to him.

The gentleman turns toward me and flatly says, "She thinks you are here to take her children away."

"Please tell this woman that we're not here to take her children."

Mrs. Mansale releases me and says something to the man. He turns to me to interpret, then I say something, and he turns back to Mrs. Mansale. She completes her thought, and we go on and on like this as we try to talk in this strange way.

We have ascertained that the woman is trying to do the best she can after being left on this island by some well-meaning rescue people. She is very close to purchasing a home for them all, so they don't have to live in the tents anymore. Please don't take her children away; she has a steady job and has almost enough money to do this.

Mrs. Mansale steps forward to take the photo out of my hand as I pull out the other one of Jason. Putting them side by side, pointing to both photos, and then to myself, I say, "Mi Pikinini, Ja son." Taking a deep breath, she blinks several times, and I repeat it. "Yu Brian, mi pikinini, Ja son."

Tears begin to roll down her face again as she slowly comprehends what this means. The man who is translating says that she knew Brian's real mother would come to claim him one day.

"Yu Ja sun, yu pikinini." She stares at me for a moment, then reaches to pull me into a firm embrace again. "Yu Ja sun, no mi pikinini, yu pikinini," she wails. "Brian no mi pikinini. Yu pikinini!"

Adrian's cellphone rings. Then he puts his hand into the circle to pull me out of Mrs. Mansale's grip. The small crowd parts to look in the direction in which Adrian is now pointing.

Two men are approaching on foot. They are approximately the same height, but one of them is large while the other is quite thin. Jake is one of the men, as there's no mistaking his hat. He must have talked someone into coming back with him, or he has found Brian.

Mrs. Mansale babbles away. When I don't understand, she turns me to face the road. "Brian," she says distinctly. "Yu pikinini, yu Ja sun."

The crowd chatters excitedly behind us. The two men are still too far away to see the young man's face clearly, although it is noticeable that the young man has a pronounced limp. Adrian takes my hand, but I'm unable to make my legs move.

"Come on," he urges. "This is what you've been waiting for."

"What if it isn't Jason?" I whisper.

"What if it is?" he replies.

We're about ten feet away when the young man stops, as we do. Jake puts a hand on the young man's shoulder and turns to say something. Then he gently nudges him forward. When we're within a few feet of the two men, the young man stands there for a few moments and then blinks a few times.

He's so thin that his cheeks and eye sockets seem hollow. When he cocks his head to the side, I immediately know who he is. He moves forward and reaches up to put a hand to my face as I reach up to touch his.

"Mom," he whispers.

I literally can't talk. My son Jason looks so different to me! His nose is broader, and he's very dark from naturally being outside in the elements. His hair is curly, not wavy, but it's unmistakably my son's voice.

"What took you so long? I've been stranded on an island waiting for you to come," he jokes. "I thought you'd never get here!"

I choke out a laugh and grab him, hanging on for dear life. "Wait a minute. You could be a phony. Lift up your shirt. I have to make sure." Under his left arm, near his armpit, is a carrot-shaped mark, and on his right thigh is a barely visible scar.

"See, it's really me. Mom, it's really you!" Jason starts to sob and hugs me for a long time.

Adrian hands Jason a handkerchief, saying, "Welcome back, son. When you're ready, we'll all go back to town on the last bus. We'll stay there for a day or two, so you can adjust to things."

We disengage for a moment when he sees his family standing off to the side. He walks toward Mrs. Mansale, and she reaches around him, pulling him to her as the others watch in silence. Then they all begin to talk at once. It looks as if they're having a private moment when Mrs. Mansale turns in Adrian's direction.

"Ol mifala kam?" Mrs. Mansale asks.

"Yes," he says, and then motions to her and the children to gather their things and get aboard the bus, as it comes to a stop near Jake.

"Nam ba wan!" Everyone stares at me. "Nam ba wan?"

"Nambawan!" Mrs. Mansale repeats, but I know she's sad. This news has rocked her unstable world. I hope that she and her children will be able to cope once we take her Brian away.

Adrian called Kensi to tell him of our success, and we could hear him yell something in the background. We assumed that he was as happy as we were. Adrian asked him to come and get us in the boat he named Peace because I was not about to get into that wicked little airplane again. Pickup will be in three days, so Jason could say his final goodbyes.

From what we can understand, through words and gestures, and what Jason could interpret for us, Mrs. Mansale, Kalima as she wants us to call her, had a feeling that Uncle Rexley was pulling the wool over her eyes. When he tried to tell her that Jason was Brian, she never quite believed him. Rexley said to her that his head injury prevented him from remembering anything.

Brian didn't recall that she was his mother. But, she knew he was not hers. For one thing, her son was left-handed, not right-handed, and he did not like the ocean, and this Brian did.

Alfred and Dani assumed that what Uncle Rexley told them was right, but Monta and Silvi had their suspicions. Even though it was not their brother--they couldn't break their Mother's heart again, not after Uncle Rexley told her that he had drowned in the ocean during one of his excursions. Then went back to her a year later to say that he had found him and was bringing him home. Kalima shared the information about traumatic brain injury with the older ones when Brian first came back.

They also helped us understand that this Brian worked hard where the other Brian was plain lazy. The new Brian was gentle and quiet. He never made a fuss that his mother made him do all the work, as the old Brian had done. The real Brian was not so nice and was often surly and nasty.

When the oil tanker took them to Pentecost Island after the cyclone, they struggled to find work, and they needed Brian more than ever to help his sisters earn a living – or else they would starve. I began to understand her struggle to tell us; I know what it's like to lose a child.

Kalima couldn't bring herself to tell the authorities, and I can't bring myself to say to this kind and brave woman that her son lies in an unmarked crypt. Nor can we tell her that her Brian died after he sustained horrific injuries, as it won't help her cope with her loss. Adrian says that what she doesn't know won't hurt her. If she needs to know more, then Dr. Malas will step in, but it won't change anything.

Jason tried to explain what happened when Uncle Rexley showed up at the hospital. He didn't know that Rexley wasn't telling him the truth, as he couldn't remember his name then. Everyone around him spoke a strange language he could neither understand or articulate. Then he thought the unfamiliar words were the language he learned as a child, and he must have forgotten it. He decided that he should learn it to survive.

Then one day, as he stared at the sea, he had a distinct impression that this was not his life. It must belong to someone named Brian. And he was not Brian. It was impossible to tell the woman who took such great care of him that he thought he was someone else. He wasn't sure she would understand him. Kalima Mansale treated him as her son. She was loving and kind. Since he couldn't remember his name, he became Brian. In time, they accepted him, and he did the same.

Knowing there was no way to communicate, Jason played along. Memories slowly came back of his former life, but it was too painful to think about it, so he tried to block them. At first, the memories began to come to him through weird dreams. Then they would pop into his head during the day. Headaches were prevalent then, most of them were pounding, while others were sharp, dagger-like pains. They were mostly in the side of his skull where surgery scars are still visible when he moves his hair aside.

It will take the rest of the week to understand what happened to Jason. We will try not to rush him; we know how difficult it will be to leave the people who were his family these last few years. The more we talk, the more the suppressed memories surface. It soon becomes clear that his accident was no accident.

Brian worked for a time at the Lonoror Airport. When someone accused him of stealing (which he adamantly says is not true), he lost his job. As we listened to Jason's story, he left out the part about how he departed the Royal Palace. He doesn't mention specific names from that time. We'll revisit that sometime in the future.

Some of his memories may stay locked up tight inside his head and may never come out. At times, he struggled to say that Kalima did her best to love and take care of all of her children, including him. That's why Adrian and I purchased a small resort on Pentecost Island. She can rename it to her liking when she gets over the shock.

I continue to write in my little notebook, snatching time in between catching up with Jason. Since we have finally reached our goal, there is no need for the step counter. It took more than the thousand steps to find him, but that's inconsequential at the moment.

Kensi blasted the airhorn on the cabin cruiser, as he approached the dock. Kalima's family were entertaining us in the marina's restaurant while we waited.

Jake stood on the dock to catch the boat line Kensi threw in his direction. Adrian pulled me aside to whisper something in my ear. When the time came to leave, we hung back to watch in silence, as Kalima and her children said goodbye to the Brian they knew and loved.

Monta took us aside yesterday to ask about her real brother, Brian. Did Uncle Rexley see him drown? Is he really dead? Adrian merely said yes.

As Jake put our suitcases on the boat, Kensi jumped off to come inside. He didn't expect Brian to recognize him, but he smiled in recognition. Kensi then introduced himself to Kalima and her family and then explained that he was a police officer from Port Vila. He had news about Uncle Rexley.

Jason stood near me to interpret, as Silvi, Monta, Alfred, and little Dani held Mrs. Mansale's hands to support her. Kensi warned them that parts of what he had to tell them would be hard to understand. When Kalima nodded her head in agreement, Kensi started off by saying that it came as no surprise that Uncle Rexley was heavily involved in the piracy that went on around the islands.

When the judge offered him amnesty during court the other day, he couldn't talk fast enough. He told the authorities that the ship called *Sea Nymph* was the one responsible for everything. Rexley had, over the years, buried some of the loot from several robberies under the large tree on Kakae Luna.

Rexley didn't dare go back there in broad daylight, because he thought someone was following him, and he feared for his life. He mentioned that he went back there a few times, but did not admit to firing at us a few days ago, but my gut said that it was him. Rexley was getting sloppy by then. He recognized Kensi as the officer who shot him in the leg when he broke the storefront window taking the necklace and ring. He also admitted throwing the jewelry into a window of a passing truck.

With a little coaxing from Kensi, Laput got into the cabin cruiser. Together, they went to Kakae Luna where they dug up several large well-wrapped sacks. The treasure, identified through serial numbers and etchings, are now back in the rightful hands of the banks and museums from whom it had initially been stolen.

The authorities were so grateful that they insisted their finder's fee was given to the Mansale family. It was in a little sack that Kensi was proudly handing to Kalima. It couldn't possibly make up for what happened to her family at Rex's unscrupulous hands, but they hoped it would help them somewhat.

According to court records, Uncle Rexley's amnesty only covered his piracy charges. No one said anything about clearing him of other things. The judge then charged him with child endangerment, and coercion of a minor, because he made Brian do his bidding as soon as he turned twelve. He most probably will stand trial for murder for what happened to him.

When Rexley fished Jason out of his net, he took him to shore with the other bodies he found, then put the strange wristwatch on one of the other bodies when it did little more than hum when the clock face lit up. Since his motto was always, finders' keepers, loser's weepers, he had one of his many helpers go back to the morgue to steal it, but it was already gone.

Rexley found it later at a pawn shop and retrieved it, using it as a way to generate interest for other stolen items when he spread that ridiculous story about the merman. Alfred mentioned that he was the one Rexley forced into spreading that ridiculous story. He also made him tell people about the odd-looking wristwatch, with the hope of generating interest for other items he wanted to sell.

Kalima and her children huddled together in disbelief. She asked about her late husband and Kensi could only say that Rexley admitted to nothing else. Adrian and I listened with rapt attention as Kensi explained how utterly selfish and manipulative some people are. Then I realized that the Mansale's had as much drama as we had over the years. No wonder Kalima hung on to Brian!

Adrian took my hand, leading me toward the dock as Jason walked toward the little group. I couldn't hear what he was saying to them, but they were all hugging him. Little Dani hung on to his thin leg as Kalima, and the others disengaged after a few moments. She wiped tears from her face and touched his face tenderly, then gently pushed him toward the cruiser.

Once we are back to our hotel on Port Vila, we will take a day to catch our breath, as Adrian makes the necessary calls home to let our family know we're okay. He tells them that we've adopted a cyclone victim and will bring him back with us. After many questions, he merely says he can't talk about it over the phone.

Adrian also arranges for Dr. Malas to examine Jason, and an anxious Gor'gena is on hand to give him support. Although he's a bit on the anemic side, supplements and good food will help him get back to a healthy weight. He has no memory of being at the hospital except for the room he was in before Rexley took him. Before we left, Dr. Malas reminded me that miracles happen every day.

"We are going home, sweetheart. A lot has changed there too. It's going to take an adjustment, but we'll see that you get help with that. We'll take it one step at a time, okay?"

Jason is quiet. We allow him to ask questions when they occur to him, but he breaks down when I tell him his Grandmother Francesca has passed. He asks about Melanie and Curlie, and we talk about his memories and stay clear of the future. We're in the here, and now, this is enough to conquer.

It's now December 18th. We say goodbye to Miss Cindy and tell her how much we appreciate what the hotel did for us, as they bestowed new clothes upon Jason, and extra food to help fatten him up. We tell her to come and visit us in Virginia; we would love to see her again. Before she turns to leave, she places a small envelope in my hand and says to read it later.

As we are about to board our airplane to Sydney, Kensi and Gor'gena come racing out of the airport toward us. They didn't know we were giving them the cruiser, until both sets of keys appeared on Kensi's desk, along with the title Mr. Zucker gave me when I purchased it. He pulls me into a bear hug and says thanks, as Gor'gena pushes him playfully aside to hug me.

Jason is grateful that they were there to help him at the hospital. It was difficult to communicate with them, because of the language barrier. As he says his goodbyes, he tenderly puts his head near Gor'gena to hum the tune she sang to him, and she starts to weep. She will know what it's like to have a son and will sing her song to him, now that she's pregnant. They have decided his name will be Jason Brian.

Adrian and Jake will keep in touch with Kensi, as there's still the unfinished business of the ***Sea Nymph***. Knowing the bloodhound that

Kensi is, it won't take very long, now that he has the means to get around on the water. They figure they'll also find Kellie and Drew.

As we board the plane bound for Australia, I think how utterly lucky and wonderful that we're going home before our time ran out. What Adrian doesn't know is that I would have allowed jellyfish to bite me, or eaten rotten oysters to get to him. He now says he never doubted me, but I know that's a crock. It was not only a Mother's intuition, but it was also sheer faith that brought us to this day!

It is indeed a Miracle for Christmas!

We're keeping things as quiet as possible, because if Dimmy finds out about Jason's 'resurrection,' there's no telling what the backlash would be. As we wait for the plane to load with passengers, I open the envelope to read Miss Cindy's note.

> *"A family is like a circle, the connection never ends,*
> *and even if at times it breaks, in time it always mends.*
> *A family is like the stars, somehow they're always there,*
> *families are those who help, who support, and always care.*
> *A family is like a book, the endings never clear,*
> *but through the pages of the book, their love is always near.*
> *A family is many things with endless words that show*
> *who they are and what they do and how they teach*
> *you so you know,*
> *but don't be weary if it's broken,*
> *or if through time it's been so worn,*
> *families are like that-they're split up and always torn,*
> *but even if this happens, your family will always be,*
> *they help define just who you are*
> *and will be a part of you eternally."*

Jason sees the tears roll down my face and reaches for my hand. "What are we going to do, Mom?" he asks quietly. "I mean, how can I go home and pretend that nothing happened?"

"We know it will be hard for you when we get home, but we think we have a long-term solution."

Jason smiles. "Like what?" It's a little like talking to a stranger, but I know it's Jason by his voice. "You have more to tell me, don't you?" he says.

"Yes, there's more. We want to call you Brian, not Jason. By leaving things the way they are, we can say we don't know anything about the real Jason. We don't know who hurt you and we don't want them to know you're alive. Can you understand that?"

Jason shakes his head in understanding.

Can we fool the people who did this to him?

"Amala…" I start to say, as he interrupts me.

"What happened to her? Is she okay? They didn't hurt her did they?" Jason suddenly gets emotional, as his armor starts to crack.

"She's fine. I can't wait for you to meet your new family. She's waiting for you back in Virginia. You can finally meet your son."

Jason can't talk for several minutes and then starts to weep. It must dredge up the night he went missing.

"Here's a picture of little BJ and Amala."

Jason chokes out a cry as tears fill his eyes. He takes the photo and touches it tenderly, as his hands begin to shake. "I don't know what to say. How did you get them out of…?"

"It's a long story. BJ looks like you did when you were a little boy. Adrian says he would have known who he was without a DNA sample. Here's the part we hope you won't mind. Adrian is already in the process of adopting you, so we'll call you Brian Thompson dash Sellers. We did that for Amala and BJ, so it'll be legal and proper."

"Thanks, Mom. I have a hyphenated last name after all."

"You remember that?"

"Yes, some things are starting to come back."

We both chuckle at the memory of our ridiculous after-dinner discussion of hyphenated names the family bantered about before Adrian, and I got married.

"It's odd how things work out. You were meant to have it anyway. You have been given back to us! Mr. Andru slash Brian slash Jason slash Brian. You are such a gift."

During the rest of the flight, we take turns filling him in on what has happened in the nearly four years since his disappearance. We tell him about the rest of the family, about our new horses, what we've done at Ashwood, and how we managed to win the Championship and the Triple Crown. He asks for details because he must feel left out.

After we arrive in Sydney, we take a day and a half to visit the places we passed on our way to fulfilling our mission, trying to build Brian up both physically and mentally. Jake has joined us for dinner on our last night together.

"Let me tell you about what's happening in locating the vanishing oil tanker named ***Sea Nymph***," he says between mouthfuls. "Capturing it has been a long time coming." When Jake uses the words tanker and ***Sea Nymph*** together in the same sentence, he stops to notice the deer-in-the-headlights expression on Brian's face.

Turning to Adrian, I say, "You know, those words could be something that triggers a long-suppressed memory."

"You're right, Ellie. What do you know about this oil tanker, Brian? Does the name ***Sea Nymph*** mean anything to you?" he asks gently.

"I think so," he says, taking in a deep breath. "Sheyanna was the one who helped me. She brought me servant's clothes and smuggled me out of the, you know. Somehow," he stops to think. "I'm sorry, I can't remember the whole thing, but I think she made me, I don't know the right word to use."

"It's okay, take your time. Dr. Malas said some things might be difficult for you to remember. He said that it's normal. There's no pressure. Maybe it would help if you write things down as they come to you." Tears swell in his eyes. "They may or may not come back. I don't mean to be a doomsayer; we can't go back, only forward."

"I'm sorry. I don't mean to be so emotional," he sniffs. "I can't help it."

"It's okay, son," Adrian says. "You've been through a lot. Go right ahead and be as emotional as you need to be."

I take out my journal and hand it to Brian. "Why don't you read this. It might help you understand what we were feeling while you were gone. Then, if you feel like it, you could try to write your name. Use up as much paper as you need. If you switch thoughts, it might help you come up with what you're trying to recall in the first place." I turn to a fresh sheet and write his new name. "Let's start here."

Adrian is sympathetic to our comfort and purchases first-class seating for us. The long flight from Sydney will take us back to the Dallas-Fort Worth International Airport to wait for our connecting flight home. It's where we'll say goodbye to Jake so that he can go home for the Christmas Holidays.

A layover of several hours gives us time to walk around to stretch our legs. As we remark about storefront windows, Brian starts to talk about his ordeal. He remembers pressing the watch face before he felt himself fall into the water and he blacked out. He has no memory of events after that or concept of time that led up to when the strange uncle showed up at the hospital.

Suddenly overcome, Brian begins to weep, leaning one hand against the wall while trying to stifle his sobs with his other hand. People stare at us as they pass, probably wondering what I've done to him. Surrounding him with my arms, he clings to me much as he did as a little boy. Oh, the horrors he must have experienced!

"It's okay, sweetheart. Let it out."

It takes about fifteen minutes before Brian can compose himself. By now, I'm weeping too, as my heart breaks for the atrocities he must have suffered. Brian's eyes are swollen and red from crying, his face is a little puffy, but he says he feels better.

"Once Rexley took me to the island, I kept telling myself that someone would come for me. When no one showed up, I thought I would have to spend the rest of my life as Brian. But I never gave up, Mom. Never!"

"I didn't either, sweetheart. Even when no one believed me, I never gave up hope. We didn't know where you were, or we would have been here sooner."

"I kept looking out to sea wishing one of you would show up."

I show him the photos I took of the black rock with the waves crashing over them. "You were there, weren't you, sweetie?"

"Yes," he whispers. "Mom, how did you get these pictures?"

"I took them. I was there with Kensi and Gor'gena. We went looking in the last place this Brian was supposed to live. I took it so you could remember."

"What do I want to remember that for?" he says mournfully.

"Many people love you. It's to remind you so that you can be grateful."

During the time between waiting for our flights, we talk with our family to prepare them for our newest member. Melanie and Curlie don't understand why we would adopt such an older person, then say the more, the merrier.

When we get into Adrian's blue convertible, it somehow reminds me of when we picked Jason and Mack up that winter they went to New York for training. Suddenly, and without warning, Brian breaks into sobs, as he must recall this memory, too.

Just what did all those years of training gain him?

It's a long and quiet ride home. Adrian and I assure Brian that things will evolve the more he remembers. When he asks about how we went about trying to find him, Adrian tells him about Levi's death. It has a profound impact on him. He feels responsible for the chain of events that led to his demise. He hangs his head, saying how sorry he is about everything.

"This is not your fault, Jas…Brian," Adrian says. "You need to stop blaming yourself, son."

"Who should I blame?" he says sullenly.

I know who to blame. "Let's blame *your* Uncle, shall we? I think he's the real reason all this happened. And let's not forget your father. Let's blame that side of the family, okay?"

Adrian must agree with me because he's quiet. It'll be interesting to see how everyone reacts when we bring him home. To the outside world, no one will know that our Jason is coming back. To prying eyes, should there be any, it will appear as if a family has adopted another child. We don't intend to let the world (or our desert cousins) know anything different. He's still my Jason on the inside, but he's going home as Brian.

It's dusk as we move along familiar roads. Adrian stops at our driveway to allow the gate to open. Brian lets out a little gasp. Twinkling lights are strewn through boughs of pine and holly along the fence. On either side of the gate, there are wreaths tied with red bows that twinkle in every window of every building. Ashwood Manor is ready for Christmas.

Adrian pulls his car up to the front door as Mona opens it. Silhouetted against the dark paneling are people waiting to greet us. As we explained earlier, we want to bring Brian in with little fanfare. Most of the family is in the living room with the drapes drawn. Mona steps aside, as Adrian takes our luggage out of the trunk, setting it inside the vestibule.

Pushing the front seat forward, I take Brian's hand to persuade him to get out. He unfolds his lithe body and stands up stiffly. He's a few pounds heavier than when we found him, but far from the person we once knew.

"Come on, sweetie, there's some people I want you to meet."

Mona closes the front door behind us, as Glen moves forward to get the luggage, then stops suddenly to grasp Mona's hand, stepping back in silence. In the next second, a little boy named BJ hollers, "Gamma, Gamma, I miss you!" As I bend to pick him up, he runs into my arms.

Turning him toward Brian, saying, "This is Little Basim. We call him BJ. BJ, this is your Daddy."

BJ blinks, putting his little hands on my cheeks, saying, "Dad dy."

"Yes BJ, this is your Daddy."

BJ squeals, "Dad dy, Dad dy, Gamma Dad dy, Papa Spesal!"

Most of the household moves into the vestibule to watch the spectacle. BJ is now holding his arms out straight to Brian, as he moves forward to take BJ in his arms. Amala's beautiful face registers shock but steps forward when Brian puts his hand out to her. She blinks several times and then runs toward him speaking Arabic, of all things.

All of a sudden, Melanie understands and lets out a scream, running to hug the brother she thought was gone forever. Then it's Curlie's turn. Then we all jostle for position around Brian, BJ, and Amala as the rest of the family stands back to wait for the hoopla to subside.

"Let's give Brian a little space," Adrian says finally.

Amala leads Brian and BJ upstairs. He needs time to adjust, and we don't want to overwhelm him. As far as Amala goes, we'll let nature take its course.

A hundred questions start hurling toward us: Why didn't I tell them what I was really up to? Why didn't I tell someone where I was going? Why did I make them worry that I ran away from home? How did I ever find him when no one else thought he was alive? Who's responsible for his injuries? And so on.

I figure that I need to say something in my defense at least. "Didn't I tell you that I joined the CIA? I couldn't jeopardize the mission, by telling any of you!"

Adrian rolls his eyes, and then shakes his head, "No, she did not."

"I knew you were up to something, Ellen!" Terre says. "A teacher mentioned the cyclone documentary. I saw it and figured you got involved with that somehow."

"In my heart, I knew Jason was alive. We don't mind what he looks like, the point is, he's home now with us."

Can we heal the places that bear no scars? Dr. Laurel said it's a special place deep within us where hurt goes when you don't know where else to put it. She also said that he needs absolution. He needs to forgive himself so that he can start to love and embrace his new life. Then, and only then, can he let go of his old self to move on with the new person he is now.

Dr. Malas told us that it would take time for Brian to regain what he lost. The possibility exists that he may not remember all of it, that in itself could be a blessing.

After we're home for a few days, Brian and I have a long conversation. He doesn't blame me for allowing him to go to Saudi. He would have gone anyway, but what he regrets most is in not letting us know how he felt sooner.

We may have lost our Jason, but we have gained a soft-spoken, gentle, and compassionate person named Brian. We will love the new Brian and help him to understand while life is full of little bumps, it's how you jump over those bumps that matter!

Amala doesn't mind that Jason's appearance is different. She does say that we need to fatten him up a little more. BJ cries when his Daddy puts him down. We are all amazed at the instant bond between them. Amala has been grooming BJ ever since he could talk. She often spoke to him about Jason, showing him pictures, telling him that his Daddy would be proud of him. She also had hoped he would return home someday.

Our three 'house spirits' can continue to guide us; Mrs. Sarah Ashwood, Old Miss Abigail, and of course, Mother Francesca. We expect a whisper occasionally from them and a happy sigh once in a while.

We will have the most wonderful Christmas, as we celebrate our very own Christmas Miracle! Our Christmas wish is for a future filled with the business of family, joy, and love.

This is not the end of the story, it is the beginning of a new chapter in the book of life!

Epilogue

Adrian knew that closure was an essential step in the healing process. That's why the information that the CIA secreted away needed to remain in their vaults. Weighing all possible repercussions, Kelvin Ingles decided to call a meeting with all parties involved. The sensitive nature of his disclosures would not only damage the CIA, but our family would be at a higher risk of danger should this get out to the world.

Kellie and Drew McGuire are now back home enjoying a much-needed break. They were already in Australia working in and around the Republic of Vanuatu when Levi and his teams discovered the signal coming from Jason's wristwatch, which alerted them that he might be alive.

Mr. and Mrs. McGuire went undercover, as they were on the trail to find the vast treasures pirated over the years. They were co-assigned by a consortium (these are the owners of the many open cases) who lost their properties over the years. It had to do with classified information, and it was just before Adrian stopped giving the family updates.

This team garnered the bulk of the intel that broke the case wide open. When the oil tanker, **Sea Nymph**, was located last week–it netted none other than Solana, aka Andrea Simmons. Kellie and Drew allowed the pirate ship to capture them, but they never dreamt Solana would spill her guts so freely in front of them.

Solana was the one who came up with the master plan against the Obagur Family and weaseled her way into Basim/Ravi's life all those years ago. Basim would have married her, except for the fact that the King would not allow it. After King Basim's guards put Solana out of the Royal Palace, it was her brothers who nearly beat Basim to death.

When King Basim announced to the world that his son was dead, no one disputed it. The funeral was done traditionally, and it satisfied the Royal Ministers. Traditional fashion meant that it included funeral prayers spoken over a shrouded body, which was laid to rest in a simple grave with no marker.

Solana had become adept at sneaking in and out of the palace for a long time. She discovered that, although Basim was severely injured, he lived. Unbeknownst to Basim, Solana gave birth to his illegitimate son, but the baby died.

The Royal Palace had many spies and many ears and knew Mr. Peter's was taking Basim out of the country. Shortly after that, Solana conspired to seek retribution by fabricating an elaborate scheme between Uncle Ruggeri *and* Fariq. She thought her plan was very clever as neither one knew about the other.

Solana was also responsible for the Andress Document scheme, our being unceremoniously dumped at Ashwood, and putting us into their phony Federal Witness Protection Program. She manipulated, coerced, and paid the many characters who came to bring harm to the Andress-Thompson family. It was she who sent 'gifts' to us, including the package with the silver bells, and taking my cellphone. She is the one who had me drugged!

Solana proceeded to tell Kellie and Drew how Khalifa caught Jason trying to sneak out of the Royal Palace. She laughed at the memory of Jason being brought onto the oil tanker, where he was beaten severely, then tossed overboard with two other bodies.

Solana's men could not convince her that the men lying dead in the morgue at a Port Vila hospital were Jason and two of their shipmates, so she sent out her network of spies, to make sure. They came back to tell her that it was not Jason. They then tried to convince her that he was somewhere else, perhaps he went back to Virginia, maybe he went back to the Royal Palace. That's when Jamaile caught her in Akdemir's library.

Once she made her way back to the **Sea Nymph**, she sent her spies out again, but this time they reported that the washed-up bodies had no identification as the tortured technician began to admit that a couple of tourists came by the morgue to ask questions. When Solana found out that Kelly and Drew was the couple snooping around, Solana sent her men to escort them to the tanker.

What Solana didn't know was that the seasoned team had their encounter planned. They hid several items that allowed them to free themselves, where they melted seamlessly into the big tanker unnoticed. When her men tied them up, it wasn't an hour later when they found the loose bindings. They couldn't tell Solana that they lost the couple, as they knew how ruthless she was. It was about that time when all the bodies started to show up on the beaches. Solana had no compunction about taking human life.

Kellie and Drew stole food from the galley, changed clothes they found along the way, and even got a message to CIA Headquarters, all without detection. At one point, they got off the tanker for several weeks to check in. They went back to reconnect with it, before authorities boarded, due to the tracking device Kellie left behind.

Kellie and Drew had a simple scheme planned for Solana and her henchmen. They and several veteran agents decided to beat her at her own game. They wanted Solana to *think* that they were attacking a vulnerable ship, when in fact, it was a decoy.

When the vessel wouldn't 'heave to,' the pirates boarded, but the agents were highly armed, Special Ops trained, and determined to stop them for good. Solana knew of the consequences of capture and turned a gun on herself. There is no question she is dead this time. The common denominator that perplexed us for so long was Solana.

A connection links the elusive criminal Uncle Rexley to Solana, which eventually led authorities to Fariq. As for Uncle Rexley, he hid his treasures inside the only tree still standing on Kakae Luna Island.

When authorities dug this up, it included such items as the necklace and pricy ring disguised in parcels attached to the roots. Rexley made sure his treasure never saw the light of day until he dug it up. His greatest fear was that the old Brian had told the new Brian about the cache. When he was sure that the new Brian was not capable of alerting the authorities about him, he started to relax. Little did he know, that this would come back to haunt him!

After much debate, Officers Laput and Kensi agreed to return the necklace and ring to Mr. Legget. All his insurance company would pay for was the window, so he was grateful when Laput put the items into his hands. It was the right thing to do, for the long-standing suffering the man endured when Rexley, (using the alias of Drexel Tambor), so rudely smashed his precious storefront window.

Our family stands united by its original version of Jason's disappearance and presumption of death. We want no further threats of recriminations, and wish for no further communications with our desert cousins.

We shall carry on as my Mother once told us to do. We will live our lives fully, now that we are a complete family again.

Did all of our ghosts sigh?

Postscript

Brain injury can happen to any person at any time! When it occurred to our family, we were unprepared to deal with this life-changing event. To cope, I started a journal the day my son suffered a traumatic brain injury. It was a way to capture the many things that occurred and document our journey. Little did I know, that writing it would eventually lead to a trilogy of books. My son's tenacity and unwillingness to give up are what convinced me that dreams do come true. I've always wanted to put the novel floating around in my head down on paper. Writing the trilogy became my therapy.

Mysteries are meant to encourage the reader to figure things out with little information. After all, if you knew everything, it wouldn't be much of a mystery. The author wants you to go on a journey of discovery, and that is what is so unique about brain injury. It too, is a journey, not only for the survivor but also for the family, because that person forever changes.

Our family's real story was used as the backdrop and woven into this fictitious trilogy storyline. During my son's recovery, I felt separated from him while he was in a rehabilitation center for nearly nine months. He couldn't communicate with us in the standard way as the accident left him in a non-responsive state. I felt all along that he needed time to recover so he could find his way home.

Our experiences correlate to several places within the storyline in all three books, and I had no idea that the journey of writing about the adventures of the Andress/Thompson-Sellers family would bring me closure until I completed it. My stories took an unconventional path, and it appears that we have come full circle.

This last book in the series was the hardest for me to write as memories kept flooding back about what we encountered during the years my son endured various therapy sessions and unconventional rehabilitation methods. But the good news is, that although my son is a different person, we have the chance to raise him again--and as my husband says, we'll do it right this time.

M.A. APPLEBY

About ***RAISING DAVID AGAIN:***

> *"Every 23 seconds, someone in the United States sustains a traumatic brain injury, 50,000 don't survive. Those that do are changed forever."*
> - Brain Injury Association of Florida

This quote comes from the *Traumatic Brain Injury TBI FACT Book*, which went into a box to start a collection of brain injury information after my son had a vehicle accident in September of 2006.

The statistics in this tiny book are quite staggering. According to the *Brain Injury Association of Florida, Inc.*, the term TBI, "is defined as a blow or jolt to the head or a penetrating head injury that disrupts the function of the brain."

Our family had no idea we would be on such a long journey with our son, or that it would take so long for him to recover–although my brother-in-law, a retired neurosurgeon told us that it would be 'epic.'

Immediately following a major tragedy, how much of what you hear goes in one ear and out the other. As a curious person, I started to devour everything about this subject, which seemed at times a bit overwhelming. Through the years, our family discovered many other sources of information that have a plethora of resources for those survivors, family, and caregivers of the brain injured.

To cope with this unique situation, I started a journal the day of my son's accident, more as a way to remember things as at times, my mind was muddled with anxiety, frustration, and lack of sleep.

I've always wanted to put the novel in my head down on paper. Using our family's story as the backdrop of this fictional story, I wove it into a trio of books called, *A Whisper of a Mystery Trilogy,* which is not my son's story, however, this group of characters suffered a life-altering tragedy.

It wasn't until the last chapter that I realized that I finally had closure and what eventually led to writing my son's story, ***RAISING DAVID AGAIN.***

You may not even be aware that the person who sits next to you may have sustained a brain injury sometime in his/her life. Or the bank teller, grocery store clerk, or anyone walking down the street, may have suffered a concussion, stroke, or head injury.

We are becoming more aware of this now that our veterans are coming back from war. The words shell-shocked doesn't begin to cover brain injury. Evidence now points to sports-related injury and how concussions affect the brain. The list goes on. I'm not an expert, but I happen to live with someone who has a brain injury.

The following keys are taken from the book I wrote after the trilogy. These are some of the issues we cope with on our daily journey through brain injury.

Our Keys To Recovery
for the Survivor of Traumatic Brain Injury:
1. Grieve for the sense of loss of who you were, handle denial and then move on
2. Practice dental hygiene and good nutrition
3. Consider a lower medication dosage/monitored by a Physician or Neurologist
4. Learn to re-train your brain
5. Do everything in moderation
6. Have patience with yourself and others
7. Use humor wherever possible - and mind your behavior
8. Care for the caregiver
9. Embrace the 'new you' and accept the 'new normal'
10. Don't forget to smile! It looks good on you!

Included in this book are courageous stories of encouragement, faith, endurance, and fortitude as caregivers shared their stories. Also, my **Brain Injury Tool Kit** has a wealth of information to help those who might be starting this long journey. It's a handy reference guide of terms, descriptions, and general knowledge we gained in our decade of discovery.

Thank you for reading my books.

And remember, don't journey through life's trials and tribulations without stopping to express your gratitude!

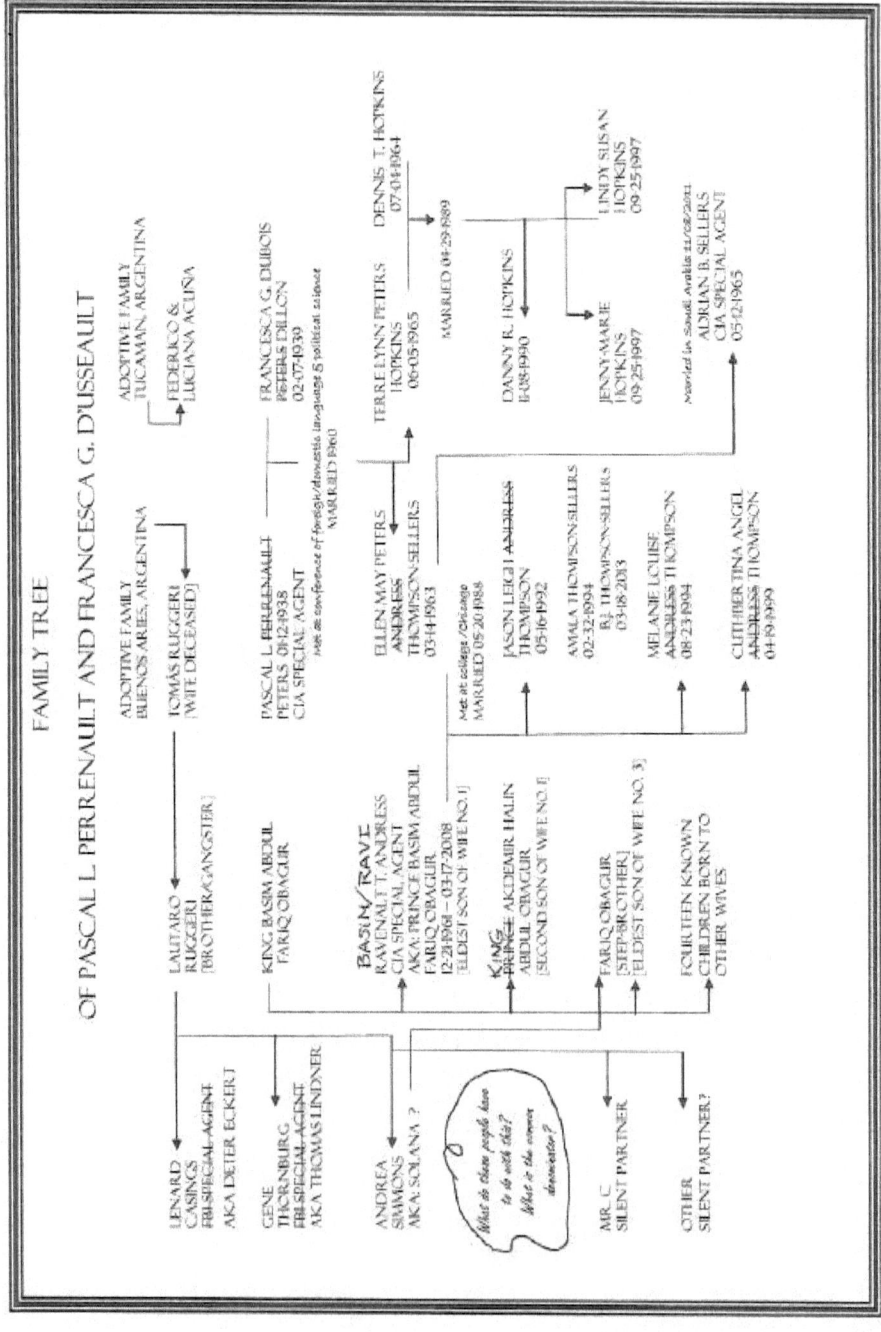

BOOKS AND RESOURCES:

Collins GEM English Dictionary, Harper Collins Publishers, New Edition 1998.

2012 Virginia Fact Book. This is a statistical guide to the Thoroughbred industry in Virginia, prepared by The Jockey Club. 01 July 2012. http://www.jockeyclub.com/factbook/StateFactbook/Virginia.pdf

DeBoskey, Dana S., Jeffrey S. Hecht, Connie J. Calub, *Educating Families of the Head Injured, A Guide to Medical, Cognitive, and Social Issues*. Aspen Publishers, Inc., Gaithersburg, Maryland, 1991.

Kushner, Harold S. *When Bad Things Happen to Good People*, distributed by Random House, Inc. 1980.

Nolte, Dorothy Law, Ph.D., Rachel Harris, *Children Learn What They Live*. Workman Publishing Co., New York. 1998. Copyright © 1972 by Dorothy Law Nolte,
http://www.empowermentresources.com/info2/childrenlearn-long_version.html

WORLD WIDE WEB/INTERNET:

A Horse Racing Controversy Surrounding an Oaklawn Trainer. 2 April 2014. This article brings to light the ethical treatment of horses by the group known as PETA. They claim there is proof a horse trainer mishandled not only the horse, but also misused drugs on horses in Kentucky and New York.http://www.fox16.com/story/d/story/a-horse-racing-controversey-surrounding-an-oaklawn/39257

Alchemy Institute of Hypnosis: 01 May 2014. Training in hypnosis, hypnotherapy sessions, retreats, workshops.
http://www.alchemyinstitute.com/grief_abandenment.html

Andy and the Gang: 22 April 2014. Andy's Gang was a children's program that ran on NBC from 1955 to 1960. A frog appeared in a puff of smoke and said "Hi Ya Kids, Hiya, Hiya!" He was always interrupting and causing trouble. http://en.wikipedia.org/wiki/Andy's_Gang

Aphasia: 14 January 2016. This is a term that describes the combination of a language and speech disorder caused by damage to the brain. It affects about one million people within the US each year. Aphasia can be caused by a cerebral vascular accident (known as a stroke and can cause impairments in speech as well as language. Aphasia can range from an occasional inability to find the right words to speak, read, or write, but does not affect intelligence. A prevalent deficit for a person who suffers aphasia is anomia, the inability to find words. Reference the National

Aphasia Association, htt://www.aphasia.org,
https://en.wikipedia.org/wiki/aphasia

Art Rooney Pace: 20 May 2014. The Art Rooney Pace was so named to remember the venerable Hall of Fame founder of the Pittsburgh Steelers annually at Yonkers Raceway. In this year's 26th edition (25 June 2016 will gather the eight top three-year-olds in training on Saturday night, May 28, for a purse of $300,000.
http://www.hambletonian.org/resources/ArtRooney2016.pdf

Battleship (game): 04 May 2014. This is the game Officer Laput refers to in the text that Kensi has put together on a grid to study oil tankers.
http://www.en.wikipedia.org/wiki/Battleship

Billingsworth Racetrack: The Thompson family takes their horses to this fictional racetrack.

Blackbirding: 24 August 2017. This is the coercion of people that is obtained through trickery and kidnapping that takes laborers which first occurred between 1842 and 1904.
http://en.wikipedia.org/wiki/Blackbirding

Blood Residue: 07 May 2014. Color of blood at a crime scene. Blood residue can be either wet or dry remnants of blood, as well as the discoloration of some surfaces on which the blood is seen to have been distributed when blood was shed. It helps CSI investigators identify what type of weapons, and helps to reconstruct a criminal action, which in turn helps to link suspects to the crime itself by analyzing samples of blood residue.
http://en.wikipedia.org/wiki/Blood_residue

Brain Injury Association of Florida: 04 May 2013. This is an organization that has several offices located in communities and trauma centers throughout Florida. Their Resource Coordinators are available to assist the TBI survivor and family members with the various phases of recovery, connecting families to the right resources and they ensure that the resources are responsive and accessible to meet the needs of the individuals.

CIA; Headquarters Virtual Tour. 16 July 2012. http://www.cia.gov/about-cia/headquarters-tour/virtual-tour-flash/index.html

Cane Pace: 12 March 2013. This is the first race in the Triple Crown of Harness Racing for Pacers. http://en.wikipedia.org/wiki/Cane_Pace CIA; Headquarters Virtual Tour. 16 July 2012. http://www.cia.gov/about-cia/headquarters-tour/virtual-tour-flash/ndex.html

Champions on Display. 08 May 2013. http://www.harnesslink.com/www/MobileArticle.cgi?ID=98621&category=Ben-Franklin Triple Crown of Harness Racing for Pacers, http://en.wikipedia.org/wiki/Triple_Crown_of_Harness_Racing_for_Pacers

Claustrophobia: 08, January 2016. Is the fear of having no escape or being closed into a small space; classified as an anxiety disorder and often results in a severe panic attack. http://en.wikipedia.org/wiki/claustrophobia

Cleithrophobia: 08, January 2016. This is similar to claustrophobia but is different in that it is the fear of being trapped or locked in an enclosed space. http://en.wikipedia.org/wiki/cleithrophobia

Clue: 05 May 2014. In this classic murder mystery game, Clue, Mr. Boddy is found dead inside of his mansion and the object of the game is to determine who the killer is, the type of murder weapon is used, and the room in which the crime was committee. This is most likely what the murder mystery parties are based upon, although they need several more 'players' as the board game is suited for players eight and up. http://www.hasbro.com/games/en_US/search.Hasbro-Games/Clue

Code of Virginia: 15 July 2012. Legislative Information System, Title 59.1 Trade and Commerce. Chapter 29—Horse Racing and Pari-Mutuel Wagering, etc. These are the rules sited in the context of this book used to demonstrate violations. http://www.gov.virginia/leg1.state.va.us/cgi-bin/legp504.exe?000+cod+59.1-69

Combined Payment Form. 17 May 2013. http://www.hambletonian.org/resources/HS772yo1.pdf

Concussion: 01January 2016. From the Latin word concutere – to shake violently. It is the most common type of traumatic brain injury and can be interchanged with other terms used to describe it; mild traumatic brain injury, mild head injury, as well as minor head trauma. There are a variety of symptoms associated with concussion both physical and cognitive and due to the large volume of information that is currently being written and discussed about this subject and if the reader is so inclined, may do his/her own research on this topic. http://www.en.wikipedia.org/wiki/concussion

Coping With Grief: 28 April 2013. http://www.webmd.com/mental-health/mental-health-coping-with-grief

Currents in Persian Gulf: 01 May 2014. As the Indian Ocean current invades the Arabian Desert, it flows through a tiny inlet between the Gulf of Oman and Iran that forms a pool of warm, almost stagnant water. https://www.en.wikipedia.org/wiki/Persion_Gulf

CWP: Concealed weapons permit. 18 May 2012. https://www.usconcealedcarry.net/Virginia

Cyclone Pam: The Naples Daily News, March 17, 2015, U.N.: 24 dead in Vanuatu after storm, by Nick Perry and Elaine Kurtenbach, Associated Press. What is interesting to note here, is that this part of the story was written in 2013, a full two years before the author read this article.

Daily racing form, [Or the daily schedule] this daily listing contains the racing information that includes news, part performance data, and handicapping.

Declaration and Condition sheet: 15 April 2013. A declaration and condition sheet specifies who owns, sponsors, services certain horses and race names, cancellation policies, estimated purse distributions, and how the winnings are divided.
http://www.google.com/#rlz=1C2SKPL_enUS425&sclient=psy-ab&q=declairation+sheet+for+pacers&oq=declairation+sheet

Diamond & Emerald Jewelry: 05 May 2014. Oval Diamond and Emerald Pendant, 1 9/10 ct. total weight, $1,600 U.S. Dollars, Diamond & Emerald Halo Ring, 14 K Gold, ½ ct. total weight, $ 5,000.
http://www.helzberg.com/product/diamond&emerald+pendent

Don't Cry for Me Argentina: 08 May 2014. María Eva Duarte de Perón was the second wife of Argentine President Juan Perón. She served as the First Lady of Argentina from 1946-52. The famous line is from "It's Only Your Lover Returning", later changed to 'Don't Cry for Me Argentina', a song from the 1978 musical *Evita,* which was put to music by Andrew Lloyd Webber and lyrics done by Tim Rice. Evita, the Movie, 1996, was distributed by Hollywood Pictures (US) and Entertainment Films (UK), Music by Andrew Lloyd Webber.
http://en.wikipedia.org/wiki/Don't_Cry_for_Me_Argentina

Downeast Cruiser: 01 January 2016. These are boats that are used in coastal New England and are often referred to as lobster boats and used for offshore cruising and fishing. Most have a cabin with sleeping berths, a head, and a place to eat. http://www.boatus.com/newtoboating/types-of-boats-powerboats.asp
http://www.nauticexpo.com/prod/sasga-yacht/product-44240-333362.html

Eng, Richard. Examining Different Levels of Competition at the Racetrack. 24 July 2012. http://www.dummies.com/hot-to/content/examining-different-levels-of-competition-at-the-racetrack

Expedia Travel. Airfares to Port Vila, Vanuatu from Virginia Beach. 10 May 2013. http://www.wotif.com/cheap-international-flights/cheap-fares-sydney-to-Port Vila-Vanuatu

Famous Male Athletes from Vanuatu: 16 April 2013. Names of people such as Dr. Malas, Jimy, Kensi, Rexley, and Laput are all fictitious. http://www.ranker.com/list/famous-male-athletes-from-vanuatu/reference

Fares from: Australia, New Zealand and New Caledonia. 10 May 2013. http://www.wotif.com/cheap-international-flights/cheap-fares-sydney-to-Port Vila-Vanuatu

Groucho Marx: 07 May 2014. Julius Henry "Groucho" Marx was an American comedian knows for his quick wit, and rapid-fire impromptu delivery. http://en.wikipedia.org/wiki/Groucho_Marx

Hamiltonian Society. Services Races: 21 April 2013.
  http://www.hambletonian.org/resources/HS772yo1.pdf
Harness Racing: 01 July 2012.
  http://en.wikipedia.or/wiki/Harness_racing
Harper, Dr. Frederick: Extension Horse Specialist Department of Animal Science, University of Tennessee, Signs of a Healthy Horse: 01 January 2014.
  http://www.animalscience.ag.utk.edu/horse/pdf/signsofahealthyhorse
Heart valve. 06 May 2013. There are four valves in the heard: tricuspid, pulmonary, mitral, and aortic. Most all heart valve operations are done to replace or repair the mitral or aortic valves. Heart valves play a key role as blood is pumped through the heart in only one direction, opening and closing with each heartbeat. They open and close as pressure changes on either side of the valve, but if they do not close tightly, it can cause them to open their flap-like door (called cusps or leaflets that causes a backflow of blood. http://en.wikipedia.org/wiki/Heart_valve
Height & Weight Rations for Males: 17 April 2013.
  http://www.livestrong.com/article/356757-height-weight-ratios-for-males
Horse Racing Glossary A-Z, Terminology, Jargon, Slang, Vocabulary: 14 July 2012.
  http://www.ildado.com.com/horse_racing_glossary.html
How to calculate betting odds and payoffs: 02 July 2012.
  http://horseracing.about.com/cs/handicapping/a/aaoddschart.htm
How to Host a Murder Mystery Party. 12 April 2013.
  http://tlc.howstuffworks.com/family/how-to-host-murder-mystery-party.htm
Hurricane Katrina. 11 May 2013. http://www.livescience.com/22522-hurricane-katrina-facts.html
Hurricane Categories. 11 May 2013. Category 1: 74-95 mile per hour winds, minimal damage Category 2: 96-110 mile per hour winds, moderate damage Category 3: 111-129 mile per hour winds, extensive damage Category 4: 130-156 mile per hour winds, extreme damage Category 5: 157 and higher mile per hour winds, catastrophic damage http://geography.about.com/od/lists/a/hurrcategories.htm
Islamic Religious Police: 08 January 2014.
  http://en.wikipedia.org/wiki/islamic_religious_police
Jasper, Virginia: Fictitious town where the Thompson's live.
Jaws: 28 March 2014. Movie Jaws II, the famous line " when you thought it was safe to go back in the water…" Written by Peter Benchley, directed by Steven Spielberg, distributed by Universal Pictures in 1978. http://en.wikipedia.org/wiki/Jaws_(film)

Languages of Vanuatu: 17 April 2013. Languages of Vanuatu. 17 April 2013. There are more than a hundred indigenous languages in Vanuatu. A recent count lists 138. Most are named after the islands they are spoken on, and some of the larger islands have several different languages with Espiritu Santo and Malakula being linguistically the most diverse, with about two dozen languages each. However, Vanuatu has three official languages, English, French, and Bislama. This is a creole language derived from English, and is what the residents of Port Vila and Luganville use first. http://en.wikipedia.org/wiki/Languages_of_Vanuatu

Laurel and Hardy: 07 May 2014. http://www.laurel-and-hardy.com

Little Brown Jug Race. 12 March 2013. This is the second of the important races that make up the Triple Crown of Harness Racing for Pacers. Named after the horse, Little Brown Jug, a pacer who won 9 consecutive races and became the United States Trotting Association Hall of Fame Immortal in 1975, had this world premium pacing event named in his honor. http://espn.go.com/horse-racing/story/_/id/7001194/little-brown-jug?src=mobile, http://www.harnesslink.com/www/Article.cgi?ID=100805

List of tropical cyclone names. 07 May 2013. https://en.wikipedia.org/wiki/Lists_of_tropical_cyclone_names

Masterpoints. 01 May 2014. Masterpoints are awarded to individuals by bridge organizations when they win competitive bridge tournaments. There are several levels, Life Master being one that most serious bridge players aspire to; 300 points, 50 black, 50 silver, 25 gold or platinum; 25 red, gold, or platinum. Grand Life Master is 10,000 points. https://en.wikipedia.org/wiki/Lists_of_tropical_cyclone_names

Maps of World. 16 July 2012. Saudi Arabia: Google Maps, http://www.mapsofworld.com/usa/states/virginia/virginia-ap.html> http://maps.google.com/maps?hl=en&tab=wl

McFerrin, Bobby: Don't Worry, Be Happy, recorded in 1988, written and sang by Bobby McFerrin. http://en.wikipedia.org/wiki.Don't_Worry,_Be Happy

Messenger Stakes. 12 March 2013. Third and final race to complete the Triple Crown of Harness Racing for Pacers. http://en.wikipedia.org/wiki/Messenger_Stakes

Muslim Baby Names. 29 March 2013. Names were obtained for the story; Khalifa, Maheer, and Raheeb, the name of Jamaile is fictitious. http://www.muslimbabynames.net/

National Geographic. 03 May 2014. The Deadliest Tsunami in History made headlines around the world when the deadly earthquake generated the great Indian Ocean tsunami December 25, 2004. According to the U.S. Geological Survey (USGS), it was estimated to have released the energy of 23,000 Hiroshima-type atomic bombs.

http://news.nationalgeographic.com/news/2004/12/1227_041226_tsunami.html

Nautical knots: 06 January 2016. Convert nautical knots into miles per hour. http://www.convert-me.com/en/convert/speed/knot.html

Nearer, My God, to Thee: 04 May 2014. Text by Sarah F. Adams, 1805-1848, sung as a hymn in many faiths, normally during a funeral.

Nomination or sustaining form: 28 May 2013.
http://www.hambletonian.org/resources/HS772yo1.pdf

Ocean Currents: 01 May 2014. Ocean currents in the South Pacific. http://www.google.com/Search?q=ocean+current+in+the+south+pacivid-tankers

Ouija Board: 06 May 2014. The Strange and Mysterious History of the Ouija Board, http://Smithsonian/history/the-strange-and-mysterious-history-of-the-Ouijaboard- 5860627/#QligyFH8aGDsthPS.99.

Oil Tankers: 17 April 2013. Classified by size; inland or coastal tankers of a few thousand metric tons of deadweight [DWT] to mammoth ultra large crude carriers [ULCCs] of 550,000 DWT.
http://en.wikipedia.org/wiki/Oil_tanker, and
http://www.reuters.com/article/2013/02/26/us-iran-sanctions-tankers

Pain Management: 28 April 2014. Coccydynia Aetiology and treatment.
http://www.coccyx.org/treatmen/inflamm.htm

Past Life Regression: 01 May 2014. The use of hypnosis helps lead patients back in time to their earliest memories. The technique of past-life regression goes even further back to examine experiences that seem to form the root of their current fears and phobias. f you can connect your current fears to a past life, those fears often disappear. http://www.oprah.com/health/does-past-life-regression-work

Pentecost Island Coordinates. 15 May 2013.
http://www.google.com/#hl=en&rlz=1C2SKPL_enUS425&sclient=ps y-&q=Pentecost+Island+coordintes&oq=Pentecost+Island+coordintes

Pentecost Island, Vanuatu. 2 May 2013.
http://en.wikipedia.org/wiki/Pentecost_Island

Persian Gulf. 17 April 2013. The Persian Gulf is a Mediterranean Sea located in Western Asia and is an extension of the Indian Ocean. It flows through the Strait of Hormuz and lies between Iran to the northeast and the Arabian Peninsula to the southwest. It is where the battlefield of 1980-1988 war between Iran-Iraq took place in which both sides attached each other's oil tankers, and the later conflict that became the Gulf War (or Desert Storm.)
http://www.geographicguide.net/asia/middleeast.htm

Purse Distribution: 20 May 2014. The term purse distribution refers to what may be the total amount of money paid out to the owners of horses racing at any particular tract over a given period of time. Or it could refer

to the percentages of a race's total purse that is awarded to each of the highest finishers of that race.
http://en.wikipedia.org/wiki/Purse_distribution

Racing Secretary. 27 January 2013.
http://en.wikipedia.org/wiki/Racing_secretary

Side view of Oil Tanker: 04 May 2014.
http://commons.wikimedia.org/wiki/File:Oil_tanker_(side_view).PNG

Spasticity: 04 July 2012. Spasticity can occur in disorders that affect the central nervous system and can be found where brain and/or spinal cords are damaged. https://en.wikipedia.org/wiki/Spasticity

Step counter: 15 January 2016. This is the device that Ellen uses to count her step toward finding Jason. It understands motions, the newest uses a 3-axis accelerometer that turns a body of movement into digital measurements when attached to the body. The device can analyze duration, frequency, intensity, and patterns of movement to count steps taken, distance traveled, and caloric intake as well as calories burned. http://help.fitbit.com/articles/en_US/Help_article/How-does-my-tracker-count-steps

Succession to the Saudi Arabian throne: 30 April 2014.
http://en.wikipedia.org/wiki/succession_to_the_Saudi_Arabian_throne

The Road to Rehabilitation Series Part 1-8: 20 May 2013.
1. Pathways to Comfort: Dealing with Pain and Brain Injury
2. Highways to Healing: Post-Traumatic Headaches and Brain Injury
3. Guideposts to Recognition: Cognition, Memory and Brain Injury
4. Navigating the Curves: Behavior Change and Brain Injury
5. Crossing the Communication Bridge: Speech, Language and Brain Injury
6. Mapping the Way: Drug Therapy and Brain Injury
7. Traveling Toward Relief: Dealing with Spasticity and Brain Injury
8. Journey Toward Understanding: Concussion and Mild Brain Injury

©Copyright 2009. Brain Injury Association. All rights reserved. Permission is granted to reprint and use information in its entirety and with credit given to the Brain Injury Association and the authors.
http://www.biausa.org/

Three Stooges: 07 May 2014. The Three Stooges were a popular film comedy team of Moe, Curly, and Larry, is best known for their slapstick comedy, eye-gouging, shin-kicking, head-knocking, and punctuated by Curly's signature 'nyuk-nyuk-nyuk' chuckle. The Stooges sparked a whole new following through TV reruns in the 60s and 70s. http://www.threestooges.com

Time zone calculator. 17 May 2013. The time zone calculator helped the author convert times in one part of the world and calculate the time difference between the two world locations, such as time in Virginia, USA and Port Vila, Vanuatu. http://www.happyzebra.com/timezones-worldclock/difference-between-Port%20Vila-and-Virginia%20Beach.php

TrackMaster Proprietary Ratings Specification, (Harness Racing): 24 July 2012. http://www.trackmaster.com/harness/infor/ratings.htm

Traumatic Brain Injury: 06 March 2011. *Brain Injury Association of Florida* defines traumatic brain injury: "is defined as a blow or jolt to the head or a penetrating head injury that disrupts the function of the brain."

Triple Crown of Harness Racing for Pacers. 18 May 2013. Consists of; 1) Cane Pace, held at Freehold Raceway in Freehold, New Jersey, 2) Little Brown Jug, held at the Delaware County Fair in Delaware, Ohio and, 3) Messenger Stakes, held at Yonkers Raceway in Yonkers, New York. http://en.wikipedia.org/wiki/Triple_Crown_of_Harness_Racing_for_Pacers

Tweedle Dee, Tweedle Dum: 11 May 2014. This is the line the twins used that comes from the play (or book Alice in Wonderland. "That's manners!" http://www.imdb.com/title/tt0043274/quotes

USGS: United States Geological Survey. 03 May 2014. The abbreviation for the U.S. government study of the landscape, natural hazards, that threatens it. It is a fact-finding research organization with no regulatory responsibility. http://en.wikipedia.org/wiki/United_States_Geological_Survey

U.S. History: 16 April 2014: Operation Desert Storm (Desert Shield, 1990) The United States came to Saudi Arab's aid, deployed over 500,000 American troops to stem an attack by Iraq. January 15 came and went without a response from the Iraqis, the next night, Desert Shield became Desert Storm. http://ushistory.org/us

Vanuatu Bislama Language, translator; important phrases. 01 May 2013. (see also Languages of Vanuatu) There are over 113 distinct languages and many more dialects throughout the islands. http://www.tripadvisor.com.au/Travel-g294143-s604/Vanuatu:Important.Phrases.html

Vanuatu, the Republic of Vanuatu; History of: 12 March 2013. Pronounced vah-new-ah-too, an island nation located in the South Pacific Ocean. An archipelago formed by volcanic action, is east of northern Australia and west of Fiji, southeast of the Solomon Islands, near New Guinea. http://en.wikipedia.org/wiki/Vanuatu

Virginia Racing Commission: 15 July 2012. http://www.vrc.virginia.gov/racinglicenses.shtml

Walking steps: 15 January 2016. Depending on the stride length, a typical number of steps per mile is between 2,000 and 2,500 steps. Rule of thumb is: if the person walks for 20 minutes and they are moving at around 3 miles per hour, then the person has walked about 2,250 steps. If the person walks for 15 minutes at around 4 miles per hour, that person

has walked about 1,940 steps.
http://walking.about.com/od/pedometer1/a/steps-per-mile.htm

What is a Cyclone? 01 May 2013. The definition of a cyclone is that it is a large-scale atmospheric wind and pressure system that is characterized by low pressure at its center and by circular wind motion, it rotates counterclockwise in the Northern Hemisphere, and rotates clockwise in the Sothern Hemisphere. It is not technically a tornado.
http://weather.about.com/od/hurricaneformation/a/cyclones.htm

What is a Millibar? 11 May 2013. A millibar can be described as a unit of atmospheric pressure equal to one thousandth (10) of a bar. Standard atmospheric pressure at sea level is about 1,013 millibars.
http://www.thefreedictionary.com/millibar White Cube. 02 May 2014. The White Cube is one of the world's leading contemporary art galleries.
http://www.google.com/white+cube+art+gallery

White Grass Ocean Resort, Tanna Island: 06 May 2013.
Http://www.google.com/#hl=en&rlz=1C2SKPL_enUS425&sclient=psy-ab&q=white+grass+resort +tanna+island&oq=White+Grass +Resort

World Atlas: Vanuatu: 15 May 2013.
http://www.worldatlas.com

Zoot suit. 10 April 2013. This is the suit that Adrian wore for the Murder Mystery Party in Chapter 11. It is from a private collector, roaring 20's costume in red and black striped material, includes a wide brimmed hat, neck tie in stripes as well as an oversized jacket with broad padded shoulders, with high-waist, wide-legged pants.
http://stores.ebay.com/DRESS-SUITS/mens-zoot-dress-suits-/_i.html?_fsub=5

GLOSSARY and OTHER INFORMATION:

Arabian Costume: The costume is of upholstery weight velvet, trimmed with hundreds of crystal and cobalt blue stones and exotic silver sequins, tassels are heavily beaded. Many pieces go with this costume; robe, headscarf, hat piece, harem-type pants with a blue shirt; horse has matching neckpiece and saddlecloth; ring to match. They can cost about upwards of $ 1,425. U.S. Dollars, refers to the **Blue and Silver costumes.**

Breeds of horses: North American harness racing is restricted to Standardbred horses. They get their name from "the early years of the Standardbred stud book; that only horses who could pace or trot a mile in a standard time or whose progeny could do so", are the only ones admitted into the book.

A Standardbred horse has shorter legs and a longer body than a Thoroughbred. It has a more easygoing temperament than a

Thoroughbred as well, which is more suitable for a horse "whose races involve more strategy and reacceleration than do Thoroughbred races."

Call to the Post: This is the bugle call that is played at horse races (and at dog racetracks) that signals that all mounts (or drivers) should be at the starting gate because the race is about to begin. Once the bugler sounds the tune, there is 5 to 10 minutes before the scheduled start time of the race.

Central Intelligence Agency: (CIA). Other services listed; Office of Intelligence & Analysis, National Clandestine Service: The branch, which is an "elite corps of men and women shaped by diverse ethnic, Educational, and professional backgrounds.

Chief Steward: This is the official that meets with each driver prior to the first race.

Cuthbertina: This is the name given to Curlie, a derivative of the old English word Cuthberta, meaning brilliant, and a feminine form of Cuthbert.

City of Nakeilen: This is the fictitious name given to the city on the fictitious Island of Kakae Luna where Ellen, Kensi, and Gor'gena visit.

Enclosure: This is the area where the runners gather for viewing before and after the race.

Frick and Frack: Fricassee and Frackamon are the nicknames of the draft horses that comprise the fictitious team for the 'Magic of Christmas'.

Glock: This is a small pistol that the woman Ellen uses for target practice; she takes it apart and puts it into containers; this is not possible to do, as airport security would spot it immediately.

Handicapping: There are many forms and methods of handicapping. Most common types are class, speed, pace, trip, and computer handicapping.

Handicapping 101: These are rules Ellen said her Daddy came up with for her to follow when she first learned how to bet at the racetrack, also found online under *Harness Charts from Harness Eye*. [See specific website under bibliography section].

Hopples: These straps connect the legs on each side of a horse's sides. Horses that pace, are faster and this is important to a better. If the horse breaks stride, the driver will take the horse to the outside until it resumes trotting or pacing again.

Horse Racing Glossary A-Z, Terminology, Jargon, Slang, Vocabulary: This glossary is a complete listing of terms from A to Z of the most often used jargon and includes slang and vocabulary that universally used around the world.

Hypothesis: This is a suggested but unproved explanation of something and based upon assumption rather than fact or reality.

Important Harness Races:
   1. The **Hamiltonian** is part of the Triple Crown of Harness Racing for 3-year old trotters.

2. The **Little Brown Jug** is part of the Triple Crown of Harness Racing for 3-year old pacers.
3. The **Breeders Crown** is a series of eight races conducted on one day at different racetracks each year. First run in 1984, today's purses, and awards total $13 million. They cover each of the traditional categories of gender, age, and gait (pace or trot).

Magic of Christmas: This is a fictitious event.

Post position: The position or stall at the starting gate from where the horse starts the race.

Post time: This is the designated time for a race to start.

Pirate activity: Any such activity, in and around the islands in the story, are purely fictitious and are added to the story for affect. Any reference to pirate and smuggling in this area are made up and comes from the mind of the author.

Race bike: (known as a sulky). The only style allowed in qualifying heats or harness racing. They are lighter in weight and the seat is smaller and harder for a driver to sit on but they are more compact and aerodynamic than the training carts.

Racing Secretary: The Racing Secretary is licensed by the government and is responsible for: the safekeeping and custody of horse papers and ownership documents. Along with forming races, and compiles a list of entries, keeps a complete record of all races, publishes and prints an accurate race program, writes the condition book, provides records for the media, and communicates with the racing commission and/or other government oversight agencies.

POEMS, PRAYERS, QUOTES, SAYINGS, & IMAGES

Angelou, Maya, 23 March 2013. "People will forget what you said, people will forget what you did, but people will never forget how you made them feel." (Chapter 15) http://musicthoughts.com/t/359

Architectural house plans found in this book are not real house plans, and therefore, are not to be used for an actual house. They are included to help guide the reader through the spaces.

Beth Ann, Stranded On The Island Of Life. 21 May 2013. (Chapter 15) http://www.poemhunter.com/poem/stranded-on-the-island-of-life

Brain Injury Association of Florida. 25 April 2014. "Every 23 seconds, someone in the United States sustains a traumatic brain injury. Fifty thousand do not survive. Those that do are changed forever." (Epilogue) http://www.biaf.org

Butterfly Image: M.A. Appleby created the image that appears at the beginning of all chapter. It is included with the copyright of this book, and may not be used in any form, unless given permission by its creator. Maps, lists, family tree, are all created for this trio of books and are fictitious in nature.

Cather, Willa, 03 March 2013. "Where there is great love, there are always miracles." (Chapter 4) http://www.goodreads.com/quotes/2637-where-there-is-great-love-there-are-always-miracles

Churchill, Winston, 09 September 2014. "Man will occasionally stumble over the truth, but most times he will pick himself up and carry on." (Chapter 1) http://quoteinvestigator.com/2012/05/26/stumble-over-truth/ "NEVER, NEVER, NEVER GIVE UP!" quote on a plaque. (Chapter 10)

Confucius, 06 March 2013. "The will to win, the desire to succeed, the urge to reach your full potential, these are the keys that will unlock the door to personal excellence." (Chapter 8) http://www.brainyquote.com/quotes/quotes/c/confucius119275.html

Elizabeth David, 04 March 2013. "Every day holds the possibility of a miracle!" http://www.michaels.com/Everyday-holds-the-possibility-of-a-miracle/ed.html

Edison, Thomas. 23 April 2014. "Our greatest weakness lies in giving up. The most certain way to succeed is time." (Chapter 11) http://www.hoofbeats-heaven.com/quotes

Greene, Vivian, 23 March 2013. "Life isn't about waiting for the storm to pass, it's about learning to dance in the rain." (Chapter 6) https://www.goodreads.com/author/quotes/769264.Vivian_Greene

Guardian Angel Prayer: 17 May 2013. "Angel of God, My Guardian Dear to whom God's love commits me here. Ever this day be at my side to light and guard and rule and guide. Amen." (Chapter 1) http://www.catholicsupply.com/existing/prangel.html

Heraclitus, 06 June 2013. "No man ever steps in the same river twice, for it's not the same river and he's not the same man." (Chapter 13) http://www.goodreads.com/quotes/117526-no-man-ever-steps-in-the-same-river-twice-for. . .

Revelations 6:8-King James Version Bible, 20 May 2013. "And I looked, and behold, a pale horse, and his name that sat on him was Death, and Hell followed with him." (Chapter 14) http://biblehub.com/kjv/revelation/6-8.htm

Lyons, John. 25 April 2014. "When your horse follows you without being asked, when he rubs his head on yours, and when you look at him and feel a tingle down your spine...you know you are loved." (Chapter 12) http://www.brainyquotes.com/quotes/topics

Mohn, Harold F. There's Always a Silver Lining. 09 April 2013. "There's always a silver lining somewhere in the sky, to bring your troubled soul new hope and lift your spirits high. When disappointments come your way accept them with a smile, for deep down in your heart you know they only last awhile. Do not believe you walk alone because you never do. Hold out your hand and you will find that God is there with you." http://www.geocities.ws/genuinesafehaven/p4/376.html

Nazarian, Vera. The Perpetual Calendar of Inspiration. 25 April 2014. "Not every puzzle is intended to be solved. Some are in place to test your limits. Others are, in fact, not puzzles at all." (Chapter 3) http://www.goodreads.com/quotes/tag/

Niebuhr, Reinhold: <u>The Serenity Prayer</u>. 06 May 2013. "God, grant me the serenity to accept the things I cannot change, the courage to change the things I can, and wisdom to know the difference." (Chapter 10) http://en.wikipedia.org/wiki/Serenity_Prayer

O'Neil, Nicole M. *A Family Is Like a Circle*. 30 November 2014. (Chapter 14) http://www.familyfriendpoems.com/poem/a-family-is-like-a-circle

Psalm 23, (King James Version 05 May 2014. The LORD is my shepherd, I lack nothing.

Radmacher, Mary Anne. 19 April 2014. "Courage doesn't always roar. Sometimes courage is the little voice at the end of the day that says I'll try again tomorrow." (Chapter 10) http://www.google.com/search?q=courage

Richter, Sylvia Irene: A Mother Mourns. 02 May 2013. "Somewhere out there a Mother mourns, 'tis impossible to explain, somewhere out there his soul is calling me, let go and banish pain. For love is rare and can't be lost, God gave that gift to us. And know for all eternity, we'll never lose that trust." This is an original poem written specifically for this book and given to the author to use in Chapter 1.

Rohn, Jim, 05 May 2013. "If you don't design your own life plan, Chances are you'll fall into someone else's plan. And guess what they have planned for you? Not much." http://www.mrselfdevelopment.com/2011/06/15-of-the-greatest-motivational-quotes (Chapter 9)

Staudacher, Carol: Beyond Grief, 16 April 2013. "Grief is like a stranger who has come to stay." http://www.awakenment-wellness.com/stages-of-grief.html **DENIAL, BARGANING, DEPRESSION, ANGER, and ACCEPTANCE**.

Unknown: 19 April 2014. "Instead of giving myself reasons why I can't, I give myself reasons why I can." (Chapter Two) http://www.inspirationalspark.com

Unknown: 02 May 2014. "If you love something let it go. If it comes back to you, it's yours forever. If it doesn't, then it was never meant to be." http://philosiblog.com/2011/07/16/if-you-love-something-let-it- go

Waters, Ethel. September 26, 2017. "Today or any day that phone may ring and bring good news." (Chapter 5) https://www.brainyquote.com/quotes/quotes/e/ethelwater314523.html?src=t_good_news

Read the National Award-Winning Non-Fiction

RAISING DAVID AGAIN
*A Guide To Understanding
The Uniqueness of Brain Injury
And How Our Faith Sustains Us*

~ ISBN: 978-1-4984-9873-9

Books by M.A. Appleby:
A Whisper of a Mystery Trilogy:
The Ancient Whisper, Book 1
~ ISBN: 978-0-6929-2129-6
Whispered Dreams, Book 2
~ ISBN: 978-0-6929-2133-3
Journey of a Thousand Steps, Book 3
~ ISBN: 978-0-6929-2134-0

Visit Author's website:
www.maappleby.com

www.ingramcontent.com/pod-product-compliance
Lightning Source LLC
LaVergne TN
LVHW052256070426
835507LV00036B/3095